The Catholic Church and Power Politics in Latin America

Critical Currents in Latin American Perspective
Ronald H. Chilcote, Series Editor

*The Catholic Church and Power Politics in Latin America:
The Dominican Case in Comparative Perspective*
Emelio Betances

*The Prophet and Power: Jean-Bertrand Aristide, the
International Community, and Haiti*
Alex Dupuy

*The Marxism of Che Guevara: Philosophy, Economics,
Revolutionary Warfare, Second Edition*
Michael Löwy

Democracy: Government of the People or Government of the Politicians?
José Nun

Cardoso's Brazil: A Land for Sale
James Petras and Henry Veltmeyer

*People's Power: Cuba's Experience with Representative Government,
Updated Edition*
Peter Roman

The Catholic Church and Power Politics in Latin America

The Dominican Case in Comparative Perspective

Emelio Betances

ROWMAN & LITTLEFIELD PUBLISHERS, INC.
Lanham • Boulder • New York • Toronto • Plymouth, UK

ROWMAN & LITTLEFIELD PUBLISHERS, INC.

Published in the United States of America
by Rowman & Littlefield Publishers, Inc.
A wholly owned subsidiary of The Rowman & Littlefield Publishing Group, Inc.
4501 Forbes Boulevard, Suite 200, Lanham, Maryland 20706
www.rowmanlittlefield.com

Estover Road, Plymouth PL6 7PY, United Kingdom

Copyright © 2007 by Rowman & Littlefield Publishers, Inc.

All rights reserved. No part of this publication may be reproduced, stored in a retrieval system, or transmitted in any form or by any means, electronic, mechanical, photocopying, recording, or otherwise, without the prior permission of the publisher.

British Library Cataloguing in Publication Information Available

Library of Congress Cataloging-in-Publication Data

Betances, Emelio.
  The Catholic Church and power politics in Latin America : the Dominican case in comparative perspective / Emelio Betances.
    p. cm. — (Critical currents in Latin American perspective)
  Includes bibliographical references and index.
  ISBN-13: 978-0-7425-5504-4 (cloth : alk. paper)
  ISBN-10: 0-7425-5504-6 (cloth : alk. paper)
  ISBN-13: 978-0-7425-5505-1 (pbk. : alk. paper)
  ISBN-10: 0-7425-5505-4 (pbk. : alk. paper)
  1. Catholic Church—Dominican Republic—History. 2. Church and state—Dominican Republic—History. 3. Catholic Church—Dominican Republic—Political activity—History. 4. Dominican Republic—Church history. I. Title.
BX1459.D6B48 2007
282'.72930904—dc22

2006101849

Printed in the United States of America

∞™ The paper used in this publication meets the minimum requirements of American National Standard for Information Sciences—Permanence of Paper for Printed Library Materials, ANSI/NISO Z39.48-1992.

To my wife Leticia Aldana de Betances and
my daughters Gabrielle and Gisele
WITH LOVE

Contents

	List of Illustrations	ix
	Acknowledgments	xi
	List of Abbreviations	xv
	Introduction	1
Chapter 1	Development of the Dominican Catholic Church: A Comparative Perspective	17
Chapter 2	Church and Politics in Four Latin American Nations	49
Chapter 3	Finding a New Role in Society	99
Chapter 4	Mediator par Excellence	143
Chapter 5	Building a New Relationship with Society	177
Chapter 6	Evangelicals and Politics: Challenges and Opportunities	209
	General Conclusions	241
	Bibliography	247
	Index	265
	About the Author	275

Illustrations

Tables

Please see the book's website for additional tables: www.rowmanlittlefield.com/isbn/0742555054

1.1	Development of the Clergy in the Dominican Republic	25
1.2	Pastoral Workforce of the Church in the Dominican Republic	33
4.1	Classification of the Clergy into Diocesan/Religious and Nationality, 1936–1976	151
4.2	Diocesan and Religious Priests by Diocese, 1993/2000	152
4.3	Distribution of Diocesan/Religious Priests by Diocese and National Origin in 2000	154
4.4	Educational and Welfare Assistance Programs	156
4.5	Mass Media and Religious Congregations	158
4.6	Construction and Renovations of Catholic Institutions by the Dominican State, 1986–1994	160
4.7	State Allocation for the Dominican Catholic Church, 1979–2000	162
5.1	Cáritas Dominicana Projects in the Diocese of Mao-Montecristi	184
5.2	Cáritas Dominicana Projects in the Diocese of La Vega	187
5.3	Cáritas Dominicana Projects in the Diocese of Barahona	193

5.4	Investments in the Diocese of San Juan de la Maguana, 1992–2001	195
5.5	Cáritas Dominicana Projects in the Diocese of San Juan de la Maguana	196
5.6	Cedail Educational and Legal Programs, 2001–2002	200
5.7	The Activities of Cedail in Social Pastoral Programs, 2001–2002	201
6.1	Growth of Evangelicals in the Dominican Republic: 1974 and 1988	221
6.2	Evangelicals and the Dominican Population: 1974 and 1987	222
6.3	Growth of Evangelicals according to Three Surveys	223
6.4	State Allocation for the Dominican Evangelical Institutions, 1979–2000	237

Figures

4.1	State Funding for the Catholic Church, Dominican Republic, 1979–2000	159
5.1	Haitians Deported from the Dominican Republic, 1991–2003	205
6.1	State Funding for the Evangelical Churches, Dominican Republic, 1979–2000	238

Acknowledgments

Writing a book is a collective enterprise where many people participate in different ways. Many friends and colleagues encouraged and supported me to get this work finished. José Luis Sáez, Franc Báez Evertsz, Cyrus Veeser, Jorge Cela, Hobart Spalding, Barbara Heisler, and Carole Bernard read the manuscript with a critical eye and gave me insightful comments that enabled me to make significant improvements over the original version. José Luis Sáez, SJ, gave me unparalleled support from the beginning to the end of this investigation, providing me with numerous documents, statistics, and contacts within the Catholic Church. In addition, he read the manuscript critically and gave me timely and intuitive comments that allowed me to develop the historical portion of the text.

Bienvenido Alvarez Vega and Adalberto Martínez gave me the key to the evangelical community in the Dominican Republic. They introduced me to the leadership of the community and ensured that key leaders gave me an interview. In addition, Alvarez Vega read the portion of the manuscript that relates to the evangelical movement and offered perceptive comments. Similarly, Alfredo Ossers Vera gave me a collection of his articles published in the Dominican press and provided me with valuable contacts within the evangelical community.

Conversations with church officials and academics in the Dominican Republic and the United States encouraged me to conclude this research. In the Dominican Republic, I want to thank Msgr. José Grullón, Msgr. Francisco José Arnáis, Msgr. Rafael Felipe, Msgr. Tomás Jerónimo Abreu, and Msgr.

Antonio Camilo González. I also thank Roberto Cassá, Rafael Durán, Bienvenido Cabrera, Mingo Ramírez, Orlando Inoa, Alejandro Jiménez, Margarita Ruiz, Antonio Lluberes, José Núñez, Pablo Mella, Regino Martínez, Pedro Ruquoy, Antonio Fernández, Abrahan Apolinario, Tomás Marrero, José Luis Alemán, Luisa Campo, and Altagracia Contreras. In the United States, my gratitude goes to Edward Brett, Edward Cleary, Bruce Calder, and the late Thomas McNamee, who read the chapter on the Catholic Church in Bolivia and Central America and furnished valuable comments that helped me fine-tune my interpretation of the mediating role of the church hierarchy in those countries. All quotations from Spanish- and French-language sources used in the text are my own translations, unless the citation comes from a secondary source in English or French.

I am indebted to many lay Catholics and evangelical leaders who supported me during my research stay in the Dominican Republic. In particular, I am grateful to Carlos Naveo, Felicia Fermín, Manuel Pérez, Juan Bolívar Díaz, Fausto Rosario Adames, Basilio Cruz, Noemi Méndez, Desiré del Rosaio, Plinio Ubiera, Freddy Báez, and Rafael Anibal (Beti) Reyes. I am obliged to those in the evangelical community who gave me valuable time and support in the course of my research. Many thanks to Ezequiel Molina, Reynaldo Aquino, Andrés Rincón, Braulio Portes, Andrés Reyes, Silverio Manuel Bello, and Manuel Estrella.

I appreciate the kindness of the Faculty Development Committee of Gettysburg College that financed my many trips to the Dominican Republic to conduct my research. Field research in the Dominican Republic and Nicaragua allowed me to incorporate substantial documentation into my text and to talk to many people within the Catholic Church and the evangelical movement. I also thank the faculty and staff of the Sociology & Anthropology Department and the Latin American Studies Program at Gettysburg College for their support during my investigation.

I am beholden to the staff of the Gettysburg College Library. I thank Robin Wagner, Susan Roach, Catherine Downton, Lisa McNamee, and Nancy Johnson. My appreciation goes to James Rutkowski, Kim S. Breighner, Sharon Birch, and Ray Miller at Instructional Technology. Also, many thanks to the staff of the Biblioteca de la Universidad Autónoma de Santo Domingo, the Universidad Tecnológica de Santo Domingo, the Pontificia Universidad Madre y Maestra de Santiago, the Universidad Católica de Santo Domingo, the Archivo de la Arquidiócesis de Santo Domingo, and the Archivo General de la Nación in Santo Domingo, and the Biblioteca de la Universidad Centroamericana in Managua, Nicaragua. My gratitude also goes to the staff at the archives of the following Dominican Newspapers: *Hoy, El Caribe, El Nacional, El Siglo,* and *El Listín Diario.*

While in Santo Domingo, I received the generous support of the Báez Rosario family. I want to thank Doña Olga Rosario de Báez, Dr. Frank Báez Evertsz, Frank Leonardo, Emmanuel, Joana, and Rosa Vanessa. They were always willing to help me during some of the most difficult times of my fieldwork.

Finally, I express my greatest gratitude and appreciation to Leticia Aldana de Betances, my wife, who helped me organize the tedious statistical work necessary to support my arguments. She also helped me prepare the manuscript and always read it with a critical eye. My deepest thanks to Gabrielle Leticia Betances and Gisele Lucie Betances, my daughters, who waited patiently while I put the finishing touches on this book. All errors and omissions are, of course, my own.

Abbreviations

ARENA	Alianza Renovadora Nacional
ASC	Asamblea de la Sociedad Civil
ASIMILE	Asociación de Ministros Evangélicos
BNV	Banco Nacional de la Vivienda
CEA	Commission of Electoral Advisers
CEA	Consejo Estatal del Azúcar
CEB	ecclesiastical base community
CED	Conferencia del Episcopado Dominicano
Cedail	Centro Dominicano de Asesorías e Investigaciones Legales
CEDES	Conferencia Episcopal de El Salvador
CEG	Conferencia Episcopal de Guatemala
CELAM	Consejo Episcopal Latinoamericano (Latin American Episcopal Council)
CEN	Conferencia Episcopal de Nicaragua
CFDC	Centro de Formación Diocesana de Cabral
CLAR	Conference of Latin American Religious
COB	Confederación Obrera Boliviana (Bolivian Workers Confederation)
CODUE	Confraternidad de Unidad Evangélica
CONE	Consejo Nacional de Educación
CONEDO	Confraternidad Evangélica Dominicana
CONELA	Confraternidad Evangélica Latinoamericana

CONIN	Consejo Nacional de Iglesias Evangélicas
COSDEGUA	Conferencia de Sacerdotes Diocesanos en Guatemala
CPH	centro de promoción humana
CR	Comando Revolucionario
CSA	Catholic Social Action
CUA	Comando Unificado Anti-reeleccionista
Demos	Encuesta Nacional de Cultura Política y Democrática
DGM	Dirección General de Migración
DR-CAFTA	Dominican Republic-Central American Free Trade Agreement
Endesa	Encuesta Demográfica y de Salud
FDR	Frente Democrático Revolucionario
FMLN	Frente Farabundo Martí para la Liberación Nacional
FSLN	Sandinista Front for National Liberation
FTZ	free-trade zone
Fundasep	Fundación de Desarrollo de Azua, San Juan y Elías Piña
IFES	International Foundation for Electoral Systems
IPF	Inter-American Peace Force
IMF	International Monetary Fund
ISAL	Iglesia y Sociedad en América Latina
JCE	Junta Central Electoral
MCC	Movimiento de Cristianos Comprometidos
MNR	Movimiento Nacional Revolucionario (National Revolutionary Movement)
MPD	Movimiento Popular Dominicano
NGO	Nongovernmental organization
NPP	national pastoral plan NPP
OAS	Organization of American States
OCSHA	Obra de Cooperación Sacerdotal Hispanoamericana
ORDEN	Organización Democrática Nacional
PLD	Partido de la Liberación Dominicana
PQD	Partido Quisqueyano Demócrata
PRD	Dominican Revolutionary Party
PRSC	Partido Revolucionario Social Cristiano
PUCMM	Pontificia Universidad Católica Madre y Maestra
UCN	Union Cívica Nacional
URNG	Unidad Revolucionaria Nacional Guatemalteca

Introduction

The Catholic Church is one of the most important pillars of Latin American societies. Its temples and cultural imprints are located in the most remote areas of the subcontinent. Latin American culture adopted many of the symbols and traditions of Catholicism, and it is impossible to disentangle the two. The transformations brought about by capitalism, military dictatorships, and democracy in the latter half of the twentieth century have not reduced the symbolic and real power of the clergy in the social, political, and cultural fields. In fact, when Latin Americans convert to other religious faiths or say they have no religion at all, they retain the basic Catholic cultural traditions. Similarly, Catholic cultural influence also embraced politics in a way that turned the church into a sociopolitical factor that permeates society.

The political relationship between the church and Latin American states began in the early years of conquest and colonization of Latin America by the Spanish and Portuguese crowns. These empires provided financial resources for the church to carry out its mission of evangelization and, in exchange, expected political support and church blessings. This relationship continued after independence in the nineteenth century and, despite interruptions in some countries, continued throughout the twentieth century into the twenty-first.

Although church groups raised questions in the past about social justice, it was not until the 1960s, following Vatican Council II, and the Episcopal Conferences of Medellín, Colombia (1968), and Puebla, Mexico (1979), that small groups of clergymen and women began to question the historical ties between the Catholic Church and the Latin American states. The Catholic hierarchy held Vatican Council II in Rome between 1962 and 1965 to update the church about changes in the modern world. Vatican II acknowledged the inalienable rights of human beings: to express themselves freely, to choose those who are to rule, and to select the form of government that exercises authority over them. These issues seemed appropriate in Europe, but when Latin American bishops raised them in Latin America, they acquired different meaning because military rulers were in charge in most of the region and they did not respect the rule of law. The Medellín and Puebla Conferences provided the ideological justification for liberation theology and the popular church and for mainstream clergymen identified with reform and modernization. Unlike Europe, in Latin America, the church needed to deal with issues of social justice, human rights violations, and widespread poverty. In the context of military repression, the church became, in many instances, the "voice of the voiceless."

Transition from military to civilian rule in the 1980s created completely different social and political conditions for the Latin American church. The end of military rule reduced gross human rights violations and political repression in most countries. The church no longer needed to be the "voice of the voiceless" because, except for Central America, the rule of law was progressively taking root in the region. The outcome of these adjustments is that the church entered into political mediations. Governments and political opponents asked church officials to mediate in their political conflicts and, at times, they did so. However, most mediation tended to occur in countries with weakly structured political institutions and under severe political crises. These political circumstances offered the church the opportunity to accommodate the process of transition to democracy as a special actor that claimed to be nonpartisan in conflict-ridden societies.

This study examines the role of the Catholic Church[1] in the context of social and political change in the Dominican Republic. The Dominican Republic is an exemplary case of a country with weak political institutions where church officials have played an important role in mediating political conflicts. The Dominican case is similar to that of Bolivia, Guatemala, Nicaragua, and El Salvador, where revolutionary forces challenged oppressive political systems and where conservative national churches tried to accommodate the new scene by mediating among governments and political opponents. In all cases, political actors called on the Catholic clergy to mediate in time of political crisis, but only in the Dominican Republic has mediation become what seems to be a permanent feature of the political system.

What factors account for this seemingly unique experience in Latin America? How has the Dominican church changed as it has attempted to deal with the challenges of democracy?

I argue that the authoritarian regime of Joaquín Balaguer (1966–1978) was an important factor that distinguishes the Dominican Republic from Bolivia and Central America. The U.S. intervention of 1965 strategically destroyed Dominican revolutionary forces, whereas in Bolivia and Central America these forces continue to be decisive political actors today. The United States installed Balaguer in power and helped him restore the authoritarian state. He was able to develop a stable relationship with the church, which became a factor of social and political cohesion. The Dominican Republic did not experience lengthy civil wars or military regimes as did Bolivia in the 1970s and early 1980s, nor did it face the development of a strong popular church movement. Balaguer brought a degree of political stability to the Dominican Republic, but his regime blocked the development of political institutions and its effects lingered in the transition to democracy.

Transition to democracy in the 1980s created new challenges for the Catholic Church and the Dominican political establishment. The first important challenge was to offer a nonpartisan political mediation during the process. Political mediation was a key aspect of church-state relationships during Balaguer's twelve years in power and subsequently became an enduring feature of the political system. The second significant challenge for the church was to rebuild its relationship with the lower echelons of society: socioeconomic changes had excluded the vast majority of the population from the benefits of capitalist modernization, leaving them in abject poverty. How did the church address these issues while accommodating the political system as mediator? I submit that the church social pastoral programs became the mainstay in building a strong relationship with the lower classes and consolidating its credibility and legitimacy in society. The third important challenge consisted of the evangelical movement.[2] The evangelical movement was not simply a religious defiance of the Catholic Church but also a political one, because the new religious leaders wanted to be part of the national political system. How have the Dominican political establishment and the Catholic Church responded to the challenges of the evangelical movement? I believe that the political elite have made the necessary adjustments to incorporate evangelicals into the body politic, and, contrary to expectations, the Catholic Church has learned to collaborate with them on political mediation and natural catastrophes, but to keep their pastoral programs separate.

Historical and Social Science Research on the Dominican Catholic Church and the Evangelical Movement

Historians have conducted most of the research available on the Dominican church. There is both a traditional and a modern school in the works of church historians. Both focus on church-state relations, that is to say, on formal interactions between two institutional entities or the official representatives of those institutions. The traditional historical studies include the anecdotal works of Carlos Nouel (1913, 1914), Msgr. Hugo Eduardo Polanco Brito (1948, 1970c, 1981), Vetilio Alfau Durán (1975), Msgr. Juan Félix Pepén (1954, 2003), Leonidas García Lluberes (1934). Nouel, Polanco Brito, and Alfau Durán are primarily concerned with institutional history and the formal relationships between the church and the state. Pepén and García Lluberes focused their attention on church influence. They are concerned with what Pepén called "the spiritual cohesion of the nation." In his essay, García Lluberes pays particular attention to the church's influence in the development of national consciousness and the active role of a sector of the clergy in the struggle for independence. The works of traditional historians provide a general historical background that is useful for understanding the role of the church in Dominican society.

Unlike the traditional school, modern historiography has sought to analyze and evaluate the interaction of the church with its environment. Frank Moya Pons wrote a valuable essay (1973) in which he developed a scheme for the periodization of the history of the church and offered a valuable synthesis of its history from the Conquest to the fall of Trujillo in 1961. Fernando Pérez Memén (1984) wrote a voluminous history that stretches from 1700 to 1853. Pérez Memén builds on the works of traditional historians who were concerned with the formal institutional history, except that he carefully studies the church-state relationships in the wider national and international contexts. He used this approach again (1985) to study the relationships between the Catholic Church and the Trujillo dictatorship (1930–1961). Luis Martínez (1995) expanded this approach by also looking at the issue of nationality in the mid-nineteenth century. Antonio Lluberes, SJ (1998), follows in the same path, except he gives us a history of the Dominican church from 1493 to 1997 and complements it with an anthology of 140 historical documents prepared by José Luis Sáez, SJ. Lluberes organized his book around the various ecclesiastical projects that attempted to build the national church.

José Luis Sáez, SJ is the most outstanding modern church historian in the Dominican Republic. His monumental work stretches from the colonial period to the present. The themes of his works include religious life (1979), church and slavery (1994), church and medical care (1996a), ecclesiastical history (1996b), and biographies of important clergymen (1996a, 1999, 2001, 2002). Remarkably, Sáez includes an anthology of the documents used in each of his books. Unlike most church historians, whose work focuses on colonial and nineteenth-century history, Sáez wrote a two-volume history of the Jesuit Order in the Dominican Republic (1988, 1990). These two volumes offer a history of the church-state relationship through an examination of the missions of the Jesuit order in both religious and secular education. Sáez's research reveals that these relationships were at times conflictive, particularly when it came to issues of school funding and the defense of human rights. Although he frames most of his research within the church-state context, he recognizes the need to study the church in relation to its social and political environment, not just in reference to interinstitutional relationships. My work will build on his significant contributions to the study of the Dominican Catholic Church.

Social science research has made modest contributions to the study of religion and politics in the Dominican Republic. Howard Wiarda (1965) examined how the church reacted to revolutionary changes in the aftermath of the Trujillo downfall and showed that it was not yet ready to embrace democracy. José Luis Alemán, SJ (1982), proposed that the church cease to legitimate social and political changes after the fall of Trujillo and, instead, selected the peasantry as its favorite clientele. In contrast, my research suggests that the church never stopped being a source of legitimacy to social and political change, nor did it remain fixed on the peasantry as Dominican society changed drastically in the 1970s. William Wipfler (1980) and Margarita Ruiz Bergés (1987) examined the church as a sociopolitical factor in society. They significantly deepened our understanding of the church's adaptation to the changing political environment.

Although the literature on the evangelical movement in the Dominican Republic is rather limited, there is a growing body of scholarly works on Latin America. For the Dominican Republic, the most important historical writings on Protestantism include William Wipfler (1966), Emilio Rodríguez Demorizi (1973), George Lockward (1982), Israel Brito (1978), and Harry Hoetink (1994). Regarding the evangelical movement itself, I could only find the works of Bienvenido Alvarez Vega (1996) and Marcos Villamán (1993). Alvarez Vega provides a historical background of the evangelical movement and Villamán gives us a social analysis of the emergence of the evangelical movement.

Theoretical Perspectives on Religion and Politics

Four powerful theoretical approaches have shaped my understanding of religion and politics in Latin America: institutional analysis; Bourdieu's theory of the religious field; Jean-Pierre Bastian's notion of mutation of the religious field; and the Marxist world systems theory. In different ways, these approaches enabled me to develop a cohesive approach to understand the relationship between organized religion and politics.

Scholars identified with institutional analysis have sought to explain the contradictory dynamic of religion and politics. This approach has been very influential in the study of religion and politics in Latin America. Ivan Vallier (1970) and Thomas Bruneau (1974, 1982) pioneered the institution analysis approach in their study of the Latin American church.

According to Bruneau, the goal of any institution is to define its relationship with its environment. Goals inform us where the institution fits into society and what it is expected to accomplish for society. The church's goal is to influence individuals and whole societies. Influence means that the goal the church gives specific and direct orientation to individuals and societies. It is "marking" the object of influence with the message of Christ. Influence, in this sense, is the capacity whereby one actor has another act in a way he ordinarily would not (Bruneau 1974, 3).

Scott Mainwaring criticizes institutional analysis because it tends to reduce the church's motivation to a mere defense of its influence. He suggests that

> most organizational analyses have understated the conflicts between different conceptions of institutional objectives—different models[3] of the church. Defending the church's interests includes such potentially contradictory goals as encouraging high mass attendance, fighting Communism, fighting for social justice, and having a close relationship with the elite. (Mainwaring 1986, 4)

For Mainwaring, goals such as institutional expansion, financial position, or influence on the elite and the state are *instrumental* objectives that the church need not pursue. He argues that "organizational approaches tend to confuse these instrumental goals with the church's ultimate objective, ignoring the possibility that some models of the church could opt not to defend certain of these interests" (1986, 5–6). For example, any particular model or orientation within the church may choose to ally themselves with the elite while another one may choose to ally itself with the downtrodden. This was the case of the popular church movement in Latin America. Mainwaring concludes that within the church there are many conflicting views of the institution's interests. Thus, depending on the orientation of a particular group of clergy, pursuing the interest of the church may be perceived as essentially right or wrong.

Mainwaring proposes to analyze the church as a political actor with a relative autonomy from both class structure and the state. He shares common conceptual grounds with Marxists such as Louis Althusser (1971), Antonio Gramsci (1971), and Otto Maduro (1980). These concerns include (a) "the way the Church responds to changes in class structures, conflicts, and ideologies and (b) the way religious practices and discourse affect the consciousness of the social classes." But he is more concerned "with the specific ways religious institutions respond to political conflict and social change" (Mainwaring 1986, 13–14). Mainwaring admits that under certain circumstance, institutions reinforce or challenge patterns of domination, as proposed by Marxists, but he refuses to see institutions such as the Catholic Church or the military as expressions of a given class. In contrast, he recommends the concept of model or orientation of church to examine the relationship between religion and politics. The concept of model of the church or orientation "suggests that the starting point for understanding the church's politics must be its conception of its mission. The way the church intervenes in politics depends fundamentally on the way it perceives its religious mission. According to this approach one must look at church goals as understood by its leaders" (1986, 7). Some leaders of the church may focus on the religious mission while others might stress the social or political dimension of the mission. These different perspectives, of course, do not change the church's mission, but political struggles generate new conceptions about society and the church's role in it.

The leading orientations of the church in Latin America include Christendom, neo-Christendom, modernization, and liberation. Christendom refers to an "integrist" view of the church, where "spiritual" and "temporal" powers are merged together as in the Middle Ages or the colonial period in Latin America.

Neo-Christendom designates a vision of the church that aims to regain the world for "Our Lord Jesus Christ" and to re-Christianize societies that have increasingly become secular. The dominant orientation in the nineteenth century and during the first half of the twentieth, the neo-Christendom vision thrives under state protection to fight secularization, Protestantism, and communism. Accordingly, the state must ensure the church receives as many privileges as possible to exert its influence in society. In the 1950s, the neo-Christendom strategy became the traditionalists and, as such, continued to promote the influence of the church in society.

The modernizing orientation, which Mainwaring called conservative modernizers, shared with traditionalists the concerns for the need of church unity, authority of the bishops, community building, fraternity, and a sense of belonging, but it was more open-minded and recognized that the Church needed to carry out its mission more effectively. It suggested disengagement from direct, partisan politics in favor of mediating political and social conflicts.

In contrast, the liberating orientation, called reformist by Mainwaring, put forward the idea that engaging in politics was a requirement of the Christian faith in order to fight social injustice and poverty. Unlike traditionalist and modernizer orientations, which were more concerned about maintaining hierarchical obedience, the liberating orientation stressed the notion of the church as the people of God (Mainwaring 1986, 37–42). These orientations of the church provide broad ecclesiastical visions to pastoral work in both human and spiritual dimensions. These are obviously not the only orientations that exist within the church, but they give us a sense of conflicting views regarding the church's relationship with secular society.

Traditional, modernizer, and liberating orientations are useful to study the church in the 1960s and 1970s. In those two decades, opposition to military dictatorships became radicalized and influential sectors within the church took up far-reaching political positions vis-à-vis repression and social justice. Liberation theology and the popular church epitomized these new developments in Brazil, Chile, Nicaragua, Bolivia, and El Salvador. In contrast, in the Dominican Republic, liberation theology and the popular church did not develop strong followings, in part, because the Dominican church was very conservative and most of the priests who arrived in the country fleeing the Cuban Revolution enhanced the conservative position of the Dominican clergy. As a result, traditional and modernizer orientations were the leading approaches in the country in the 1960s and 1970s.

In the 1980s and 1990s, traditional, modernizing, and liberating orientations underwent significant changes because Latin American politics lost its radical steam as transition to democracy unfolded. In addition, the shifting conservative policies of the Vatican diminished support for liberation theology and the popular church. Traditional and modernizing orientations actually merged into a neoconservative orientation that proposes participation in mediation as a way to reincorporate the church into the political realities that came into sight because of transition to democracy in the 1980s. The Vatican's conservative shift significantly diminished the number of bishops who supported the liberating orientation and the popular church; therefore, they are at least out of the limelight, if not extremely marginalized. The successful reincorporation of the church into the mainstream of politics turned the neoconservative orientation into the hegemonic force within the Latin American church. In 1980s and 1990s, the Dominican church came to mirror the larger reality of the Latin American church.

Mainwaring's orientations of the church approach enable us to capture the changing dynamic of religion and politics. However, it does not tell us much about the changing dynamic of the religious field. For example, why has evangelical Protestantism grown so rapidly over the last four decades? What are the consequences of this new development for the relationship between religion and politics? If evangelical Protestantism signals the end of the Catholic monopoly of the religious field, what are its implications for the relationship between religion and politics?

Two important schools of thought have emerged in the literature to explain the growth of the evangelical movement in Latin America. The first school suggests that Latin American evangelicals are really an expression of a continuum of the Protestant effervescence that occurs in the context of "rival civilizations." This continuum occurs in three waves: Puritanism, Methodism, and Pentecostalism. It began with eighteenth-century English Methodism and North American Pentecostalism in the twentieth century. This first expansion constituted the first wave of expansion, whereas the second wave extended to Latin America in the nineteenth and early twentieth centuries. Latin American evangelicals comprise the third wave of Protestant expansion and domination in what used to be a Catholic-dominated territory. For David Martin, the evangelical explosion in Latin America embodies the vitality of the Protestant religious culture. This evangelical wave symbolizes the premise of religious reform in Latin America with long-term political and social consequences. According to Martin, "Methodism and Pentecostalism alike construct models of equality, fraternity and peaceability in the religious enclave of culture . . . [which] . . . are sociologically consonant with democratic polities and provide part of the popular cultural base on which such polities might rest" (Martin 1990, 22).

Martin expands on the conclusions reached by Emilio Willems, who wrote about Brazil and Chile in the early 1960s. Willems concluded that evangelicals spread the Protestant virtues of discipline, thrift, honesty, and sobriety and contribute to revolutionizing culture. Despite widespread poverty in their milieu, he was convinced that their new lifestyle—hard work and saving—plus the elimination of alcohol, womanizing, and gambling would encourage evangelicals to aspire to middle-class status. He did recognize, however, that two opposing principles are operative in the Pentecostal (or evangelical) sects, one "democratic" and the other "authoritarian." These principles tend to emerge in times of conflicts and words such as *caudillo*[4] and *cacique*[5] are freely used to refer to the attitude of pastors. Nonetheless, Willems reduces the importance of these conflicts when he emphasizes that congregations are conducive to the development of democratic values. The congregation "minimizes the social distance between the common members and the pastor, between laity and clergy. It is an institutionalized way of keeping authority within the group in a state of continuous flux" (Willems 1967, 139). Willems was enthusiastic about the democratic possibilities of the evangelicals even though the movement was in its infancy. Writing in the 1990s, David Stoll echoes Willems when he writes that "evangelical Protestants are giving Latin Americans a new form of social organization and a new way to express their hopes. (Stoll 1990, 331). In conclusion, Martin, Willems, and Stoll tend to see evangelicals as a modernizing force for capitalist development and liberal democracy.

In contrast, the second school explains the growth of the evangelicals in terms of change in the Latin American religious field rather than as a continuity of historical Protestantism. Jean-Pierre Bastian (1992) believes that evangelical Protestants emerged because of dramatic mutations of Latin American popular religious culture.

> Current heterodox religious effervescence in Latin America is nothing but a redeployment of "popular religion," that is to say, rural Catholicism without priests. Thus, rather than talking about Protestantism, we must ask whether Latin American Protestantism, in existence for more than a century, has not experienced a mutation. This mutation is the sum total of a religious field that burst out as it was liberated by the social and economic transformations that were imposed on Latin American societies after the 1960s. (Bastian 1992, 329)

In the context of mutations of the Latin American religious field, we have seen a mixture and inculturation of evangelical Protestantism into the practices and values of folk Catholicism. Evangelical Protestantism embraces the whole of Latin American culture with all its implications.

Bastian builds on the early work of Christian Lalive d'Epinay (1969), who understood sectarian Protestant societies as countersocieties who reconstructed the *hacienda*[6] model within the evangelical churches. Lalive d'Epinay concluded that

> Pentecostalism . . . puts forward a reconstitution of the great family represented by the hacienda; it validates personal relationships by giving them a brotherly dimension and an elating finality . . . it symbolizes the old image of *patron*[7] by replacing faith in obedience with obedience in faith, and in doing this gives

new life to the *relationship of dependence*, which is the primary axis of a nascent community. (Lalive d'Epinay 1969, 83–88)

Unlike Martin, Willems, and Stoll, Bastian finds that today most of the evangelical churches have leaders who are chiefs, owners, *caciques*, and *caudillos* of a religious movement created by themselves and transmitted from father to son in a patrimonial and nepotistic model of reproduction. According to Bastian, it is this adaptation and the socioeconomic transformation of the region that explain the success of the evangelical religion in Latin America. Thus, contrary to Stoll's interpretation that "Latin America is turning Protestant," Protestantism is becoming Latin American. Rather than promoting modes of "equality, fraternity and peaceability" (Martin) or "minimizing the social distance" (Willems), evangelicals embrace the most authoritarian features of Latin American culture.

The debate on the dramatic changes that have taken place in the Latin American religious field and whether these changes will strengthen democratic or authoritarian values is still open. It is hard to establish whether the evangelical churches will be the standard bearers of capitalist development and liberal democracy as Max Weber saw it in the beginning of capitalism in Western Europe. Neither is it necessarily the case that because Latin American popular religious culture is authoritarian, some form of liberal democracy cannot successfully develop in the region. Notwithstanding these shortcomings, the debate on the growth and political implications of evangelicals is useful to frame the analysis of their relationship with politics. At a minimum, it forces us to examine how the political consequences of changes in the religious field relate to political power.

It would be inaccurate, then, to study religion and politics in Latin America without taking into account the dramatic changes that have occurred in the religious field. I thus propose to broaden Mainwaring's institutional analysis and combine it with Pierre Bourdieu's theory of the religious field, Bastian's notion of mutation of the religious field, and the Marxist world systems theory to explain the role of the Catholic Church in politics and the emergence of the evangelical movement into the mainstream of politics.

For Bourdieu, the religious field is a separate space within the social space. As a result, it is possible to establish positions, relationships, and activities that can be differentiated within the social space. In this sense, one could speak of the religious field, the economic field, the political field, and so on. The religious field is the theoretical space where one can reconstruct the logic of intervention between agents and institutions that produces and distributes symbolic salvation goods. A supply-and-demand dynamic emerges, where people can "buy" symbolic salvation goods. Agents and institutions that produce salvation goods enter into competition for religious capital and religious power in historically determined religious fields. They also enter into competition with other fields in the social space. For example, the relationship between political and religious power is notable. Bourdieu indicates that

> [T]he structure of relationships between the religious field and the field of power requires, in each conjuncture, the configuration of the structure of relationships constitutive of the religious field. The religious field fulfills an external function of legitimization of the established order as long as the maintenance of the symbolic order contributes directly to maintenance of the political order.... The proper function [of the religious field] is to contribute by imposing, inculcating schemes of perception, thought, and objective action agreed upon with the political structures. (Bourdieu 1971, 328–29)

The relationship established between the church in the religious field and the different factions of the dominant classes in the political field allows the church to contribute to the maintenance of religious and political order. However, this complementary relationship does not exclude tensions and conflicts between the religious and political field. Depending on historical circumstances, church and state may complement each other—sign concordats to legalize their relationships—or may encounter conflicts because the latter inhibit the influence of church in society.

While the concept of religious fields allows us to understand the logic between religious agents and public institutions, the notion of mutation in the religious field illuminates our understanding of Latin America, where liberal modernity was not established based on a religious reform that could permit the eventual mutation of corporative mentalities. This explains why a form of oligarchic liberalism, neo-corporatist populism, and caudillismo[8] followed nineteenth-century liberal reforms. Latin American liberals could not reconcile conservative Catholicism with liberal modernity and ended up embracing it. Similarly, evangelicalism in the twentieth century follows in the tracks of Latin American folk Catholicism and adopts many of its authoritarian traditions.

The concepts of religious field and mutation of the religious field open up new opportunities to comprehend the emerging dialectic between religion and politics as new agents appear in the religious market place. These new agents bring a greater degree of cultural pluralism and, as such, exert a considerable influence on society and politics.

Changes in the religious field occur in the context of the transformation of the world economy and the political field. The world systems theory can help explain the milieu in which transformations in the religious field take place. This theory states that starting in the sixteenth century, a capitalist world economy began to develop and, from then to the present, societies ceased to be isolated entities and became part of an increasingly interdependent world system. The boundaries of the world economy originally included most of Europe and Latin America, but subsequently came to cover the whole planet (Wallerstein 1974, 1981). In the words of Wallerstein:

> I assume that this totality is a system, that is, that it has been relatively autonomous of external forces; or to put it another way, that its patterns are explicable largely in terms of its internal dynamics. I assume that it is a *historical* system, that is, that it was born, has developed, and will one day cease to exist (through disintegration or fundamental transformation). I assume lastly that it is the dynamics of the system itself that explain its historically changing characteristics. Hence, insofar as it is a system, it has structures and these structures manifest themselves in cyclical rhythms, that is, mechanisms which reflect and ensure repetitious patterns (Wallerstein 2003, 448).

The world economic system profoundly reshapes all aspects of society. The world systems theory recommends studying social change in the context of the dynamics introduced by modern capitalism. Although this theory tends to overstate the economic factors, it does provide a solid theoretical framework with which to examine the relationship between religion and politics. It posits that abrupt changes in the worldwide economy provide the context for the interplay between the fields of religion and politics. Certainly, a careful application of Wallerstein's master theory can shed light on radical economic changes in the Dominican Republic and other parts of Latin America in the past fifty years. This research will follow the recommendations of the world systems theory on issues of economic change, but it will tend to privilege the analysis of the effects of economic changes on the state. It will define the state as the basic alliance, the basic "pact of domination," and the norms, which guarantee the domination of the ruling classes over the subordinate strata of society. I will draw a distinction between the state and the political regime. The political regime refers to "formal rules that link the main political institutions (legislature to the executive, executive to the judiciary, and party system to them all), as well as the issues of the political nature that lies between citizens and rulers" (Cardoso 1979, 38). Religious institutions, Catholic and evangelical, operate in the context of the changing dynamic of the state as they seek to exert influence in the religious field.

In writing this book, I relied on primary and secondary source materials in the United States and the Dominican Republic. As a Dominican, I have benefited from real-time contact with the country, which enabled me to have an inside perspective on cultural, social, and political developments. During the last fourteen years, I have traveled to the country every year and have spent at least the last five summers doing fieldwork on religion and politics. I visited the nine dioceses and two archdioceses of the Dominican church and interviewed their bishops and archbishops as well as more than sixty priests, nuns, and Catholic lay workers.[9] These visits familiarized me with the social pastoral work of the church and the challenge of the evangelical movement. To broaden my perspective, I interviewed twenty-five evangelical pastors, including national ecclesiastical leaders of the evangelical religion. I also reviewed the most important daily newspapers and magazines as well as the local Catholic and evangelical printed media and discussed my project with important Dominican Catholic and evangelical scholars. Further, I worked in the personal library of Msgr. Hugo Eduardo Polanco Brito and reviewed a collection of newspaper articles dealing with church political mediation at the Pontificia Universidad Católica Madre y Maestra. What emerged from this research is not a history of the relationship between religion and politics, but an interpretation of the Catholic Church in a changing political environment.

Summary of Chapters

The text contains six chapters and a conclusion. Chapter 1 offers a comparative and historical context of the church in Latin America in the nineteenth and twentieth centuries and then gives an account of the Dominican church from 1844 to 1961. It examines various attempts to build a national church along the lines of the neo-Christendom orientation and discusses how the Dominican church is an exemplary case of church subordination to the state.

Chapter 2 introduces the national churches of Bolivia, Guatemala, Nicaragua, and El Salvador. It examines exemplary cases of political mediation in countries with weak democratic institutions. I argue here that the clergy identified with the modernization approach in those churches tended to promote and participate in political mediation as a means to foster transition to democracy and re-accommodate the new political situation.

Chapter 3 returns to the Dominican Republic to explain how the church responded to social and political changes and how it became reintegrated into the post-Trujillo society. It shows that through political mediation the church became a factor of cohesion that helped to consolidate the authoritarian regime of Joaquín Balaguer.

Chapter 4 looks at the context in which the Dominican church consolidates its role of mediator. It submits that, as in Bolivia and Central America, the modernization approach merges with traditional conservative forces forming a neoconservative church orientation that promotes liberal democracy and political mediation as the best mechanism to resolve conflicts.

Chapter 5 analyzes the social pastoral programs of the Dominican church as an attempt to fulfill its evangelical mission but also to rebuild its ties with the lower echelons of society and strengthen its legitimacy in society. It argues that the entire church agrees with the social pastoral approach, but those who actually promote it have a history of identification with modernizing and liberating orientations.

Chapter 6 explores the emergence and political integration of the evangelical movement in Latin America and, in particular, the Dominican Republic. It posits that evangelicals are a competitor to the Catholic Church in the area of religion, financial resources, and political mediation.

The conclusion proposes that in the near future both Catholics and evangelical institutions will play important roles in society and politics. The weakness of Dominican democracy and the incapacity of political parties to reach significant agreements regarding lasting political and economic reforms make the presence of the clergy necessary to mediate political conflicts. These circumstances have provided the occasion for the complete reintegration of the Catholic Church and the evangelical institutions into the mainstream of society.

Notes

1. It is important to clarify what I mean by "the church" at the outset of this introduction. Following Thomas Bruneau (1974, 1), the church is defined "by four closely interrelated components: a message, an institution and its relationship with the Universal Church and the state." This investigation will focus primarily on the church's relationship with the state, but it will, when appropriate, highlight the role of the universal church or the Vatican in the life of the Latin American church and, in particular, the Dominican church.

2. I will use the term evangelical to refer to a wide range of Protestants. However, I will divide them into two groups: historical Protestants and evangelicals or Pentecostals. The term *historical Protestant* is used to refer to the mainline churches that established themselves in Latin America in the nineteenth and early twentieth centuries. These churches generally followed the theological orientation of their mother

churches in Europe and the United States. The term *evangelical* or *Pentecostal* refers to "ecstatic forms of Protestantism defined in terms of special gifts bestowed by the Holy Spirit. Whereas only a minority of North American missionaries are Pentecostals, most Latin American evangelicals are" (Stoll, 1990, 4). In any case, most Latin American Pentecostals refer to themselves as *evangélicos*. I, too, will use the term evangelical to refer to this religious movement.

3. For the sake of clarity, I will use the term orientation or ecclesiastical view of the church instead of models of the church as used by Mainwaring.

4. A strong regional or national leader who wields complete power over subordinates.

5. A local boss who exercises power over subordinates.

6. A large estate in Latin America.

7. A person with power and authority.

8. Refers to a set of patron-client personal ties of dominance and submission and the common desire to obtain political power or wealth. Caudillismo flourishes in the context of a lack of institutionalized means of succession to political office.

9. See the references for a list of all my interviews with Catholic and evangelical leaders.

CHAPTER ONE

Development of the Dominican Catholic Church: A Comparative Perspective

The Dominican Catholic Church shares a similar history with its Latin American counterparts when it comes to the development of its relationship with politics. In this sense, a comparative historical perspective is useful for understanding the role of the church in society. It enables us to comprehend differences and similarities in the region and see how the Dominican church fits within the general pattern of church politics in the region. This chapter thus begins by placing the Dominican church in the context of church and politics in Latin America. It then explores the development of the church from independence in 1844 to the end of the dictatorship of Rafael Trujillo in 1961. The core of the chapter first examines church politics by looking at the ecclesiastical governments of Tomás Portes (1848–1858), Fernando A. Meriño (1885–1906), Alejandro Nouel (1906–1931), and Ricardo Pittini (1935–1961). It then analyzes the church institutional consolidation during the Trujillo dictatorship and the subsequent political crisis. It submits that despite its institutional weakness the church served as a factor of social and political cohesion to Dominican society in the nineteenth and twentieth centuries.

The Latin American Church and Politics

The relationship of the Catholic Church with Latin American politics dates back to the Conquest, extended throughout the colonial period, and underwent significant structural changes as a result of independence from Spain and Portugal in the 1820s. Despite the political changes resulting from the break of colonial ties, the legacy of colonialism set the tone for church-state relations in the nineteenth and twentieth centuries. As a consequence, the presence of the church is important in the political process that led to independence and the establishment of the new republics.

The church hierarchy sided with the Spanish Crown in the struggle for independence and went on to support the conservative political factions that took power shortly after independence movements in the early 1820s. However, a small number of influential priests did not follow the hierarchy and joined the independence movement. This was the case, for example, of Miguel Hidalgo and José María Morelos, who led the independence movement in Mexico. The church opposed liberalism across Latin America during the nineteenth century and resisted the various political offsprings of liberalism in the twentieth century such as socialism and communism. Church opposition to liberalism was due to the liberal program of reducing the power of the church. Nineteenth-century liberals wanted to separate the church from the state and curtail its access to public resources. During that time, a small but active group of priests and nuns sided with social and political movements that sought the overthrow of authoritarian regimes.

These nineteenth- and twentieth-century political developments show that the church was not a monolithic institution, but rather one that harbored diverse ecclesiastic and political views. Nonetheless, across Latin America the neo-Christendom orientation became the hegemonic force and the clergy accepted subordination to the state as an adequate way to obtain financial resources in exchange for church blessings.

As the church confronted liberal attacks, it remained confined to a neo-Christendom vision of the world. This legacy would linger on in Latin America, where Spanish and Portuguese forged new societies that mimicked European cultures. Thus, the Latin American church evolved along with the colonial state apparatus as one of the principal pillars of society. However, when Latin America broke colonial ties with Spain (1810–1824) and Portugal (1822) in the nineteenth century and created new nation states, the Christendom orientation began to decline. The church struggled throughout the nineteenth century to regain its previous status in society and to reconstitute its relations with Latin American states, but it could not turn back the wheels of history; instead, it modified its Christendom vision into a neo-Christendom worldview.

The process of re-Christianizing society began in the later years of the nineteenth century but did not flower and bear fruits until the 1920s (Mainwaring 1986, 25–42). While making those claims on the ideological realm, the Catholic hierarchy built political alliances with conservative regimes. Conservatives protected the church and helped it exert its control over the education system, social welfare, baptism, burials, and morality. In exchange, the church legitimated the authority of conservative governments, regardless of how oppressive conservatives were. A relationship of convenience with Latin American authoritarian rulers developed over time as the church implemented its neo-Christendom orientation of the world. The Catholic hierarchy did not perceive relationships with social economic elites or the state as political but as a natural projection of its religious outlook on the world and life.

The pattern of church hierarchy involvement in Latin American politics varies significantly across the region. We can note at least three types of patterns within Latin America: church-state ruptures, church-state integration, and church subordination to the state. By church-state ruptures, I mean abolition of church privileges; freedom of worship and the press; civil marriage and divorce; secular civil registers, cemeteries, and education; and suppression of religious orders, including contemplative ones. In contrast, church integration refers to a situation where the church is an essential element of the social order and plays a major role in various aspects of life. Church-state integration is the orientation of the traditional ideal of Christendom, as opposed to neo-Christendom, where the church adapts to, rather than fights, the civil authorities. Church subordination to the state refers to a condition in which the church is so poor and structurally weak that it needs state economic support to carry out its mission. In these circumstances, the church seeks to implement a neo-Christendom orientation, where it tries to accommodate the political establishment.

Church-State Ruptures

Mexico, Cuba, Guatemala, and Chile are cases of ruptured church-state relationships. In Mexico, Benito Juárez curtailed church prerogatives and broke diplomatic ties with the Vatican (1858). The church had been a key ally of the conservative forces that lost half of Mexican territory in the U.S.-Mexican War (1846–1848). Mexico would not renew its diplomatic ties with the Vatican until the early 1990s. Similarly, in Guatemala, the liberal regime of Justo Rufino Barrios (1871) expelled the Jesuits and the bishop and reduced the power of the church by cutting state economic support and prohibiting public religious processions. Barrios even visited the United States to invite Protestant pastors to preach in his country. In 1887, General Manuel Lisandro Barilla, Barrios's successor, went further by forbidding foreign clergy to enter his country. The government expelled the archbishop and did not allow him to return until 1897. Church-state tensions quieted down for two decades but flared up again in 1920, when General José María Orellana renewed the anticlerical campaign and exiled the archbishop.

In 1925, liberals took power in Chile and began to extricate the church from the state, seeking to reduce its influence. The church and conservative governments had had such a close relationship in Chile that the church had veto power over conservative presidents. Anticlerical liberals had always wanted to end this type of relationship (Stewart-Gambino 1992, 13–26).

In Cuba, the socialist revolution of 1959 produced the most complete reduction of church influence. The revolution not only expelled the priests who supported the counterrevolution, it also reduced the church's presence in Cuba as a whole. Church opposition to the government was equally strong and it would not issue a pastoral letter criticizing the U.S. economic blockade of the island until 1968, when it began to accept that Christians were participating in the state efforts to promote development (Dussel 1992, 421–24).

Church and State Integration

Colombia stands alone as a case of church integration. In Colombia, the political conflict between liberals and conservatives left a lasting legacy in church-state relations. After a long liberal reign (1848–1887), the conservatives took power and ruled until 1930. During this time, they signed a concordat with the Vatican in 1887 that regulated church-state relations and turned the church into an essential element of the political order. The church was a pillar of society that endured after liberals overthrew the conservatives, which occurred in 1930.

According to the concordat, the Catholic religion was to be taught at all levels of education. The church was charged with registering births, and parish records were considered more important that civil records. The government turned all cemeteries over to ecclesiastic authorities. "Civil divorce did not exist, and civil marriage for baptized Catholics was made contingent on a public declaration of abandonment of the faith. These statements were supposed to be made before a judge, posted publicly, and communicated to the bishop" (Levine 1981, 70).

Despite the liberal upheaval of 1948, when the church was attacked nationwide and even the archbishop's palace in Bogotá was burned down, subsequent liberal return to power in the 1960s did not curtail the church's role in Colombian life. In fact, the church renegotiated the concordat of 1887 in 1973, but the only significant change was the possibility of a civil divorce without public apostasy. Nonetheless, by the 1950s, the church had largely withdrawn from active participation in partisan politics and had begun to stress the need for unity and an end to the violence that had been so dramatic in nineteenth- and twentieth-century Colombia. Subsequently, members of the church served as mediators in political conflicts rather than taking sides in those conflicts.

This peculiarity of the Colombian case might be explained by the early institutional development of the Colombian church. In 1903, the church in Colombia had already constituted a National Conference of Bishops, an institution that Latin American churches would not create until the 1950s. The national conference brought bishops from different dioceses together and enabled them to establish nationwide pastoral programs and seminaries to educate and increase the clergy as well as the laity. In the 1940s, the conference began to create an extensive network of Catholic Action groups, trade unions, adult education programs, and community organizations. By 1972, it had developed a permanent professional secretariat that coordinated the work of all the dioceses (Levine 1981, 72–74). These educational programs enabled the church to maintain a strong influence on the state and society.

Church Subordination to the State

Church subordination to the state is the most common model of church-state relationship in Latin America. In Central and South America, with the exception of Chile and Colombia, the church became weak as a result of the liberal period. This partly explains the church hierarchy's acceptance of the Estado Novo of Getulio Vargas in Brazil (1930) and the regime of Juan Domingo Perón (1946) in Argentina. The church needed to enlist the support of these regimes to promote its neo-Christendom orientation. In Venezuela, the church played the role of a junior partner. In fact, until 1964, state control was extensive there. For example, under the Law of Ecclesiastical Patronage of 1824, the church did not have a juridical status and it could not own property or enter into any contract (Levine 1981, 71). In Central America, the church was equally subordinated to the dictatorships that ruled the region in the nineteenth and twentieth centuries.

The Dominican church fits nicely within this model of church subordination to the state. It mirrors the larger reality of those nations where the church evolved from a weak institution that needed to enlist state support to carry out its neo-Christendom vision of the world. Let us now examine the Dominican church to illustrate a case of church building along the lines of the neo-Christendom orientation where the church is subordinated to the state.

The Dominican Church under Colonial Rule

The history of the church in the Dominican Republic begins with the conquest and colonization of what the Europeans called the New World. Church and state relations were established through the papal bull *Inter Caetera*, issued in May 1493, shortly after Christopher Columbus returned from his first voyage. By so doing, Pope Alexander VI ceded to the Spanish Crown complete and perpetual dominion in America. In exchange, Spain would spread Catholicism in the New World. On July 28, 1508, Pope Julius II issued the bull *Universalis Ecclesiae regimini*, in which he gave King Ferdinand and his successors the right to present to Rome candidates for offices from archbishop downward. This new mechanism was known as *Real Patronato* (Royal Patronage) (Metzler 1991, 104–7). Subsequently, the Royal and Supreme Council of Indies[1] ran the entire machinery of the *Real Patronato*. In practice, the pope gave the Spanish Crown full control of the church in the New World.

The church had been an intricate part of Iberian society, and Spanish authorities wanted to develop it in the New World the way they knew it back home. In Spain, church, state, and society were intertwined, which does not necessarily mean that the church dominated everything. Church and state had a relationship of interdependence, and lay groups and agencies often used the latter for their own advancements (Lockhart and Schwartz 1996, 13).

However, the historic circumstances of the New World were quite different from those of the Iberian Peninsula, and the church had to adapt to the new social and cultural environment. This included eventually accepting elements of indigenous and African religions. This was difficult for the church because not everyone within the institution agreed with its proximity to the conquerors. Early in the process of conquest and colonization in the Caribbean, small but dynamic and committed groups of priests led by Fathers Antón de Montesino and Bartolomé de las Casas protested the injustices the Spanish committed against the indigenous population. These protests were eventually followed by legislation that regulated the treatment of Indians in the New World. Nonetheless, one central element remained unchanged: the Catholic clergy would be linked closely to the Spanish colonial oligarchy and the state that developed after the conquest of the indigenous civilizations.

The Dominican Church under the Haitian Occupation, 1822–1844

Dominican independence is a unique event in Latin American history because it was obtained from a Caribbean nation state. Dominicans gained their first independence from Spain in 1821, but the newly established Spanish Haiti, as the new republic was called, was not yet ready for self-rule and it accepted its annexation by Haiti in 1822. However, church political involvement in the process was similar to the Latin American experience. For example, the church opposed Haitian liberalism that rejected the existence of corporate entities. During the occupation, the Haitian government confiscated church properties; closed the University of Santo Domingo, which had been under church administration; and forced the clergy to obey the liberal Constitution of Haiti (1816).

In 1824, a church-inspired plot against the Haitian government failed. This complicated church relations with the government and eventually led Bishop Pedro Valera y Jiménez (1809–1830) to leave the island for Cuba (Henríquez Ureña 1991, 31). It was this conflictive political relationship that led many clergymen to support the movement for the separation of Santo Domingo from Haiti (1838–1844). Vicar General Tomás Portes (1830–1848), successor of Bishop Valera y Jiménez, did not support independence. A Hispanophile, Portes thought that Spanish rule had to be restored, but because of his close relationship with the French consul in Santo Domingo and the uncertainties of restoration of Spanish rule, he was apparently willing to consider annexation by France.

A number of local priests shared Portes's pro-French views, whereas others, such as Gaspar Hernández (a Peruvian royalist) and Pedro Pamies, a Spaniard, had remained pro-Spanish. Notwithstanding these views, many rank-and-file priests from the Cibao (northern region), where there was significant support for independence, did not follow the vicar general's political views and supported independence. Priests in favor of independence included Manuel González Regalado, Anselmo Ramírez, Silvestre Núñez, Domingo Solano, and Anselmo Rodríguez (Polanco Brito 1980, 22–24). The political divisions of the clergy did not prevent them from joining the independence movement, because nearly everyone opposed the Haitian despotic version of liberalism.

Clerical participation in the independence movement left its influence in the Dominican Constitution of 1844. The Constituent Assembly had twenty-nine members, eight of whom were priests. In fact, the president of this assembly, Manuel María Valencia was consecrated as a Catholic priest four years later. The priests were quite influential in the discussions and drafting of the first Dominican constitution. For example, the commission charged with framing the constitution was composed of five members, three of whom were priests. These priests played an important role in ensuring that Catholicism would be the official religion of the new independent state. Today, Catholicism figures prominently in the symbols of the state: the Bible and the cross are displayed in the National Shield, encircled by the words *Dios, Patria y Libertad* (God, Fatherland, and Freedom). Clearly, the clergy legitimated the birth of the new nation state and its constitution, thereby setting the pattern for a complex political relationship between the state and the church.

The Dominican church mirrored the larger realities of nineteenth-century Latin America in its participation in the emancipation movement. In Brazil, the archbishop presided over the commission that drafted the constitution in 1822. In Ecuador, the bishop of Quito became president of the newly created republic. In Central America, the clergy played an active role in the Cortes of Cadiz[2] in 1812 and later participated in drafting a constitution for the region. Of forty-nine notables invited to participate in the sessions, seventeen were clergymen. Although Dominican independence took place some twenty years later, it resembled the process that took place elsewhere in the region and thus fit the general pattern of church-state relations.

Portes and the Search for a National Church, 1844–1858

Despite the involvement of many of its members in the independence movement and in drafting the constitution, the church had its own historical project. This project consisted of celebrating a synod to reestablish the church hierarchy, founding a conciliar seminary to train priests, exerting cultural influence in society, and setting up the church along the lines of the neo-Christendom orientation. The importance of this project should not be underestimated. The French and Haitian occupations had dealt a mortal blow to the church and, as a result, the church had lost its economic base, its role in education, and its social assistance programs. The number of priests, which was sixty-eight in 1827, had not changed by 1861 (see table 1.1), the year that the country was annexed by Spain.

The church leadership had to adapt to the social and political circumstances of the time to implement its project. Portes was ready to make this

Table 1.1. Development of the Clergy in the Dominican Republic

Year	Foreign Born	Dominican	Unknown Nationality	Total
1827*	26	42		68
1861*	17	27	15	69
1884**	23	24		47
1902***	5	58		63
1923***	13	51		64
1936****	43	28		71
1953*****	87	40		127

Sources: *private correspondence with José Luis Sáez, SJ, August 4, 2000, and March 10, 2000; **Lluberes (1998, 120); ***Sáez (1979, 76–77); ****Tomé (1963, 712); ***** Instituto Nacional de Pastoral (1993, 360).

political move. He ignored his Hispanophile political sentiments and decided to support Pedro Santana, the first Dominican president (1844–1848). In a pastoral letter issued in July 1844, he threatened excommunication to anyone obstructing the "wise government" of Santana (Martínez 1995, 75). This explains why Portes's request for government support to get his papal appointment as archbishop of Santo Domingo was approved. Pope Pius IX appointed him archbishop in 1848, an event perceived by national authorities as papal recognition of Dominican independence.

Despite the nonexistence of a concordat,[3] Archbishop Portes, with state support, founded the Seminario Conciliar (Conciliar Seminary) Santo Tomás de Aquino in 1848. The government promised a subsidy of 12,000 pesos annually, then a substantial sum, for the seminary from the public treasury and gave the church four of the best houses in the city of Santo Domingo and the produce of the Ingenio Frías (a plantation near the city). It also gave twelve scholarships for equal numbers of students from the republic's provinces (Polanco Brito 1948, 30–40; Sáez 1996a, 39–42). The Conciliar Seminary was the first educational institution founded in the postindependence period and it was not only meant to train priests in theology but also to teach medicine, humanities, and jurisprudence. The Dominican government did not sign a concordat with the Vatican, but the church received state economic support nonetheless.

Regardless of support for the church, the Dominican state did not return its properties, which Haitian authorities had confiscated during their occupation of the country. This created a problem for the relations between the two entities. Although not as strict as the Haitian constitution, the Dominican constitution was also liberal and eliminated chaplaincies and other church prerogatives. Santana noted that Archbishop Portes wanted to make the church autonomous from state control. This was the main source of church-state political conflicts. Santana made concessions to the church by abolishing divorce and declaring civil marriage invalid, but he also tolerated the presence of Protestants and Jews. In short, nineteenth-century Dominican governments intervened in church affairs by limiting its prerogatives, but they never played as important a role as governments did in other countries in Central and South America.

Buenaventura Báez (1849–1853) was a political enemy of Santana and, as such, he wanted to enlist church support. He thus encouraged the archbishop to hold a diocesan synod while he was in office. In 1851, Archbishop Portes held the VIII Diocesan Synod to update the church regarding the new social and political circumstances of the nation. When the issue of church-state relations came up, the clergy had a sympathetic ear in the government. Báez, wanting to get along with the church, abolished the constitutional articles and laws that limited church prerogatives (Pérez Memén 1984, 654). However, when Santana returned to the presidency (1853–1856), he summoned the archbishop to Congress, where he asked him, in public, to take the oath of allegiance to the Constitution of 1844. The archbishop engaged in a duel of words with the president and refused to take the oath. The president threatened to exile him. Ill and demoralized, Portes instructed a subordinate to take the oath of allegiance on his behalf (Rodríguez Demorizi 1969, 99–102). Santana then restored the articles and laws that governed church-state relations.

Due to the instability of the state and the changing fortunes of the political *caudillo* (strongman) Báez, who supported the church, Portes's project did not produce significant results. The government did not restore the church's prerogatives, and the seminary only graduated thirteen priests during Portes's leadership (1848–1858). Portes died in 1858, and with him also died a weak national project to build the Dominican church as an autonomous entity.

From Colonial Rule to Institutional Crisis, 1861–1884

From 1848 to 1861, the struggles between Santana and Báez had colored political events. From the outset of independence, both of them sought a foreign power to take over the newly established state. This search included pro-Spain, pro-U.S., pro-England, and pro-France groups. These efforts did not succeed until the United States was in the midst of the Civil War (1861–1865). In this context, Santana, becoming president for the third time (1858–1861), requested Spanish annexation. In 1861, when Spain annexed the Dominican Republic, the colonial church was reestablished as well, and a Spaniard, Bienvenido Monzón, was appointed archbishop of Santo Domingo. Monzón came to reestablish order in a church where the hierarchy had nearly collapsed. Gaspar Hernández, Portes's successor, fearing Santana's repression, left the country. Shortly before dying, he delegated his functions to Martín J. Niewindt, bishop of Curacao.[4]

Rather than improving its institutional organization, the reestablishment of Spanish colonial rule in the Dominican Republic weakened and divided the church. Archbishop Monzón started a crusade to bring both the clergy and the population under strict church discipline. Upon his arrival, he noted the existence of Masonic lodges, Protestant churches, relaxed customs among priests, and illegitimate marriages (see chapter 6). In 1863, he issued a pastoral letter in which he outlined his apostolic project, which banned public religious ceremonies other than Catholic ones. Monzón's strategy backfired and stimulated opposition to Spanish rule. Many priests and seminarians joined the rebels who had been fighting the reestablishment of colonial rule. General José de la Gandara, head of the Spanish forces in Santo Domingo, blamed Monzón for his difficulties in the war effort, which the Spanish were losing. Monzón went to Spain to defend his case, but Spain could no longer afford to pay for the war and decided to withdraw its forces in 1865 (Guerrero Cano 1991, 23–33, 65–89).

Church-state relations deteriorated after the Spanish departure, and the hierarchy nearly collapsed once more. Political instability was partly to blame, because neither nationalists nor annexationists were able to sustain power for any considerable length of time. Nationalists wanted the Vatican to appoint a Dominican priest to lead the church, while a faction of the annexationists, led by Báez (Santana died in 1864), were willing to work with a foreigner. Again, the church was caught between the two predominant political forces of the time and, as usual, the clergy was politically divided. Prior to departing for Spain, Monzón delegated his authority to Blas Díaz de Arcaya. Clearly, Monzón left the Dominican church in a complete state of confusion.

In 1866, the Vatican, apparently following Spanish advice, appointed a series of three European apostolic vicars who were generally rejected by liberal nationalist governments. These vicars included Luis Nicolás Buggenons, a Redemptoris, (1868–1873), Leopold A. Santaché de Aguasanta, a Franciscan (1870–1874), and Roco Cocchia, a Capuchine, (1874–1884). After a difficult beginning, Cocchia succeeded in gaining the support of the local liberal elite. He organized the IX Synod of the Dominican church in 1878, which brought significant stability to the church. Cocchia's Synod was dedicated to the celebration of the sacraments, catechism, preaching, clergy life, and culture. He reestablished the church hierarchy and prepared conditions for the return of a Dominican priest to lead the local institution (Bello Peguero 1997, 99–240; Sáez 1993, 90–94; González 2001, 13–16).

From 1865 to 1878, the Dominican Republic endured one of the most unstable periods in its history. Except for Báez, who installed a dictatorship (1868–1873), most Dominican governments did not complete their terms in office because political opponents overthrew them. The short-lived liberal governments that ruled after Báez were overthrown and never achieved meaningful international recognition because the liberals did not want to acknowledge foreign debts incurred by Báez. In these circumstances, the state did not have the capacity to support a church that was in the midst of an institutional crisis. Meanwhile, local political rivalries ensnared the church and prevented it from reestablishing the hierarchy until the arrival of Cocchia. Nonetheless, the church's institutional links to Rome saved it from collapsing along with the Dominican state.

Meriño and the Development of a Dominican Clergy, 1885–1906

Fernando Arturo de Meriño continued Archbishop Portes's nationalist project to make the church less dependent on foreign priests. He was one of the thirteen Dominican priests who graduated from the Conciliar Seminary founded by Portes in 1848 and was apostolic administrator for a brief period (1860–1862). He was forced into exile by the Spanish forces that occupied the country in 1861 because of his identification with the nationalist political project, and his nationalist sympathies eventually led him to accept the presidency of the republic for a brief time (1880–1882). Prior to Meriño's appointment as archbishop of Santo Domingo (1885–1906), he had been the apostolic administrator (1882–1884). His appointment provided institutional continuity, which helped consolidate the church as an institution.

Meriño was a leading force in the church and a man with clearly defined nationalist ideas. He believed that the church needed to develop a national clergy to accomplish its objectives. His nationalism led him to oppose the importation of foreign clergy to aid him with the education of Dominican priests. In fact, he undertook this task personally by taking the leadership of the Conciliar Seminary upon completing his presidential term. There were forty-seven priests (twenty-four Dominicans and twenty-three foreigners) when Meriño was appointed archbishop (1885). In 1902, the number had increased to sixty-three (fifty-eight Dominicans and five foreigners) (see table

1.1). Meriño inverted the ratio of national/foreign priests, and this gave the church a minimum of quantitative growth. However, as an institution the church remained weak and subordinated to the state. Meriño did not make any deliberate attempts to contradict the policies of Ulises Heureaux, the dictator who led the nation during most of his ecclesiastical government.[5]

In President Heureaux's first term as president (1882–1884), the Dominican government renewed earlier efforts to get a concordat with the Vatican. In 1884, Collin de Paradis, a diplomatic agent who had worked for various Latin American nations in Europe, was appointed as special envoy by the Dominican government. De Paradis negotiated a concordat with the Vatican that, in fact, was approved by the Dominican Congress. However, the final document was never exchanged with Vatican authorities, a necessary action according to international church or state diplomacy. In this document, the Dominican state recognized Catholicism as the official state religion and agreed to exercise the *Patronato*, and support the church economically. In addition, "the archbishop would be loyal and obey the government established by the Constitution of the Republic and would not start any activity, directly or indirectly, against the established interests of the State" (Alfau Durán 1975, 82–84; Peralta Brito and Chez Checo 1979, 90–91). Clearly, despite its financial incapacity to support the church, the Dominican state still sought to subordinate it by its involvement in the appointment of the archbishop. Why wasn't the final document exchanged with Vatican authorities? Simply put: the Dominican government wanted to fill the post of archbishop of Santo Domingo and Meriño was its candidate. Once this objective was achieved, the government ignored the diplomatic issues relating to the concordat. Meriño himself was trapped in local politics, which apparently prevented him from following up on the diplomatic details of the concordat.

Despite his acceptance of the legal framework of the state, Meriño fought government support for positivist ideas in education. He fought against the ideas of the Puerto Rican philosopher, Eugenio María de Hostos, who had taken up residence in the country in the 1870s and became an established personality in public life, particularly in education. Hostos founded the Escuela Normal, a type of school geared to training teachers. He believed that schools had to be secular and that religious education had to be excluded from public schools. Hostos's Escuela Normal held several graduation exercises, and despite his expulsion from the country (1888) due to his opposition to the Heureaux regime, the school system he founded continued to operate until 1895. His ideas had a profound influence on Dominican education that continued well into the twentieth century.

Meriño, of course, opposed Hostos's ideas forcefully and sought to include religious education in public schools. He pushed for and obtained a reform in education that suppressed Hostos's Escuela Normal and replaced it with two central schools located in Santo Domingo and Santiago. Catholic religious education was mandatory in the new schools (Lluberes 1998, 119–25; Peralta Brito and Chez Checo 1979, 37–45). However, these were public schools and not Catholic schools; the church did not have schools or hospitals at that time. Still, Meriños's church project had a relative success in terms of getting the state to change its education policy, ensuring that most Catholic priests were native Dominicans, and having the state continue to recognize Catholicism as the official state religion. Significantly, despite its institutional weakness, the church had a legitimating power that the state had to consider.

Nouel and the Development of a Dependent Church, 1906–1931

Dominican political instability inhibited the development and consolidation of the church. The collapse of the Heureaux regime in 1899 affected all aspects of Dominican society, and a period of political instability ensued that lasted until Ramón Cáceres (1906–1911) rose to power. Dominican customhouses were briefly occupied by the U.S. Marines to secure Dominican political stability and the payments of the nation's foreign debt. Cáceres was able to provide a minimum of stability because of a convention he signed with the United States in 1907, which, in fact, only legalized actions already implemented by the latter.

Adolfo Alejandro Nouel Bobadilla was appointed archbishop coadjutor *jure sucessionis* (1904–1906) because of Meriño's advanced age and illness. Nouel became archbishop when Meriño died in 1906. The Dominican government accepted this but reminded Nouel that he was violating the concordat signed in 1884. As noted above, the concordat was never exchanged, so it was not legally binding. In any case, when Nouel went to the Vatican in 1904, he carried a signed letter by the minister of foreign relations (Alfau Durán 1975, 92). Dominican authorities knew that Nouel was a conservative member of the local elite, educated in Rome, and that it could not reject him. Nonetheless, it needed to remind the clergy that it was under the political influence of Dominican civil authorities.

The conflicts that emerged in church-state relations at the beginning of the twentieth century might be considered low intensity compared to the political confrontations between Santana and Portes in the nineteenth century.

However, they point to conflicts of interest between the two entities. For example, there were disputes in 1908 about the church's right to erect a mausoleum for the interment of Meriño's body in the Cathedral of Santo Domingo. The National Congress claimed that the state owned church buildings and, consequently, that the clergy needed permission from Congress to erect the mausoleum. Nouel accepted the state's claim, but he reminded the minister of interior that he had violated a church prerogative. Again that same year, Nouel complained that whereas the Constitution of 1908 recognized Catholicism as the official religion, it suppressed God's invocation (Jiménez 1987, 28–31; Lluberes 1998, 149). It is interesting to note that when there were conflicts between church and state, Nouel was willing to resolve them through negotiation.

These political frictions did not obviate the fact that the church was accepted as a legitimate and major force in the nation. In fact, after Cáceres was assassinated in 1911, and political instability returned, Nouel was asked to assume the provisional presidency, and he accepted, albeit reluctantly in 1912. He soon realized that he could not resolve the political crisis that unfolded. Rival factions put political pressure on him to accept their political positions. He could not take such pressures and resigned just a few months after his inauguration.

The unrest culminated with U.S. military occupation (1916–1924)[6] (Betances 1995, 48–55; Veeser 2002, 126–61). Nouel assumed a cautious political position about the U.S. occupation. In 1916, he agreed to lead the Commission on Public Instruction, and in 1919, he participated in the consulting commission set up by the occupation government to look into complaints regarding abuses by the U.S. Marines. Not everyone in the clergy shared Nouel's cautious approach. Shortly after the U.S. occupation began, *Boletín Eclesiástico*, the main church publication, issued an editorial declaring the day of the invasion as the "saddest day . . . a day of mourning." Fr. Rafael Castellanos, a nationalist priest, considered the invasion as "an oppressing and humiliating event" (Lluberes 1998, 141–42). In 1920, in the midst of widespread nationalist protests against the American occupation, Nouel sent a letter to U.S. minister Russell saying:

> It is true that the Dominican people in its political disturbance have seen more than once unjust persecution, violations of individual rights, summary executions, etc. However, it never knew about the Chinese water torture, burning of women and children, rope twisting, hunting men in the savannah as if they were savage animals, and dragging a seventy-year-old man by the tail of a horse in broad day light in the main square of Hato Mayor. (Jiménez 1987, 34)

Nouel saw the need to disassociate the church from the abuses of the U.S. military government. He would protest again in 1924, when government reform curtailed church prerogatives regarding marriages. In 1930, despite his illness, he protested a Supreme Court decision to suspend the juridical status of the church. Fr. Rafael Castellanos, one of his successors, joined him in these efforts, but this issue had to wait until a new government was established in 1930. Except for his letter to Minister Russell, which was forceful and patriotic, all of Nouel's protests were measured, and he always sought negotiated solutions whenever he could.

Nouel disagreed with Meriño about the development of the clergy. He thought the Dominican church did not have the necessary resources to train and staff local parishes. In the context of a new activism for re-Christianizing Latin American societies, Nouel started a pattern whereby the church would essentially rely on foreign religious priests to accomplish this goal. Opening the church's doors to different religious orders, in 1909, he asked the Spanish Franciscan religious order for help in staffing several parishes. The Eudists order had arrived from France two years earlier to take charge of the Conciliar Seminary (1907–1916); however, their stay in the country was short because of the outbreak of World War I. It was not until 1923 that priests from the Claretian order of the United States arrived in the country to replace the Eudists in the Conciliar Seminary. This explains, in part, Nouel's lack of success in ordaining priests during his administration (the Conciliar Seminary only graduated twenty-three priests during his twenty-six years of leadership).

The Dominican church was still weak and fragile when Nouel completed his ecclesiastical government. If one recalls that in 1902 there were sixty-three priests, then the church had not made significant progress: twenty-one years later, there were only sixty-four priests (see table 1.1) (Sáez 1979, 70–77). As noted in table 1.2 below, this picture had not changed by 1936. In importing religious priests to staff parishes and to lead the Conciliar Seminary, Nouel made a complete break from the Meriño period, when church authorities refused to import priests and, in particular, religious priests. This orientation of development continued through the twentieth century and its effects still linger on.

The Church and the Trujillo Dictatorship

Trujillo reorganized and consolidated the modern nation state in the Dominican Republic. The regime he installed in 1930 was the outcome of the U.S. occupation of 1916–1924. The United States laid the basic institutional infrastructures that permitted Trujillo to become a rising star within

Table 1.2. Pastoral Workforce of the Church in the Dominican Republic

Year	Diocese	Parish	Dom. Diocesan Priests	Foreign Diocesan Priests	Foreign Religious Priests	Dominican Religious Priests	Brothers (None Priests)	Religious Laymen	Religious Women
1936	1	59	28	28	15	0	8	0	75
1963	5	123	64	21	240*	5	98	927	835

Year	Ed. Inst.	Seminary (Major and Minor)	Hospital	Retirement Home	Male Rel. Comm.	Female Rel. Comm.	Religious House	Radio Station
1936	6	1	4	9	5	4	1	0
1963	29	1	7	2	21	25	8	1

Sources: Boletín Eclesiástico de la Arquidiócesis de Santo Domingo (1936); Tomé (1963).

* The massive increase of foreign religious priests and other church personnel in 1963 was due to the impressive immigration of Cuban and Spanish who left Cuba after the Revolution of 1959. In contrast, in 1953 there were only 127 priests in the country (87 foreigners and 40 Dominicans), whereas by 1963 this figure increased to 330 (69 Dominicans and 261 foreign born).

the Dominican National Guard. He joined the U.S.-created National Guard in 1919, moved successfully through its upper ranks, and led its transformation into a national army under his protector, President Horacio Vásquez (1924–1930). He became a military *caudillo* and soon began plotting to overthrow the government. In 1930 he staged a simulated rebellion, whose political dimension the president apparently did not understand. Though simulated, the rebellion obtained its purpose by getting Vásquez to resign in a confusing political situation. Trujillo used this opportunity to get a figurehead president to succeed Vásquez. He then organized fraudulent elections where he was the official candidate and won by a landslide. The political opposition had to withdraw from the electoral race because of the repression unleashed by state-supported paramilitary groups.

Shortly after Trujillo became president, a strong hurricane hit the country and disrupted both political and economic activities. Trujillo seized this opportunity to build internal and external support for his regime and consolidate his power. He then moved to develop a special relationship with the church. He was aware that his government did not have legitimacy in the eyes of politically active Dominicans, and he knew that the church was important and that he could not ignore it. He expressed this awareness in his welcoming speech to Papal Internuncio Giuseppe Fietta[7] in February 1931. He said:

> The nexuses that unite the Holy See and the Dominican Republic are truly immortal. I will be personally and actively interested in consolidating these nexuses while I am in charge of the National Executive. I trust that your efforts will be fruitful under the protection and cooperation that my government will offer you.
>
> I believe in the spiritual force of our religion and think that it will be always an unquenchable source of comfort and a moral element of powerful influence in establishing progress, well-being, independence and our definitive constitutional stability. (Castillo de Aza 1961, 216)

Trujillo knew about the church's role in Dominican society and recognized that it was important for ordinary people. He was also aware that it lacked economic resources, was institutionally weak, and was anxious to regain its juridical personality. The clergy continued to play a significant role in the nation's cultural and political life. It is worth recalling that Haitians closed down the University of Santo Domingo in 1822 and it was not reopened until 1916. During this period, the church's seminary was the only institution of higher learning. This institution was not just dedicated to training priests; the nation's elite attended the seminary, where they could study medicine, law, and commerce. Thus, except for the very wealthy, who sent their children to study in Europe, the church educated most of the professionals in the country.

Therefore, the church exerted considerable influence in Dominican life. In addition, past and present priest-politicians had substantial power over the population, and Trujillo wanted to find ways to reduce their influence or, better, bring it under his authority. This explains why in March 1931, both houses of Congress discussed and urgently approved a bill to recognize the juridical personality of the church. Congress extended this privilege in 1943 when it declared that all the juridical acts carried out by the church were "valid and firm, and not confiscable under the allegation that the church did not have juridical personality. This was true even for acts carried out prior to April 20, 1931" (Pérez Memén 1985, 170).

Trujillo offered great privileges to the church, but he also demanded its obedience, something not everyone in the church was willing to accept. The Vatican appointed Fr. Rafael Castellano as apostolic administrator to succeed Meriño. In his new post, Castellano was one whose voice rose against Trujillo. However, Msgr. Castellanos's episcopal government (1932–1934) lasted for barely two years because he died of a heart attack. The Vatican appointed Fr. Eliseo Pérez Sánchez to succeed him as apostolic administrator, but did not choose him for the position of archbishop of Santo Domingo. Fr. Ricardo Pittini, an Italian of the Salesian order, was appointed to the post. Fr. Pittini had been a missionary in Uruguay, Paraguay, and the United States, where he learned English. He reportedly impressed Trujillo favorably.

This appointment disrupted the succession of Dominican prelates in the leadership of the church, which had caused so many problems in the nineteenth century. However, politics had changed significantly since then, and now the nation had a strong leader who did not have a credible political opposition and who was willing to accept a break with the past. Significantly, Internuncio Msgr. Guiseppe Fietta was convinced that it was feasible to have a foreign archbishop in the country and had recommended Pittini to the Vatican (Belza 1976, 63–69).

Unlike his predecessors, Archbishop Pittini succeeded in implementing a project for a modern national church with Trujillo's support. He collaborated closely with Trujillo for twenty-six years (1935–1961), and during this period, he enlarged and modernized the church. Archbishop Pittini outlined the objectives of his ecclesiastical project in a letter addressed to the clergy and church's followers in September 1939. One of the main points of his address was the foundation of the Minor Seminary of Santo Cerro in the province of La Vega. He noted the need to increase the number of priests per soul and to upgrade the seminary, where the number of students barely reached twenty-five. This task required a "suitable place, a group of educators with great intellectual and moral capacity, and an increasing pool of candidates that may favor a careful selection. The seminary will have to elevate the prestige of the priesthood to the highest possible status. This is the only way to make the priesthood attractive and thus to stimulate priestly vocations" (Msgr. Pittini's letter is in Document No. 113, Lluberes 1998, 535–36). The seminary needed public support to cover its budget, and Pittini knew that he could count on the government for financial assistance. This assistance became the archbishop's Achilles' heel, forcing him to act cautiously. In a circular letter written in 1937, he affirmed:

> The best way, if not the only way a priest can participate in politics, is by fulfilling his civil duties and contributing efficiently with public authorities to advance the country's progress and well-being. The priest must put in this contribution his prestige, culture, and indifference to profit. As such, we belong to the people and the homeland. Anything of interest to the homeland cannot be foreign to us. (Belza 1976, 85–86)

This letter shows that Pittini wanted his church to be loyal to public authorities and to make a contribution to the progress as understood by the regime. Writing in 1948, he assessed his accomplishments: "I dictate these lines thirteen years after assuming the direction of the Episcopal Government and thank God because I have been able to put on my side the cooperation of the people, the clergy, and civilian authorities" (Pittini 1949, 93).

The achievements of Pittini's ecclesiastical government were extraordinary in terms of the expansion and consolidation of the church. In 1938, Pittini held the X Diocesan Synod to bring the Dominican church up to date with canon law and the changes that had taken place in the church and society. However, the synod did not change Nouel's strategy of importing priests to accomplish the church's mission. As can be observed in table 1.2, Pittini strengthened this tendency started by Nouel as he sought to expand the pastoral workforce of the church. Pittini's contribution is seen in the institutional growth of the church (i.e., the number of dioceses, parishes, educational institutions, health institutions, and religious communities; see table 1.2). The church's institutional improvement was significant, and it led Pope Pius XII, in 1953, to issue the bull *Si Magna et Excelsa* to create the Ecclesiastic Province of Santo Domingo. This bull established the Dioceses of Santiago, La Vega, and the Prelate nullius of San Juan de la Maguana. Three years later, the Vatican made the following bishopric appointments: Fr. Hugo Polanco Brito (Dominican) in Santiago, Fr. Francisco Panal (a Spanish Capuchine) in La Vega, and Fr. Thomas F. Reilly[8] (a North American Redemptorist) in San Juan de la Maguana. In 1959, Fr. Juan Felix Pepén (Dominican) was appointed bishop of the new Diocese of Altagracia in Higuey. The creation of the new dioceses increased the number of parishes, as noted in table 1.2. These new developments established the modern basis of the Dominican church and consolidated the neo-Christendom orientation whose legacy would linger on in the aftermath of Trujillo's assassination.

Pittini's close collaboration with Trujillo did not mean that the relationship was straightforward. José Luis Sáez (2002, 34–35) alludes to three occasions when frictions between Trujillo and Pittini became public. The first occurred in August 1940, when Pittini criticized Trujillo during the Te Deum held to celebrate the Restoration of Dominican independence. The second took place in 1941, when Pittini criticized the United States and England during a sermon and went on to praise totalitarian methods. As a result of these critiques, the Dominican minister of foreign relations informed the American legation in Santo Domingo that it was "considering requesting the Vatican to withdraw Msgr. Pittini from his post" (Vega 1985, 340). The third occurred on May 30, 1947, when Pittini reportedly confessed to the U.S. ambassador, George H. Butler, that the "monopolistic nature of the regime is a heavy load on the Dominican people. . . . Previously he had been able to approach Trujillo about these abuses, but now he feared that such action could mean problems for the Catholic Church" (Vega 1984, 421). The U.S. legation investigated the issue and found that Pittini had, in fact, given various antidemocratic sermons. However, the issue was put to rest when the legation reported that it did not consider Pittini a sympathizer of the Axis. Notwithstanding these frictions, Pittini was a collaborator of the regime as illustrated by his willingness to hand carry, on February 25, 1938, a check for $250,000 to "compensate" Haiti for a massacre conducted by the Dominican government that cost the lives of 5,000 to 10,000 Haitians[9] (Sáez 2002, 33).

The Concordat and the End of the Trujillo Dictatorship

The Dominican Republic was the first country in twentieth-century Latin America to sign a concordat with the Vatican (1954). It was then followed by Colombia, which, as noted earlier, signed a concordat in 1973. These are the only two countries in the region that have signed a concordat with the Vatican. Argentina (1957), Bolivia (1958), Paraguay (1960), El Salvador (1968), and Ecuador (1978) signed agreements on religious assistance to the military, and Venezuela signed a general agreement in 1964. In 1966, Haiti signed a protocol in which the government gave up its privileges of presenting the names of bishops for appointments (de Agar 2000, 881–87).

Dominican authorities used the concordat signed by Francisco Franco of Spain (1953) as a blueprint for negotiations with the Vatican. Trujillo had excellent relations with Franco and thus was able to use the services of the Spanish ambassador in Santo Domingo to guide the Ministry of Foreign Relations in the negotiations that led up to the signing ceremony in Vatican City. Trujillo traveled to Rome for the occasion and the document was signed on June 16, 1954. This concordat is still in force, and the church still considers it as a binding agreement. This position has been accepted by the different administrations that have ruled the country since the death of Trujillo.

Trujillo perceived the concordat as a legal instrument that would give his regime prestige at home and abroad. When Msgr. Ricardo Pittini was appointed archbishop of Santo Domingo in 1935, he began to cultivate a special relationship with Trujillo, which allowed him to consolidate and expand the work of the church. Archbishop Pittini blessed and legitimized the regime and, in exchange, Trujillo gave significant donations to the church enabling Pittini to expand the national network of parishes and pastoral work. Dominican historian Frank Moya Pons calculates that Trujillo gave the church $26 million during the period of his dictatorship (Moya Pons 1973, 15).

According to the concordat, the state recognized the church as an ecclesiastic society and guaranteed it the free and full exercise of its spiritual powers. The state guaranteed its jurisdiction, granted juridical personality to all the religious associations and institutions, and allowed the appointment of archbishops and bishops once the government had been notified of the person chosen in order to determine if there were any objections to him. The state also exempted foreign clergy from payment of immigration taxes and other taxes. Similarly, it recognized and guaranteed the property of the church and declared that temples and religious buildings belonged to the church. Further, it created military chaplains, recognized church holidays, recognized only Catholic marriages, and did not allow divorce. The concordat did not grant immunity to priests, but it established a system through which, if there was an accusation against a priest, the judge would communicate it to the religious authority, and, in the event of a conviction, the convict would serve his sentence separated from lay persons (Gaceta Official del Gobierno Dominicano 1954, 3–16; Lockward 1993, 252–67).

This treaty was the highest degree of understanding between church and state. The state recognized, in theory, the existence of a parallel power within its own jurisdiction. In addition, the state was willing to finance the operation of this parallel power. The treaty was a victory for the church, but it was no less so for Trujillo. By signing it, Trujillo not only got the annulment of a previous marriage by the Vatican, it also provided him great publicity abroad that affirmed his proclaimed Catholicism and his anticommunism.

In theory, the concordat suggests the existence of some form of church-state integration. In practice, however, the opposite happened. As noted above, the church had a long history of legitimating political public institutions and political struggles through priests who were also politicians. This was problematic for the Trujillo regime, and he sought to eliminate the influence of the clergy in national politics. In fact, he kept the representatives of the institutional church busy doing things that were beneficial rather than dangerous to the state, such as administering the technical schools, Catholic schools, hospitals, retirement homes, and so on (Alemán 1982, 397–98). Unlike Colombia, where the church was a strong pillar in society and where its prerogatives did not change after the liberals overthrew the conservatives in 1930, the Dominican church was small, separate, and relegated to the religious sphere. This was demonstrated by its refusal to denounce the abusive policies of the state and by the state's financial support of the numerous educational and welfare institutions of the church. Thus, in practice, the concordat did not eliminate the subordinated status of the church.

The Conflict between Trujillo and the Church

Despite this high level of understanding and subordination, Trujillo's relations with the church began to deteriorate in the late 1950s. Why did the church begin to withdraw political support to the dictator who had been so generous? To understand this radical shift, we must look at changes in the global institution. Prior to Vatican II, the Roman Catholic Church had been revising its social teaching in light of its twentieth-century experience vis-à-vis politics.

In Latin America, the First Bishop Conference had been held in 1954 in Rio de Janeiro, Brazil, and Latin American bishops were beginning to discuss regional religious, social, and political developments. Subsequently, the Cuban Revolution would have an important impact on Latin American politics. In Brazil and Chile, reform-minded bishops had questioned the traditional neo-Christendom ecclesiology, which viewed a closed relationship with the ruling elites as positive and necessary for the church to carry out its mission. These bishops suggested distancing the church from dictatorial regimes and proposed a greater degree of autonomy of the church vis-à-vis public authorities (Fleet and Smith 1997, 46–53; Mainwaring 1986, 43–59).

The Dominican church, however, was reluctant to question its neo-Christendom orientation. In regard to relationships with public authorities, it was comparable to Nicaragua, where the hierarchy had given full support to the dictatorship of Anastacio Somoza (1936–1954); Haiti, where François Duvalier (1957–1971) basically co-opted it; or Guatemala (1954–1985) and Argentina (1976–1983), where the hierarchy supported military rulers (Greene 1993, 111–14; Kirk 1992, 33–57; Klaiber 1998, 67–92, 217–39). Archbishop José Antonio Lezcano y Artega in Nicaragua, Archbishop Wolf Ligondé in Haiti, Archbishop Mario Casariego in Guatemala, Raúl Cardinal Primatesta (archbishop of Córdoba), and Carlos Cardinal Aramburu (archbishop of Buenos Aires from 1975 to 1990) acted in the same way as Archbishop Ricardo Pittini in the Dominican Republic. They all shared a neo-Christendom orientation of the church and an anticommunist ideology, which justified their support for dictatorial regimes. These archbishops legitimated these regimes and, in exchange, received financial support to carry out their mission. The Vatican had to act forcefully to distance these local churches from the political regimes that gave them financial resources in exchange for moral support and a source of legitimacy.

The Vatican reviewed the relationship between church and state under Trujillo and sought to distance itself from his regime. The ecclesiastic hierarchy kept silent when an armed expedition, coming from Cuba, arrived in the country on June 14, 1959. Two days later, Msgr. Lino Zanini was appointed nuncio to the Dominican Republic. However, it is noteworthy that Msgr. Zanini did not arrive in the country until October 25, 1959, the day after the birthday of Trujillo. He could have arrived earlier, but he chose to stop over for a few days in Puerto Rico to avoid participating in the ceremonies held to praise Trujillo (Lluberes 1998, 168; Sáez 1999, 12). In symbolic terms, the church sent a message to Trujillo saying that relationships between the Vatican and his regime had changed.

Zanini's presence in the country is associated with a collective pastoral letter, signed by the five bishops, calling for the avoidance of excesses in the treatment of the political opposition. This letter, made public on January 21, 1960, revealed that the bishops had promised special prayers to God wishing that "none of the relatives of the Authority ever experienced, in their existence, the sufferings that now afflict the hearts of so many parents, children, so many mothers and Dominican wives" (Conferencia del Episcopado Dominicano 1990, 43). This statement might have been moderate, but in the context of the Trujillo dictatorship it was a political challenge to a regime that did not permit any kind of dissidence.

The collective pastoral letter marks a turning point in church-state relationships, but it did not lead to a complete rupture comparable to that in Mexico (1858), Guatemala (1857), Chile (1925), or Cuba (1959). Rather, relations between the church and the Trujillo regime entered into a political crisis as a result of the repression unleashed against the entire church. The campaign included negative press coverage, profanation of temples, arrests of seminarians, deportation of priests, and harassment of bishops. In the midst of the crisis, the regime promoted the idea of a plebiscite asking the church to award Trujillo the title of benefactor of the church. On March 31, 1960—more than two months after the publication of the collective pastoral letter—Trujillo decided to support such a request while ordering the Ministry of Interior and Religious Affairs to cover the deficit of the Seminario Superior Santo Tomás de Aquino (Saint Thomas Aquinas Seminary) (Lluberes 1998, 552–53). In this way, Trujillo reassured the church that he supported it, but at the same time, reminded the bishops of their economic subordination to the regime.

The regime picked the two foreign bishops (Francisco Panal, a Spaniard who led the Diocese of La Vega, and Thomas Reilly, a North American who headed the Prelate Nullius of San Juan de la Maguana) as targets because they were the most vocal in opposition to Trujillo's repressive measures. Trujillo even sent his minister of foreign relations to Rome to express his views regarding the nuncio and the local hierarchy. However, Pope John XXIII announced that the Vatican agreed with the collective pastoral letter published by the bishops (Vega 1999, 71–73). Nonetheless, at the local level, both the nuncio and the bishops tried to talk to Trujillo and encouraged him to end his aggressive acts. In fact, the nuncio, Lino Zanini, on February 15, 1960, wrote to Joaquín Balaguer, the nominal president at the time, asking him to serve as a channel of communication and urging him to renew the financial assistance to the Colegio Agrícola San Ignacio de Loyola in Dajabón[10] (Vega 1999, 94–97).

Interestingly, the U.S. Embassy in Santo Domingo courted the nuncio and embassy personnel talked to Vatican officials in Rome, expressing sympathy for the church's position concerning the Trujillo dictatorship. The United States wanted to know if the position of the local church was also that of the Vatican and how it perceived the Dominican political situation. Msgr. Samoré, secretary of the Vatican, told U.S. diplomatic authorities in Rome that "the bishops of Santo Domingo started their own action, opposing Trujillo's policies, and that it merely coincided with the arrival of Zanini" (Vega 1999, 149). However, the U.S. Department of State knew better, because reports from the U.S. Embassy in Santo Domingo indicate that the nuncio was behind the pastoral letter and quite active defending the local church hierarchy. Obviously, the nuncio was not acting without clear guidance from the Vatican, but the United States apparently wanted to appear as an ally of the Catholic Church opposing Trujillo when, in fact, it had supported the dictator for thirty-one years. In the meantime, the Trujillo regime declared Nuncio Zanini persona non grata, and he left the country on May 21, 1960.

The Dominican church did not seek a rupture in church-state relationships. Instead, the church hierarchy wanted a moderation of the regime's policies. Trujillo himself did not want to break political ties with the church, as demonstrated by the visit of his minister of foreign relations to Rome. This situation is completely different from the case of Mexico (1858), Guatemala (1871), Chile (1925), or Cuba (1959), where the state sought a complete rupture with the church. The Dominican church wanted to continue to operate within the framework of the concordat that Trujillo had signed with the Vatican. The letters of the nuncio and the hierarchy to Balaguer and Trujillo repeatedly asked them to recognize the concordat and said that they wanted to harmonize their relationships with public authorities. In fact, in a memorandum prepared for an interview with Trujillo nearly a year after the publication of the collective pastoral letter, the bishops stated that they proposed to:

- remind, once more, all priests of the norms to follow regarding politics
- seek all just means to harmonize and cooperate with authorities
- be careful and act within the framework of their responsibilities
- try, by all means available, to avoid the most elementary friction and distrust of the authorities
- take the government's suggestions into account, study them carefully, particularly regarding the request of religious ceremonies by authorities. (Lluberes 1998, 557–58)

The bishops stated that they expected civil authorities to get along with the clergy and to avoid interfering with ecclesiastic-religious matters. They also asked the authorities to stop the radio and press campaigns against the church, to allow deported priests to return to the country, to respect the contract signed with religious foundations, and to respect the concordat. Despite the moderate tone of this memorandum and the conversation with Trujillo regarding church-state relationships, the bishops held their ground when it came to responding to Trujillo's request for the title of benefactor of the church. They wrote to Balaguer and all the ministers of state on February 6, 1961, nearly a year after Trujillo advanced the claim for such a title, stating that they could not support the initiative to award the title because granting it was an attribute reserved for the Holy See (Lluberes 1998, 559–60).

The regime reacted strongly against the bishops' rejection. Bishops Panal and Reilly received the brunt of the attacks because of their continuous denunciations. Bishop Panal took advantage of Trujillo's presence at a mass held in La Vega, March 4, 1961, to tell him about the suffering of the Dominican people. He ordered Trujillo to his knees while asking the congregation to repeat: "Long live the Catholic, Apostolic, and Roman Church! Long live the Roman Pope, Vicar of Christ, Supreme Pastor of all Christians, and long live the Dominican ecclesiastic hierarchy!" Bishop Reilly of San Juan de la Maguana used another mass, on March 12, 1961, to denounce human rights violations and to proclaim the rights of the church (Lluberes 1998, 561–68).

The regime intensified its attacks against Bishops Panal and Reilly because Trujillo and his advisors thought that these two were the source of the problems with the church. Panal and Reilly were the only foreigners among the bishops and had no relatives in the country; thus, they were not vulnerable to Trujillo's threats. Even so, the local press accused Reilly of plotting to overthrow the regime. On April 10, army officers and soldiers dressed as peasants marched toward the offices of Bishop Reilly in San Juan de la Maguana. Word reached the bishop about the march, and he promptly fled to Santo Domingo, one hour before the so-called peasants attacked and ransacked his office. The U.S. embassy issued a protest before the Inter-American Peace Commission against the persecution of Bishop Reilly and the Catholic Church. This protest complicated Trujillo's relationship with the Organization of American States (OAS), which infuriated him. On May 29, 1961, Trujillo issued orders to arrest Bishops Panal and Reilly and put them in jail. The order was not carried out because Trujillo was assassinated on May 30, 1961. Balaguer canceled the arrest order the following day (Crassweller 1968, 390–403; Rodríguez de León 1996, 299–314; Wipfler 1980, 108–47).

The assassination of Trujillo unleashed an unprecedented wave of repression against anyone suspected of collaborating with the plotters who killed him. Ramfis Trujillo, the dictator's son, flew directly from Paris to the Dominican Republic. Immediately upon his arrival, he took control of the armed forces and personally directed the search for his father's killers. All the participants in the plot, except for Amiama Tio and Antonio Imbert Barrera, were assassinated. The Catholic hierarchy was indeed relieved and held masses nationwide to honor Trujillo in the midst of widespread political repression.

Once Balaguer and Ramfis had the political situation under control, the United States proceeded to press the Trujillo family to leave the country. The United States said that it would not release Dominican funds held in U.S. banks until all of Trujillo's brothers left the country. The United States held Dominican funds as political pressure exerted against Trujillo by the OAS. The OAS had broken diplomatic ties with Trujillo when his agents nearly killed Rómulo Betancourt, Venezuelan president, in the summer of 1960. Trujilllo's agents attempted to kill Betancourt because he gave refuge to Dominican exiles who wanted to overthrow Trujillo. Ramfis and Trujillo's brothers left only when the United States threatened them militarily by making a "show of force" right across from the Dominican National Palace, which is off the coast of the Caribbean. Balaguer was not satisfied when his presidential powers were reduced by the Council of State, which was seeking to organize free and fair elections. With help from the military, he tried to overthrow the Council of State, but he failed to do so. Afraid that violence might reach him, Balaguer took refuge in the residence of the papal nuncio. Subsequently, he received safe passage to leave the country. The Council of State organized elections on December 20, 1962, and Juan Bosch, a writer and politician who had lived in exile for over twenty-four years, was elected by a landslide.

Conclusions

This chapter identified two types of projects to build a national church in the Dominican Republic: (1) a nationalist project, which proposed to develop seminaries to train local priests to carry out the church mission; and, (2) a dependent church model, which relied on the importation of priests to do this type of work. Despite differences in their strategy, both types sought to implement the neo-Christendom orientation of the church. Archbishops Portes and Meriño represented the nationalist attempts to build the church; Nouel and Pittini represented a more dependent model. Nouel concluded that the nationalist project was not viable and proposed to rely on religious orders to help the church in its mission of evangelization. Pittini continued this policy, while also promoting the foundation of seminaries to train local priests.

The development of the Dominican church fits within the general pattern of subordination to the state that most Latin American churches experienced from independence to 1960. The nineteenth-century church in Central and South America had to deal with liberal governments that sought to limit its prerogatives, whereas conservative governments protected the church and helped it fight secularization and Protestantism.

The church's political alliances with conservative political forces continued in the twentieth century, as it sought to implement its neo-Christendom vision of the world. Unlike other Latin American churches, the Dominican church was not able to profit from conservative political support following the restoration of independence in 1865 due to the near collapse of the hierarchy. However, the church resolved its internal problems in the late 1870s and reclaimed its strong position in the country. Two clergymen (Meriño and Nouel) served as presidents of the republic for brief periods, which illustrates that the church had restored its power in society. The involvement of the clergy in politics gave the church a special role legitimating political, cultural, and social events.

The ecclesiastical government of Pittini laid the modern basis of the church in the Dominican Republic. He expanded the institutional basis of the church from one to five dioceses, created a minor seminar, and increased the number of Catholic schools and services organizations. In addition, he conducted the negotiations that led to signing the concordat that framed church-state relations until today. However, he had to subordinate the church to Trujillo's regime, which provided the financial resources in exchange for political and ideological support. As a consequence of this relationship, the church was secluded in the sacristy where it remained silent.

Changes in the transnational church prepared the conditions for the local hierarchy to issue a critique of the Trujillo regime. This seemingly moderate critique led to a political crisis between the church and a regime that was already in a rapid process of decomposition. Despite Trujillo's repressive measures, the local church hierarchy never sought to break ties with the regime. On the contrary, it wanted to patch up its relations with Trujillo and thus to continue under a subordinated status to the state.

Pittini's relationship with Trujillo was comparable to the relationship developed by church leaders in countries where the church was subordinated to the state. In Central America, twentieth-century dictators subordinated the church in exchange for favors and protection. This also happened in Bolivia, Peru, Paraguay, Venezuela, Argentina, Brazil, and so on. The leaders of these churches had a neo-Christendom vision of the world. They thought that only from the position of power could the church have influence in society. The effects of this legacy linger in the Latin American church as it looks to support more open and democratic societies. The next chapter reviews how several Latin American churches made the transition from being collaborators of dictatorial regimes to mediators of political conflicts.

Notes

1. The Royal and Supreme of the Indies came into existence in 1524 in response to the expansion of the territories conquered by Hernán Cortes and to the need to upgrade Spanish central administration. This body was firmly resident in Spain and operated as a department in charge of Indies affairs.

2. The Cortes of Cadiz was made up of the provincial juntas of the Spanish resistance to France that had occupied Spain and taken the Spanish king prisoner in 1808. The Cortes of Cadiz met in the context of the Spanish American War of Emancipation and it wanted to attract support from the Spanish American colonies for its imperial plans. This is why it promulgated a constitution that declared that Spain and America were one nation.

3. Under a concordat, the state undertakes the protection of religion; recognizes the rights of the church; and supports the bishop and his diocesan curia, the seminary and parish priests, economically. Latin American nation states signed concordats with the Vatican during the years of conservative rule (Guatemala in 1852, Costa Rica in 1852, Nicaragua in 1861, El Salvador in 1862, Haiti in 1860, and Colombia in 1887). However, the Dominican Republic was not able to sign a concordat, in part due to the weakness of the ruling political groups who did not show much interest in signing a concordat with the Vatican. Instead, these groups were concerned about a Haitian invasion. Haiti did not recognize Dominican independence until 1856 and invaded the new republic several times between 1844 and 1856.

4. What followed was a power struggle between Santana and the clergy over who would lead the Dominican church. Calixto Ma. Pina and Fernando A. Meriño led the church for brief periods until Monzón arrived (1862–1865) to reestablish the colonial church. Monzón filled the cathedral chapter and the seminary with Spanish priests, whereas the Dominican clergy, which had generally supported annexation by Spain, was ignored. In 1961, there were sixty-nine priests in the country, and twenty-four of them signed the document of annexation; interestingly, twelve of the signers were Dominicans (Lluberes 1998, 96; see table 1.1).

5. Ulises Heureaux had been a liberal nationalist who fought against the Spanish annexation in the 1860s. He rose from humble beginnings to the presidency (1882–1884) and (1886–1899). During these two periods, he forged an alliance with the emerging sugar planters and merchants in the 1880s. In common with many other Latin American liberal rulers in the latter third of the nineteenth century, he became a conservative who was willing to support the church. During Heureaux's second term in office, Archbishop Meriño went to him for personal favors, and Heureaux generally acquiesced. However, Meriño never raised any major political issue, except to oppose Heureaux's legislation that did not recognize religious marriage ceremonies.

6. The United States established a military government in the Dominican Republic from 1916 to 1924. The United States no longer trusted that its local allies were going to pay the government foreign debts and decided to occupy the country

to protect its bankers and the emerging sugar industry, also owned by American concerns.

7. Fietta was the first papal nuncio in the Dominican Republic, but one should refer to him as papal internuncio because he was also papal nuncio in Port-au-Prince, Haiti. There were nuncios in the country before Fietta's appointment, but they were considered delegates.

8. Both of these priests were religious and appointing them as bishops was not a common occurrence.

9. There are at least two ideas regarding Trujillo's reasons for ordering the massacre of Haitian peasants. The first suggests racist motivation. Accordingly, Trujillo used this opportunity to settle historical accounts that go back to atrocities committed by Haitian soldiers during the invasions of 1801 and 1805. The second suggests that although there may have been racial factors involved in the motivation to order the massacre, Trujillo's main concern was to secure his rule over the national territory. During the first fifteen years of his regime (1930–1945), Trujillo implemented programs to exert political, economic, social, and cultural control over the border region. Thousands of Haitian peasants had established themselves on the Dominican side of the border, and their trade reached as far as Santiago de los Caballeros in the heart of the Republic. Trujillo feared that Dominican guerrillas could use this area to fight his regime (Betances 1995; Castor 1983; Cuello 1985; Vega 1988, 1995).

10. Currently, this school is called Instituto Agronómico San Ignacio de Loyola.

CHAPTER TWO

Church and Politics in Four Latin American Nations

The process of reincorporation of the Catholic Church into the mainstream of post-Trujillo life in the Dominican Republic occurred in the context of epoch-making changes in Latin America from the 1960s to 2000. These changes included the Cuban Revolution, the Latin American military regimes of the 1960s and 1970s, the subsequent implementation of neoliberal economic policies in the 1980s and 1990s, and transition to liberal democracy. The Catholic Church had no choice but to embrace these changes and make the necessary adjustments to accommodate the changing political reality. In some countries, it initially supported military takeovers, but soon realized that those new regimes had long-term goals that conflicted with its social doctrine. However, the way the church responded to both military regimes and the transition to democracy varies from nation to nation. Because this variability is so broad, this chapter focuses on the role of the church in Bolivia, Guatemala, Nicaragua, and El Salvador. These countries are comparable to the Dominican Republic in terms of political history, socioeconomic polarization, and the mediating role of the church. Comparing parallels and differences between those churches and the Dominican case can illuminate our understanding of the process of reinsertion of the Dominican church into post-Trujillo society.

The chapter begins with a review of the tenets of Vatican Council II and the Latin American Episcopal Conferences of Medellín and Puebla and the subsequent conservative shifts. It then breaks into four sections to discuss the role of the church in the four nations selected for study. Each section summarizes the political and historical context in which the church operates, reviews the role of the hierarchy and the popular church in national politics, and analyzes the reinsertion of the church into politics and society. I posit that in the process of reincorporation into the political system, traditional and modernization visions merged into a neoconservative orientation that regards participation in mediation as the best political role for the church. Clergymen associated with this orientation claim to be nonpartisan vis-à-vis political parties and movements and promote liberal democracy as the only game in town.

Church and Politics in Latin America after Vatican II

Vatican Council II provided the framework for the reconceptualization of the church mission in Latin America. Scholars and religious actors consider Vatican II one of the most important events in history. For the first time ever, 600 Latin American bishops traveled to Rome to participate in a church council. This meeting allowed Latin American bishops to recognize each other as members of a region that shared similar histories, cultural perspectives, and political problems.

According to theologian Gustavo Gutiérrez, a Peruvian Dominican, Vatican II expected the church to be present in three different worlds: the modern world, the Christian world, and the religious world. Gutiérrez says that the attitude of openness to the modern world is revealed in the sixteen documents of Vatican II (Gutiérrez 1990, 11). Vatican II reiterated issues raised by Pope John XXIII's 1963 encyclical *Pacem in Terris* ("Peace on Earth"), where he acknowledges the inalienable rights of human beings, including the right to life, to bodily integrity, to assembly and association, to express one's opinions freely, to take an active part in public life, to choose those who are to rule, and to select the form of government in which authority is to be exercised. This position was reaffirmed in 1965 in *Gaudium et Spes* ("The Pastoral Constitution of the Church in the Modern World"), which stated that "the choice of government and the method of selecting leaders is left to the free will of citizens" (Fleet and Smith 1997, 2). Vatican II legitimated greater participation in the decision-making process within the church and encouraged a more collegial exercise of authority among pope, bishops, priests, nuns, and the laity.

The bishops' conferences of Medellín (1968) and Puebla (1979) consisted of interpretations of the Latin American situation in light of Vatican II. Pope John XXIII called for *aggiornamento* of the church of the developed world, which meant bringing up to date the European church on issues of faith in the scientific age. Aggiornamento meant something completely different when seen from a Latin American perspective. It

> entailed the pain of a creative enterprise . . . uprooting of the Latin Americans from their European theological soil . . . growing on their own, away from the parental trunk, though clearly remaining an offshoot . . . a process similar to that of a young man thinking his own thoughts and making his own plans, though guided by teachers and parents. (Cleary 1985, 24)

Before the conference at Medellín took place, national churches were consulted, a series of regional preparatory meetings were held, and a number of important documents emerged. Pope John Paul VI traveled to Colombia to give the inaugural address, thus becoming the first pope ever to visit Latin America. His four-day visit attracted the attention of the press all over the world. After his departure, the bishops settled down to discuss the position papers that had emerged from regional meetings. The Consejo Episcopal Latinoamericano, CELAM (Latin American Episcopal Council), published these papers and the subsequent conclusions as *The Church in the Present-Day Transformation of Latin America in the Light of the Council*, Vol. 1: *Position Papers*, and Vol. II, *Conclusions*. In the conclusions, the 130 bishops who met in Medellín stated that the church operates in unjust societies marked by structured inequalities, which they defined as sinful. "The reason is obvious: excessive inequality systematically prevents the satisfaction of the legitimate aspirations of the ignored sectors and breeds increasing frustrations" (CELAM 1970, Document 2, sections 1 and 4). The bishops called for social change and expressed their desire to participate in the process through education, evangelization, and lay participation. A liberating education was called for to address the situation:

> Our reflection on this subject leads us to propose a vision of education more in conformity with the integral development that we are seeking in our continent. We could call it "liberating education," that is, that which converts the student into the subject of his own development. Education is actually the key instrument for liberating the masses from all servitude and for causing them to ascend "from less human to a more human condition." . . . A deafening cry pours from the throats of millions of men, asking their pastors for a liberation that reaches them from nowhere else. (CELAM 1970, *Conclusions*, Document 4, section 8, and Document 14, section 2)

Military governments ruled in all but five Latin American countries when the Latin American bishops met in Medellín, Colombia. The church appeared to be between military regimes that defended the status quo and an upsurge of guerrilla movements that sought to overthrow the established social political order. Despite their claims to defend Western Christianity, the military suppressed all political opposition and attacked those in the church who dared question their policies.

In Brazil, the bishops approved the military that took over in 1964, but soon realized that the coup leaders had long-range plans (Klaiber 1998, 24–25). The church hierarchy withdrew its support for the military and began to protest their policies. As a result, the military proceeded to kill lay Catholics, killed or deported priests, and searched the residences of some bishops. In January 1972, Archbishop Paulo Evaristo Arns of São Paulo founded the Commission of Peace and Justice to defend human rights and provide protection for those persecuted for political reasons.

In Chile, the bishops were divided over the 1973 military coup against the elected socialist government of Salvador Allende, and at first, the hierarchy acted cautiously. But soon it realized that General Augusto Pinochet, the coup leader, wanted to impose a military dictatorship. Raul Silva Henriquez, archbishop of Santiago, became one of the principal critics of General Pinochet, whose repressive measures had reached the church. As in Brazil, General Pinochet arrested and deported a number of priests. Msgr. Silva Enrique founded the Vicariate of Solidarity in 1976, which was based on earlier efforts to offer help to those persecuted for political reasons (Klaiber 1998, 50).

As noted below, similar developments took place in Bolivia and Central America. In those years, the church became the "voice of the voiceless" and thus contributed significantly to help move Latin American nations to more open and democratic societies in the 1980s. In this context, many bishops thought that it was necessary to make a Christian commitment because it was a Gospel imperative.

Making a Christian commitment meant denouncing human rights violations and taking sides with the downtrodden. The Vatican approved those conclusions and recognized their historical importance, but conservatives in and out of the church felt offended, while moderates and progressives thought the conclusions were in line with Vatican II. Many progressive bishops, priests, nuns, and lay Catholics found the Medellín conclusions inspirational. The conference inspired liberation theology, a reflection about the relationship between salvation and the historical process of liberation of man. According to Gustavo Gutiérrez, "only with this approach will theology be a serious discourse, aware of itself, in full possession of its conceptual elements . . . (it) also refer(s) to a clear and critical attitude regarding economic and socio-cultural issues in the life and reflection of the Christian Community" (Gutiérrez 1973, 11).

The conference also inspired the ecclesiastical base communities (CEBs), small grassroots groups organized by pastoral workers to discuss faith and social issues that deal with their survival, such as housing, employment, and human rights. In short, it created the political and theological foundation to justify the commitment of many Christians to fight against social and political oppression. CEBs were part of a larger social and religious movement that came to be known as the "popular church," through which Christian activists organized various national organizations concerned with social justice and political activities. The best-known organizations include Oficina Nacional de Información, ONIS (National Office of Information) in Peru; Iglesia y Sociedad en America Latina, ISAL (Church and Society in Latin America) in Bolivia; Priests for the Third World in Argentina; the Group of Eighty in Chile; and the Golconda Movement in Colombia. Latin American theologians felt inspired as well. Gustavo Gutiérrez published *Teología de la Liberación* (1971), which became a reference book for many involved in the CEBs movement in the 1970s and 1980s.

However, conservatives wasted no time or energy and soon exerted control over CELAM, which had been actively promoting the Medellín conclusions throughout the region. The progressive direction of CELAM changed in 1972, when conservative Colombian archbishop Alfonso López Trujillo was elected secretary general and shifted its political direction. When López Trujillo secured control of CELAM, he stopped supporting regional seminars and conferences, and publications decreased. This action had a significant impact on the burgeoning CEBs movement in countries where the full support of bishops was lacking.

The Third Latin American Bishops' Conference took place in Puebla, Mexico, in 1979. Elected in 1978 to replace Pope John Paul I, John Paul II traveled to Mexico to inaugurate the conference. Unlike the Medellín conference, which was largely controlled by church experts, the Puebla conference was carefully managed and organized by the bishops. Archbishop López Trujillo selected committee members who produced a document that was almost universally rejected by national episcopal conferences for being "too timid, too general, and too spiritualizing" (Cleary 1985, 47). Evidently, the legacy of the Medellín conference lingered on, and conservatives could not impose their position.

Participants in the Puebla conference began by considering the human and religious situation in Latin America. The 191 bishops who attended the conference found that the Latin American situation was as bleak and hopeless as it was in 1968: human rights violations and social polarization had increased throughout the region. In the final document, published as *Puebla and Beyond* (Eagleson and Scharper, 1979), the bishops examined the roots of social injustice and concluded:

- We see the continuing operation of economic systems that do not regard the human being as the center of society.
- There is economic, technological, political, and cultural dependence; the presence of multinational conglomerates that often look after only their own interests at the expense of the welfare of the country that welcomes them in.
- There is a lack of structural reforms in agriculture that adequately deal with specific realities and decisively attack the grave social and economic problems of the peasantry.
- We see a crisis of moral values: public and private corruption; greed for exorbitant profit; venality; lack of real effort; the absence of any social sense of practical justice and solidarity.
- Finally, speaking as pastors and without trying to determine the technical character of these underlying roots, we ourselves see that at bottom there lies a mystery of sinfulness. This is evident when the human person, called to have dominion over the world, impregnates the mechanisms of society with materialistic values. (Eagleson and Scharper 1979, Final Document, sections 64–70)

The Puebla conference continued in the same vein as the conclusions reached at Medellín. It even went a step further, however, declaring a commitment to accompany and support the oppressed in their struggles for a better life. Undoubtedly, the bishops were trying to shift from a hierarchical to a more communal church. The Medellín conclusions were deepened at the Puebla conference, but the universal church began to move in a different direction with the election of John Paul II.

Pope John Paul II and the Conservative Shift in Church Mission

This section examines the impact of the papacy of John Paul II in the Latin American church as it sought to redefine its role in the post-Puebla context. After the Puebla conference, Latin American nations went through a transition from military to civilian rule, and the gross human rights violations of the 1960s and 1970s decreased. In those years, the church became the "voice of the voiceless" and a primary defender of human rights. With the transition to democracy, the church was no longer needed to protect those persecuted for political reasons. In many countries, the hierarchies read the "signs of the time" and sought ways to reincorporate themselves into the mainstream by promoting liberal democracy as the most adequate political system.

The election of John Paul II (1978) to the papacy strengthened the traditional clergy in Latin America. John Paul II represented a conservative shift in the church compared to his predecessors, who had advocated the implementation of Vatican II. The new pope believed that it was necessary to strengthen church authority, unity, and religious conformity. In Latin America, the most visible aspect of this conservative shift was the appointment of new bishops and the pope's reaction to liberation theology. Bishops who identified with liberation theology, such as Helder Camara of the Diocese Olimba and Recife, Brazil; Sergio Méndez Arceo of Cuernavaca, Mexico; Samuel Ruiz of Chiapas, Mexico; and Archbishop Raul Silva Henríquez of Santiago, Chile, were, in time, replaced with conservative clergy.

Another visible factor of church authority is the role papal nuncios played in promoting the new orientation of the Vatican guidelines. Papal nuncios not only represent the pope before local governments, they also prepare reports on the local church, which are sent to the Vatican. In these reports, nuncios expressed their opinions concerning the local hierarchy and recommend those who should be promoted to the rank of bishop. Pope John Paul II noted the role various conservative nuncios played in Latin America during the military dictatorships, and these nuncios were promoted for their conservative actions.

Three of these deserve attention: Sabastiano Baggio was nuncio in Brazil (1964–1969) during the worst repression of the military; Angelo Sodano was stationed in Chile (1977–1988), again during the very repressive years of Pinochet. Pío Laghi served in Argentina (1974–1980) when the military waged a dirty war against urban guerrillas and all those who opposed their heavy-handed policies. John Paul II appointed these conservative nuncios to key posts in the Vatican. Baggio was appointed prefect of the Congregation of Bishops (1973–1984) and president of the Pontifical Commission for Latin America. Two archbishops from Latin America also received appointments. Eduardo Pironio, the progressive bishop of Mar de la Plata (Argentina) and president of CELAM and Alfonso López Trujillo, archbishop of Medellín (Colombia) and Pironio's successor as president of CELAM (1979–1983). Pironio was appointed to the Congregation of Religious and López Trujillo the Pontifical Commission on the Family. Except for Pironio, all the appointments went to conservative figures. These nuncios had supported the worst kind of dictatorship, and López Trujillo was the leader of a campaign against liberation theology and the popular church in Latin America (Klaiber 1998, 14).

The new conservative direction of the church created tensions with the liberation movement that had developed within the church in the 1960s and 1970s. In 1983, John Paul II announced his "New Evangelization" pastoral in Latin America, which was essentially a drive to attract the masses to the church. In response to this call, the Conference of Latin American Religious (CLAR), representing over 355,000 men and women from religious orders and congregations, announced its "World life" program. This program proclaimed, "Evangelization should start with the 'Word of God' as experienced by the Latin American people themselves." The Vatican responded quickly by requesting to withdraw the "World life" program and reminding CLAR that "bishops are the teachers of faith and truth" (Stewart-Gambino 1994, 131). The program sponsored by CLAR was based on the Medellín (1968) and Puebla conferences (1979).

Unlike the Medellín and Puebla conferences, where the new pope and the Vatican bureaucracy apparently failed to defeat the liberation movement within the church, Vatican leaders went well prepared to the Fourth Latin American Bishops' Conference held in Santo Domingo in 1992. The national conferences of bishops had rejected two drafts prepared by the conservative-dominated CELAM for the Santo Domingo Document, but the Vatican bureaucracy was reassured that its main points would not be seriously challenged. The Vatican appointed three conservative co-presidents to organize the Santo Domingo meeting, including Angelo Sodano and his Chilean protégé, Jorge Medina.

Despite the conservative bias of the Vatican appointees, the result of the Santo Domingo conference was a compromise called "New Evangelization, Human Development, and Christian Culture." Some of the ideas of the popular church movement may be noted in the sections dealing with the methodology of "see, judge, act" as well as in the church's role concerning ecology, race relations, urbanization, economic justice, human rights, and women's issues. Despite the retention of these progressive ideas, a conservative shift that separated the church from the Medellín and Puebla conclusions was consolidated in the Santo Domingo conclusions (Hennelly 1993; Stewart-Gambino 1994).

The political significance of the Fourth Latin American Bishops' Conference was quite different from that of Medellín (1968) or Puebla (1979). Renowned theologian Jon Sobrino noted that the significance of this conference can be evaluated in terms of the reaction of the United States. In 1968, Nelson Rockefeller, governor of New York, published a report on his visit to Latin America, raising suspicions about the direction of the Catholic Church, and Ronald Reagan's advisors did likewise regarding the Puebla conference. The United States did not issue any declaration regarding the Santo Domingo conference, which indicates that the position adopted there did not affect its interest (Sobrino 1993, 175).

The church may not agree with the U.S. government regarding particular regimes and policies in Latin America, but it does support liberal democracy as the most viable political system. Church concerns with nonpartisan politics, mediation, and conciliation complement rather than contradict U.S. interests in the region. Despite these general agreements, the church has substantial political differences with the United States and local regimes concerning social justice and human rights violations. Hence, the publication of pastoral letters critical of government policies concerning these topics. These criticisms are worded as nonpartisan statements that promote the common good and, as such, the church appears above social groups and political parties seeking power. In countries with weak political institutions, this position turns the church into the only national institution with the necessary moral authority to call on all social and political forces to enter into a real dialogue. We now examine a few countries to illustrate how political mediation[1] is a channel to reincorporate the church into the mainstream of life in Latin America.

Case Studies of the Latin American Catholic Church and Politics

The next four sections look at the Catholic Church in Bolivia, Nicaragua, El Salvador, and Guatemala as exemplary cases of political mediation in countries with weak political institutions. I use the notion of orientations of the church to examine the role of the hierarchy and the popular church in Latin American politics.

Bolivia

The Bolivian Revolution of 1952 furnished the context for the reintegration of the church into the mainstream of society. The revolution ended oligarchic rule and destroyed the regime that served it. The Movimiento Nacional Revolucionario, MNR (National Revolutionary Movement) emerged as the party of the revolution and proposed to create an inclusive society that brought peasants (Indians), workers, and middle-class groups into the mainstream of Bolivian society. The revolution produced moderate agrarian reform, nationalized the mining sector, and offered jobs in the public sector to the middle class. However, neither the MNR, the military, nor the left was ever able to exercise hegemony in Bolivian politics and society. All political groups have had a difficult time maintaining themselves in power and, as a consequence, political institutions have not been strengthened. Instability has been the main feature of Bolivian social and political life over the last fifty years (Klein 1992, 227–86).

The fragmentation of the Bolivian political landscape led to the formation of two wings within the MNR: a moderate conservative faction, led by Victor Paz Estenssoro, and a moderate left, led by Hernán Siles Suazo. These two leaders alternated being in control until the military took power in 1964. However, neither Paz Estenssoro nor Siles Suazo was capable of exerting control over the powerful Confederación Obrera Boliviana, COB (Bolivian Workers Confederation), led by Juan Lechín. The COB was mostly comprised of miners and occasionally enjoyed the support of peasant movements that had their own political agenda. The COB had a socialist agenda for the unionized working class and, at times, created a virtual co-governing power with the MNR or the military government (Spalding 1977; Zavaleta Mercado 1970).

The leaders of the reconstituted armed forces that emerged from the revolution consolidated their political position within the state after the military coup of 1964. General René Barrientos Ortuño overthrew the government of Paz Estenssoro and established a military government (1964–1969). General Barrientos realized that the COB was becoming a threat to the state and decided to curtail the political freedoms offered by MNR governments. Nonetheless, Barrientos presented himself as a revolutionary and promised to deepen the revolution, using a populist rhetoric to lure the middle, working, and peasant classes. However, like Paz Estenssoro and Siles Suazo, he was unable to gain the support of the miners, and his relationship with peasant organizations was unstable. Led by the COB, the miners had their own political agenda: their leadership proposed to create a socialist society in Bolivia, but it failed to gain the support of the moderate political faction of the MNR to promote this project. This failure was due, in part, to the incompatibility of the ultimate strategies of the two organizations.

The military rulers who followed General Barrientos shared his perception that the COB was a threat to the status quo. These rulers included General Alfredo Ovando (1969–1971), Hugo Banzer (1971–1978), and the various regimes that resulted from the unstable political crises that followed the end of the so-called Banzerato. General Juan José Torres was the exception to this rule. He ruled for nearly a year (October 7, 1970, to August 21, 1971), but was an ineffective leader who had no control over the military or over the COB and the popular movement. "The hallmark of the Torres interlude was a lack of central authority. It was a situation driven by forces beyond the management of the state or any specific government." (Malloy and Gamarra 1988, 55). General Hugo Banzer took advantage of this situation to overthrow Torres and install a dictatorial military regime that eventually outlawed all political parties and labor union activities. Banzer's repressive policies also affected the pastoral work of the Catholic Church, particularly in the mining areas. The residences of priests, nuns, and bishops were raided by security personnel.

Growth and Consolidation of the Church in Bolivia
There was a remarkable expansion of the church in Bolivia in the latter third of the twentieth century. The church felt the impact of the liberal legislation at the beginning of the twentieth century, but it continued to enjoy government protection. Like most Andean, Central American, and Caribbean churches, the Bolivian church was small, conservative, and fearful of communism and Protestantism. It, too, relied on the importation of priests because it could not educate enough of them at the national level.

In the nineteenth century, the main orders in Bolivia were the Jesuits and the Salesians. The twentieth century saw the arrival of the Vincentians, Augustians, Society of Maryknoll, Josephines, Oblates of Mary Immaculate, the Dominicans, and others (Klaiber 1998, 122). The *Annuarium Statisticum Ecclesiae* published by the Vatican does not identify priests by nationality, but it does classify them as diocesan and religious.[2] More recent statistics show that in the 1970s and 1980s, the number of diocesan priests was still markedly low compared to religious priests. Diocesan priests increased, but at a very slow pace from 1970 to 1990. For example, there were 262 in 1970, 255 in 1980, and 256 in 1990. However, in the 1990s, there was a large increase, so the total reached 399 in 1998. In contrast, there were 610 religious priests in 1970, 674 in 1980, 671 in 1990, and 649 in 1998. In Bolivia, the historical tendency is for religious to outnumber diocesan priests (see web table 2A and Maldonado Villagrán 1991, 187).

The increase in the number of diocesan priests may be explained, in part, by the significant expansion of the institutions of the Catholic Church in Bolivia. The number of dioceses increased from nine in 1980 to fifteen in 1998, while that of archbishops increased from four in 1980 to eight in 1998. Seminaries decreased from nineteen in 1970 to eight in 1980, but rebounded to twenty-six in 1998.

As part of this expansion, parishes with priests increased from 290 in 1970 to 343 in 1980, to 358 in 1990, and to 442 in 1998. There are still many parishes without priests, though. There were 88 parishes without priests in 1970, 92 in 1980, 124 in 1990, and 100 in 1998. There was a slight decline in educational institutions from 1,012 in 1980 to 864 in 1990, but, as with seminaries, there was a recovery in 1998 when the number of educational institutions increased to 942. The pattern of growth of welfare institutions was similarly unstable: they went from 447 in 1980 to 1,085 in 1990, but decreased to 697 in 1998. However, the number of religious women working in Bolivia increased from 1,638 in 1970 to 1,682 in 1980 to 1,781 in 1990 and to 2,379 in 1998 (see web tables 2A, 2B, 2C, and 2D).

In general, the Bolivian church expanded and consolidated itself in the 1980s and 1990s, giving it more visibility and a larger role in mediating political conflicts in the 1980s and 1990s. This new role enabled it to reintegrate itself into the mainstream of society as a special actor that claims to be above partisan politics.

The Bolivian Church and Politics
Understanding the role of Bolivian church politics after the 1952 revolution requires distinguishing between the hierarchy and the popular church. Through much of this period, the hierarchy, represented by the Conferencia Episcopal Boliviana (Bolivian Episcopal Conference) was rather conservative, preaching conciliation and accommodating political regimes regardless of their political affiliation. However, within the Bolivian Episcopal Conference a group of dynamic bishops raised their voices to protest injustices and to speak on behalf of those suffering political oppression. These bishops often supported the popular church, led mostly, but not exclusively, by foreign-born religious priests. These bishops included Jorge Manríque and Jesús López Lama, who supported the Oblate priests, known as priest-miners. In 1965, the archbishop of La Paz, Abel Atezama, along with 126 priests, signed a document supporting the demands of the miners. However, this was not the position of the Bolivian Episcopal Conference as a whole. In fact, under the leadership of Cardinal Vincent Maurer, archbishop of Sucre (1951–1983), the Bolivian Episcopal Conference adopted a conservative political position vis-à-vis the military regimes that were in power from 1964 to 1978. Cardinal Maurer, president of the Conferencia Episcopal Boliviana for three terms from 1966 to 1979, ensured that the hierarchy kept its distance from radical religious priests and that it maintained a cordial relationship with military governments.

Notwithstanding this conservative position, the hierarchy recognized the need to preach political conciliation and, in various instances, agreed to mediate political conflicts. For example, in 1968 it mediated a political conflict between President René Barrientos Ortuño (1966–1969) and the COB. The COB demands included higher wages, better fringe benefits, and other prerogatives. Barrientos rejected their demands, but after months of negotiations brokered by the Catholic Church, he signed an agreement with the COB as the basis for a new social peace. The agreement was signed in the presence of Cardinal Vincent Maurer, archbishop of Sucre; Jorge Manríque, archbishop of La Paz, the papal nuncio; and other bishops. Barrientos recognized the role of the church in this mediation as well as its work in the health and education of the miners (Klaiber 1998, 123; Valda Palma 1995, 326–40).

The Role of the Popular Church
The political involvement of the prophetic or popular church increased as a result of the military coup against the populist General Juan José Torres led by General Hugo Banzer in August 1971. Banzer unleashed an unprecedented repression, ending open and legal political activities. Over 19,000 Bolivians were exiled, many more were detained, and hundreds were tortured. Universities were closed, political parties were banned, and union activity stopped. Church temples were raided; priests and nuns were arrested. By the end of 1972, eighteen priests had to leave the country. Three Protestant pastors and four Catholic religious women were forced into exile as well. Fifteen religious houses were raided in searches for political activists. The Convento of Recoleta in Sucre, which traditionally served as a refugee center for politicians, was raided, and four university students were arrested. Bishops Manríque, Gutiérrez, and López Lama were slandered in the press. The residence of Jesús López Lama was raided twice (Testimonios de Cristianos 1976, 33–35). In response, the bishops of Bolivia issued a message that stated:

> While recognizing a move towards a period of greater stability, we cannot hide our sadness when we see the number of dead and wounded, the mourning, the pain, the detentions, exile, and poverty that had come to deepen the separation of our people, threatening them with the creation of hatred and reprisals. . . . The Church is committed to the process of transformation that our society requires . . . (but) it proclaims that this commitment is above party politics. . . . In the midst of special circumstances, many members of the Church carry out activities . . . that go beyond what has been traditionally recognized as specific priestly functions. . . . We regret the violation of the tradition of asylum in institutions of the Church. . . . The Church will defend these traditions for humanitarian reasons and evangelical charity. (Testimonios de Cristianos 1976, 22–24)

As a group, the bishops expressed the views of the Boliviana Episcopal Conference, which was generally conservative, cautious, and pastoral. Individual bishops also expressed their views, however. For example, Adhemar Esquivel, auxiliary bishop of La Paz, published a letter in *Presencia*, the Catholic newspaper, in support of Jesús López Lama, bishop of the Prelature of Corocoro, whose residence had been raided by security personnel, and Jorge Manríque, archbishop of La Paz, sent a communiqué to the Ministry of Interior after the raid on the Jesuit residence in La Paz. This raid had violated an agreement reached between church hierarchy and the government whereby the latter agreed to respect religious houses according to Bolivian tradition (Testimonios de Cristianos 1976, 37–39, 44–45).

In contrast to the Bolivian Episcopal Conference, the priests, particularly the foreign-born religious priests, took a more radical position. At least two factors explain the radicalization of these priests. First, many of them arrived in the context of the reforms proposed in Vatican Council II (1962–1965). Second, when religious priests arrived in Bolivia to carry out their priestly functions and to accompany the Bolivian people, they found poverty, racism, political exclusion, and repression. It was difficult for many of them to preach the Gospel and ignore the realities that their Christian communities had to confront. In addition, unlike most Bolivian diocesan priests, they did not have relatives in the country who might suffer because of their involvement in political activities. This explains, in part, why religious priests became the backbone of the prophetic church and why we find so many of them preparing and signing the document titled "Evangelio y Violencia" ("Gospel and Violence"). This document was published on January 19, 1973, to denounce the political repression conducted by Banzer since 1971. Ninety-nine priests, religious women, and pastors signed the document covering the following points:

1. It is true that the church has raised its voice of protest on some occasions, but it has been to defend its priests, its privileges, or interests.
2. In the last few months, we have regressed because we have not been able to use the tradition of asylum, which has saved so many lives in our history.
3. We denounce the assassinations, tortures, arbitrary detentions, negation of due process, freedom of expression, attacks on defenseless citizens, the lack of autonomy of the judicial system, corruption, the clandestine military operations (left or right), the injustices in the distribution of public employment, etc.
4. In conclusion, it is urgent to immediately break the spiral of silence. The more we wait to stop it, the greater will be the suffering of our peo-

ple and the bloody reactions of the political swing (Testimonios de Cristianos, 1976, 53–59).

This document circulated nationwide and abroad and shocked collegial relations within the Bolivian Episcopal Conference. It marked a high point in the political involvement of the popular church in politics and gave progressive priests visibility and prestige in the eyes of the oppressed. Despite the importance of the role of progressive priests in Bolivia, we must remember that they were a minority of the clergy. In 1970, there were 872 priests in Bolivia (262 diocesan and 610 religious) (see web table 2A). Thus, the vast majority did not sign "Evangelio y Violencia" or appear to sympathize with the popular church. Several bishops knew about the document being prepared or supported it, but most sent strong criticisms to Cardinal Maurer, then president of the Bolivian Episcopal Conference. One bishop wrote to Cardinal Maurer: "I consider that the Bolivian Episcopal Conference is obliged to emphatically reject the notion that this publication has the right to interpret in any form the position of the Church because the hierarchy has always abstained from making direct political judgments" (Barnadas 2000, 235).

Despite differences of opinion within the Bolivian Episcopal Conference and the priesthood in general, the hierarchy approved the creation of the Comisión de Justicia y Paz (Justice and Peace Commission) in January 1973. The commission was presided over by the vice president and secretary of the Bolivian Episcopal Conference, Jorge Manríque and Gerardo Pratta, bishops who traditionally supported the popular church. The daily activities of the Justice and Peace Commission were handled by lay Catholics and priests.

The commission received many requests to help free political prisoners, to investigate the whereabouts of missing people, and to issue communiqués denouncing human rights violations. Throughout 1973, the Justice and Peace Commission became one of the principal defenders of human rights in Bolivia, and the government was not pleased. In March 1975, two priests, Eric de Wasseige, a Dominican and president of the commission, and Jorge Wavreille, an oblate who collaborated with it, were expelled from the country. Jorge Manríque, archbishop of La Paz, learned about the expulsion when he arrived back from a trip to Rome. He immediately issued a message to all of his parishes protesting and denouncing their expulsion (Testimonios de Cristianos 1976, 75–90, 153–55). The remaining members of the commission were relieved by the Manríque protest, but their relief did not last long because in March 1975, the Bolivian Episcopal Conference put the commission in "recess."

In contrast to Manríque, Cardinal Maurer, president of the Bolivian Episcopal Conference, favored the expulsions. He wrote to one of the superiors of the exiled priests:

> Frankly, I will tell you that his style of speaking about politics has created many difficulties for us. Since he is a foreigner, we made repetitive requests asking him to moderate his politics, but he did not listen. He caused a lot of tension between the Government and the church. Consequently, the majority of the bishops do not wish his return. (Barnadas 2000, 236)

These two different responses show that the hierarchy was divided, but the majority of Bolivian bishops seemed to support the position of Cardinal Maurer.

The end of the Justice and Peace Commission did not end the church's concerns with human rights violations. A small section of the commission continued to work to help political prisoners, but in a more subdued manner. In 1977, the Permanent Assembly on Human Rights was created and headed by Luis Adolfo Siles Salinas, an important practicing lay Catholic and former president of Bolivia (April–September 1969). The hierarchy supported this organization, but it was independent of the official church and it was ecumenical. In any case, the assembly filled the vacuum left by the Peace and Justice Commission.

The Catholic hierarchy had numerous other conflicts with radical priests who were involved in politics. In 1969, the Bolivian Episcopal Conference did not renew contracts to the Obra de Cooperación Sacerdotal Hispanoamericana, OCSHA (a Spanish missionary society for cooperation with Latin America), to administer a seminary in Cochabamba. The OCSHA priests were considered too progressive, and the Bolivian Episcopal Conference was afraid of their possible influence on younger priests. In 1971, the OCSHA priests were not allowed to return to Bolivia. Another important crisis took place between the hierarchy and Iglesia y Sociedad en América Latina, ISAL (Church and Society in Latin America), a progressive ecumenical group that accompanied the miners, was involved in campaigns to denounce human rights violations, and was known for approving socialism. ISAL operated from offices located in the Archdiocese of La Paz, but when it openly criticized the conservative position of the Bolivian Episcopal Conference and the role of the nuncio in Bolivia, the group was asked to leave. The Bolivian Episcopal Conference made it clear that ISAL was not an organ of the church. ISAL had to leave the country when Banzer took over in 1971.

The Mediating Role of the Church Hierarchy
This section examines how the church became the mediator par excellence in a society ridden with social and political conflicts. Whether or not the church intended to, its participation mediating political and social conflicts reintegrated it into the life of post-Banzer Bolivia (1978–1982) and the subsequent process of democratization (1982–2000).

The role of the church focused increasingly on mediation, as the Banzer military regime confronted a devastating political crisis. These mediations were largely, but not exclusively, promoted by a small group of bishops identified with the modernization orientation of the church. Unlike the traditional conservative clergy, these bishops supported the popular church and worked tirelessly to promote dialogue as the means to resolve political conflicts.

The collapse in the prices of Bolivia's exports spurred the consolidation of a formidable political opposition to the regime of General Hugo Banzer. Banzer had been able to maneuver in the turbulent waters of Bolivian politics because of impressive GDP growth rates. The GDP grew from 4.94 in 1971 to 6.8 in 1976. These remarkable growth rates were due partly to favorable prices of Bolivian exports in the early 1970s, but when those prices collapsed, the rates of growth decreased noticeably. Growth decreased to 4.0 in 1977 and to 3.3 in 1978 (Malloy and Gamarra 1988, 233). Economic conditions soon affected the political scene negatively because Banzer no longer had sufficient public resources to maintain his political clientele.

A hunger strike triggered a national movement that eventually forced Banzer to reconsider his political position. Four women declared a hunger strike in December 1977, to demand a general amnesty for all political prisoners and the return of exiles. With permission from Archbishop Manríque, they used the premises of the Archdiocese of La Paz to protest. Soon they received support from twenty-eight different groups from various cities across Bolivia. In January, the police stormed the buildings where the strikers were located, but Archbishop Manríque threatened to put La Paz under interdict, which increased the pressure on Banzer (Klaiber 1998, 129–30). Banzer then had to negotiate with a movement that threatened his decaying regime. The Permanent Assembly on Human Rights began to mediate in the negotiations, but eventually Cardinal Maurer became involved in the negotiations, and as a result, Banzer spoke on television and announced a general amnesty and later scheduled elections for July 1978. Contrary to his own political wishes, Banzer appointed General Juan Pareda Asbún as the official candidate. When it became evident that the opposition candidate, Hernán Siles

Suazo, would win the elections, General Pareda committed massive fraud, bringing Bolivia into a period of political instability that lasted until 1982.

The church mediated successfully through the subsequent series of crises. Archbishop Manrique mediated in the impasse created by the 1979 electoral crisis where no candidate won a clear majority. Congress appointed Walter Guevara Arce as interim president. The church also mediated when General Alberto Natush Busch overthrew Guevara Arce after he had been in office for only a brief period. As result of these mediations, Lydia Gueiler became president, but she was overthrown by General Luis García Meza (1980–1981).

García Meza installed the most brutal, corrupt, and destructive regime in Bolivian history. Political repression reached all levels of society and church personnel, and Catholic lay workers were arrested, tortured, and exiled. The U.S. Drug Enforcement Agency accused high-ranking government officials of involvement in the international traffic of cocaine. The Bolivian Episcopal Conference issued a message titled "Dignity and Liberty," denouncing political repression and listing a series of rights that it felt were violated, including individual rights, social rights, the right to work, the right to form unions, the right to political participation, and the right to freedom of political choice. The bishops ended their message citing church freedom to spread the Gospel, which it felt had also been violated by the García Meza regime (Conferencia Episcopal de Bolivia 1992, 13–23). Lay Catholics and priests associated with the popular church applauded this message, and the church offered to mediate in the conflicts that emerged as a result of the García Meza dictatorship.

The Bolivian Episcopal Conference calls for conciliation and political moderation continued throughout the 1980s and 1990s. In 1981 it mediated in a miners' strike in Huanuni, drafting a document that was acceptable both to the miners and the government, and union rights were eventually restored. In 1982, the church called on all political parties to participate in a national dialogue to seek ways to strengthen democracy by creating a national consensus on certain basic principles and agreements.

This first stage of the dialogue helped resolve a crisis that resulted from a presidential hunger strike. President Siles Suazo (1982–1985) had actually gone on a hunger strike in a desperate attempt to press the opposition parties and the COB to give him a political hiatus. As a result of church mediation, the hunger strike was ended, the parties in conflict signed an agreement that created the basis for a new national consensus, and President Siles Suazo obtained the truce he wanted.

In the second stage of dialogue, the COB was not satisfied with the results and claimed that the new political pact and the truce granted to Siles Suazo conflicted with the demands of the workers. Walter Delgadillo, the COB representative, explained: "We believe that the Church has extended its hand to the rich and powerful, but not to the dispossessed of this country" (Klaiber 1998, 135). Despite these criticisms, the church was called on to mediate by governments, unions, and political parties in 1985, 1986, and 1987. These mediations helped avoid the continuation of crises that would have had terrible consequences for Bolivia.

Although the church hierarchy was mostly concerned with calls for conciliation and offering its good offices to mediate political conflicts, it also issued strong messages criticizing government policies. The best example of this is a document signed by Julio Terrazas, CSSR, bishop of Oruro and president of the Bolivian Episcopal Conference. This document responded to the neoliberal economic policies contained in presidential decree 21060 of 1985, which dissolved state-owned mining companies, downsized public administration, banned monopolies in the production of public services, dissolved decentralized state agencies, proposed new regulation of internal debts, freed exchange rates, lowered trade tariffs, issued new administrative directives to suspend anyone employed in the state banking sector who does not abide by the law, and proposed the relocation of downsized employees in both the private and public sector. Terrazas raised a series of concerns about the social impact of the new economic policies. Here are some of his questions:

> What social sectors would benefit and how? Will these new policies deepen social differences and widen the gap between rich and poor? How will they protect national industries and the resulting unemployment? Will they not aid currency speculation and "money laundering" coming from narco-traffic? Could they generate a "loyal competition" in the assignment of resources? Will they not gravely affect the national production of goods and services? What complementary policies are proposed, for example, in the area of taxation to help redistribute income and wealth? How will they overcome social conditions and economic depression in the peasant sector? (Centro de Promoción del Laicado 1985, 18)

The mere raising of these concerns led many in the business community to accuse the church of meddling in politics by proposing "concrete technical alternatives" to Bolivian economic problems, as if they were the only ones who could issue an opinion on the social impact of neoliberal economic policies. The government's reaction was more cautious: it stated that the church document was positive and declared its willingness to participate in a church-sponsored dialogue.

The ability of the church to mediate, but also to offer a critical position on social and economic issues, earned it a place in the Bolivian political landscape. For those affiliated with the popular church movement, moderates within the hierarchy were raising topics with which they had been concerned for a long time. Conservatives within the church now also supported the promotion of dialogue and mediation, which moderates had supported and directed since the late 1970s.

Despite much imperfection, transition to democracy in the 1980s provided the opportunity for the church to accommodate the new political scene. Repeated calls for mediation by different sectors of Bolivian society demonstrate the church's reintegration into the political system as a nonpartisan actor who defends and promotes liberal democracy. This new status has melded the previously conflictive views of traditionals and moderates to create a neoconservative church orientation that identifies with liberal democracy as the most adequate political system. Despite this conservative turn, it is important to note that members of the Bolivian Episcopal Conference continued to denounce social injustice and human rights violations throughout the 1990s and the first years of the twenty-first century.

Guatemala
As in Bolivia, the Guatemalan Catholic Church identified with conservative oligarchs in the nineteenth and twentieth centuries. It was the strongest in Central America until liberal oligarchs came to power in 1871. Liberal oligarchs saw the church as a powerful institution that could offset their policies, and they sought to reduce its role in society. They introduced a series of laws that eliminated the church's role in education, abolished the tithe, confiscated church property, outlawed religious orders, and exiled most religious priests and nuns.

The church lost control of marriage and cemeteries, and the clergy were banned from holding government offices. When the church retaliated by excommunicating President Justo Rufino Barrios and holding public processions, the government outlawed such religious processions and sent the archbishop into exile. President Barrios traveled to New York to invite Protestant pastors to go to Guatemala in a move to counteract Catholic influence in the country. All these measures were legislated and codified in the Constitution of 1879. As a result, the number of priests declined from 314 before the new legislation, to 119 in 1880, and 78 in 1928 (Brett 2003, 23; Calder 1970, 11–46). This significant reduction in the church pastoral workforce diminished its role in society as a whole and the church worked mostly with the elite of Guatemala City and a few other urban centers. Local priests came from the elite classes, and few ventured into the rural areas where the vast majority of the inhabitants were Indians who did not speak Spanish.

The church hierarchy developed a good relationship with the Guatemalan state in the twentieth century. When Mariano Rossell Arellano was named archbishop of Guatemala in 1939, he realized that the liberal dictator of the time, Jorge Ubico (1931–1944), would become the Guatemalan version of Francisco Franco of Spain, whom he admired. His predecessors had fought liberal regimes, but Rossell Arellano thought that he could work out an agreement with Ubico, hoping that the government would give the church some basic concessions, which, in fact, Ubico did by allowing the Jesuits and the Maryknoll, Salesian, Marist, Franciscan, and Dominican priests to return to the country. Ubico also accepted a papal nuncio and allowed the church to celebrate mass publicly. Ubico made all these concessions personally, but he never repealed the legislation enacted in 1879. This left the church in legal limbo and totally subordinated to the state (Brett 2003, 23–24).

The overthrow of Ubico in 1944 by nationalist reformist forces brought back political frictions, but no persecution. Rossell Arellano welcomed the new regime because he hoped the new government would rescind the legislation that constrained the development of the Catholic Church. He was disappointed, however, when the Constitution of 1945 was published with all the anticlerical legislation of 1879. Even worse, he perceived that the new government, led by Juan José Arévalo (1945–1950) showed some favoritism to Protestants, allowing a large number of non-Catholic pastors to enter the country, allegedly to neutralize Catholic influence. Rossell Arellano warned Guatemalans about communist influence in the government and, prior to the 1950 elections, advised them not to vote for any candidate suspected of communist sympathy. He was clearly referring to Jacobo Arbenz Guzmán (1951–1954), the official candidate, whom Arévalo expected would add to the reforms started in his government (Brett 2003, 25).

Arévalo and Arbenz Guzmán attempted to modernize the Guatemalan economy, society, and politics. Their plans called for the establishment of a modern labor code, new education and health policies, establishment of a social security program, and agrarian and political reforms that would have laid the basis for a modern society. The labor code sought to modernize labor relations in both the urban and rural areas. Political reforms entailed creating a modern electoral system that permitted free and fair elections. Agrarian reforms were intended to build a solid stratum among the peasantry that could expand production and internal markets. The government planned to buy uncultivated lands from the local landed oligarchy and the U.S.-based United Fruit Company. However, local elites, the Catholic Church, and the

U.S. government opposed these plans. They accused Arévalo and especially Arbenz Guzmán of close association with communists, which the United States, in the midst of the cold war with Russia, perceived as a real threat (Tischler Visquera 1998, 266–87).

The United States moved swiftly to approve a plan to overthrow Arbenz Guzmán. The Central Intelligence Agency (CIA) was charged with organizing secret operations in collaboration with Colonel Carlos Castillo Armas. With CIA support, Castillo Armas trained a band of counterrevolutionary guerrillas to invade Guatemala. Arbenz Guzmán did not have strong support within his own armed forces, so Castillo Armas did not encounter major resistance when he invaded in 1954, and the government quickly dissolved, thus ending Guatemala's experiment with democracy.

The overthrow of the Arbenz Guzmán regime marks a turning point in church-state relations in Guatemala. The United States and Guatemalan elites saw the church as a vital ally in the struggles against communism. Castillo Armas and his successor, Miguel Ydígoras Fuentes (1958–1963), repealed all the anticlerical legislation dating back to 1879 and gave the church everything it wanted except to make Catholicism the official state religion. They even declared Rossell Arellano a national hero. Nonetheless, these concessions did not completely eliminate political frictions with the church; Rossell Arellano disapproved of the use of violence as an instrument to eradicate communism. The frictions led President Ydígoras Fuentes to negotiate an agreement with the papal nuncio, José Paupini, whereby all church documents, including those of the archbishop, were to be approved by the nunciature prior to their publication. This agreement created conflicts between Paupini and Rossell Arellano, which the former tried to mend by recommending the appointment of Fr. Mario Casariego Acevedo to the Vatican as auxiliary bishop. Casariego Acevedo had been educated under Rossell Arellano and had excellent contacts in high places both in Guatemala and in Rome, but he was also a good friend of Paupini. When Rossell Arellano retired in 1964, Mario Casariego Acevedo was named archbishop (1964–1983) to replace him (Bendaña 1985, 374–76; Calder 1970, 153–71).

Casariego Acevedo led the Guatemalan church toward significant changes at international and national levels. Internationally, the United States supported a broad role for the Latin American military to contain communism. This was particularly the case in Guatemala, where the military had overthrown the Arbenz Guzmán regime and broadened its power base within the country. The Vatican named Casariego Acevedo, archbishop of Guatemala, to lead the national church in the context of these new changes. However, he was a pre-Vatican II man who was more interested in raising the banner of anticommunism than in redefining the role of the Catholic Church. This partly explains his close political association with top military and conservative civilian leaders. Like Archbishop Pittini in the Dominican Republic, Casariego Acevedo saw his relationship with the government as an opportunity to expand the role of the church, not as a critical voice, but rather as one that supported the status quo. This political attitude is comparable to that of Cardinal Maurer in Bolivia, who also sought to maintain cordial relations with military governments to obtain privileges for the church. In all these cases, the leadership of the church identified with the church's traditional orientation.

Expansion and Consolidation of the Church in Guatemala
The relationship Casariego Acevedo built with the Guatemalan state allowed him to continue expanding the institutional basis of the church by importing large numbers of religious priests. Institutional growth allowed the church to become more visible and to play a larger role in society. There were two stages involved in building the Guatemalan church in the twentieth century. The first one (1939–1964) was led by Rossell Arellano and the second one (1965–1984) by Casariego Acevedo.

When Rossell Arellano was appointed to lead the church in 1939, he had to start from scratch to build the pastoral workforce. This was necessarily slow due to the political circumstances of the time. As Archbishops Nouel and Pittini in the Dominican Republic or Maurer in Bolivia had done, Rossell Arellano wanted to build the national clergy, but he did not have the resources to do it and had to import religious priests. This was one of the greatest challenges for the archbishop because diocesan priests (mostly Guatemalans) actually decreased from seventy-three in 1945 to sixty in 1950, whereas religious priests (mostly foreign born) increased from forty-one in 1945 to seventy-two in 1950.

This pattern strengthened in the second half of the twentieth century under Casariego Acevedo. For example, diocesan priests increased from 115 in 1959 to 196 in 1965. Numbers slipped to 185 in 1970, but there were 206 in 1980, increasing to 236 in 1990 and 353 in 1998. At the same time, religious priests increased from 231 in 1959 to 298 in 1965. There were 423 in 1970, 493 in 1980, 449 in 1990, and 582 in 1998 (see web table 2A).

An increase in the pastoral workforce led to an expansion in the number of ecclesiastical jurisdictions and parishes. The Guatemalan church expanded from 7 dioceses and one apostolic administration in 1951 to 15 in 1991 with 21 bishops. Parishes with priests increased from 273 in 1970 to 300 in 1980, and 403 in 1998, whereas parishes without priests increased from 29 in 1970 to 39 in 1980 and 44 in 1998. Similarly, seminaries increased from 8 in 1970 to 13 in 1980 and 30 in 1998. Catholic educational institutions decreased in the 1980s from 251 to 208, but picked up by 1998, when the number reached 882. The number of welfare institutions actually decreased in the 1980s from 710 to 701 in the 1990s. However, these rebounded to 1,247 by 1998. As in Bolivia, it is worth noting that the number of religious women increased from 792 in 1970 to 1,191 in 1980, and from 1,531 in 1990 to 1,608 in 1998 (see web tables 2A, 2B, 2C, and 2D; Bendaña 1985, 464; Calder 1970, 47–62).

The overwhelming presence of foreign-born religious priests helped expand the structural basis of the church, but it also created problems. Unlike Rossell Arellano, a Guatemalan, Casariego Acevedo was a religious priest born in Spain but raised and educated in Guatemala. Casariego Acevedo was more open to the importation of religious clergy than Rossell Arellano, who was more interested in developing the national clergy. Religious priests were better educated than Guatemalans and, as a result, ended up occupying key positions within the local church, which local diocesan priests resented. These complaints were expressed by the Conferencia de Sacerdotes Diocesanos en Guatemala, COSDEGUA (Conference of Guatemala Diocesan Priests).

COSDEGUA was founded on April 30, 1968, by sixteen diocesan priests, all of them Guatemalans, except for one German. Their organization was created to promote the implementation of the postulate of Vatican II as well as the social, economic, and intellectual condition of diocesan priests. In one of its first pronouncements, COSDEGUA, composed mostly of priests from poor urban parishes, revealed the conflict created by the massive presence of foreign-born religious priests who came from wealthy countries such as the United States, Spain, and Germany.

> In particular, we repudiate foreign priests and bishops who use their economic power and staff in an arrogant fashion. We equally deplore and reproach the disloyal attitude of some Guatemalan priests and bishops who, due to their nature and behavior, seem to betray the Fatherland and the church. Because of this, we finally declare that our confrontation is a struggle of mentality rather than nationality. (Chea 1988, 212)

COSDEGUA complained most strongly against Spanish priests, who spoke loudly and authoritatively, always pointing their fingers. This was reminiscent of a colonial mentality the Guatemalan church had not yet eradicated. COSDEGUA reserved its most severe criticism for Archbishop Casariego Acevedo, whom they considered an ally of the military government. Unlike other Latin American organizations of priests, such as Chile's Group of Eighty, Argentina's

Priests for the Third World, or Peru's ONIS, whose objectives transcended internal church conflicts, COSDEGUA revealed rebelliousness within the church, and its claims were concrete: there were abnormalities and injustices within the Guatemalan church, disapproval over imposition of a foreign mentality, complaints about Cardinal Casariego Acevedo, and discussions of social injustice (Chea 1988, 215). Despite its efforts, COSDEGUA was not able to gather much support among the diocesan priests, much less among the religious clergy. The Conferencia Episcopal de Guatemala, CEG (Guatemalan Episcopal Conference) had doubts about their nationalism and thought their rebellious attitudes unacceptable. Eventually, COSDEGUA lost political steam and disappeared.

Religious Priests and Their Pastoral Work with the Indigenous
Foreign-born religious priests lived in remote rural settings that were transformed by economic changes in the 1960s. Unlike their Central American counterparts, where religious priests tended to live in urban settings, these priests lived in inhospitable zones, where the church had been absent for decades. Inhabited mostly by indigenous people, who constitute about 60 percent of the Guatemalan population, these regions were socially explosive. Like Bolivia, Guatemala experienced impressive growth rates in the 1970s. For example, the GDP grew on average by 6.1 percent between 1970 and 1978. Industrial production comprised 50 percent of the value of agricultural production. This industrial push benefited from significant foreign investments. However, this prosperity did not benefit the vast majority of Guatemalans. In relation to 1970, the value of the minimum wage had diminished by 46.8 percent in 1979. In the same period, industrial wages lost 31 percent, whereas unemployment and underemployment reached 34.2 percent. In addition, the Guatemalan poor suffered the consequences of the 1976 earthquake, which left 22,000 dead and 1 million homeless (Samandu, Siebers, and Sierra 1990, 38–40). In short, religious priests went to work in the most socially explosive regions of the country.

The experience of many missionaries in Guatemala is comparable to that of foreign religious priests in Bolivia, who encountered a social reality that transformed their lives. Many of them brought an innovative religious discourse and received support from Guatemalan bishops who shared the teachings of Vatican II and Medellín. They began to work in such places as Petén, Quiché, Huehuetenango, and Alta Verapaz, regions ridden with social and political conflicts. Prior to their arrival, Catholic Social Action (CSA) had worked in those regions but had played a rather conservative role. CSA pastoral work had been pietistic and conservative and, as such, supported the ideological project of the counterrevolutionary military government. It also supported the military regimes of the 1950s and 1960s by developing infrastructural projects in areas not reached by the state. CSA promoted social movements that limited their demands to basic necessities, claiming to be apolitical. One such movement was Ligas Campesinas (Peasant Leagues), created in the 1960s to defend the interests of indigenous people against *ladinos* (racially mixed people) and local authorities. Ligas Campesinas eventually established links to the Christian Democratic Party.

Religious priests soon realized that it was impossible to preach the word of God without a social commitment. They first encountered opposition within the church hierarchy that disagreed with their pastoral approach to implement the teachings of Vatican II and Medellín. These conflicts deepened in 1961 when they founded the Confederación de Religiosos Guatemaltecos (Guatemalan Conference of Religious). Many of these religious priests had turned from being anticommunists when they first arrived in Guatemala, to being progressives who questioned the conservative political attitudes of the hierarchy. A number of them attempted to develop cooperative, ecclesiastical-basis communities and to support the claims of the indigenous people with whom they worked and lived.

A small group of them decided to join guerrilla forces to overthrow the military government. The names of Thomas and Marjorie Melville became well known in the United States. The Melvilles had joined a guerrilla force, but apparently a member of their order, the Maryknoll, denounced them. This led the U.S. Embassy and their religious superior to order them out of the country. There were other lesser-known cases that were more coherent in the combination of denunciation and action than that of the Melvilles. These included members of the Jesuit order, the Sacred Heart, and the Congregation of the Immaculate Heart of Mary (Chea 1988, 233–57).

As in Bolivia, repression against the church's pastoral work force was widespread. Between 1978 and 1985, the military assassinated five diocesan priests, eight religious, and two non-priest religious. Eleven of these clergymen were foreign born and four were Guatemalan. As a result of military repression between 1980 and 1981, over ninety-one priests and sixty-four religious women left the country; six Catholic radio stations were either destroyed or silenced; and ten Catholic schools as well as forty-two centers for religious education were closed. Msgr. Juan Gerardi was nearly killed in July 1980 and then almost forced to close down the Diocese of El Quiché. Gerardi traveled to Rome to explain what had happened, but when he returned he was not allowed into the country. He was exiled to Costa Rica (Samandu et al. 1990, 59–61).

Casariego Acevedo and the Political Division of the Hierarchy
Despite the repressive measures against Catholic personnel, Casariego Acevedo did not voice any protest. Throughout the 1970s, there were multiple signs within the church indicating that a large number of clergymen and religious women did not agree with the archbishop. For example, while Casariego Acevedo was in Rome for promotion to the rank of cardinal in March 29, 1969, a group of priests wrote a letter making grave accusations against him and asking the pope to keep Casariego Acevedo from returning to Guatemala. On April 29, 1970, 200 priests signed a letter to Pope Paul VI asking him to remove the archbishop within thirty days.

The following year, shortly after Independence Day, a group of Christian leaders including bishops, priests, and evangelicals asked for a return to the rule of law and for the use of humanistic means to resolve differences of opinion. Msgr. Ramiro Pellecer, speaking on behalf of the CEG accused the group of "meddling in politics." A few days later, the military government expelled the foreign priests who signed the letter and the national priests were threatened seriously. Even Gerardo Flores, a bishop who signed the letter, was forced to leave the country temporarily (Bendaña 1985, 471–72).

The CEG was politically divided as a result of the positions taken by the archbishop. A number of bishops were concerned with the violence and poverty that permeated society. In 1974, the bishops published a collective letter on violence, but Casariego Acevedo and two other bishops refused to sign it. Again, on the occasion of the elections of 1978, the bishops prepared a letter to advise the faithful. The archbishop took the document, eliminated the parts he did not like, and published it without consulting the bishops. This infuriated a group of bishops, who wrote a letter to Pope Paul VI asking for Casariego Acevedo's removal from office (Berryman 1994, 107–44; Calder 1970, 139–52; Klaiber 1998, 228). Casariego Acevedo's partisan position divided the church and prevented it from acting in a more cohesive manner. The church remained divided until Casariego Acevedo passed away on June 15, 1984.

The Resurgence and Mediation of the Church in Guatemala
The promotion of dialogue, political mediation, and the defense of human rights became the center of the church work following the appointment of Próspero Penados del Barrio as archbishop of Guatemala (1984–2005). The new archbishop had been an important voice among those criticizing the use of violence to resolve political and social issues. When President Vinicio Cerezo (1986–1991) wanted to have a dialogue with the guerrilla insurgency, Penados del Barrio applauded the initiative. The president seemed interested

in ending a long social and political conflict that dated back to the overthrow of the Arbenz Guzmán regime in 1954.

Guatemala had gone through various waves of guerrilla warfare, and most of them had been defeated by the army, but after 1982 the various guerrilla groups put behind them sectarian attitudes and banded together under the Unidad Revolucionaria Nacional Guatemalteca, URNG (National Revolutionary Union of Guatemala). Despite this unity, however, the URNG was strategically defeated by the army. The army waged a scorched-earth campaign from 1981 to 1983 that destroyed more than 440 villages. As a result, over 150,000 civilians were killed or disappeared. In addition, over 200,000 went to Mexico as refugees.

These genocidal policies were meant not only to eliminate the guerrillas, but to destroy the culture, identity, and communal structures of the indigenous population (Jonas 2000, 24). Many Catholic clergy as well as the laity criticized this genocidal campaign and paid dearly, either with their lives, exile, or jail. This is why Archbishop Penados del Barrio welcomed Cerezo's proposal for dialogue with the guerrillas.

The church's promotion of dialogue received a significant endorsement from the agreement that became widely known as Esquipulas II, after the place where it was signed in Guatemala. The Central American presidents agreed, despite political pressure from Washington to the contrary, to a peaceful solution to national and regional conflicts. They rejected foreign interference in the region and purely military solutions in favor of negotiated peace. They signed an agreement promoted by the Contadora group, comprising Venezuela, Colombia, and Mexico. This agreement pushed Nicaraguans and Salvadorans to negotiate peace settlements in the 1990s. Like his counterparts in Nicaragua and El Salvador, President Vinicio Cerezo of Guatemala wanted to improve his country's image and respond to international pressure to end human rights violations. Aware of their strategic victory over the guerrilla insurgency, the Guatemalan military did not support Cerezo wholeheartedly and, on at least three occasions (May and August 1988 and May 1989), sought to overthrow him (Klaiber 1998, 229).

Despite military uneasiness, the Guatemalan peace process moved through four stages, and the Catholic Church, represented by Bishop Rodolfo Quezada Toruño, mediated in the first three stages. Quezada Toruño received the title of conciliator to mediate between the URNG and the government from 1987 to 1995. The church was critical of both sides in the conflict. For example, Quezada Toruño criticized both sides for their refusal to declare a cease-fire, for their use of the negotiations to take political advantage, and for their rejection of a compromise (Calder 2001, 793). The various governments that succeeded Vinicio Cerezo were uncomfortable with the church's critical position and accused Quezada Toruño of being the "Fourth URNG Comandante." Quezada Toruño played an instrumental role in laying the basis for the United Nations to come into the country in 1996 and complete the peace settlements successfully (Calder 2001, 793; Jonas 2000, 39–50; Klaiber 1998, 229–36).

The Guatemalan church was part of a movement that pushed for a national dialogue and peace that had been inspired by the Esquipulas II agreements. In February 1989, the National Dialogue Commission was established and, at its first meeting, brought together eighty-nine delegates from forty-seven different organizations. In addition to the Catholic Church, the commission included twenty-six representatives from six accredited religious institutions, including the Evangelical Alliance of Guatemala, a large conservative confederation of Pentecostal churches; the conference of evangelical churches of Guatemala, a small, progressive confederation of individual Protestant churches; the Jewish community of Guatemala; the Episcopal Church; and the Permanent Assembly of Christian Groups. Neither the URNG nor The Comité Coordinador de Asociaciones de Comercio, Industria y Finanzas (Coordinating Committee of Associations of Agriculture, Trade, Industry, and Finance) were represented at this meeting, but political pressure from the National Dialogue Commission was significant in forcing them to eventually compromise on key issues (Calder 2001, 779; Klaiber 1998, 231).

Another important factor in the development of a peace movement in Guatemala was the Asamblea de la Sociedad Civil, ASC (Association of the Civil Society) founded in May 1994. Like the National Dialogue Commission, the ASC expressed the frustration of the large sectors of society that were excluded from the peace process. Comprising the same groups that participated in the National Dialogue Commission in 1989, the ASC was created as part of the Framework Accord of 1994. The accord provided the mechanism for the United Nations to take over the negotiation of the peace process. Quezada Toruño stepped aside from the mediation process, but prominent members of ASC asked him to preside over their organization. Under the leadership of Quezada Toruño, the ASC prepared a series of documents that became blueprints for the peace negotiations. Despite the ASC attempts to balance the interests of the different parties in the conflict, right-wing sectors within the government and the military claimed that Quezada Toruño was biased toward the URNG, which at times took ideas from the ASC. The bishop responded by observing that "coincidences are inevitable; however, we do hope that the documents coincide with the poor and the marginalized of Guatemala." He resigned from the ASC in February 1995, saying that the church had reached the conclusion that "it was time to work from below, no longer in an official capacity" (Jonas 2000, 69–92; Klaiber 1998, 236).

Quezada Toruño continued to support the Human Rights Office of the archdiocese, which had been formed in 1989. Bishop Juan Gerardi presided over the commission charged with the investigation of human rights violations and on April 24, 1998, presented a 1,400-page document entitled "Guatemala: Never Again." The document was part of a "Project to Recover the Historical Memory" (Recuperemos la Memoria Histórica). The report was based on 7,000 interviews with victims and eyewitnesses of violence. The findings of the commission showed that 83.4 percent of the violence was committed by official security forces during the thirty-six years of conflict. This type of report was unprecedented in Guatemala, and those who had been the backbone of the military regime were angry about its publication. Bishop Girardi was killed by assassins just forty-eight hours after presenting his report (Klaiber 1998, 49–84). The murder indicates how dangerous it has been for the church to be involved in the promotion of peace and justice.

The role of the church in Bolivia and Guatemala runs parallel in many ways. In these two cases, one finds the massive presence of foreign-born religious priests who work with indigenous people. A significant number of these priests are engaged in the popular church and work for human rights. In both cases, a group of bishops supports the popular church, causing a division of the hierarchy, led by the conservative cardinals. The presence of a progressive group of bishops in both hierarchies had an important impact in defining the role of the church in its transition to democracy. This presence probably made it possible for the modernization orientation of the church to succeed in promoting political mediation and dialogue while remaining critical of the political process.

Nicaragua

The Somoza dynasty (1936–1979) laid the foundation for the development of modern twentieth-century Nicaragua. It also left a lasting legacy on the Nicaraguan church, and its effects are still lingering today. What follows is a brief description of Somoza's relationship with the Catholic Church as a necessary background to understand church-state relations during the Sandinista period (1979–1990).

Anastasio Somoza García and his children created a dynasty that ruled Nicaragua from 1936 to 1979. He took power in 1936 and ruled until he was assassinated in 1956. During the entire period of his regime, Somoza García had the political and economic support of the United States, which helped him become director of the National Guard and eventually president of the country. Like Trujillo in the Dominican Republic, Somoza García was a product of U.S. military occupations in Central America and the Caribbean. These occupations prepared the conditions for the emergence of dictatorial regimes whose authoritarian legacy permeates those societies today.

When Somoza García was assassinated in 1956, his children, Luis and Anastasio, continued to run the country as a family affair until the Sandinistas took power in 1979. Luis and Anastasio Somoza Debayle ended their father's populist approach[3] to political domination, and thus increasingly distanced Nicaraguan elites from government. Luis's death in 1967 left power in the hands of his older brother, Anastasio, who alienated the Nicaraguan elite even further. However, the event that crowned the end of a political relationship between Somoza Debayle and the elite was a massacre of more than 300 people who participated in a rally called by the Conservative Party. The massacre occurred in 1967 and it had a high political cost for Somoza Debayle. After the massacre, he allowed a civilian triumvirate to take over the government in 1971, but he retained complete control over the National Guard. The Managua earthquake in 1972 provided the occasion for Somoza Debayle to thrust aside the civilian triumvirate and seize control of the entire government.

If the massacre of 1967 soured Somoza Debayle's relationship with the elite, the Managua earthquake marked the beginning of a crisis that culminated with the Sandinista Revolution in 1979. Somoza Debayle created order in the chaos that resulted from the earthquake, and, at the same time, took advantage of the earthquake to enrich himself with the aid that came into the country. Somoza Debayle pocketed a great deal of the aid and allowed National Guardsmen to pillage the incoming goods that came in to help needy Nicaraguans.

The Nicaraguan dictator set up construction companies to rebuild parts of Managua and to manufacture bricks to be sold to different municipalities in the country to repair streets. His corruption expanded into various areas. Phillip Berryman reports, for example, of a Somoza Debayle military aid purchase of 93.6 acres for $71,428 in July 1975 that was sold to the government for $1.7 million just two months later (Berryman 1994, 65). Somoza Debayle's behavior further estranged the elite, who could not profit from the reconstruction of Managua. This helped prepare the conditions for the emergence of a social movement comprising the peasantry and the working- and middle-class people who were disenchanted with his rule. The Catholic Church, one of the dynasty's key allies, was also alienated.

The Catholic Church and Somoza García

The role of the Nicaraguan church under the Somoza dynasty parallels its Central American and Dominican counterparts. The Nicaraguan church accommodated the Somoza family regime and was slow in responding to the need for change in society. Archbishop José Antonio Lezcano y Ortega (1913–1953) worked with both liberals and conservatives to regain the church's position in Nicaragua. He made sure, however, that the political elite knew that he objected to the nationalist guerrillas of Augusto César Sandino in the late 1920s. Sandino organized an armed resistance to the presence of U.S. Marines in Nicaragua from the mid-1920s to early 1930s. In fact, the archbishop urged Sandino and his followers to support the occupying forces. He recommended humility and resignation to Nicaraguan Catholics.

When Somoza García took power in 1936, Lezcano y Ortega was ready to support him because he thought that Somoza García could protect the church from Protestantism and international communism, which he believed was the greatest threat of his time. The archbishop was aware of the repressive nature of Somoza García, but he believed that the government only pursued enemies of the common good: "It is a clear fact that, on the Government's side, nobody is punished or persecuted unless they are involved in revolutionary conspiracies or acts of disloyalty against public order" (Kirk 1992, 51).

Lezcano y Ortega's successor, Vicente Alejandro González y Robledo (1953–1968), continued the same type of relationship with the regime when Somoza was assassinated in 1956. Except for Octavio José Calderón y Padilla (1947–1970), archbishop of Matagalpa, no other member of the Nicaraguan hierarchy dared criticize the Somozas. Calderón y Padilla promoted Rural Catholic Action and the CEBs. Later, his pastoral work had an important impact on the development of the popular church in Nicaragua. When Miguel Obando y Bravo was appointed archbishop of Managua in 1970, he began to criticize the Somoza regime and mediated in conflicts with the Sandinista guerrillas and the government, but, as noted below, he eventually became a foe of the Sandinista Revolution.

Institutional Expansion of the Nicaraguan Church

The Nicaraguan church significantly expanded in the 1980s and 1990s. The most notable increase can be observed in the pastoral workforce. This institutional development made the church more noticeable and allowed it to play a larger role in society. As with the Bolivian church, the Nicaraguan church relied on the importation of priests. For example, there were 121 diocesans in 1970, 119 in 1980, 134 in 1990, and 253 in 1998. In contrast, religious priests increased from 186 in 1970 to 221 in 1980 and 173 in 1990 (see web table 2A). There were not as many religious priests as in Bolivia, but they still were a significant group. Unlike Bolivia, however, the number of Nicaraguan-born priests has increased substantially in recent years. According to Andrew J. Stein, it increased from 42.6 percent in 1962–1979 to 75.9 percent in 1980–1990. Interestingly, this figure rose to 94.1 percent in the 1990s. In contrast, religious priests comprised 57.4 percent in 1962–1979, 24.1 percent in 1980–1989, and dropped sharply to 5.9 percent in 1990–1993 (Stein 1998, 342). However, as noted above, the number of religious priests rebounded substantially in the decade, though it remained below that of diocesan priests.

As in Bolivia and Guatemala, the Nicaraguan church increased the number of ecclesiastical jurisdictions. In 1998, there was 1 archdiocese (Managua), 4 dioceses, 2 prelatures, and 1 apostolic vicariate. Seminaries increased somewhat from 5 in 1970 to 6 in 1980 to 8 in 1990 and to 11 in 1998. Parishes with priests increased from 129 in 1970 to 159 in 1980, and 227 in 1998. Noticeably, there was an increase in the number of parishes without priests from 15 in 1970 to 23 in 1980, but these diminished to 16 in 1990 and 5 by 1998. Educational institutions diminished from 237 in 1980 to 208 in 1990, but they bounced back by 1998 when they increased to 704. Welfare institutions also increased from 73 in 1980 to 212 in 1998. The number of religious women increased from 497 in 1970 to 692 in 1980, 663 in 1990, and 946 in 1998 (see web tables 2A, 2B, and 2D). This impressive growth parallels those of Bolivia and Guatemala, where the institutional growth of the church made it more discernible and permitted it to accommodate the new political scenario created by the Sandinista Revolution.

The Emergence of the Popular Church in Nicaragua
Religious priests played an important role in the development of the popular church throughout Latin America, particularly in Nicaragua. Jesuits were one of the most involved orders, but they were not the only ones. In 1968, a pastoral encounter called "Facing the Future of the Church in Nicaragua" brought together 250 priests and religious as well as three of the nine Nicaraguan bishops. This event marked a key moment in the post-Vatican II Nicaraguan church and in future relations between the church and the Somoza Debayle's regime. According to the organizers of this event, the Nicaraguan church was pre-Vatican and it needed to be updated. A Jesuit priest, Noel García, noted that the Nicaraguan hierarchy was removed from the Nicaraguan reality:

(The hierarchy is) decrepit, conservative, stationary, advanced in age, apathetic, negative, disunited, hardly accessible to the public, some of whom have no idea about—or interest in—the hierarchy. It represents the desire to do nothing, merely repeating coldly and compulsively timeworn positions. . . . The church in Nicaragua is sorely lacking true spiritual leadership from its pastors. (Noel García, as cited in Kirk 1992, 53)

Noel García and his colleagues wanted the hierarchy to be more open, as mandated by Vatican II and the bishop conferences of Medellín and Puebla. They thought that the church had to denounce injustice and defend human rights, as was happening elsewhere in Latin America. The official church cautioned against this radical approach and reminded clergy and laity that the church should not get involved in daily matters and lose its spiritual mission.

Fr. García's speech echoed the emergence of the popular church in Nicaragua. One of the most important developments was the founding of Fr. Ernesto Cardenal's religious community of Solentiname in 1966 on Lake Nicaragua in the south of the country. Cardenal's community encouraged peasants to reflect on their living conditions according to the teachings of the Gospel. In 1966, the Spanish priest José de la Jara founded another community called "14 de Septiembre" (September 14) in Managua, and he, too, encouraged Catholics to think about their social reality. Like Fr. Cardenal, he moved to the community and lived in the barrio with the poor people. He was later joined by a number of religious women from the Maryknoll sisters. Similarly, Fr. Pedro Vílchez organized a program to train peasant leaders who worked in rural communities.

The Capuchins of the Atlantic Coast were also involved in training peasant leaders and the Delegate of the Word to take priestly functions in parishes without priests. Fr. Uriel Molina, a Franciscan, developed a project similar to that of Fr. De la Jara in the early 1970s, except that the latter worked with university students. Fr. Molina had been professor at the Jesuit-run Universidad Centroamericana, and he encouraged a significant number of the students to join his parish at the Barrio Riguero in eastern Managua. Inspired by Fr. Molina's community, a group of students founded the Revolutionary Christian Movement, a close ally of the Sandinistas in the revolutionary struggle that led up to the overthrow of Somoza Debayle. Molina told me that many of the leaders of the Sandinista Front for National Liberation (Frente Sandinista de Liberación Nacional, FSLN) came out of his community (Fr. Molina, interview with the author, Managua, July 17, 1997).

The radical role these and many other priests played should not lead us to believe that most Nicaraguan priests (religious and diocesan) supported the popular church. Again, as in Bolivia and Guatemala, the number of priests who became involved in the activities of the popular church was relatively small. For example, a 1982–1983 survey of 220 priests (i.e., 60 percent of the total number of priests in the country) reported that 46 percent supported the Sandinista Revolution and 54 percent were opposed to it. In his study, Philip William (1989, 77–78) made the following estimates of the political stance of the clergy:

- Direct or active collaboration   15–20 percent
- Passive collaboration   20 percent
- Passive opposition   40–45 percent
- Active opposition   20 percent

These are estimates, but if they reflect reality, then most of the clergy were anti-Sandinistas. Most priests (i.e., 60–65 percent) avoided extreme political positions.

Another important element to consider when looking at the political behavior of priests in Nicaragua in the 1980s is that religious priests were heavily concentrated in Managua, the capital city, the seat of the only archdiocese in the country, and the source of most conflicts with the Sandinista government. There were 50 diocesan and 102 religious priests in the archdiocese of Managua in 1983. The proportion of diocesan/religious was relatively balanced in the rest of the dioceses. For example, if one looks at the larger dioceses, in Estelí there were fourteen diocesan and seventeen religious; in Granada there were sixteen diocesan and twenty-two religious; in León there twenty-two diocesan and seventeen religious; in Matagalpa there were twelve diocesan and thirteen religious (William 1989, 78). Because most religious priests were in the Archdiocese of Managua, a large number of them were involved in the popular church or supported the government in the church-state conflict during the Sandinista regime. Though small in number, this group of priests had superior educations and commitment as compared to the rest of the clergy. They had a significant impact on church-state relations in the period leading up to the revolution and during the Sandinista regime.

Church-State Relations: From Conflict to Mediation
Church-state relations during the Sandinista regime moved through various stages, which included initial sympathy, opposition to the government, and, subsequently, mediation between the government and the National

Resistance, better known as the Contras. On November 17, 1979, four months after the Sandinistas entered Managua victoriously, the Conferencia Episcopal de Nicaragua, CEN (Nicaragua Episcopal Conference) published a pastoral letter greeting the revolution, recognizing the valor and legitimacy of the triumphant insurrection, discussing the construction of a new man, declaring the legitimacy of socialism, recognizing the mission of the FSLN, and supporting the "preferential option for the poor." The bishops only asked for the necessary space to continue the evangelizing mission of the church without any privileges (Conferencia Episcopal de Nicaragua 1979). Church-state relations were cordial and even included a visit to the pope by Fr. Miguel D'Escoto, minister of foreign relations. Three other priests occupied important cabinet positions in government—Ernesto Cardenal, Fernando Cardenal, and Alvaro Arguello.

In October 1980, the FSLN published a communiqué on religion in which it laid out its position on the issue. The communiqué states that Christians have been an integral part of Nicaraguan revolutionary history, to a degree unprecedented in any other revolutionary movement in Latin America, and possibly the world. It lists a series of inalienable rights, such as freedom of religious practice, respect of religious celebrations, and the right of all Nicaraguans to participate in the country's decision-making process (FSLN 1983).

Despite the good intentions of the FSLN, relations with the church began to sour even before the communiqué on religion was issued. Thus, shortly after publishing the pastoral letter that greeted the revolution, the CEN called on the priests who occupied cabinet posts in the government to resign because the exceptional period had ended. This call poisoned the cordiality of church-state relations. The priests rejected the call and expressed their commitment to the Sandinista Popular Revolution. The rejection was followed by Archbishop Obando y Bravo's refusal to attend the celebration of the successful culmination of the National Literacy Crusade in July 1980, which had been led by Fernando Cardenal, SJ. The following year the CEN said that education must be based on Christian principles. It ignored the fact that Nicaraguan educational policies were under the direction of a Catholic priest who was the minister of education and, instead, it chose to tolerate a group of lay conservative Catholics when it launched a campaign through the daily, *La Prensa*, denouncing Sandinista intentions to establish an atheist and Marxist education.

The positions of the CEN began to move from criticism of government policies to publication of pastoral letters that coincided with the political views of the opposition. In August 1983, the CEN published a pastoral letter in which it strongly condemned the government's plan to establish a military service law at a time when the country was being attacked by the U.S.-supported Contras from Honduras. On April 22, 1984, the CEN published a controversial pastoral letter: it demanded that the government begin a dialogue with the Contras, which was exactly the same position put forward by the Contras in December 1983 and the Reagan administration. This letter was published in the wake of the CIA's mining of Nicaraguan ports, and the CEN did not even mention the incident when it suggested that all Nicaraguan sectors must be included in the dialogue. On March 22, 1985, the bishops offered themselves as mediators in an "internal dialogue." In fact, this is what the Contras wanted, and the bishops appeared to be going along with their position (William 1989, 83–95). The CEN denied that it took a partisan position on the various issues mentioned here, but the way they conducted themselves publicly leaves no doubt that they sided with the political opposition.

Notwithstanding this seemingly monolithic position of the CEN, three bishops did not share the extreme political position of the hardliners. These were Rubén López Ardón, bishop of Estelí, who supported the revolution but had to be abroad most of the time because of poor health; Salvador Shaefer, bishop of Bluefields, who had differences with Obando y Bravo over the Sandinistas but did not want a radical political change; and Msgr. Barni of Matagalpa, who seemed to be open to the popular church (Rochet Coronado 1987, 7). Despite the importance of their dioceses, these bishops were unable to counter the positions of Obando y Bravo in the Archdiocese of Managua.

Msgrs. Pablo Vega, Miguel Obando y Bravo, and Bismarck Carballo represented the hardliners within the CEN. Obando y Bravo led the group and took the most hostile position, questioning, for example, the validity of the 1984 elections and using every opportunity to deny any legitimacy to the government. It is worth recalling that shortly before the Sandinistas came to power in 1979, the hierarchy openly supported the overthrow of Somoza, but at the same time Obando y Bravo was looking for ways to avoid a Sandinista triumph. On July 17, 1979, just a few days prior to the Sandinista victory, Obando y Bravo was in Venezuela accompanying Enrique Dreyfus, president of COSEP, the main business group in Nicaragua, Esteban González Rapacciolli, a businessman, and Humberto Belli, the most representative personality of the extreme right in Nicaragua (Selser 1989, 42–44). The objective of this visit was to seek support for a moderate alternative to Somoza Debayle and thus avoid a Sandinista victory.

After the revolution triumphed, Obando y Bravo became one of its principal critics and at times behaved as if he were a member of the political opposition. He seemed to have the support of Pope John Paul II and CELAM in his struggle against the Sandinista government. Several assistants of Obando y Bravo traveled to the United States and Europe seeking support for the Contras. Pope John Paul II himself visited Nicaragua in March 1983, as part of a Central American tour, but failed to improve church-state relations. In fact, the pope promoted Obando y Bravo to the rank of cardinal in April 1985, an indication that Obando y Bravo enjoyed support for his policies in Rome. In June, Obando y Bravo celebrated mass in Miami, not in Managua, surrounded by the Contra leadership. This event put to rest any doubt about the official church relationship with the Nicaraguan opposition.

The Contras' inability to topple the Sandinistas, despite massive aid from the United States and changing political circumstances in Central America modified the pope's position vis-à-vis the Nicaraguan government. Several factors may help explain a change in the Vatican's perception of Nicaraguan political reality: (1) the Sandinistas held elections in 1984 and demonstrated a genuine interest in moving Nicaragua from participatory to Western-style democracy. This represented a shift in Sandinista political thinking and strategy despite their revolutionary rhetoric as socialist revolutionaries; (2) in spite of U.S. assistance, the Contras were unable to take any Nicaraguan territory from the Sandinistas and always had to retreat to their bases in Honduras; (3) the active opposition of the U.S. Episcopal Conference to the Contras in Nicaragua; (4) U.S. congressional opposition to the American presence in Nicaragua, and last, but not least, the agreement of the Central American presidents in Esquipulas II in 1987.

The Vatican response to the changing political circumstances in Nicaragua came in July 1986, with the new apostolic nuncio, Msgr. Paolo Giglio, who persuaded both Obando y Bravo and the Sandinistas to begin discussions. Giglio was an experienced diplomat who had mediated between the church and the state in China. Once in Nicaragua, he declared himself in favor of dialogue between the United States and Nicaragua and offered to mediate if both sides considered it necessary. However, Obando y Bravo took up the task of mediating between the Sandinistas and the Contras. In fact, President Daniel Ortega appointed Obando y Bravo to lead the National Commission of Reconciliation.

The first important agreement was reached in 1988 in Sapoá, a community near the border with Costa Rica. Observers of Latin American political developments were surprised when it was announced that the parties in conflict had reached fundamental agreements. The United States opposed these agreements, thus complicating the peace process, but it did start negotiations that eventually ended the military conflict. It was because of these negotiations that, in 1989, President Ortega announced that the elections scheduled for November 1990 would be moved up to February. The Sandinistas lost these elections and, in an unprecedented action in Latin America, handed power over to the opposition in a peaceful transition in 1990 (Berryman 1994, 23–62; Klaiber 1998, 208–12).

The CEN and Obando y Bravo were partial toward the administration of Violeta Barrios de Chamorro (1990–1996). During the Chamorro administration, the church played an active role demobilizing the Contras and reducing the Sandinista Army by criticizing the Chamorro administration for not retiring General Humberto Ortega from the armed forces. General Ortega presided over the reorganization of the Sandinista Army into a national army. However, the CEN did not hide its pleasure when Chamorro implemented policies that dismantled educational and health plans implemented by the Sandinistas that it considered to be contrary to Catholic teachings. The new Ministry of Education and Health guidelines included public morality issues, religious values, and sex education. "Unlike Sandinista policy, which favored greater preventive measures and contraception, the 1994 sex education program—as seen in a draft policy paper—stressed abstinence and morality rather than merely informing students" (Stein 1997, 240). These policies were continued under the Arnoldo Alemán administration (1996–1999) and pleased the hierarchy.

Unlike the Bolivian and Guatemalan churches, which took a critical approach to politics, in Nicaragua there was not a significant political division within the hierarchy. The CEN first welcomed the Sandinista Revolution, but shortly thereafter it moved to the political opposition. With strong encouragement from the Vatican, the hierarchy played a positive role in mediating between the government and the Contras; however, once the Sandinistas were voted out of office in 1990, it returned to its old position. Nicaragua is a case where the hierarchy leans toward the conservative side and, consequently, the modernization orientation did not gain strong support among key members of hierarchy. This may be because the popular church grew to unprecedented levels and developed an alliance with the Sandinista Revolution, and the hierarchy perceived the unity of the institution as seriously threatened. This experience contrasts sharply with Bolivia and Guatemala, where a group of bishops supported the popular church, took on a moderate approach to politics criticizing both sides on the conflict, and denounced injustice and human rights violations.

El Salvador

The emergence of powerful social and political movements in the 1970s and 1980s framed the circumstances for church reinsertion in politics in El Salvador. What follows is a brief description of these movements to understand the development of the church as a mediator of political conflicts. Despite its conservative tradition and identification with the elite of the country, the actions of a few dynamic archbishops set the stage for the reinsertion of the church into politics.

Salvadoran social movements emerged in response to military repression unleashed by governments that served the interests of a small but powerful elite, popularly known as the fourteen families. Coffee constituted the economic base of the elite during the nineteenth and twentieth centuries. The vast majority of the population was excluded from the prosperity derived from the coffee economy, and consequently the elite lived in fear of possible popular uprisings. In fact, the roots of the Salvadoran social and political conflict during the 1970s and 1980s date back to 1932, when the security forces massacred over 30,000 people, most of whom had not rebelled or planned to but who objected to the social injustices created by the coffee economy.

From 1932 to 1982, the Salvadoran military ruled the country with an iron fist, leaving little political space for any opposition. However, capitalist modernization of the economy and the creation of the Central American Common Market in the 1960s stimulated the expansion of the middle classes, which, in turn, led to the formation of new political parties and labor unions. The repressive nature of the military regime radicalized the emerging social movement (Vilas 1995, 13–40). Unlike Nicaragua, where the opposition targeted the Somoza dynasty as the cause of the nation's problems, in El Salvador there was no one visible personality on whom to place the blame because the original fourteen families had expanded the upper echelons of society, and each military ruler lasted only a relatively short time.

The 1970s saw the development of a powerful social movement both in rural and urban settings that set the stage for the emergence of powerful guerrilla organizations. The most important rural organizations were the Federación Cristiana de Campesinos Salvadoreños (Christian Federation of Salvadoran Peasants) and the Unión de Trabajadores del Campo (Union of Rural Workers). Urban workers had formed their organizations in the 1950s. For example, the Central General de Trabajadores Salvadoreños (Salvadoran General Confederation of Labor Unions) was founded in 1957. This was a militant organization with strong antigovernment positions. In response, the government created the Confederación de Sindicatos Salvadoreños (General Confederation of Salvadoran Unions). Students, historically a political force in El Salvador, strengthened the Asociación General de Estudiantes Salvadoreños (General Association of Salvadoran Students), founded by Farabundo Martí, the leader of the 1932 failed uprising. Another important urban organization that consolidated was the Asociación Nacional de Educadores Salvadoreños (National Association of Educators of El Salvador) (Ramírez López 1987, 90–93).

In the 1970s, the government created paramilitary groups to help the security forces maintain control over the sprawling popular organizations. The most notorious of these paramilitary groups were the Unión de Guerreros Blancos (White Warrior Union) and the Organización Democrática Nacional, ORDEN (National Democratic Organization). These organizations were responsible for the disappearance of numerous peasant and urban leaders who opposed government policies.

The tense political atmosphere of the late 1970s led to the creation of the Frente Farabundo Martí para la Liberación Nacional, FMLN (Farabundo Martí Front for National Liberation) by five leftist guerrilla organizations in 1980. Subsequently, the FMLN developed a political alliance with the more moderate Frente Democrático Revolucionario, FDR (Revolutionary Democratic Front). The FDR brought together many different political organizations, including labor unions and peasant and popular organizations. While the FMLN conducted the military operations against the Salvadoran armed forces, the FDR sought to develop the mechanism for a negotiated political solution to the civil war. Throughout the 1980s, the FMLN developed a strong revolutionary army that could have easily defeated the Salvadoran armed forces had the latter not had U.S. economic and military support. The United States perceived the war in El Salvador as part of Soviet-Cuban expansionism in the region and did not believe that the conflict was homegrown. In response to a major offensive launched by the FMLN, the United States increased military assistance to El Salvador from $5.9 million in 1980 to $82 million. This powerful infusion of money led to the expansion of the Salvadoran armed forces from 17,000 in 1980 to 59,000 in 1987 (Klaiber 1998, 170).

The expansion of the armed forces turned them into a powerhouse and into human rights violators. Human rights violations increased, provoking an outcry both at home and abroad. This outcry was even heard in the U.S. Congress as the result of the assassination of four American nuns in El Salvador in November 1980. Congress demanded that the president guarantee that the armed forces respect human rights. However, President Reagan found ways to increase military assistance to El Salvador despite denunciations of gross human rights violations by security forces. These are the circumstances that framed the reincorporation of the Catholic Church into the Salvadoran political process.

The Growth of the Catholic Church in El Salvador
The Salvadoran church experienced significant expansion in the latter third of the twentieth century. Like the Bolivian, Guatemalan, and Nicaraguan churches, the Salvadoran church is relatively small and most of its activities are concentrated in the Archdiocese of San Salvador. The archbishop of San Salvador is an important national figure whose opinions are taken into account seriously. The Salvadoran church suffered the consequences of the nineteenth-century liberal legislation, but it was later able to adjust to the demands of the landowning oligarchy that ruled the country. However, unlike Bolivia, Guatemala, and Nicaragua, the Salvadoran church has a more balanced proportion of diocesan to religious priests. There were 222 diocesan priests in 1970, 154 in 1980, 257 in 1990, and 394 in 1998. In contrast, there were 213 religious priests in 1970, 207 in 1980, 187 in 1990, and 208 in 1998 (see web table 2A). In 1990, the majority of the 257 diocesan priests were native born, whereas the majority of the religious were foreign born. The Salvadoran church expanded significantly from 4 dioceses in 1980 to 8 in 1990. However, there was a decrease in parishes with priests from 196 in 1970 to 172 in 1980. Similarly, there was an increase of parishes without priests from 13 in 1970 to 65 in 1980. Many parishes were staffed in the 1990s, when parishes with priests went up to 219 and then to 353 in 1998.

Similarly, seminaries increased from 7 in 1970 to nine in 1980, 12 in 1990, and 27 in 1998. The number of educational institutions expanded from 133 in 1980 to 225 in 1990, but declined to 212 in 1998. However, welfare institutions increased from 163 in 1980 to 180 in 1990 and to 1,608 in 1998. The number of religious women increased from 687 in 1970 to 836 in 1980, 1,174 in 1990, and 1,279 in 1998 (see web tables 2A, 2B, 2C, and 2D). The decrease in the number of parishes with priests and without priests reported in the 1980s was due to the war, which forced the massive relocation of people. Notwithstanding this decline, in general the Salvadoran church expanded its institutional basis, making it more modern and visible. This helped its reincorporation into the mainstream of society and politics.

The Catholic Church responded to the development of social and political conflicts by evolving slowly from the moderate position of Archbishop Luis Chávez y González (1938–1977) to the at first conservative and then progressive positions of Archbishop Oscar Romero (1977–1980), and then to the mediations led by Archbishop Arturo Rivera y Damas (1983–1994).

Archbishop Luis Chávez y González promoted important changes in the church following the Medellín conference. Chávez promoted Catholic Action, Christian unions, the reforms of Vatican II, and the spirit of Medellín. On August 6, 1966, Archbishop Chávez González published a pastoral letter entitled "The Responsibility of the Laity in the Ordering of Temporal Life." This letter put distance between the church and the military, criticized capitalism, and led to a near rupture with the socioeconomic elite.

Significantly, Archbishop Chávez González supported the work of Fr. Rutilio Grande and three other Jesuits who, in 1972, began to carry out pastoral work in the town of Aguilares, twenty miles north of San Salvador. Aware that the proportion of priests to parishioners was 1 to 10,000 during the 1970s (this proportion worsened during the 1980s, climbing to 1 to 20,000 due to the assassination of a dozen priests and expulsion or exile of another sixty), the archbishop worked hard to develop centers to prepare catechists and Delegates of the Word. The archdiocese established seven of these centers between 1970 and 1976 and trained approximately 15,000 lay leaders who had various responsibilities, including prebaptismal instruction, catechism, youth work, music groups, and CEBs (Montgomery 1983, 69–75). The work of these agents was exclusively pastoral, but the content of their message, drawn from the Bible, was profoundly radicalizing in political and religious terms. Members of the CEBs discussed biblical passages and sought ways to relate them to their lives. It was not hard for them to make the connection between their daily lives, filled with multiple hurdles, and biblical passages dealing with political and social oppression such as those narrated in the Book of Exodus.

Jesuit priests also worked at the Universidad Centroamericana José Simeón Cañas (UCA), a Catholic university, where they educated the children of the elite on the social and economic reality of the country. The socioeconomic elite provided financial support to found the university in 1966 but soon realized that their children were not receiving the type of education they wanted, and thus funds began to dry up. The UCA became a critical center in Salvadoran political life, and neither the government nor the elite was satisfied with its political direction.[4]

The Conferencia Episcopal de El Salvador, CEDES (Episcopal Conference of El Salvador) was deeply divided over the direction Archbishop Chávez González (1938–1977) gave to the church in the 1970s. This division came out in the open in 1970, when the CEDES agreed to hold a "pastoral week." The more conservative bishops thought the conclusions of the pastoral week were too extreme and that the denunciations of their connivance with the local oligarchy were not fair. They also thought that CEBs were more political than religious and needed to cut their affiliation with secular movements. Bishop Oscar Arnulfo Romero was among those who opposed the CEBs and the work done by Jesuits priests at the UCA. In fact, he was selected for the post of archbishop of Salvador because of his conservative political views. Bishop Arturo Rivera y Damas, a moderate and close ally of Archbishop Chávez González, was bypassed when the Vatican chose Romero to lead the Salvadoran church.

The political situation of El Salvador transformed Romero into a progressive archbishop. This began with his concern for the poor wages that coffee planters paid their workers, then deepened following the assassination of Fr. Rutilio Grande. With the support of all the priests of his archdiocese, Romero decided to suspend all masses throughout the Archdiocese of San Salvador, except for the one he would celebrate at the cathedral. He wanted people to reflect on the meaning of the death of Fr. Rutilio Grande. However, the nuncio and the conservative bishops of the CEDES opposed him. Rivera y Damas was the only one who supported Romero.

Nonetheless, the mass went on. Romero's radical denunciations of human rights violations by Salvadoran paramilitary forces cost him dearly in Rome. Conservative Salvadoran bishops sent continuous reports to the Vatican that portrayed Romero in a negative light. Romero traveled to Rome to defend himself on several occasions. He always had the support of Rivera y Damas, who traveled with him to Rome. The ultraright of the Salvadoran political establishment could not tolerate Romero's continuous denunciations, particularly his call to Salvadoran soldiers to stop the killing. Romero was assassinated while celebrating a mass on March 24, 1980 (Brockman 1999, 80–133). The United Nations Truth Commission reported years later that Roberto D'Aubuison, head of ORDEN, was the intellectual author of the murder.[5]

Church Mediation in Politics

Romero's assassination demonstrated that political polarization had reached unprecedented levels in Salvadoran history. Backed by the United States, the Salvadoran armed forces saw no other course than violence as a way to resolve the political impasse. The FMLN considered negotiation, but fought with determination to overthrow the Salvadoran government and replace it with a democratic revolutionary one. This was the context in which Msgr. Arturo Rivera y Damas was appointed apostolic administrator to succeed Romero in the Archdiocese of San Salvador (1980–1983) and then archbishop of the Archdiocese of San Salvador (1983–1994). Romero's supporters wanted Rivera y Damas to follow in Romero's footsteps, whereas conservative bishops wanted him to take the lead of CEDES. Rivera y Damas walked a tightrope, treating the FMLN and the Salvadoran government evenhandedly, but he did not always succeed in the tense political atmosphere of the time.

Rivera y Damas was convinced that the Salvadoran conflict could be resolved peacefully. He used his close relationship with Christian Democrats and particularly with President Napoleón Duarte (1984–1989), a leader of the party and close friend of his, to promote his peace agenda. Similarly, within the FMLN/FDR political alliance there were key leaders, such as Rubén Zamora and Guillermo Ungo, who had been affiliated with the Christian Democratic Party. Thanks to these connections, Rivera y Damas was able to transmit messages to both sides of the conflict and eventually organize important meetings to negotiate a solution to the civil war.

There are two important stages in Rivera y Damas's involvement in the process of mediation. These two stages include the promotion of mediations prior to the Esquipulas II Agreements of 1987 and the mediation that took place after it.

During the first stage (1983–1987), Rivera y Damas arranged a meeting between President Duarte and representatives of the FMLN and the FDR, which took place at La Palma on October 15, 1984. Though no substantial agreement was reached there, it was the first time the parties in conflict had met. The second meeting occurred on November 29 at Ayagualo, but it was less auspicious because the following day the FMLN launched an offensive that killed Colonel Domingo Monterrosa, commander of the eastern region. The third important mediation involved the kidnapping of President Duarte's daughter, Inéz Guadalupe Duarte, and her friend, Ana Cecilia Villeda. This incident occurred on September 10, 1985. Rivera y Damas went to the town of Guazapa, north of San Salvador, to negotiate with the FMLN for the girls' release. The FMLN wanted to exchange war prisoners. Unlike previous mediations, the archbishop acted both as mediator and representative of the president. After lengthy negotiations, the FMLN released the president's daughter and the government freed 22 prisoners. Later, the government and FMLN exchanged 25 mayors for 101 wounded guerrillas, who received safe conduct to leave the country. In this instance, the archbishop traveled to rebel-controlled territory, where he saw the conditions under which people lived and showed that he was on both sides of the conflict (Klaiber 1998, 178–82; Sobrino 1986, 84–85).

The second stage of the church mediation began with the Esquipulas II agreement of 1987. This agreement facilitated church mediation until the United Nations took over the peace process in 1990. President Duarte explained the agreement to the bishops and immediately proposed a high-level meeting, which took place at the papal nunciature in San Salvador on October 4 and 5, 1987. The nunciature meeting was a watershed compared to La Palma and Ayagualo because this time both parties to the conflict were apparently ready to make key concessions.

In the communiqué published after the meeting, the government and the FMLN agreed to implement the Esquipulas II agreement, in accordance with which each government in the region with internal conflicts would establish dialogue with the rebels, declare a cease-fire, and create a commission of reconciliation. According to the communiqué, two commissions would be created: one to examine the possibilities of the cease-fire and the second one to study Esquipulas II. The parties in conflict named Archbishop Rivera y Damas to head the two commissions, an action that shows that both parties held him in high regard.

Both the government and the FMLN acknowledged the meeting at the papal nunciature as a landmark in the process of resolving the Salvadoran conflict (Presidencia de la República de El Salvador, FDR, and FMLN 1987, 746–47). However, this landmark was clouded by the assassination of Herbert Anaya Sanabria on October 26. Anaya Sanabria was the coordinator of the nongovernmental Human Rights Commission and a critic of the government. Following the Anaya Sanabria assassination, the FMLN withdrew from the negotiation process and did not attend a meeting in Mexico that had been scheduled to discuss the peace process.

Despite this setback in 1988, Rivera y Damas moved on to promote a National Debate for Peace, hoping to achieve a wider acceptance to end the civil war. In response to this call for dialogue and peace, the church sponsored a conference with the participation of all the political forces, except the ultraright represented by the Alianza Renovadora Nacional, ARENA (National Renovating Alliance). According to a survey prepared by the church, 82 percent of the participants condemned the war as a solution to the country's problems. In addition, 82 percent held that "elections by themselves would not guarantee democracy." There was total unanimity on the proposition that "dialogue constitutes the most rational, just, and Christian method for a solution to the conflict"(*Estudios Centroamericanos* 1988, 713–29; Klaiber 1998, 184–85). The National Debate for Peace generated credibility for the church among the popular sectors and the FMLN, and Rivera y Damas was accepted as the key promoter of peace and reconciliation.

The Christian Democrats lost the 1989 election to Alfredo Cristiani of ARENA, a party founded by Roberto D'Aubuisson, also a leader of ORDEN.

ARENA was obviously anticommunist, anti-Social Democrat, anti-North American, and represented the most extreme factions of the Salvadoran political spectrum. Nonetheless, Cristiani, the son of one of the important coffee families and a graduate of Georgetown University, announced his intention to have a dialogue with the FMLN. He represented the moderate faction of the ultraright. The rise of Cristiani to the presidency distanced Rivera y Damas from the negotiations. He no longer had contacts in the president's office as he had had with President Duarte, a Christian Democrat. Cristiani, on the other hand, preferred to deal with Bishop Romeo Tovar, the conservative president of the Episcopal Conference. As Cristiani came into office, the United Nations took over the negotiation process and the church progressively withdrew from the technical aspects of the peace settlement that ended the war in 1992 (Cañas 1989, 669–81; Ellacuría 1989, 683–93; Harto de Vera 1993, 29–38; Klaiber 1998, 186–87).

Rivera y Damas laid the foundation for dialogue and reconciliation. He made strong moves to turn the church into a special political actor that could reconcile antagonistic forces. In doing this, however, Rivera y Damas, as head of the church, also legitimized the new political order that emerged from the civil war. Perhaps unwillingly, the church became a pillar of the new conservative political order (Rivera y Damas 1987, 859–63).

Rivera y Damas passed away in 1994 and was soon replaced by Archbishop Fernando Sáenz Lacalle, whose conservative positions brought the church back to the old warm relationship with both the government and the socioeconomic elite. This may be explained, in part, because the political situation had changed and there were no bishops willing and able to continue the policies initiated by Rivera y Damas. In this sense, the Salvadoran case parallels that of Nicaragua, where the hierarchy seems to feel at ease with both conservative governments and the elite. Neither of these hierarchies had a significant number of progressive bishops who could support the popular church.

The second papal visit to El Salvador in 1996 demonstrated how far the church was willing to let the government and the elite organize the event. In the midst of multiple cuts to social spending in health care and education ordered by the International Monetary Fund, the government was willing not only to repair the cathedral for the visit, but to cover a great deal of other expenses to make the papal visit a success. The government and the local elite presented the papal visit as a sign of reconciliation between church and state (Cardenal 1996, 29–45). It was a symbolic gesture indicating that the church had to return to the previous status quo.

Conclusions

What is most revealing about religion and politics in Latin America is that the radical pronouncements of Medellín and Puebla were turned around with the rightward shift in the universal church. The actions of the episcopal conferences of Bolivia and Central America were caught in between. Except for a small group of active bishops in Bolivia and Guatemala who supported the modernizing church orientations, these conferences were conservative and pleased with the new direction given to the church by John Paul II.

All the churches discussed in this chapter participated in political mediations because of social and political pressures. Nonetheless, this participation provided the occasion for the church to reaccommodate the new political circumstances. The revolutions that rocked Bolivia and Central America prepared the conditions for the church to reincorporate itself into the new political scenario. The hierarchies realized that they could no longer continue their business-as-usual policies vis-à-vis national politics. Naturally, as churchmen sought to react to national political issues they experienced political divisions, but they closed ranks in responding to the emergence of a popular church that joined national liberation movements to fight injustice and human rights violations. Both conservatives and moderates within the church preferred conciliation and political mediation to confrontation.

All church leaders claim that their mediation is nonpartisan, but their promotion of liberal democracy as the most viable political system and their overlapping interests with the powers that be turn them into defenders of the status quo rather than true nonpartisan actors. Furthermore, the connections of bishops with political and economic elites and the privileges enjoyed by the church in Latin American societies make it nearly impossible for it to be truly nonpartisan. However, as an institution rooted in history, society, and culture, the church enjoys a type of legitimacy and credibility that no other political actors can claim. Unlike politicians, bishops do not have to run for office every four years, nor do they have to be held accountable for failed economic policies. This is what makes the church a special political actor.

Despite these general similarities, there are clear-cut differences among the churches studied in this chapter. Although deeply divided over the issue of the popular church, important sectors within the Bolivian and Guatemalan hierarchies became critical voices in society and supported clergymen associated with the CEBs. Those bishops were associated with the modernizing church orientation and played key roles mediating political conflicts while remaining critical of the status quo. Despite Rivera y Damas's successful mediation to reach a negotiated settlement to the civil war in El

Salvador, his moderate policies were discontinued following his death in 1994. His successor, Archbishop Fernando Saenz Lacalle, brought the church back to the old comfortable relationship with the state and the socioeconomic elite. In Nicaragua, Archbishop Obando y Bravo, who became a foe of the Sandinistas and an open supporter of the opposition, continued his homey relationship with the post-Sandinista regime. The paths of the Nicaraguan and Salvadoran churches are deeply conservative, whereas those of Bolivia and Guatemala seem more critical of the status quo. In all cases, however, the church played an important role mediating political conflicts, reincorporated itself into the political scenario, and contributed to the transition to democracy through political mediation.

Notes

1. The role of the Catholic Church in political mediation in Latin America has not received much attention in the transition literature (Booth and Seligson 1989; Diamond, Linz, and Lipset 1989; Gunther et al. 1995; Linz 1990; Mainwaring et al. 1992; Malloy and Gamara 1988; O'Donnell 1994, 1996; Oxhorn and Ducatenzeiler 1998; Przeworski 1991; Schmitter 1994; Vilas 1993). Church scholars, on the other hand, have produced a substantial amount of literature on church and politics, but few have focused their research on the issue of mediation (Blancarte 1992; Bruneau 1974, 1982; Camp 1997; Keogh 1990; Levine 1981, 1996; Mainwaring 1986; Meyer 1999; Smith 1982; Stewart-Gambino 1992). Although not exclusively dedicated to the issue of mediation, the works of Jeffrey Klaiber (1998), Michael Fleet and Brian Smith (1997), Jean Meyer (2000), Bruce Calder (2001), and Edward Brett (2002) make seminal contributions to the study of church mediation. This chapter attempts to build on their work by looking at the role played by a small group of bishops in the process of political mediation in Bolivia and Central America.

2. A diocesan priest belongs to a diocese permanently, whereas religious priests belong to a religious order. Religious priests may serve under contract to a diocese and may be transferred to other countries or dioceses according to the superiors of their religious order. In Latin America, religious priests are mostly foreign born, whereas diocesan priests tend to be native born.

3. This populist approach was known in Nicaragua as the policy of the three Ps. Palos (stick) for the undecided, Plata (silver) for his friends, and Plomo (lead) for his enemies. From the early days of his regime, Somoza García sought to gain support for his regime and used government resources to reassure a minimum of legitimacy in the eyes of the population.

4. Throughout the 1970s and 1980s, UCA played a key role promoting peace and negotiation in the midst of a civil war and as such suffered the consequences. On November 16, 1989, while FMLN forces seized portions of San Salvador, a group of soldiers from the Atlacatl Battalion entered UCA and killed six Jesuit priests and their

cook. The victims included Fr. Ignacio Ellacuría (rector), Ignacio Martín-Baró (vice-rector), Segundo Montes, Amando López, and Ramón Moreno, all of whom were professors at the university.

5. On September 3, 2004, a civil court in Fresno, California, recognized Alvaro Rafael Saravia, former captain in the Salvadoran armed forces, as the man who killed Romero. Saravia, trained in Taiwan, was Roberto D'Aubuisson's right-hand man and founder of a death squadron in El Salvador. A California judge sentenced him in absentia to pay $10 million to Romero's relatives. The main witness in the case was Robert White, former U.S. Ambassador to El Salvador. Ambassador White said that D'Aubuisson planned the murder and Saravia carried it out. According to White, financing for the assassination came from the so-called Grupo de Miami (Miami Group), also known as the "Group of the Six." This group had channeled millions of dollars to D'Aubuisson to destabilize the moderate government that took power in October 15, 1979 (Fazio 2004).

CHAPTER THREE

Finding a New Role in Society

The Catholic Church allied with state and social economic elites, a culture of political subordination, and powerful revolutionary upheavals are common characteristics in the history of the Dominican Republic, Bolivia, and Central America. The reaction of the Dominican church to the social changes brought about by the fall of Trujillo and the subsequent revolution of 1965 parallels that of its counterparts in Bolivia, Guatemala, Nicaragua, and El Salvador. What seems unique about the Dominican Republic is the direct U.S. military intervention of 1965, the near-defeat of revolutionary forces, and the installation of Joaquín Balaguer in power (1966–1978).

The United States supported repressive regimes and sponsored counter-revolutionary guerrillas in Central America, but never sent its own forces to crush a revolution. But it did in the Dominican Republic. Aided by U.S. intervention, Balaguer was able to restore the authoritarian features of the state and create the framework to reincorporate the church into mainstream life and politics. In this context, I posit that rather than simply playing a nonpartisan role, church mediation became a factor of cohesion that enabled Balaguer and subsequent regimes to retain the basic authoritarian design of the Dominican state. In contrast, the popular church, despite its small size, was able to show an alternative ecclesiastical orientation, a new style of relating the church to the people.

The chapter is divided into two major sections. The first section (covering 1961–1966) focuses on the events that let up to the revolution of 1965, the U.S. military intervention and the defeat of revolutionary forces, the mediation of the papal nuncio, and the emergence of the popular church. The second portion (covering 1966–1978) examines the regime of Joaquín Balaguer (1966–1978), the role of the church hierarchy as mediator of political conflicts, and the role of the popular church as part of a movement that proposed an alternative orientation of church politics.[1]

The Dominican Church and Post-Trujillo Society, 1961–1966

Trujillo truncated the development of the socioeconomic elite and the subordinated social groups. The elite did not have much experience in the political domain; consequently, they were not prepared for a democratic regime and could only think of authoritarian methods to handle political dissent. This section examines the political instability that followed the demise of Trujillo and how the church, a segment of the elite, tried to reinsert itself into post-Trujillo society.

The political history of the Dominican church parallels those of Bolivia and Central America because they, too, had lived politically subordinate to the wishes of dictatorial regimes. When these regimes disappeared, ecclesiastical authorities did not understand the "signs of the times." As noted in chapter 1, the Dominican church hierarchy challenged Trujillo and contributed to his downfall, but it was too afraid of communism and suspicious of those who either tolerated or collaborated with communists.

The emergence of new political parties, labor unions, and student movements of different ideological persuasions challenged the Dominican church hierarchy. It regarded these new political actors as threats to the established order. For example, the Dominican Revolutionary Party (PRD), a liberal democratic party founded in Havana in 1939, introduced a modern discourse that called for democracy, whereas various small leftist political parties proposed a radical socialist revolution. These leftist parties included, among others, the Movimiento Revolucionario 14 de Junio (June 14 Revolutionary Movement), the Movimiento Popular Dominicano, MPD (Dominican Popular Movement), and the Partido Socialista Popular (Socialist Popular Party).

A group of politically active laymen and women founded the Partido Revolucionario Social Cristiano, PRSC (Revolutionary Social Christian Party), in 1961. This party was created with support from the Christian Democrats of Venezuela as a moderate alternative to the left-wing political parties. The church hierarchy never gave it public support, but Jesuit priests oriented many of the organizations of the party. These organizations included workers, peasants, and high school and university students. The Jesuit presence indicated that the hierarchy tolerated their participation (Wipfler 1980, 163–68). The ideology of the PRSC was generally based on the social doctrine of the church and opposed communism. In practice, though, the church tacitly supported the Union Cívica Nacional, UCN (National Civic Union), a political party closely associated with the socioeconomic elite that sought to control the unstable political situation that developed following the elimination of Trujillo. The church reserved its main criticisms for Juan Bosch of the PRD, who posed the main challenge to the UCN. Thus, the Dominican clergy followed the Latin American pattern of church-state relationship where hierarchies supported the status quo and opposed those who challenged it.

The Church and the Bosch Government

The significant presence of Jesuits who had fled the Cuban Revolution and the anti-Cuban propaganda and personal histories of some of these religious clergy strengthened the anticommunist sentiment in the Dominican church (Moya Pons 1973, 17). Various members of the clergy actively participated in local politics and even accused Juan Bosch, the leader and presidential candidate of the PRD, of being a communist. In the midst of a tense political situation, Bosch threatened to pull out of the race unless the church withdrew its accusation. Fr. Lautico García had published a newspaper article reiterating the church's allegations, and he soon represented those who claimed that Bosch was a communist. Bosch challenged Fr. García to a televised debate to discuss Fr. García's allegations. The debate was held on December 17, three days before the elections of 1962. Fr. García was unable to prove that Bosch was a communist, which cleared Bosch's name (Bosch 1998, 33–37; De la Cruz 1998, 15–42).

The claim that Bosch was a communist placed the church on the side of the UCN, a right-wing political party that represented the interests of the oligarchy. No matter what the church hierarchy said to the contrary, it was obvious that Fr. García took the place of Viriato A. Fiallo, the UNC candidate, in the debate; in the eyes of the voting population, he was the church's candidate. Interestingly, Bosch never threatened to take away any of the privileges that the church enjoyed through the concordat signed by Trujillo in 1954. In fact, he sought a dialogue with the bishops to prove that he was not a communist. However, in the context of the Cuban Revolution and the cold war, it was apparently impossible for the hierarchy to distinguish a democrat from a communist (Guerrero 1993, 161–80; Wiarda 1965, 239–54).

Bosch won the 1962 presidential elections by a landslide, despite the opposition of the Catholic oligarchy and the military (Bosch and Fiallo received

58.7 percent and 30.1 percent of the votes, respectively; the PRSC received 5.2 percent; and the remaining 6 percent went to smaller political parties) (Gleijeses 1978, 86). This victory did not stop the church's political opposition to Bosch, which intensified after his inauguration. The church promoted a series of demonstrations of Christian reaffirmation that had political overtones. Bosch viewed these demonstrations as clear evidence that church authorities were involved in a larger campaign of causing political instability. Bosch even expelled Fr. Rafael Marcial Silva as chaplain of the Dominican Air Force because of his involvement in promoting the so-called Christian reaffirmation campaign within the air force. According to Bosch, Fr. Marcial had asked many air force officers to watch Bosch carefully because he was a communist (Bosch 1964, 127).

The anticommunist hysteria reached all levels with which the church had contact among the population, including Catholic schools, Catholic welfare institutions, Sunday masses, confessions, and Catholic Radio Santa Maria, which aimed its programs at the countryside. There is no doubt that this campaign helped antigovernment forces, which on September 25, 1963, overthrew Bosch and replaced him with an illegal triumvirate government led by Donald Reid Cabral. In a book published a year after the coup, Bosch explained that the Catholic hierarchy's political opposition to his regime was partially due to the fact that it

> behaved like the members of the Dominican upper middle class, perhaps without realizing it. The Catholic hierarchy of the country lived in the environment of the upper middle class and elite people; they did not have any contact with the popular masses and did not understand them. They were ignorant of their existence as a social group with aspirations; they only knew that social group as the poor to whom one gives charity once in a while and as people whose souls they must pursue for the sake of the faith. This elevated Catholic hierarchy was not above the social milieu in which it carried on its business. (Bosch 1964, 125)

According to Bosch, the social background of the Catholic hierarchy prevented it from accepting a constitution that was framed by a constitutional assembly composed of congressional members, including workers, students, housewives, and men whose surnames were not among the elite. The hierarchy could not accept a constitution that did not mention the concordat, that recognized the rights of workers to share in the profits of the companies in which they worked, that put limits on the extension of landownership in agriculture, and that respected public liberties. In a document signed by all the bishops, the hierarchy said that the Constitution of 1963 did not recognize "the rights of God and the Church" and that "no Catholic could be a communist . . . no true Dominican can be a communist. If a Dominican chooses to be a communist, then he ceases to be a Dominican" (Conferencia del Episcopado Dominicano, 1990, 86–111).

This document put the hierarchy on a collision course with Bosch's government. It did not recognize the constitution and refused to participate in the ceremony held to proclaim it the law of the land. The conflict had a lasting effect on Dominican politics because the hierarchy would always treat Bosch with suspicion. As Bosch noted, the hierarchy felt more comfortable with conservative elite politicians and distrusted popular leaders.

The identification of the Dominican nationality with Catholicism demonstrates that the hierarchy still embraced a traditional pre-Vatican II vision of church-state relations. It did not recognize the separation of the church and the state and rejected political and religious plurality. The hierarchy was far behind the times and would have serious difficulties adjusting to the changes proposed in Vatican II. This was a church that had completely identified with a dictator who viewed the world through the narrow lens of primitive anticommunism. However, as noted in chapter 2, this parallels developments in Bolivia and Central America, where the church had a history of a symbiotic relationship with the state.

The Dominican Revolution and U.S. Military Intervention

What distinguishes the Dominican revolution from the Bolivian and Central American revolutions is the unprecedented military response of the United States. The Dominican revolution began as a traditional military coup d'état that overthrew the illegal triumvirate government led by Donald Reid Cabral in April 24, 1965. A group of young military officers and their civilian allies distributed weapons from bases near Santo Domingo to their supporters. Civilians organized themselves into commandos, or politico-military units, that defended the barrios of Santo Domingo. The young officers who led the uprising wanted to restore Bosch and the Constitution of 1963 to power. They became known as the Constitutionalists and the conservative military faction who opposed them were called Loyalists.

The military confrontation between Constitutionalists and Loyalists led to open civil war. The young officers, led by Colonel Francisco Caamaño, defeated the Loyalists in a three-day battle. Colonel Elías Wessin y Wessin, head of the Centro de Enseñanzas de las Fuerzas Armadas (Armed Forces Training Center) and a member of the conservative movement for Christian reaffirmation, led the Loyalist forces. Aware that the Loyalists were defeated, Caamaño sought the mediation of U.S. ambassador William Tapley Bennett, but he refused, claiming that it was time for Caamaño to surrender rather than negotiate. Caamaño went back to the battlefront, captured the entire city of Santo Domingo, and forced the Loyalists to retreat to the San Isidro Air Base outside the city. What Caamaño did not know is that the United States was already preparing a military occupation of the entire country.

The United States invaded on April 28, 1965, and soon deployed over 23,000 marines, whose objective was to suppress an upheaval meant to restore a democratically elected government. The United States claimed that it intervened to "save the lives of Americans" who lived in Santo Domingo and to prevent a communist takeover. American policy makers thought that the Dominican Republic was "a carbon copy" of Cuba, where a nationalist revolution had turned socialist. However, there was no resemblance between Cuba and the Dominican Republic. Fidel Castro had led a guerrilla war against Fulgencio Batista, a Cuban dictator, whereas Caamaño was leading an urban insurrection to restore the rule of law and democracy. This sharp contrast apparently did not matter in the eyes of U.S. cold war policy makers, who were concerned about "losing" another Caribbean island to communism or to unpredictable nationalist leaders. It appears that the difference did not matter much anyway.

The U.S. military intervention changed the political scenario immediately. Caamaño's forces were soon cornered in the old section of Santo Domingo, where the business district was located. Caamaño prepared to resist the U.S. occupation and threatened to blow up the city's business district if the U.S. Marines continued to attack his forces. In the meantime, the PRD called the members of Congress who were elected in 1962 for a special assembly. This assembly elected Caamaño constitutional president in lieu of Juan Bosch, who was still in Puerto Rico and was unable to travel to the Dominican Republic. Caamaño led the negotiations with the occupying forces, which were operating under the banner of the Organización de Estados Americanos, OAS (Organization of American States). The United States had violated the charter of the OAS, which prohibited intervention in the internal affairs of the member states. However, the OAS was under the political hegemony of the United States, so it was not difficult to arrange for two-thirds of the member states to approve the organization of a military force better known as Fuerzas Interamericana de Paz, IPF (Inter-American Peace Force).

Various conservative Latin American governments sent small military and police units to join the U.S. forces in Santo Domingo and make the operation look like it was a broad international effort to bring peace to a war-torn nation. In actuality, a U.S. commander led the IPF and a U.S. presidential envoy conducted the negotiation. The Constitutionalists had to negotiate under continuous military threats. In fact, when negotiations stalled, the U.S. Marines attacked the positions of the Constitutionalists, forcing them to accept U.S. terms in the negotiations.

There is no need to repeat here what others scholars have written about in detail (Chester 2001; Draper 1968; Gleijeses 1978; Lowenthal 1972; Slater 1970). In short, the Constitutionalists were forced to accept U.S. terms in the negotiations, which included disarming Caamaño's forces, creating a provisional government led by a man acceptable to the United States, and holding presidential elections within nine months. Among other things, the Constitutionalists proposed reintegrating their combatants into the Dominican armed forces, providing a general amnesty for those who participated in the war, arranging the immediate departure of the IPF, and keeping their weapons and controlling the old section of Santo Domingo.

In the end, a general amnesty was declared, but it only benefited right-wing political prisoners; the Constitutionalists did not have lawyers who could support them to build their case in a court of law. Caamaño was sent to England as military attaché and other leaders and combatants were sent into exile. Subsequently, hundreds of combatants who stayed in the country were thrown into jail or assassinated in broad daylight in the streets of Santo Domingo in what appeared to be a coordinated campaign by security forces. The defeat would have decisive political repercussions for both nationalist and leftist political tendencies in the years to come. As noted below, it facilitated the restoration of the authoritarian state under Joaquín Balaguer (1966–1978) and the reincorporation of the Catholic Church into the mainstream of society. This reinsertion into the postrevolutionary order helped the political regime acquire a degree of cohesion.

The Church and the Revolution

The church's anticommunist ideology and its elitist background hindered it from understanding Dominican political realities. Church authorities acted as if they had nothing to do with the process that led to the coup against Bosch and proceeded to organize the Sixth Mariological Congress and the Eleventh Marian Congress scheduled for March 17–22 and March 22–25, 1965, respectively. The Vatican announced on July 6, 1964, that it had chosen the Dominican Republic to hold these important congresses, and the local church hierarchy wanted to make sure that they were successful. So, shortly after the news from the Vatican, the local church announced that it would continue the construction of the huge Basilica of the Virgin of Altagracia, which had been started by Trujillo in the town of Higuey after he signed the concordat with the Vatican.

The triumvirate government saw this as an opportunity to improve its international image and offered economic support both to the two congresses and to the construction of the basilica. The campaign leading up to the congresses included many articles in newspapers describing a drive at the national and international levels to raise funds for the construction of the basilica. The articles explained that Pope Paul VI chose the country for this occasion because it was where the first mass was celebrated in the New World, where the first cathedral was built, and where the people were devoted to the Mother of Jesus.

Ignoring the political tensions that existed in the country resulting from the illegality of the government, continuous national strikes, and nationwide protests against rampant government corruption, the church held the two congresses and organized a lavish dinner in the National Palace to honor the distinguished guests who attended. This dinner was televised to a country where the vast majority of the population was in abject poverty. The church also accepted the government's offer to use the building of the National Congress to hold its meetings (Wipfler 1980, 206–13). None of the members of the hierarchy acknowledged that the Dominican Republic was in the midst of a political crisis and that appearing too close to an illegal government distanced the church from the people it sought to serve and represent.

A small group of Catholic youth criticized the church in an event organized at the Colegio Don Bosco in Santo Domingo in the last day of the Marian Congress. One of the speakers, Miguel Angel Heredia Bonetti, said: "We want less commitment with governments and corrupt political systems and closer relations with the exploited masses that seek redemption" (Sáez 1990, 66). Another speaker, Juan Bolivar Díaz Santana, recognized that the church was perhaps responsible for the alienation of students, and that it offered no solution, other than accusing them of being communist.

The Dominican bishops did not attend the meeting at Colegio Don Bosco, but the papal nuncio Emanuelle Clarizio (1962–1967); Raúl Cardinal Silva Henríquez, archbishop of Santiago de Chile; Tomás Alberto Clavel Méndez, archbishop of Panama; and Giuseeppe Cardinal Ferreto, bishop of Sabina, did attend. Both Clarizio and Silva Henríquez expressed their disapproval of the event and complained that the speakers took advantage of the presence of foreigners to make denunciations rather than helping the poor. Archbishop Clavel Méndez of Panama approved the initiative taken by the youth, which suggests that there was not complete agreement among the hierarchy (Sáez 1990, 66).

The dissenting voices of the Catholic youth were yet another indication that Dominican society was in crisis and that the church was not paying enough attention to a rapidly changing political scenario. Similar voices had already been heard in the youth branch of the PRSC, which led to a split in the party. Although the radical wing of the PRSC was not really successful in getting a strong following in the peasantry or the urban poor, it did gain some popularity with the Catholic youth. As a matter of fact, a group of Catholic community leaders supported the revolutionary commandos of the Constitutionalists during the civil war of 1965. This group would later join the popular church movement within the church, which pushed for a more open and democratic society.

If the traditional conservative hierarchy was not prepared to listen to the Catholic youth, it was even less prepared to respond to the civil war that followed the coup against the triumvirate government of Reid Cabral. At first, the hierarchy ordered priests to open the church's temples and facilities to U.S. soldiers, running from the heavy rains of April and the attacks of Dominican Constitutionalists. Fr. James A. Clark, a North American, recalls:

> Without judging whether the intervention was right or wrong, the church assisted the American troops. She recognized them as the one source of protection for the society and the people. . . . The Church sought to calm the people when the soldiers began arriving during the initial terror-filled days at the end of April. When the people realized the Church accepted and had decided to work with the soldiers, they did the same.
>
> With thousands of American troops moving in, the problems of language interpretation were massive. The Church provided many of the necessary interpreters through religious who spoke both languages. . . . Further, the Church blessed the inauguration of the OAS Peace Force and provided services for the soldiers. I remember hearing confessions in fields and saying Mass on Jeep hoods as a member of a corps of priests organized by the Church to assist military chaplains with the spiritual needs of the boys. (Clark 1967, 106)

The revolution turned critical after the arrival of U.S. troops because the Constitutionalists were forced to use their strategic position in the old section of Santo Domingo to repel the aggression of the U.S.–OAS-backed Loyalists. Apparently fearing a communist takeover, Msgr. Octavio Beras Rojas, archbishop of Santo Domingo, asked most of his priests to leave the war zone soon after the U.S. intervened. He left for Puerto Rico and did not return to Santo Domingo until early August when he visited the parish of San Miguel inside the war zone. It is possible that his removal from the post of archbishop in December of 1965 was related to this action. In any case, the hierarchy was not available to issue a continuous call for peace, nor could they mediate between the parties in conflict (Sáez 1990, 74–75).

Clarizio, the Revolution, and Political Mediation

The political mediation of Nuncio Emanuelle Clarizio shows how a church diplomat reacted to the Dominican revolution when the local hierarchy was not available to respond to a crisis. This mediation was the first step in preparing the church to accommodate the post-Trujillo society. Clarizio had arrived in the country on February 27, 1962, almost two years after the departure of Lino Zanini, his predecessor. He followed the traditional conservative orientation that permeated the Dominican church and joined forces with the bishops who opposed the government of Juan Bosch. In fact, he exerted political pressure on Bosch regarding the recognition of the concordat by the constitution. Bosch reminded Clarizio that he knew how a democracy worked and, consequently, the president should not tell Congress what to do. The revolution caught Clarizio out of the country, but he hurriedly returned on April 28, 1965, just as U.S. forces were disembarking in the country. On his arrival, the OAS, which was already involved in the crisis, asked him to make arrangements for a cease-fire. Clarizio met with the Constitutionalist leadership, led by Colonel Francisco Caamaño, in the old section of Santo Domingo and later on traveled to the San Isidro Air Base, outside Santo Domingo, to talk with the Loyalists.

The terms of the cease-fire were simple: protection for the individuals involved in the negotiations and the acceptance of the OAS as arbitrator. The secretary general of the OAS, José A. Mora, arrived in Santo Domingo in May 1, 1965. The cease-fire secured under OAS supervision was fragile. Dressed in his white cassock at all times, Clarizio drove his car around the city with the Vatican's flag in front. He traveled between the Constitutionalist zone in the southern section of the city and the Loyalists in the northern sector to talk to both factions. He served as a mediator during the four months of the conflict.

Clarizio's role, however, was not limited to mediating. He also turned the nunciature into an information center for the families of the missing. This center later opened two other branches: one in the Constitutionalist zone, where Jesuit priests coordinated a food distribution outlet, and another in the northern section, controlled by U.S. troops. In the absence of the Dominican bishops, who had left the city following the U.S. military occupation, Clarizio distributed six papal messages to the press calling for peace and reconciliation. The pope sent four of these messages during the first weeks of the conflict. The local church hierarchy kept silent until May 22, 1965, when the bishops issued their first call for peace and reconciliation. It appears that Clarizio and the OAS had exerted some pressure on the bishops to speak. "We have been asked to speak and to look for a satisfactory solution to the national tragedy. We cannot avoid our responsibility" (Conferencia del Episcopado Dominicano 1990, 129). Then they repeated the basic proposition of the United States and the OAS, which called for the formation of a provisional government.

Clarizio's mediation did not go unchallenged. Right-wing political groups accused him of being a communist and even painted a sign on the outside wall of the nunciature calling it a "communist embassy." These groups had links with the Dominican military, which thought Clarizio's mediation saved the Constitutionalists from a complete defeat shortly after the United States arrived. Vatican Radio announced that right-wing groups were offering $10,000 for Clarizio's head, which demonstrates that threats on his life were serious. Although the Constitutionalists respected Clarizio's efforts, they could not avoid associating him with the right-wing forces that were seeking to disarm them, although through diplomatic means rather than military force. Except for Msgr. Hugo Polanco Brito, all the bishops were opposed to the Constitutionalists and supported the U.S.-backed Loyalists. Nonetheless, Clarizio had the support of the Vatican, and he reassured the Constitutionalists that, at least publicly, the bishops would distance themselves from the Loyalists (De Broucker 1966, 12–18; Leveque 1972, 5).

The revolution and the mediation process transformed Clarizio from a traditional conservative clergyman to someone who appeared to identify with the modernizing orientation of the church. In this new capacity, Clarizio aspired to direct the Dominican church into playing a nonpartisan political role in society. He was recognized by many in the Dominican Republic as a great diplomat who could converse with all the different groups and who grew to be a progressive and popular personality. Many saw him as a "friend of the people." His contact with the popular masses during these mediating efforts earned him the trust and sympathy of those who had thought that the church was an unconditional ally of right-wing governments (Figueredo 1971, 11).

The Emergence of the Popular Church

The emergence of a small group of priests and religious brothers who were willing to risk their lives shows that the church is not a monolithic institution, but one that harbors different ecclesiastical orientations. The following two sections examine the response of grassroots priests and nuns to the crisis that resulted from the revolutionary upheaval and the subsequent U.S. military intervention.

Though unintentional, the pastoral work of the "three priests of the San Miguel parish" laid the groundwork for the emergence of the popular church in the country. These foreign-born religious priests went to the old section of Santo Domingo as the hierarchy and its priests left the city. They were Jesuit priests who came to the country from Cuba and decided to go to the war zone to help at the Billini Hospital located in the Constitutionalist zone. This group was comprised of Frs. Tomás Marrero, José A. Moreno, and Manuel Ortega. They joined two Capuchin priests, three native Dominican brothers (non-priests), and the De la Salle brothers who refused to leave the war zone (Leveque 1972, 6).

The three Jesuit priests lived in Manresa,[2] a Jesuit residence on the outskirts of Santo Domingo, and decided to go to the Constitutionalist zone to help with the wounded. They took care of the parishes that were left abandoned by most of the clergy. This meant saying mass; taking care of the wounded and sick; helping administer the Billini, Luis E. Aybar, and Moscoso Puello Hospitals; conducting weddings; and serving first communion in the war zone. They performed these duties to give a sense of normalcy to those living in a city filled with war tensions (interview with Fr. Tomás Marrero, July 10, 2001).

The Jesuit priests turned the parish of San Miguel into their center of operation. When the U.S.-led Inter-American Peace Force bombed the area, the Jesuits opened the temples so people could take cover from the bombs, and when the firing was over they picked up the wounded and brought them to the Billini Hospital. They did this for the first three weeks of the war. Then they set up a food distribution center at the parish using identity cards, which were given to each family. On Wednesdays, wearing their cassocks, the priests drove trucks across the line that divided the Constitutionalists from the Inter-American Peace Force to get the food that Nuncio Clarizio received from Caritas; then they returned to the Constitutionalist zone.

Back in the parish, the Jesuits would work through the night preparing small bags with rations that included oil, rice, and flour. They would drive their trucks around the city distributing food to the noncombatants because the Constitutionalists had their own supply system (interview with Fr. Marrero, July 10, 2001). José Antonio Moreno wrote a PhD dissertation that was later published as *Barrios in Arms* (1970, 66–84). In this book, Moreno provides a detailed analysis of the revolution, the Jesuit's work in the hospitals, the parish of San Miguel, the role of the revolutionary commandos, and life in the barrios of Santo Domingo during the revolution (Moreno 1970, 66–84).

The social work of the three priests of San Miguel did not always go smoothly. Because of their identification with the people during the four months of war, various radio commentators began to compare them with worker-priests of Paris. The foreign anti-Castro press took advantage of the presence of Jesuits in the Constitutionalist zone to suggest that Dominican revolutionaries were killing priests. Once the war was over and the provisional government was installed, the victorious U.S.-backed Loyalists tried to search the parish of San Miguel, claiming that there were weapons hidden under the altar. Msgr. Hugo Eduardo Polanco Brito, the apostolic administrator of Santo Domingo had to intervene to prevent the search (Sáez 1990, 78). The three priests of San Miguel showed a new style of relationship between church and the people and, as such, experienced the early history of the popular church in the country.

Catholic Nuns and the Revolution
Catholic nuns also contributed significantly to the beginnings of the popular church. Although few scholars have paid attention to the role of nuns, their actions during the revolution of 1965 were important. The revolution had a huge impact on the lives of both foreign and Dominican religious women. A North American sister of the Dominican order based in Adrian, Michigan, revealed how this epoch-making event affected her life: "The occupation of 42,000 [sic] Marines made me feel ashamed of being a North American. I felt offended when I saw the soldiers of my country occupying this beloved island. It also saddened me a great deal that families would lose their loved ones in the battle that took place during the first week of the revolution of 1965" (Ruiz Bergés 2001, 29).

Another sister of the same congregation, but a native Dominican who had to leave the country, was perplexed because no one in her congregation could understand why she supported the Constitutionalists:

> I lived the most traumatic experience of my life in the Colegio de Santo Domingo in April 1965, when the war broke out. I listened to the radio, I talked over the phone with my relatives and friends and I knew very well that the conflict had to be resolved between Dominican men and women. At all times, I identified with those who struggled for the return to constitutionality and I was very familiar with our country's painful history.... I played the part of the voice crying in the wilderness, when I tried to defend and to explain the facts without being listened to or understood by those who saw Communism everywhere. I observed in perplexity how my own sisters listened only to North American priests, bishops, and their embassy. (Ruiz Bergés 2001, 29)

The Salesian Sisters had varying sentiments regarding the revolution. These ranged from those who thought that the Dominican Republic could have gone the Cuban road to socialism to those who sympathized with the Constitutionalists. The U.S. Marines installed a military station in the Colegio María

Auxiliadora, where nuns carried out domestic work such as washing and ironing clothes for the military while they shared their food and medicine with them. These religious women witnessed the crossfire in their neighborhood and saw how the sisters of the Colegio Sagrado Corazón lacked sufficient food to eat. Many of the Salesian Sisters hid under their beds, as did everyone else, either because of fear or to protect themselves (Ruiz Bergés 2001, 30). When circumstances permitted, these nuns also offered their help to those who needed protection or simply some food.

The Sisters of Mercy were more committed to work in the battlefield, risking their lives while offering their services and donating their blood to the wounded. They expressed their feelings toward the suffering of everyone involved in the revolution:

> The revolution of 1965 was a challenge to the commitment of the sisters in the province. Many of them came from different communities and repeatedly offered their services to help out. They were even willing to donate their blood to help the wounded. Despite urging from the General Government of the Province to abandon the war zone, many of them, supported by the provincial government, decided to stay in the battlefield to help the wounded and sick of both factions, which earned their respect and affection. (Ruiz Bergés 2001, 30)

The priests and nuns who joined with lay people in the special circumstances created by the revolution laid the groundwork for the emergence of the popular church. As noted below, in 1972, Fr. Marrero joined a group of Jesuits that took up residence in a northern barrio of Santo Domingo and created the first Ecclesial Base Communities (ECBs). Similarly, in 1973, Adrian (Michigan) Dominican sisters donated Hermanas del Colegio de Santo Domingo, an elite Catholic school, to the Archdiocese of Santo Domingo so they could work with the poor. The work of those who risked their lives not only showed the human face of the church, but it laid down the seed for the development of the popular church as an alternative way for the church to relate to the state and society. This early experience of the Dominican popular church mirrors the larger reality of the popular church in Bolivia and Central America, where clergymen moved to live in poor neighborhoods to accompany fellow Christians.

The Church and Post-Trujillo Society, 1966–1978

This section focuses on the twelve-year regime of Joaquín Balaguer, the emergence of the church as a factor of cohesion for state and society, the mediation of Msgr. Hugo Eduardo Polanco Brito, and the political activities of the popular church. Neither Bolivia nor Central America produced an authoritarian leader who restored the authoritarian design of the state, provided the framework for the reincorporation of the church to the mainstream of society and politics, and kept the democratic opposition at bay and completed the destruction of the revolutionary left. The Dominican Republic was an exception because of U.S. military intervention and its subsequent economic and political support of the regime of Joaquín Balaguer.

The Balaguer Regime, 1966–1978

The regime of Joaquín Balaguer restored the authoritarian features of the state and prepared the conditions for the full reintegration of the church into the mainstream of society. Balaguer was one of the few government officers who served Trujillo during the entire period of his dictatorship. He reorganized the core membership of Trujillo's Dominican Party and used it to establish the Reformist Party in 1964. In the midst of the 1965 war, the United States allowed Balaguer to return home from New York, ostensibly to visit his dying mother for seventy-two hours in the summer months of 1965. When the war ended, Balaguer announced that he would run for president as the candidate of his Reformist Party. The United States was pleased with his announcement and supported efforts to hold general elections in the summer of 1966 (McPherson 2003, 127–46; Vega 2004, 117–67).

Bosch agreed to run as the PRD's presidential candidate, supposedly as a way to get the U.S.-backed Inter-American Peace Force to leave the country. However, he was not able to run a normal campaign due to numerous threats on his life. As a consequence, he used the radio as the main means of communication during his campaign. He was literally under house arrest. Balaguer, on the other hand, used a helicopter to travel throughout the country, announcing a "bloodless revolution." The church did not lead any demonstrations against Bosch during the campaign, but the hierarchy published a document expressing the view that Catholics should not vote for a candidate who "[makes] attempt[s] against the Christian order, such as the Marxist-Communist parties" (Conferencia del Episcopado Dominicano 1990, 145). Balaguer won the elections by a landslide (Balaguer and Bosch received 56.4 percent and 30 percent of the votes, whereas the PRSC received 2.2 percent of the votes; the remaining 4.5 percent went to smaller parties (Ruiz Bergés 1987, 48).

It is remarkable that the vote preference had been basically inverted compared to the general election results of 1962, when Bosch defeated the right-wing candidate 58.7 percent to 30.1 percent. The PRSC had also seen its numbers significantly reduced compared to 1962, when it received 5.1

percent. This demonstrated that, unlike Venezuela, Chile, and El Salvador, where Christian democratic parties had emerged as mainstream political forces, Christian democracy failed to take root in the Dominican Republic because the hierarchy did not see Christian democracy as a means to influence political events. The hierarchy was more comfortable with conservative Balaguer than with populist Juan Bosch, whose political ideology it viewed with suspicion. The fact is that the political process had changed completely. The left-leaning social and political movements that had supported Bosch were nearly crushed during the U.S. military intervention, and the oligarchy, along with the church, rallied behind Balaguer as a savior.

The newly elected government would have had great difficulties succeeding, had it not been for massive U.S. assistance. The United States helped him rescue the entire state apparatus, which had nearly collapsed during the revolution, and resurrected the Dominican armed forces and police, placing them under direct U.S. command and assuming total responsibility for the payment of salaries, clothing, food, and military equipment. It also took control of the nonmilitary apparatus of the state, paid salaries, and placed U.S. agents in important government posts, for example, in the ministries of finance, agriculture, industry and commerce, health, education, and communications; the internal revenue services; the central bank and the reserve bank; the National Office of Statistics; and other decentralized government agencies (Betances 1995, 117–18).

Balaguer used the power of the restored authoritarian regime to finish crushing the left and to keep the social democratic opposition in check. He filled Dominican jails with political prisoners, hunted down leftist revolutionaries, and sent into exile social democratic leaders who could pose a threat to his regime.[3] The authoritarian regime's success at crushing the political left and holding the democratic opposition at bay can be explained, in part, by the economic prosperity of the Dominican export sectors. Rising international market prices for Dominican products brought a significant increase in state revenues. These products included sugar, cacao, coffee, and minerals. Sugar sold at record prices ($.61 per pound) in the early 1970s. Interestingly, these developments parallel economic performance in Bolivia and Central America during the same period.

The government initiated a series of public works projects aimed at modernizing infrastructure, strengthening the state, and gaining public support. Balaguer traveled in a government-owned helicopter deep into the country to inaugurate small and large public projects, such as schools, roads, hydroelectric dams, Catholic temples, and hospitals, and to inaugurate projects of the Oficina para el Desarrollo de la Communidad (Office for Community

Development). He also launched a huge government-sponsored construction program to broaden the streets of Santo Domingo and Santiago and to construct new avenues to speed up traffic. Along with government-owned enterprises—all of Trujillo's sugar mills and multiple other holdings were nationalized and the state became a huge administrator of public assets—the construction industry created new jobs, which helped calm urban protests. The visibility of public construction gave the main urban centers a veneer of modernity and upper-middle-class urban dwellers began to enjoy a degree of comfort.

The regime's political machine began to decline as the international economic and political environment changed after the mid-1970s. Two important events determined the political fate of Balaguer's government in 1978: the dramatic decline in the international prices of Dominican export products after 1976 and the election of Jimmy Carter as president of the United States. The fall in international market prices left Balaguer without financial resources to sustain his clientelistic political machine, and the election of Carter left him without the political backing of the United States.

Despite massive use of state resources to stay in power, Balaguer could not get the support of the electorate in 1978 and had to hand over power to S. Antonio Guzman, the victorious candidate.[4] He retained control of the Senate through political negotiations, showing that conservative sectors still supported him.

The case of Balaguer is rather unique in Latin America, where most of the authoritarian rulers in the 1960s and 1970s had been generals. Unlike the military dictators of Bolivia and Central America, Balaguer was a civilian politician who served under Trujillo for thirty-one years. He made a series of agreements with neo-Trujillista political forces in order to succeed during his twelve years in office. This is why important personalities within the Trujillo dictatorship served under his various administrations and why he did not dismantle the basic design of the state built during the Trujillo dictatorship. Balaguer served as a channel of communication between the Catholic hierarchy and Trujillo during the crisis that erupted as a result of the church denunciation of political oppression in the last two years of his dictatorship.

Unlike General Hugo Banzer of Bolivia (1971–1979), Balaguer exerted complete control over the military and, as noted below, developed a good relationship with the Catholic hierarchy. The military rulers of Central America did not allow any civilians to gain sufficient power to become independent, as Balaguer did in the Dominican Republic. Further, serving Trujillo for thirty-one years taught Balaguer how to navigate the troubled waters of the Dominican political environment. He was thus prepared to accommodate the needs of the Catholic hierarchy, whose blessing he needed to legitimize a regime that was the result of fraudulent elections held under the U.S. military occupation. He continued Trujillo's policy of providing substantial financial assistance to the church in exchange for its political support and blessings (see chapter 4).

The Church and Balaguer
Balaguer's regime provided the framework for the church to reintegrate into post-Trujillo society. This restoration occurred simultaneously with the changes the Vatican effected in the Dominican hierarchy to bring it in line with the precepts and conclusions of Vatican II. The Vatican began to introduce changes in the Dominican church shortly after the revolution ended. On December 10, 1965, it accepted the resignation of Msgr. Francisco Panal, who was blind. In the same month, it removed Msgr. Octavio Beras Rojas as archbishop of Santo Domingo and appointed Bishop Hugo Eduardo Polanco Brito, of the Diocese of Santiago, as apostolic administrator of the Archdiocese of Santo Domingo. Msgr. Polanco Brito had demonstrated greater acceptance of the changes produced by Vatican II, whereas Beras Rojas was a traditional conservative archbishop who developed most of his career during the Trujillo period and abandoned his post in the critical days of the revolution of 1965. In 1966, Fr. Roque Adames, considered a progressive, was appointed bishop of the Diocese of Santiago, while Fr. Juan Flores Santana, believed to be in line with the modernizing orientation, was appointed bishop of the Diocese of La Vega (Wipfler 1980, 239–42). The influence of Nuncio Clarizio is quite noticeable in these choices.

Msgr. Polanco Brito's messages and public statements showed that there was a new modern leadership in the Archdiocese of Santo Domingo. For example, in January 1966, Polanco Brito issued a message in which he called on the most important sectors of society for help. He urged the military to turn itself into a guardian of national integrity, the economic elite to recognize the need for a better distribution of wealth, and the workers to act with more responsibility when they called strikes. He also encouraged the politicians not to contribute to chaos and to teach the people how to live in a democracy. Finally, he asked peasants to recognize that they were the majority of the population, and, as such, to sustain the national economy (Wipfler 1980, 238). This exhortation was important because a leader of the Catholic Church was calling on all sectors of society, rather than just the elite (as in the past). Following in the tracks paved by Nuncio Clarizio, Msgr. Polanco Brito was clearly seeking to establish the church as a special political actor.

The public statements of the new archbishop were followed by declarations from Msgrs. Adames of Santiago and Juan Félix Pepén of La Altagracia. In February 1967 Msgr. Adames called on the priests of his diocese to hold a three-day conference on the political situation of the country and called on the government to implement agrarian reform (Wipfler 1980, 257). Msgr. Pepén issued a pastoral letter in February 1969 calling for the attention of the faithful of the Diocese of La Altagracia to agrarian issues. He stated that the economic misfortune of the peasants concerned the church because those who lack the basic necessities of life are not in a condition to be good Christians. After recognizing the necessity for better distribution of the land, the letter stated that the church had defended the right to private property more than any other entity. Pepén insisted that, according to Vatican II, private property had a social function and that "when it is easily forgotten, it turns into a multiple temptation of ambitions and serious disorders. This way it gives excuses to its objectors to doubt the validity of such a right." The letter did not blame anyone for the situation of the peasants, but it "argued that the system had created the ills of latifundia and minifundia. Nonetheless, it is significant the letter ends calling on the peasants to organize" (Lluberes 1998, 585–89).

Reactions to the letter appeared in the press immediately. Landowners accused the church of intervening in politics and agitating the peasants to occupy lands. The priests of the Diocese of La Altagracia responded to these criticisms with a document that clarified that the bishop's letter was not asking to take things lightly, but to study the situation carefully because the land issue was complex (Lluberes 1998, 601). The letter suggests that Msgr. Pepén was taking the most radical position and thus *appeared* politically close to the popular church movement, but he never became its defender before the Conferencia del Episcopado Dominicano, CED (Dominican Episcopal Conference).

How can we explain the church's approach to the peasants? Was the church turning radical? Did it take sides with the peasantry? Was it in competition with Balaguer or was it pushing him to implement a modernizing capitalist agrarian reform? The concern of the hierarchy about social issues can be traced back to the exhortations, messages, and pastoral letters of the CED issued in the early 1960s. Fr. José Luis Alemán, SJ, argues that the failure of the church's initiative in the aftermath of Trujillo's downfall indicates that it could not rely on Dominican folk Catholicism alone. Under these conditions, it was necessary to look for other channels to reach the concrete objective of the church: evangelization. This led to the rural pastoral work through which the church sought to abbreviate the distance between "folk" and "official" religiosity, emphasizing the social dimension of Christianity.

Working with the peasantry, which was 70 percent of the population in the early 1960s, while proclaiming that it was not interested in exercising direct or indirect political control of state power, the church declared itself nonpartisan but enunciated its position concerning social justice (Alemán 1982, 406–10).

Rather than become radical or take a partisan political position when opting for the peasants as a favored social group, the church sought to emphasize its concern for social issues such as human rights and land ownership. In the Declaration on the Rural Situation (1967), the CED stated that "the intention of the hierarchy was to call the attention of men of good will in the Republic to the peasants' problems and to propose the church's own outlook on life: a global vision of men" (Conferencia del Episcopado Dominicano 1990, 155). The declaration summarizes the problems of Dominican peasants and points out the possible consequences if affairs were mishandled. It recommended that landowners not block the agrarian reform laws and called on them to appropriate their lands for the settlement of poor peasants.

The individual declarations of bishops did not deviate from the main tenets of the CED concerning the peasantry. In fact, the church was supporting the agrarian reform laws promoted by Balaguer. However, the landowners and the Gulf & Western Corporation, which basically owned almost all the arable land in the eastern regions of the country, opposed any kind of agrarian reform. In this sense, the church was not being radical, but rather was pushing a modernizing capitalist project that sought to balance out the uneven distribution of land ownership. It was working to bring social cohesion to society, which the regime needed desperately, given its lack of political legitimacy. However, given the previous association with the dominant elite and the government, this marked a turning point in church-state relations, because the hierarchy now approved a pastoral action that supported the peasantry. These actions created political friction between the hierarchy and Balaguer, but they were smoothed out in private meetings.

The political context in which the bishops made their positions public was filled with tensions. In a highly contentious situation, many critics made excessively politicized interpretations of their messages. For example, the Communist Party openly supported Balaguer's agrarian reform laws. Some critics ended up thinking that the church position coincided with the left on the agrarian problem, when, in fact, neither the social democratic opposition, led by the PRD, nor the socialist left seemed to understand the bishops' intent. During his inauguration as bishop of the Diocese of Santiago in June 1966, Msgr. Roque Adames, considered progressive by many, declared that the church did not have as its immediate mission the political, economic, or social order; its mission was religious. However, it could not completely disengage itself because it must be concerned with the social order, as Vatican II indicates: "that which can contribute to a better organization of human society, is not foreign to the Kingdom of God" (Rodríguez Núñez 1991, 186). Msgr. Roque Adames and the other bishops thought that the church, as an ecclesiastical society, had its own mission and objectives, which should not be confused with the objectives of society and the public authorities.

The Dominican hierarchy was politically divided concerning the government's social policy. From 1966 to 1970, four bishops (Adames, Santana, Pepén, and Polanco Brito) pressured Balaguer to carry out profound agrarian reforms. This group proposed a modernizing orientation of pastoral action that called for land reform and the implementation of programs to fight poverty, improve health standards, and so on. A second group comprised of traditional conservatives such as Beras and Tomás F. Reilly were comfortable with Balaguer's conservative perspective for the country. Although these two groups espoused different ecclesiastic views, they had one thing in common: they both distrusted the emerging popular church that was inspired by liberation theology (Ruiz Bergés 1987, 252–67; Wipfler 1980, 247–90).

Despite the different approaches within the church hierarchy, its relationship with Balaguer seemed unproblematic. The hierarchy seemed to feel quite at ease with Balaguer, who respected the concordat signed by Trujillo, which continued to frame church-state relations, and the government, in turn, did not interrupt the construction of Catholic temples. It also granted great privileges to the institution through subsidies to Catholic schools, universities, and various other church welfare institutions, such as dispensaries and hospitals.

The news that Msgr. Beras Rojas was reappointed archbishop of Santo Domingo in January 1970 was well received by the government. Beras Rojas spent most of his career in the Trujillo dictatorship and replaced Msgr. Ricardo Pittini as archbishop of Santo Domingo. The Vatican also abolished the post of apostolic administrator and named Polanco Brito coadjutor to the archbishop of Santo Domingo. Earlier, 1967, the Vatican had replaced Nuncio Clarizio with Msgr. Antonio del Guidice (1967–1971), a conservative, who possibly had a degree of influence in the new changes.[5] Progressives within the church saw these appointments as measures that reinforced traditional conservatives within the hierarchy. This conservative shift within the church helped bring cohesion to the authoritarian government of Balaguer, whose legitimacy was questioned by the democratic opposition. The church promoted conciliation and political compromises through the office of Msgr. Polanco Brito. In short, the Dominican church hierarchy was in synchronization with that of its peers in Bolivia and Central America, where the majority of bishops and archbishops had a comfortable relationship with military rulers during the same period.

The Political Mediation of Polanco Brito
The political mediations of Msgr. Polanco Brito constitute the second church attempt to intervene in important political conflicts in the post-Trujillo period. The actions of Polanco Brito—mediating political crises, calling for the freedom of political prisoners, and criticizing government policies—showed that he wanted a nonpartisan role for the church. However, his overlapping interests with the powers that be made him more of a defender of the status quo than a true nonpartisan influence. For example, when he pressed the opposition to participate in negotiations, it helped the government regularize conflicts and gave an impression of cooperation on both sides. In addition, his efforts to help political prisoners leave the country relieved the government of problematic individuals.

In this section, I briefly review Polanco Brito's mediation in the political kidnapping of Colonel Donald J. Crowley, U.S. air attaché, the intervention to arrange for political prisoners to go into exile, the intercession between the government and political opposition in the elections of 1974, and the negotiations to release foreign diplomats kidnapped by a revolutionary commando at the Venezuelan consulate in the same year.

The kidnapping of Colonel Donald J. Crowley occurred in the midst of Balaguer's second bid for the presidency. The Comando Unificado Anti-reeleccionista, CUA (Anti-reelection Unified Command), abducted Crowley on March 24, 1970. The CUA was made up of members of the Movimiento Popular Dominicano, MPD (Dominican Popular Movement), a Marxist-Leninist political party, which demanded the liberation of twenty-one political prisoners. Maximiliano Gómez, the leader of the MPD, was the first man on the list of prisoners. The CUA said that it had no time to waste and gave the government a short deadline to free the prisoners at Parque Duarte in Santo Domingo. The kidnappers asked Msgr. Polanco Brito to lead a mediating commission along with Dr. Rafael Kasse Acta, president of the Universidad Autónoma de Santo Domingo (UASD), and Dr. Bienvenido Mejía y Mejía, president of the Asociación Dominicana de Abogados (Dominican Bar Association).[6]

The government refused to release the prisoners in Parque Duarte, claiming that it would be tantamount to demanding the president's resignation, but offered to give them safe passage to leave the country in exchange for Crowley's freedom. The CUA refused the government's offer and demanded that the government withdraw all security personnel from Parque Duarte and release the prisoners. It threatened to kill Crowley if the government did not fulfill its demands.

After tense hours of negotiation, the CUA accepted Balaguer's offer because they feared that if the national police released the prisoners in Parque Duarte, security forces would then assassinate them. According to the agreement negotiated by the mediating commission, the prisoners received safe passage to Mexico including a charter plane to fly directly from Santo Domingo to Mexico City; enough money to cover basic necessities in Mexico; and the government's agreement to receive the prisoners in the Mexican Embassy, where the ambassador would meet them and drive them to the airport. To strengthen the guarantees offered, the mediating commission asked the papal nuncio and the ambassadors of Costa Rica, El Salvador, Spain, and Great Britain to be present at the airport when the prisoners arrived. As part of the agreement, Polanco Brito agreed to go with the prisoners to Mexico City. When he arrived in Mexico City, he would call the Mexican ambassador in Santo Domingo to let him know that they had arrived safely. In exchange, the CUA agreed to release Crowley unharmed to the Mexican Embassy as the plane departed for Mexico City.

Despite minor glitches, the prisoners reached Mexico City on March 26, three days after the seizure, and Crowley was released behind the building of the Santo Tomás de Aquino Seminary in Santo Domingo. A transit policeman took him to the head of the national police, who, in turn, drove him to the Mexican Embassy, as previously agreed (Polanco Brito 1970a, 1–14). There was a sense of relief in the population when the kidnapping was resolved, and national newspapers wrote editorials praising Polanco Brito and the other members of the mediating commission. Polanco Brito demonstrated his usefulness to the government in a time of crisis and raised the prestige and credibility of the church.

For the Dominican government, the Crowley case was not yet closed. It wanted the members of the CUA to be physically eliminated. The national police concluded that Otto Morales and Amin Abel Hasbum, two prominent leftist leaders, were responsible for Crowley's kidnapping. The way the police killed them suggests that they were not interested in arresting the leaders, but wanted to assassinate them. In both cases, the police conducted raids where it thought the kidnappers could be. When they found Morales and Abel Hasbum, they shot them on the spot. Most of the exiled prisoners left Mexico for Cuba and Europe where many were eventually killed in strange circumstances. For example, Maximiliano Gómez died of asphyxiation in his apartment in Brussels, Belgium.[7] Gómez's body was returned to the Dominican

Republic on May 28, 1971. Polanco Brito and the mediating commission went to the airport to receive his remains (Polanco Brito 1970b).

Protests for the freedom of political prisoners continued to be on top of the opposition's political agenda. The government met public demonstrations with police repression through the use of a paramilitary group known as "La Banda Colorada," (The Red Band), a name identified with the colors of Balaguer's official party. This group also identified itself as anticommunist and took it upon itself to eliminate government opponents. Polanco Brito called on the government to stop the actions of La Banda Colorada because it was destroying the principle of authority and imposing terror in the population (Polanco Brito 1971, 18). Balaguer responded by saying that La Banda Colorada was an uncontrollable group when, in fact, it was public knowledge that it operated jointly with the national police as a paramilitary force.

Police repression intensified after January 12, 1972, when combined forces of the national police and the national army fought a group of revolutionaries led by Amaury Germán Aristy and Virgilio Perdomo Pérez on the highway to the Airport of the Americas, outside Santo Domingo. The national police accused them of robbing $60,000 dollars from the Royal Bank of Canada on November 8, 1971. It took security forces more than eight hours to defeat the revolutionary group. After the battle of January 12, the national police also looked for Plinio Matos Moquete and Harry Jiménez Castillo because it claimed that they had also participated in the robbing of the Royal Bank of Canada.

The search for Matos Moquete and Jiménez Castillo brought fear to their relatives and friends, who asked Polanco Brito to form a mediating commission to guarantee their lives. Polanco Brito was joined in this new mediating commission by a new nuncio, Luciano Storero (1971–1973), who replaced Antonio del Guidice; Salvador Pittaluga Nivar, a well-known television journalist; Rafael Kasse Acta, president of UASD; and German Ornes Coiscou, owner of *El Caribe*, a Dominican daily. Matos Moquete refused to surrender to the mediating commission because he wanted to remain in the country to organize the revolution. Unlike Matos Moquete, Jiménez Castillo accepted their mediation to arrange his exile at the Mexican Embassy. When Jiménez Castillo received safe passage to leave the country, Polanco Brito accompanied him to Willenstad, Curaçao. Subsequently, the nacional police arrested Matos Moquete (Polanco Brito 1972a, 1–14).

Polanco Brito, Nuncio Luiciano Storeno, and Pittaluga Nivar established themselves as nationally recognized mediators. Relatives of political prisoners looked to them as intermediaries with power to intercede for them with President Balaguer. They were open to requests across the political spectrum.

When La Banda was restructured by Balaguer in 1973, Ramón Pérez Martínez (Macorís), its leader, claimed political persecution from both the left and the right. Polanco Brito and Pittaluga Nivar interceded so he could travel to Europe. This mediation was highly criticized because Pérez Martínez had been involved in various political crimes. Despite these criticisms, most analysts and relatives of the political prisoners praised their mediating efforts (Polanco Brito 1972b, 53).

The CED supported Polanco Brito wholeheartedly in his efforts to obtain the freedom of political prisoners. Shortly before Christmas Eve in 1972, the CED sent a special commission, composed of Msgrs. Polanco Brito, Tomás O'Reilly, and Roque Adames, to meet with Juan Aristides Taveras Guzmán, attorney general of the republic. The CED said that "it joined the petition of mothers, wives, and relatives of political prisoners that demand a general amnesty for their relatives from the President of the Republic." The CED also wrote to President Balaguer, who responded by saying: "The government highly appreciates the humanitarian efforts of the Conferencia Episcopado Dominicano and it will do whatever it can to respond to your request as far as circumstances permit" (Polanco Brito 1972–1973, 72–74). The CED's call for the freeing of political prisoners and its support of Polanco Brito's mediation indicate that traditional conservative bishops and those identified with a modernizing church orientation were acting together to transform the church into an institution that cared for solutions to national problems.

The movement to free political prisoners ended in February 1973 when Francisco Caamaño arrived in San José de Ocoa, a town on the southern coast of the country, with a group of guerrillas from Cuba. These guerrillas wanted to set up a force that would eventually develop into an army with popular support and then overthrow Balaguer's regime. Political attention shifted to the guerrilla movement, while relatives of the guerrillas asked Polanco Brito to form yet another mediating commission to intercede with the government so that the bodies of three dead guerrillas could be identified. This commission never began its work because the government refused to allow them to reach the battlefront. Government forces quickly defeated the guerrillas, and only three of the nine guerrillas led by Caamaño survived; Hamlet Herman, Torivio Peña Jaquez, and Claudio Caamaño were arrested by security forces and subsequently deported.

Communication between the government and the political opposition broke off during the government's confrontation with the guerrillas. The government suspected that Bosch and Peña Gómez supported the guerrillas, and these leaders had to go into hiding to avoid persecution. On February 22, 1973, *Listín Diario* published a letter from a group of notable citizens who urged the government and the opposition to start a dialogue. The letter asked Polanco Brito to lead a mediating commission. Polanco Brito declared "I have been present whenever I have been able to make a contribution to the search for peace and understanding among all groups. However, this time, for reasons I do not wish to reveal, I decline the offer." (Polanco Brito 1973a, 29).

Polanco Brito would not participate as a mediator again until September 1973, when Manfredo Casado Villar kidnapped Cuitlahuac Villar, the son of the Mexican ambassador. Casado Villar had been a refugee in the Mexican Embassy for a year, but he had not received political asylum to go to Mexico. He abducted young Cuitlahuac Villar, apparently to press the Mexican ambassador and the Dominican government to give him safe passage to leave the country. Casado Villar asked Polanco Brito; Jottin Cury, the president of the UASD; and journalists Radhamés Gómez Pepín, Silvio Herasme Peña, and Rafael Herrera to form a commission to mediate the matter.

In the tense situation, Polanco Brito offered himself in exchange for the child, but Casado Villar did not accept the offer. The Dominican government did not want to give Casado Villar safe passage to leave the country because he had been tried by a tribunal and found guilty of a crime before taking refuge in the embassy. Polanco Brito and the mediating commission worked hard to find a country that would grant him political asylum. He received it in France, but did not release the child until he was inside the plane, ready to go. He handed the child over to Polanco Brito, and Radhamés Gómez Pepín accompanied him to his final destination (Polanco Brito 1973b, 70). Once again, Polanco Brito and the commission mediated to get a kidnapper out of the country and, in a way, resolved a problem for the government.

Polanco Brito's successful mediation was followed by an outpouring of requests by relatives of political prisoners and by the Comité Permanente Pro-Libertad de los Presos Políticos (Permanent Committee for the Freedom of Political Prisoners) to arrange for political prisoners to leave the country. The committee led a campaign to occupy Catholic temples as a way to pressure the church and the government to speed the freedom of political prisoners. The hierarchy appeared divided on this issue, with some bishops allowing for the occupation of temples in their dioceses, while others did not. In May 1974, Msgr. Roque Adames of the Diocese of Santiago gave permission for Catholic temples to be used, but Msgr. Juan Flores of the Diocese of La Vega warned that he would call the police if they occupied temples in his diocese (Polanco Brito 1974a, 114–19). Polanco Brito was already on record as opposing the occupation of temples for political purposes.[8]

Polanco Brito continued to mediate in political conflicts throughout 1973 and 1974. He repeatedly called for negotiations between the political opposition and President Balaguer. The political opposition formed a coalition to participate in the presidential elections of 1974. This coalition, extending from the left to the right, was called the Acuerdo de Santiago, or Santiago Accord. It included the leftist MPD, the moderate PRD, the conservative PRSC, and the right-wing Partido Quisqueyano Demócrata, PQD (Quisqueyan Democratic Party), led by General Elías Wessín y Wessín. Wessín y Wessín was exiled by Balaguer in 1971 after Balaguer found him culpable of a conspiracy to overthrow the government.

It is worth noting, however, that Juan Bosch had left the PRD for political and ideological reasons in November 1973 and later formed the Partido de la Liberación Dominicana, PLD (Dominican Liberation Party). The PLD and various other leftist parties refused to work within the larger Acuerdo de Santiago to participate in the presidential elections of 1974 because Balaguer would not allow the opposition to freely run an electoral campaign.

The Acuerdo de Santiago excluded Bosch's PLD and other small left-wing parties, and President Balaguer took advantage of these political divisions in the opposition. Troops from the army and police participated in Balaguer's electoral campaign. They shouted slogans, waved the official party flag, and called for reelection. The campaign became so violent that the candidate of the Acuerdo de Santiago, S. Antonio Guzmán, did not dare go in the streets to campaign. And the vice presidential candidate, Elías Wessín y Wessín, was not allowed to return home to participate in the campaign. These were the circumstances in which the Acuerdo de Santiago decided to withdraw from the electoral race just two days before the presidential elections of May 16, 1974.

Polanco Brito hurriedly formed another mediating commission with Dr. Pedro Troncoso Sanchez and Rafael Herrera, both recognized as notable citizens. They reportedly wanted to secure the participation of the Acuerdo de Santiago in the elections because otherwise there would be no opposition voice in the National Congress to counterbalance the executive. After many hours of discussions with the mediating commission, the Acuerdo leaders proposed the following conditions to participate in the elections:

1. Reschedule the elections for July 1.
2. Allow General Elías Wessín y Wessín, vice presidential candidate, to return home from exile.
3. Free political prisoners.

4. Reassure the apolitical status of the armed forces and the national police.
5. Implement the electoral law and the electoral registry in its original form and repeal the last resolutions of the Central Electoral Board because they were contrary to the spirit of the law. (Polanco Brito 1974b, 191–94).

President Balaguer was willing to accept items 3, 4, and 5, but he was not eager to reschedule the elections, ostensibly because it violated the constitution. He agreed to allow General Wessín y Wessín to return home if he was duly elected. Despite Balaguer's concessions, the Acuerdo withdrew from the elections.

The Acuerdo leadership criticized the mediating commission for its insistence on negotiations. The commission knew the Acuerdo's reasons for withdrawing from the electoral race in May 14. Saturnino Gil Morales, an Acuerdo leader, said:

> The commission took away from us the little time we had to orient our militants about our electoral abstention. We wanted to avoid what in reality happened: the government and interest groups wanted to retain power by whatever means necessary. They used the means of communication at their disposal and closed down ours. This way, they created confusion, spreading the false news throughout the country that we had agreed to participate in the elections under the government conditions and that we would participate in the elections on May 16. (Polanco Brito, 1974c, 218)

Polanco Brito and his mediating commission claimed to see farther than the immediate interests of a particular political party. They believed Dominican society needed to strengthen its democratic institutions and that electoral abstention did not contribute to this end:

> The mediating commission tried to look for compromises so the Acuerdo de Santiago would participate in the elections of May 16. The democratic process demanded participation in the electoral race even if all the conditions were not met, that is to say, all the conditions that each group demanded. It seemed to us that it was possible to arrive at a negotiation. Each part had to give up something of what they thought belongs to them. (Polanco Brito 1974d, 163)

The mediating commission's attempts to make last-minute arrangements between an opposition that had already decided to withdraw from the elections and a president who wanted to retain power at whatever cost colored their otherwise nonpartisan role.

The role of Polanco Brito was further compromised shortly after the elections when he called on the political parties of the opposition to join the government. He was still hoping that the government and the opposition were going to find a negotiated solution to their political differences. In fact, he noted: "Personally, I believe that, once the elections of whatever period in Dominican history are finished, once the political differences between the political parties are ironed out, every Dominican must be ready to offer his talent, his training, and his experience to society" (Polanco Brito 1974e, 11–20). The Acuerdo de Santiago denounced Polanco Brito for exerting pressure on the opposition to collaborate with the government. Oscar A. Robles Toledano, a prominent conservative priest, wrote a letter to the *Listin Diario* on June 4, 1974, under the pseudonym of P. R. Thompson, in which he stated:

> How can anyone, with a clear conscience, join a regime characterized for its partisan spirit, one that sometimes demands that a person renounce his own convictions to accept a job in government? The words of the Monsignor still stir the air and we still have not recovered from the astonishment caused by the accusation that appeared in the press concerning the dismissal in the Central Bank—an entity for technocrats, if they exist—of a dozen technical experts because, using their right, they presented themselves as candidates for elective posts with the opposition or manifested their sympathy for parties that oppose the regime. . . . If the government sincerely aspires to obtain the collaboration of the best human resources of the country, as Monsignor Polanco wants, it must guarantee its offerings, with irrefutable facts and inviolable agreements. It must begin by previously sterilizing its own house. (Polanco Brito 1974e, 20)

Polanco Brito's political autonomy from President Balaguer appeared to have been diminished during the summer of 1974. However, on September 24, 1974, he gave a homily to honor the Virgen de las Mercedes, in which he restated his political independence from the president. Balaguer and members of his cabinet were present during the sermon, in which Polanco Brito candidly said: "Your excellence, you have ahead of you a four-year period that will be the hardest, the most committed, and one in which the nation hopes to consolidate the works initiated eight years ago. I am going to speak as if it were the Dominican people talking to their president." He continued:

1. You have proclaimed the agrarian reform and have carried it out with tenacity, but there is a lot more that needs to be done. I ask that in the next four years Your Excellency help the peasants with all your might so they can be "more" Dominican.

2. I have traveled throughout the country over the last few years and have been able to ponder over the huge government efforts carried out to help the population in the provinces. . . . I want to congratulate Your Excellence, but I also want to convey the clamor of many villages and cities that ask for a more equitable distribution of national resources.
3. Our streets see thousands of people wandering without work. These are men and women who have not had an opportunity in life or who have lost it. They, too, need the effort of the government and private entities to break one of the chains that hold down the country's progress.
4. Our youth need more schools, more sports facilities, better attention from the parents and teachers to educate the future Dominican man.
5. Sugar constitutes the greatest source of Dominican wealth. . . . The solution to human problems involving cultivating cane, cutting it, and manufacturing sugar takes a lot of the time of a president. I request that you study this issue. . . . It is (also) necessary to address the human problem of Haitian cane cutters who are our brothers who share the island that saw our birth.

We all know there are "jailed politicians" (*políticos presos*) and "political prisoners" (*presos políticos*). . . . I humbly confess that I do not know which is the best way to resolve this problem, but I dare ask Your Excellence to implement a plan which you already proposed when you created by decree the Prison Commission. . . . I ask you to accelerate the review of the process of so many unknown prisoners who do not receive an immediate sentence because they are poor and abandoned men. . . . Personally, I do not believe that the so-called political prisoners are all politicians; neither do I believe that those who proclaimed themselves to be political prisoners are heroes for the simple fact that they proclaim themselves persecuted for ideological/political reasons. . . . Nonetheless, I request that the government reopen these cases for review. (Polanco Brito 1974f, 194)

In this homily, Polanco Brito appeared as the "voice of the voiceless," as other archbishops had done in Bolivia, El Salvador, Guatemala, Brazil, Chile, and elsewhere. He told President Balaguer what many wanted him to hear directly. The critiques of Polanco Brito were praised in the press, but just a few days after his sermon (on September 27, 1974), a group that called itself Comando Revolucionario, CR (Revolutionary Commando), kidnapped several diplomats in the Venezuelan Consulate, and the political scene changed completely. The diplomats abducted included Barbara Hutchinson, head of the U.S. Information Services, who was kidnapped outside her office and taken to the Venezuelan Consulate. She was kept there with Gregorio del Corral, Venezuelan consul; Aldemar Alvarado; their secretaries, Dulce Maria and Abrosina Ares; and Santiago Fuente, a Spanish priest who happened to be at the consulate translating for Pablo Chan, a Taiwanese businessman who was looking for a visa to go to Venezuela. The CR demanded the release of thirty-six political prisoners, including Plinio Matos Moquete. They also asked for $1 million in exchange for the hijacked diplomats. Radhamés Méndez Vargas, leader of the CR, called the press and asked Polanco Brito; Pittaluga Nivar; Rafael Herrera; and Hugo Tolentino Dipp, president of the UASD, to lead a mediating commission. The last two members of the proposed commission were not in the country at the moment but said that they could return home to participate if necessary. The CR claimed that they had twenty-three heavily armed revolutionaries ready to die, and they threatened to blow up the consulate if the police attacked them (Polanco Brito, 1974g, 164–86).

Unlike the Crowley kidnapping, the abduction at the Venezuelan Consulate lasted thirteen days and the national and international press covered it widely. It was also dangerous for those involved in the negotiations. Perhaps because of the danger, Polanco Brito's attempt to mediate was cut short, but he initiated the whole process. In a diary covering the event, Polanco Brito wrote that on September 30, he talked to Méndez Vargas at the consulate and tried to persuade him to accept the government's guarantees to respect the lives of the kidnapped victims and provide medical attention to a wounded captor, if they would give themselves up. But Méndez Vargas rejected the offer, asserting that the demands were not negotiable. The next time Polanco Brito went to the consulate, he tried to persuade Méndez Vargas to release the three women and to let him take the wounded hostage taker to the U.S., Spanish, or Mexican Embassy. This was also rejected. Later that day, U.S. ambassador Robert Hurwitch told Polanco Brito that no more food was going to be allowed into the consulate. Polanco Brito was afraid that the police would storm the building, but the U.S. ambassador assured him that President Balaguer pledged this would not happen. The ambassador promised to call him later, which he did (Polanco Brito 1974g, 221–26).

The ambassadors of the United States and Spain and the Venezuelan chargé d'affaires took over the delivery of food and negotiations with the hostage takers. On October 5, Méndez Vargas met with the diplomats outside the consulate to discuss the CR's demands. By this point, Méndez Vargas had scaled down his demands significantly and accepted a reduction in the number of prisoners to ten and safe passage to either Peru or Mexico. President Balaguer agreed to give the kidnappers safe passage but did not release any political prisoners. Neither Mexico nor Peru agreed to grant political asylum, but Panama agreed to give them sanctuary. The kidnappers left (alone) for Panama on October 10, 1974 (Polanco Brito 1974g, 128–86).

Despite recognition of Polanco Brito as an excellent mediator by both the government and the opposition, the papal nunciature announced on December 5, 1975, that the Vatican had named him to replace Msgr. Félix Pepén of the Diocese of Altagracia as archbishop-bishop. This announcement came as a big surprise, and the local press speculated that Gulf & Western and other landowners in the eastern region, had pressured the Catholic hierarchy to obtain Msgr. Pepén's resignation. However, Pepén himself told the press that he resigned for health reasons and he accepted the transfer to the Archdiocese of Santo Domingo as auxiliary bishop to Beras Rojas. In his memoirs, Pepén says:

> Around my voluntary resignation, personal and made of good conscience, there were lots of speculations then and later. Whether economic and political sectors exerted pressures, supposedly resentful of the minimum human liberating process promoted by the social pastoral work of the Diocese of the Altagracia and its bishop, or the result of the pressure exerted by landowners, or subject of an economic transaction. None of this is true. (Pepén 2003, 181)

Pepén's reference to an "economic transaction" refers to a widely circulated rumor among informed people that Gulf & Western donated sugar to the Vatican so it could, in turn, give it to the Palestinian people. The economic transaction consisted of "trading the bishop for sugar," that is to say, obtaining his resignation of the post of bishop of Diocese of La Altagracia.

Similarly, there was much speculation concerning the appointment of Polanco Brito to the Diocese of La Altagracia. Many perceived Polanco Brito to be a conservative clergyman who pushed the political opposition to accept compromises with President Balaguer. Reportedly, Gulf & Western and local landowners wanted Polanco Brito to go to La Altagracia to bring the situation under control. Contrary to expectations, however, when he went to the Diocese of La Altagracia, Polanco Brito continued to support the work of Msgr. Pepén, who was identified with the struggles of landless peasants in the region. He shored up the priests who counseled landless peasants—considered agitators by the region's landowners—and called on the government to deepen agrarian reform. Notwithstanding these initiatives, Polanco Brito did not continue in the ways of Pepén and eventually accommodated the status quo. In any case, his transfer to the Diocese of La Altagracia reduced his national role as mediator and slowly relegated him to regional issues (Polanco Brito 1975, 81–105; 1976, 73–81).

The Role of the Popular Church

This section examines two aspects of the popular church. The first portion addresses the popular church as a movement that seeks to promote human development and denounce social injustice and human rights violations. The second segment focuses on the development of the ecclesiastical base communities (CEBs). Despite its relatively small size, the Dominican popular church played an important political role, showing that the Catholic Church is not a monolithic institution but one with diverse ecclesiastical views.

A Different Approach to Life and Politics
The popular church is an alternative approach to the official church's style of relating to social issues. The priests and nuns who worked in the church's social welfare programs faced social problems directly and had little choice but to become active critics of government policies. As in Bolivia and Central America, most of the leaders of the Dominican popular church tended to be foreign-born religious priests. For example, Fr. Lucas Lafleur, MSC, a Canadian, founded Plan Nagua in 1970 as a nongovernmental organization that operated in the city of Nagua, in the northern Cibao region. This plan consisted of a series of projects whose objectives were to help peasants transport their goods to the market, to rebuild roads, to conduct sanitation campaigns, to build latrines, and to assist the Federación Dominicana de Cooperativas (Dominican Federation of Cooperatives).

The landowners of the area opposed the activities of Fr. Lafleur, who supported peasant land claims. Some of the peasant demonstrations turned violent, and, at least on one occasion, angry peasants occupied the parish's temple, despite Fr. Lafleur's objections. The police intervened, arrested protesters, and threatened Fr. Lafleur, accusing him of being a communist. In these circumstances, Plan Nagua offered assistance to get the peasants out of jail with the cooperation of progressive lawyers. Fr. Lafleur also visited peasants in jail and used his contacts with regional police commanders to get them out of jail, but he did not always succeed because the provincial governor herself thought that Fr. Lafluer was a communist (interview with Fr. Lafleur, June 13, 2000).

Various parishes administered by Jesuit priests were also targets of harassment. In Loma de Cabrera, located near Dajabón in the northern border with Haiti, Fr. Ramón Dubert, SJ, initiated a new style of identification with the parish community. When he went to Lomas de Cabrera (1966–1974), the area was teeming with problems. For example, in the community of El Pino, peasants were under constant threat of paramilitary bands and repression unleashed against the peanut growers, who asked for higher prices for their product. In addition, on his arrival, a prominent agrarian leader, Henry Segarra Santos, "disappeared" from the Dajabón military fortress in July

1969. Although Fr. Dubert only listened to the demands of the peasants, that was enough for the police to file a report accusing him of exciting the peasants who occupied the lands of Alfonso Mera, an important landowner in the area (Sáez 1990, 168–69).

In the parish of Dajabón, Fr. Ernesto Martín Fusté, SJ, learned that the regional military commander, Colonel José Demetrio Almonte Mayer, who claimed to be a devout Catholic and went to mass on Sundays, was involved in torturing prisoners. Fr. Martín called on Almonte Mayer several times in his office, but the latter was never available. After becoming aware of Colonel Almonte Mayer's reputation as an agent of repression, Fr. Eladio Pastor, SJ, said that in good conscience, he could not give him Holy Communion. This became a public issue, with people showing signs in front of the parish calling for "No Communion for Colonel Almonte Mayer." The conflict between the Jesuits and Colonel Almonte Mayer was not limited to the issue of Holy Communion but to local authorities interested in taking away the Colegio Agrícola San Ignacio de Loyola from the Jesuits, a technical school they founded and had administered for over three decades. In the end, the Jesuits had to give Holy Communion to Colonel Almonte Mayer and Fr. Martín had to leave Dajabón (Sáez 1990, 170–73).

A more dramatic case was that of Fr. Sergio Figueredo, SJ, who was not permitted to return to the country after a short stay in Puerto Rico. Fr. Figueredo was a well-known figure in Santo Domingo because of his critical newspaper and magazine articles and his appearance on television. Along with Figueredo, Fr. Gratiniano Varona, OP, was also not allowed to return home. Both were highly involved in political issues. Figueredo worked in Santo Domingo, where he criticized government social policies and human rights violations. Varona worked in the eastern province of Higuey, where he supported landless peasants who occupied uncultivated lands as a way of pressuring the government to implement agrarian reform in the region.

As a result of these governmental actions, eighteen religious organizations protested and issued a joint declaration criticizing repression of foreign priests. They also called on the government to stop its repression against the people and the church. These organizations pressured the bishops who identified with the modernizing orientation of pastoral action within the CED to ask that President Balaguer allow the priests to return home. Subsequently, the hierarchy did so (Ruiz Bergés 1987, 69). However, neither Varona nor Figueredo were able to continue their social work.

Figueredo's television program was suspended for three months after he returned because of pressure from business groups who did not like his criticism. After consulting with the CED, Msgr. Polanco Brito recommended that the Jesuits transfer Figueredo to another country, which suggests that they, too, were uncomfortable with his public position. It seems that Figueredo did not have much support within the Jesuit community either. Thus, he went to Chile to finish his studies. Msgr. Luciano Storeno, the nuncio, joined Polanco Brito stating, "the best for everyone would be that he stay in Chile, where, according to him, the government is creating the best conditions" (Sáez 1990, 131–32). In an unprecedented break with his recent past, Fr. Varona, in 1970, accepted a post as first lieutenant in the national army, suggesting that he must have accepted disciplinary actions recommended by higher church authorities.

The pressure from priests continued in the 1970s through letters, protests, and, in some cases, allowing the occupation of churches. For example, on February 24, 1970, forty-seven priests of the Archdiocese of Santo Domingo signed a document in which they said, "The country is in a state of violence and political turmoil that we should avoid." They also said that they were going to "neither speak nor write or counsel people on their rights to express themselves as citizens in the next elections." They added that they were not going to "give mass or give blessing that might be interpreted to favor any candidate" (Ruiz Bergés 1987, 76). Msgr. Beras Rojas said that the document signed by the priests did not reflect the position of the CED. That way, the hierarchy avoided any association with dissenting priests or groups that wanted to distance the church from the existing power structure. The hierarchy was also aware that this was a relatively small number of priests, who were located mostly in the Archdiocese of Santo Domingo.

The popular church was not limited to priests who denounced political oppression. It also included laypeople who had either participated in the PRSC or in other Catholic organizations. In 1969, after reflecting on the meaning of the Medellín conclusions, a group of clergy and lay Catholics issued a document that called for the formation of the Movimiento de Cristianos Comprometidos, MCC (Movement of Committed Christians) This group was the Dominican equivalent of Christians for Socialism in Chile, Priests for the Third World in Argentina, and the National Office of Social Information in Peru. Among other things, the MCC called for ending the concordat, dismissing the military chaplain, rejecting the blessing of state-sponsored ceremonies, stopping the collection of money to build monumental temples, increasing lay participation in the decisions of the church, reevaluating the role of Catholic schools, and elaborating a catechesis conducive to Christian commitment (Wipfler 1980, 275). This group, however, did not have much influence on the Dominican hierarchy.

Nuns also played a very important role in response to the repressive regime of Joaquín Balaguer. For example, the radicalization of the Adrian Dominican Sisters did not end with their support for the war wounded in 1965. In 1973, the congregation decided to donate the Hermanas del Colegio de Santo Domingo, an elite Catholic school, to the Archdiocese of Santo Domingo. The sisters questioned whether the religious women who taught at the colegio could serve and also respond to the issues of poverty and social justice that the poor and oppressed suffered in Santo Domingo. In fact, they hired a Colombian consulting firm to conduct a thorough study of the educational mission so that they would have sufficient information to make their decision. The sisters questioned the motives of middle- and upper-middle-class parents and students. Did they select the colegio for its prestige, or were they concerned with social justice? After much dialogue concerning the impossibility of converting middle- and upper-middle-class youths into real committed Christians and social agents of change, the Adrian Dominican Sisters decided to donate the colegio to the archdiocese as their contribution to the Dominican people. A few years later, the sisters abandoned their residence to work in the poorest communities (Ruiz Bergés 2001, 30).

Another important case was that of the Daughters of Charity, who lived at the hospital in San Francisco de Macoris, a city in the northern Cibao Valley. They had complete control of the hospital in 1971, when they began to assess their work with the community. They concluded that they had to leave the institution and integrate themselves into the community, believing that if they wanted to work in conditions of equality and poverty, they had to "return to the source" and be faithful to their calling. "They felt that they could not serve from the structures of power, that it was not sufficient to work for the poor, it was necessary to live among them, with them, and, when conditions permit, just like them" (Ruiz Bergés 2001, 55).

A similar case was that of the Sisters of Cardinal Sanchas. They decided to work in Gualey, a barrio near Guachupita and Los Guanduales, where the Jesuits had established themselves, too. These sisters also went to work in the countryside to collaborate in the rural pastoral work. Apostolic houses were established in Jánico (1970), near Santiago in northern Cibao, and in Enriquillo (1971) in the southern region of the country. As with priests, the number of nuns participating in the popular church was relatively small.

The experience of both priests and nuns during Balaguer's twelve years in office demonstrates that the Dominican popular church movement within the church mirrored the larger reality of the Latin American church. Balaguer's security forces did not kill any priests or nuns, death and deportation were constant threats. As in Bolivia and Central America, the Dominican popular church "brought fresh air" into the church and showed the people that the church could associate itself with the downtrodden. Nevertheless, the Dominican popular church movement was incapable of building a strong network among the laity and did not have much influence on the hierarchy.

Unlike Bolivia or Guatemala, where a number of bishops supported the popular church, the Dominican popular church could not count on a dedicated bishop who would support it and speak on its behalf at the CED. Msgr. Pepén of La Altagracia and Roque Adames of Santiago expressed support for the initiatives of their priests, but did not lend their support to the popular church. The Dominican case resembles that of Nicaragua, where only Msgr. Octavio José Calderón y Padilla (1947–1970) supported the CEBs, or that of El Salvador with Msgr. Luis Chávez y González (1938–1977), and subsequently Msgr. Oscar Arnulfo Romero (1977–1980) and Arturo Rivera y Damas (1983–1994).

Fr. Sergio Figueredo, SJ, lamented that whatever support the popular church received from the hierarchy was short lived. In 1970, he was perceptive in describing how the popular church movement was short-circuited:

> It must be recognized that 1969 was the *peak year* in the relationship between the church and the Dominican *people*. But in 1970, suddenly and unexpectedly, this weak but existing line of progress and commitment that marked our church ended abruptly. This line of progress had started during the Revolution of 1965, in which Nuncio Clarizio played an outstanding role. It turned into an *attitude* of increasing *indifference* regarding the human problems that afflict the Dominican people. The church hierarchy gradually accommodated the dominant economic, political, and military powers. This occurred precisely in a moment of profound national crisis, which demanded that the church make a firm, decisive, and vigorous defense of *human rights*!
>
> This is not the time to examine in detail the concrete causes that regrettably produced this lamentable regression of the Dominican church. It suffices to say that after the first few months of 1970, the image that our church is projecting to the people is that of a community which is gradually absent from national reality, tightly linked to the government, present in too many official events, and above all, skillfully used by sectors lacking social consciousness who feel satisfied "having conquered, once more, an old ally." (Figueredo 1971, 12)

Despite lack of support from the hierarchy, the popular church offered an alternative voice to the official church in the 1970s. As a high school student, I saw how priests worked with the youth in Licey, Santiago, how they strengthened ties with youth organizations, and how they were even willing to risk their lives to rescue students persecuted by the police. Similarly, the Hermanos de la Salle and scores of religious and diocesan priests left a lasting legacy among the youth that made them better persons. In sum, the popular church inaugurated a different style of relating to society and politics, which enables the entire church to enhance its legitimacy and credibility.

The Ecclesiastical Base Communities

The popular church as a protest movement tells only half of the story of the liberation movement within the church. The second part consists of the development of the ecclesiastical base communities, or CEBs. Frei Betto, the noted Brazilian theologian, defined these communities as

> small groups, organized around a parish (urban) or chapel (rural) and initiated by lay men, priests or bishops. These are communities because they bring together people with the same faith, belong to the same church and live in the same region. Motivated by their faith, these people live together and discuss issues that deal with their survival such as housing, struggle for better living conditions, desires and liberating hopes. They are ecclesiastical because they belong to the church as basic nuclei of communities of faith. People who work with their hands integrate these communities and this is what makes them base communities (popular classes). (Betto n.d., 10)

CEBs should not be confused with popular organizations that are autonomous from the church and whose objectives are completely secular. CEBs are a special way of living the Christian faith in the midst of secular life; that is, they are people who are brought together fraternally and guided by the word of God. If the CEBs were confused with popular organizations, they would lose their ecclesiastic identity. They were a new type of organization composed of people who had a novel way of looking at the world and life. They claimed to live the gospel according to the perspective of Vatican II and proposed a new style of the church that was not associated with civil authorities.

These communities recognized that they had to make a contribution to society through constructive criticism of civil authorities, proposing dialogue as a method of resolving pressing demands that affected poor urban and rural dwellers. Thus, it was fundamental for CEB members to work with others in the community to seek solutions to public issues. Unlike traditional conservatives or modernizers who were tightly linked to civil authorities, the new style of church proposed by the CEBs demanded that the state fulfill its duties and the church become the "voice of the voiceless." The CEBs proposed participation of laymen and -women in the decision-making process in the church.

The novelty of the CEBs attracted the attention of priests and nuns, as well as laymen and -women in Latin America. The success of the CEBs depended on the support they received from bishops. The episcopal conferences throughout Latin America supported the emergence of CEBs, but the actual development of the communities varied depending on the commitment of local bishops. The bishops who identified with the popular church supported CEBs wholeheartedly. Among the main supporters of the CEBs in Latin America were Helder Camara in Recife, Brazil; Méndes Arceo in Cuernavaca, Mexico; Samuel Ruiz in Chiapas, Mexico; Jorge Manrique in La Paz, Bolivia; and Oscar Romero in San Salvador, El Salvador.

The experiment of the CEBs in the Dominican Republic began in the early 1970s, when a group of Jesuit priests decided to move to Guachupita, a poor barrio in the northern section of Santo Domingo. Before the move, the group of five priests (Frs. Tomás Marrero, José Fernández Olmo, Jaime González Vallejo, Benjamín González Buelta, and Jorge Cela) went to study for a year at the Lumen Vitae Institute in Brussels, Belgium, in 1971. The Lumen Vitae Institute is an international institution that gives special preparation to missionaries who go to Latin America, Africa, and other parts of the world. Many of the professors who taught at the institute had been at the Vatican II council and were proponents of the emerging liberation theology.

The priests' preparation consisted of designing a project for insertion into a poor urban community in Santo Domingo. Fr. Tomas Marrero recalls that they wrote hundred of pages, but the project consisted, basically, of having no project at all because it had to be developed within the community. "The people of the community had to tell us how we could insert the administration of the church into their neighborhood" (interview with Fr. Marrero, July 10, 2001). The priests returned to Santo Domingo and on October 12, 1972, they moved to Guachupita where they had rented an apartment in a building constructed by the government. Ten years later, Fr. Benjamín González Buelta recalled:

> The insertion into the community was sort of a material exigency for us because it had to make our solidarity with the cause real and comprehensible. In some respects, we were poorer than the people. We reviewed each step we took and carefully examined our expenses. We subjected ourselves to a complete reeducation. We even wanted to learn to entertain ourselves as poor people did. (González Buelta cited in Sáez 1990, 187–88)

The priests' experiences show that they were middle-class people who decided to live and work with the poor, where they expected to develop meaningful CEBs. Fr. Jorge Cela acknowledged this when he said of their time in Guachupita: "We are not Dominicans . . . we only know the Dominican elite, we have an international culture which we learned during our education . . . and we must orient ourselves towards the people, not towards an elite enveloped into a universal culture" (Cela cited in Sáez 1990, 85).

If we recall the political context in which the Jesuit priests were inserting themselves in Guachupita—Balaguer's repressive campaign was in full swing against those who questioned his political tactics—this was not an easy task. They were foreigners, and the people themselves began to ask themselves what these white people were doing in a poor barrio. Later, they noticed that the secret police were observing their activities, and the official political party, the Reformist Party, would accuse them of being leftists.

Despite these and other problems, their work went on, and from 1974 to 1978, the group experienced modest growth as new priests and professed religious women joined them. During this time, they had an organization of five parishes and had developed work methods in which laypeople actively participated. Members of the CEB would come together and work with the priests to discuss the gospel and the type of questions they wanted to be raised at Sunday mass.

Slowly, people began to take more responsibility in the parish, and authentic communities developed. This commitment was not limited to living a Christian life (i.e., having strong faith, attending Sunday mass, and taking Holy Communion). Living as part of a CEB also demanded a degree of commitment to help others. The CEBs raised people's level of social consciousness, which, in turn, led them to address public issues, such as demanding that civil authorities repair schools and buy seats for students. This was the case, for example, in the school of Jobo Bonito in Guachupita, where Fr. Marrero was the principal. The parents went to the Ministry of Education and to the president to demand seats, blackboards, office paper, and so on. (interview with Fr. Marrero, July 10, 2001).

The Jesuits laid the groundwork for the development of the CEBs in Santo Domingo. They created working *equipos comunitarios* (community groups) whose pastoral action went beyond welfarism and the sacraments. By the late 1970s, they had some twenty working community groups that were led by *animadores* (coordinators) who sought to link the Word of God with the reality in which they lived (Sáez 1990, 190). Through the 1970s and the 1980s, neither the government nor the Catholic hierarchy felt comfortable with the community work of the CEBs. Most of the bishops perceived that the CEBs worked too closely with leftist political organizations. Nevertheless, the CEBs began to build bridges with the poor of the barrios and thus strengthened both the spiritual and human dimension of the church's mission. The experience was limited to the northern barrios of Santo Domingo, but the network of CEBs later expanded to the other areas of the city and, in a limited way, to other parts of the country.

Conclusions

The U.S. defeat of the revolution of 1965 and the restoration of the authoritarian features of the Dominican state by the Balaguer regime provided the framework for reinsertion of the Catholic Church into the mainstream of society and politics. The Balaguer regime is the fundamental factor that distinguishes the Dominican Republic from Bolivia and Central America. Aided by the United States, Balaguer was able to consolidate an authoritarian regime that kept the social democratic opposition at bay for twelve years and crushed the remaining left-wing groups. It is worth recalling that in Bolivia neither the military nor the nationalists were able to bring the revolutionary left under their hegemony. Similarly, in Nicaragua the Sandinistas held power for ten years and still constitute a formidable political opposition. In El Salvador, the FMLN negotiated a peaceful solution to the civil war and turned itself into a mainstream social democratic party and still identifies itself as part of the democratic left. Likewise, in Guatemala, the revolutionary guerrillas led by the URNG negotiated a solution to the civil war and integrated itself to mainstream politics as well.

In all these cases, revolutionaries left a legacy of struggles and political gains that one cannot find in the Dominican Republic. This explains why the Dominican popular church did not become viable as it did in Bolivia and Central America. It also explains why the Dominican Catholic hierarchy could ignore the popular church and reincorporate itself into the mainstream of politics. Notwithstanding this lack of recognition, the Dominican popular church and the CEBs offered an alternative approach to society and politics.

Like its Bolivian and Central American equivalents, the Dominican church began to reintegrate itself into the mainstream of society as a political mediator. In its early years of reincorporation, the Dominican church resembled that of Nicaragua during the Sandinista years in power. Like Nicaraguan church officials, the Dominican hierarchy identified with the power elite so they could not serve even as mediators. It was the papal nuncio, Emanuelle Clarizio, who took up the task of mediating during the revolution of 1965. It was only after the retirement of some pre-Vatican II clergy and new bishopric appointments that Polanco Brito could become a mediator of political conflicts.

The mediations of Clarizio and Polanco Brito legitimated the reincorporation of the church into Dominican society and politics, but at the cost of helping consolidate an authoritarian state. Many recognized that Clarizio was a great diplomat and a "friend of the people" who was concerned about issues of social justice, but the Constitutionalists could not help but see him as part of the established order that sought their defeat. Polanco Brito earned considerable national recognition because of his mediations in the kidnappings of diplomats and the arrangement for the release and subsequent exile of political prisoners. Nonetheless, his well-intended actions significantly strengthened Balaguer's repressive regime. In any case, Clarizio and Polanco Brito laid the groundwork for the church to become the mediator par excellence in contemporary Dominican society.

Notes

1. This chapter draws on extensive interviews with the following church scholars José Luis Sáez, Jorge Cela, Antonio Lluberes, Franklyn Pimentel, Antonio Camilo González, José Luis Alemán, Pablo Mella, José Francisco Arnáiz, Abrahan Apolinario, Margarita Ruiz, Fernando Ferrand, José Luis Guigni, Fausto Rosario Adames, and Juan Bolivar Díaz Santana.

2. José A. Moreno reports in his book (1970, 66) that he lived in a house at Independencia Avenue located in an upper-middle-class sector of Santo Domingo and not in Manresa as reported to me by Fr. Marrero.

3. In the 1970 presidential elections, Balaguer ran against two small parties: Movimiento de Integración Democrática Anti-releccionista, MIDA (Movement of Democratic Integration), presided over by Augusto Lora, and the Partido Quisqueyano Demócrata, PQD, led by Elías Wessín y Wessín. In these elections, Balaguer officially received 57 percent of the vote; MIDA and PQD combined received 29.8 percent. The remaining 13.2 percent was distributed among four smaller parties (Hartlyn 1998, 113; Ruiz 1987, 75). The PRD, the only credible opponent in these elections, withdrew in protest of the massive repression waged against its leadership and party members.

In 1974, Balaguer met a more serious challenge because the PRD formed a powerful coalition that included both right- and left-wing parties. As noted below, the church hierarchy—mostly through the office of Msgr. Polanco Brito—played a key role mediating to bring the PRD's coalition and Balaguer to the negotiating table. However, these negotiations failed because the PRD coalition withdrew two days before Election Day, May 16, 1974. Balaguer had run against a tiny political party, which gave the election a veil of legality, and officially received 84.6 percent of the vote; his opponent, Luis Homero Lajara Burgos of the Partido Democrata Popular (Popular Democratic Party) received 15.3 percent (Ruiz Bergés 1987, 166). Balaguer was reelected in both elections, but his legitimacy was seriously tarnished because the credible democratic opposition withdrew from the electoral races.

4. Although S. Antonio Guzmán, the PRD candidate, had won the presidential and congressional elections (Guzmán, Balaguer, and Bosch received 51.7 percent, 42.2 percent, and 1.1 percent of votes, respectively; the remaining 5 percent went to smaller parties) (Espinal and Hartlyn 1999, 484), he had to negotiate a deal with Balaguer, known as "fallo histórico"(historical decision) whereby Balaguer gave up the presidency in exchange for the control of Congress. The PRD gave Balaguer four provinces where it had won so Balaguer's party could have a majority in Congress.

5. Clarizio left the country on July 10, 1967, and moved to Canada where the Vatican had named him apostolic delegate. On June 14, 1969, he was appointed archbishop tit. of Anzio and charged with the Pontifical Pastoral on Migration and Tourism (Sáez 2005, 2).

6. An accomplished church historian and academic, Polanco Brito (1918–1996) was the founder (1962) and first president of the Pontificia Universidad Católica Madre y Maestra. He kept a diary where he described his role on the Crowley kidnapping. The diary is included in a volume entitled *Documentos sobre el Secuestro del Coronel Donald J. Crowley, 1970* (Polanco Brito 1970a). As noted in the bibliography, Polanco Brito collected newspaper clippings on the activities of the church in Dominican society. He collected numerous volumes of newspaper clippings that stretch back to the 1940s. These volumes, his personal archives, and library are housed at the Central Library of the Pontificia Universidad Católica Madre y Maestra in Santiago, Dominican Republic.

7. I inquired in Dominican left-wing circles about the circumstances in which Maximiliano Gómez died. When he was killed, Gómez was accompanied by Mirian Pinedo, the wife of Otto Morales, the second-most-important leader of the MPD. Pinedo survived asphyxiation, but she was later kidnapped and her body torn apart. Some believe that a paid CIA agent who infiltrated the group was responsible for this mysterious death; others believe that it was the product of political and ideological rivalries within the group. I have not been able to find any substantial account based on documents that would explain how this incident took place. It may be necessary to travel to Belgium to look at police records to find out the results of a police investigation.

8. Polanco Brito, for example, had opposed the occupation of the cathedral in Santo Domingo in 1969 and even issued a letter calling for the police to prevent protestors from using the Catholic temples for political ends. Striking workers from Metales Dominicanos (Dominican Metals) had occupied the cathedral of Santo Domingo and some paintings were damaged during the occupation. The workers issued a communiqué explaining the agent provocateurs had done it and that they opposed such actions (Polanco Brito 1969, 22–23).

CHAPTER FOUR

Mediator par Excellence

The transition to democracy and the socioeconomic transformations that occurred in Latin America in the 1980s provided the framework for church participation in political mediation. It was a turning point in the reformation of all political actors, particularly in the ways they related to the state. In common with other social and political actors in the region, the Catholic Church faced formidable challenges as it sought to redefine its political role. This chapter looks at the church's reincorporation into the mainstream of Dominican politics in the context of transition to democracy and economic change. In a period teeming with social and political conflicts, the church deepened its commitment to political mediation and consolidated its relationships with the state.

This chapter is made up of four sections. The first one briefly examines the Dominican transition to democracy and the process of socioeconomic transformation to provide the context in which the church carries out its functions. The second focuses on the institutional expansion of the church and how this enabled it to have a greater presence in society. The third looks at public funding and the church: it demonstrates that throughout the democratic transition, regardless of which political party was in office, the church received funding. The final portion returns to the issue of mediation and examines the role of the church in the tripartite dialogue and the elections of 1986 and 1994. I argue that the fragility of Dominican democracy, the socioeconomic transformation of the 1980s, and threats from below provided the occasion for the reinsertion of the church into the mainstream of Dominican politics and society as the mediator par excellence.[1]

The Dominican Transition to Democracy

The type of regime that emerged from the Dominican transition was a delegative democracy. This type of democracy

> rests on the premise that whoever wins the election to the presidency is thereby entitled to govern as he or she sees fit, constrained only by the hard facts of existing power relations and by a constitutionally limited term of office. The president is taken to be the embodiment of the nation and the main custodian and definer of its interests. The policies of his government need bear no resemblance to the promises of his campaign—has not the president been authorized to govern as he (or she) thinks best? (O'Donnell 1994, 59–60)

Delegative democracy reinforces the authoritarian features of the state in societies where the chief executive traditionally exercises an incredible amount of power. Ruling by decree (*decretismo*) was the norm in most Latin American nations. The neoliberal presidents of the 1980s felt quite comfortable with the institutions of delegative democracy because they enabled the presidents to issue decrees, bypassing national congresses. These types of presidents spoke as democrats, but when it was time to apply the recommendations of the International Monetary Fund (IMF), they forgot campaign promises and implemented policies that restructured the economy and left the basic needs of the population unattended.

Unlike most Latin American nations, the Dominican Republic did not have a military regime that held power for nearly two decades. Nonetheless, the regime was authoritarian, and although it held elections every four years, these were neither free nor fair. As noted in chapter 3, the collapse of the prices of Dominican exports, the election of Jimmy Carter, and a massive social and political movement that supported S. Antonio Guzmán Fernández, the PRD candidate in the 1978 elections, forced Balaguer out of office.

This was a new dawn for Dominican society, and it increased expectations for change. However, Guzmán Fernández and his successor, Salvador Jorge Blanco (1982–1986), were unable to go beyond cosmetic changes, so they could not alter the basic design of the authoritarian regime. For example, they were powerless to introduce legislation to eliminate laws in the Dominican Constitution that granted indefinite reelection of the president, allowed for the concentration of power in the hands of the executive, or reformed the Central Electoral Board. Balaguer's control of the Senate (1978–1982) and political divisions within the PRD (1982–1986) inhibited these types of legislation. In these circumstances, Guzman Fernández and

Jorge Blanco ruled by decree and further weakened institutions they had promised to modernize and consolidate.

Today the regime remains a delegative democracy that inhibits the modernization and consolidation of political institutions. Despite advances of basic democratic freedoms, the institutions of democracy remain weak and fragile, which is why the mediation of the Catholic Church has become an integral part of the Dominican political system

Economic Changes in the 1980s and 1990s
The economic transformations of the 1980s and 1990s provided the social context for the transition to democracy and the reincorporation of the church as mediator in political conflicts. Dominican transition to democracy occurred in the context of a vast social and economic transformation. These changes were of three types, occurring at the same time: (1) transition from agro-export to a service economy, such as tourism; (2) rapid development of free-trade zones; and (3) increased remittances, as the 1980s and 1990s saw a dramatic increase in Dominican international migration. What follows is an analysis of how these changes impacted the state's abilities to perform in the context of a polarized society.

From Agro-Export to a Service Economy
The changing patterns of international consumption and the inability of the Dominican state to offer protection to local producers partly explains the remarkable decline in the export of sugar, cacao, tobacco, and coffee. In addition, beginning in the late 1970s, there was an increase in health awareness in the United States and Europe that eventually translated into far less consumption of what the republic exported. At the same time, corn syrup began to be used in the United States as a substitute for cane sugar. This meant that the United States imposed higher tariffs on foreign sugar to protect its own producers. Traditional exports gradually declined from a peak of $1,188 billion in 1981 to only $530 million in 1993. For example, the value of raw sugar dropped from $513 million in 1981 to $112 million in 1993 (Hartlyn 1998, 138). This pattern continues for all Dominican traditional exports.

The dramatic transformation of the Dominican economy meant thousands of workers were laid off in agriculture, forcing them to move to the already congested cities of Santo Domingo and Santiago, the country's two most important urban centers. In 1960, nearly 70 percent of the population lived in the rural areas and most of the labor force was engaged in agriculture. Over the last four decades, the situation reversed itself. Thus, by the late 1990s, around 70 percent of the population lived in urban settings and some

30 percent in the rural areas. A dramatic exodus of over a million people to the United States, the Caribbean islands, and Europe helped the economy significantly because those who left sent remittances home. Over the last thirty years, remittances have become a pillar in the Dominican economy.

The development of the tourism industry began in 1971 with the enactment of special legislation. Law 153-71, on the Promotion and Incentives to the Development of Tourism, provided the legal framework. For ten years, the tourism industry was completely exempt from incorporation taxation, import/export duties, construction permits, and income tax. In addition, it received significant economic support through loans that were channeled through Infraestructura Turísca (INFRATUR), an agency of the Banco Central de la República Dominicana (Central Bank of the Dominican Republic), whose objective was to promote the industry. The public funds used by INFRATUR to promote tourism reached 1.1 percent of the GNP (PNUD 2005, 64–88). Thus, the Dominican state invested heavily to promote the tourism industry and subsidize its growth in the early years.

The tourism industry had its fastest rates of growth in the 1980s and consolidated in the 1990s. The number of tourists grew from 600,000 in 1980 to 1.4 million in 1992.[2] Earnings from tourism increased from $206 million in 1981 to $877 million in 1991 (Hartlyn 1998, 140–43). This pattern continued through the end of the twentieth century (see web table 4A). Contrary to the free-trade zones (FTZs), whose contribution to the GNP was 2.3 percent in 2003, the tourism industry's contribution increased from 1.3 percent in 1980 to 6.8 percent in 2000. In terms of job creation, tourism trailed behind the FTZs. In 2003, the FTZs employed 5.2 percent of the economically active workforce, whereas tourism employed 5 percent (PNUD 2005, 76). In contrast, tourism makes a significant fiscal contribution to the state, whereas FTZs do not.

Free-Trade Zones

The principal new sectors in the Dominican economy included free-trade zones (FTZs), tourism, and remittances sent by Dominicans residing abroad. The first legislation to establish FTZs was approved by the National Congress in 1969–1970. Law 299 on industrial incentives provided a legal framework and protection. It turned FTZs into an economic sector that enjoys exemption from income taxes and duties. Despite these incentives, FTZs did not grow significantly until the 1980s. Dominican FTZs are really the result of the U.S. Caribbean Basin Initiative, created under President Ronald Reagan in 1982 to promote foreign investments in the region. This program catapulted exports from $117 million in 1980, to $517 million in 1988, to $1.7

billion in 1995 (Safa 1999, 2). The number of firms operating in the FTZs increased from 446 in 1997 to 531 in 2003. The active workforce employed by these firms increased from 1.2 percent in 1983 to 6 percent in 1991. FTZs consolidated throughout the 1990s, but they never experienced rates of growth comparable to those of the 1980s. From 1991–2003, rates of growth in exports were moderate, and by 2003 job creation had declined slightly to 5.2 percent of the active workforce. Despite all the fanfare about the FTZs, they had only increased the GNP by 2.3 percent in 2003 (PNUD 2005, 92–95).

Remittances

Remittances sent by Dominicans living out of the country are the third-largest source of income in the Dominican Republic. By the end of the 1970s, estimates of the numbers of Dominican immigrants ranged from 206,000 to 300,000.[3] Dominican emigration was dramatic in the next two decades, as registered migration increased from 220,131 in 1980, to 454,754 in 1990, to 732,299 in 2000[4] (PNUD 2005, 121, 124).

A significant number of Dominican migrants send remittances back to their relatives and make a vital contribution to the economy. Remittances rival earnings from tourism, and have increased from $427 million in 1988, to $528 million in 1992, to $1 billion in 1995 (Hartlyn 1998, 140–43). The contribution of remittances to the economy is comparable to those of the FTZs and tourism combined (see web table 4B). Further, remittances go directly to Dominican families and actually help more than any other sector of the economy to alleviate poverty.

The Process of Inclusion/Exclusion and External Pressures on the State

The inclusion of large numbers of women into the workforce and the reduction of the financial resources of the state are two important by-products of the transition from agro-exports to a service economy. Tourism and the FTZ zones opened new opportunities for low-income women. The number of women in the labor force grew from less than 10 percent in 1960 to 38 percent in 1990. In 1992, 60 percent of workers employed in the FTZ were women; 30 percent of workers in the tourism industry were women; and 19 percent of workers in agro-industry were women (Hartlyn 1998, 140–41).

As noted by Safa (1995), incorporation of women into the labor force has had important implications for gender relations. Working women have become less dependent on their husbands for their economic sustenance at the same time that employment for males has decreased. The cultural implications are also far reaching. For example, it is no longer surprising to find women working nightshifts in the tourism industry. In the 1960s, women working in these types of jobs were considered prostitutes, and middle-class parents would not allow their daughters to take such jobs. Today, however, working in the tourism industry or the FTZs is seen as a sign of economic independence and thus encouraged. These industries have also led to an increase in the number of people who study foreign languages, such as English, German, Italian, and French. Hotel and restaurant schools have also proliferated nationwide as the demands for middle-level management increased.

The new economy diminished the capacity of the state to extract resources from the fastest-growing sectors. Unlike agro-exports, which the state could easily tax at the ports, FTZs, by definition, do not pay taxes. The Dominican tourist industry is largely controlled by international hotels and tour operators, which means that the state cannot extract more than the agreed-on taxes. In the 1980s, the state continued to receive revenues through import taxation, but this also declined due to the changing international economic environment that demanded economic reforms. A state that needed to increase its revenues had no other choice but to accept the policy "recommendations" of the IMF.

Salvador Jorge Blanco (1982–1986) implemented IMF-inspired policies that increased social exclusion, and these met stiff resistance from the impoverished population. The new economic policies were announced while thousands of people were vacationing during Holy Week in 1984. On returning home, they found that the government had devalued the currency and significantly reduced their buying power. A week of riots followed, and the police reportedly killed over 150 people and arrested thousands nationwide. The riots were unprecedented, and the government responded with unusually harsh and repressive measures to control the situation (Cassá 1995; Pérez 1996; Pérez and Artiles 1992).

Jorge Blanco earned respect with the local socioeconomic elites and his international backers, but lost legitimacy in the eyes of those who elected him. These riots were not repeated during his period in office, but his successor, Joaquín Balaguer (1986–1990, 1990–1994), saw the emergence of a powerful social movement that organized frequent regional and nationwide strikes demanding wage increases, employment, and social services. These strikes paralyzed economic activities and, at times, threatened the nation's social fabric. Both the social and political elites viewed these social protests with concern.

Reduction in revenues made it difficult for the state to make its foreign debt payments. In the late 1980s, Balaguer refused to pay the foreign debt, arguing he would pay only according to what was possible. Foreign financial sources dried up, and in the early 1990s, he, too, was forced to implement IMF-style policies, which further reduced public spending. In the context of an expanding U.S. economy and increased foreign investments in late 1990s, the Dominican economy reached a significant macroeconomic stability and a degree of prosperity. But the implementation of IMF policies did not allow any government to substantially increase social spending and improve the lives of most poor people because the state was forced to pay its escalating foreign debt. This debt increased from $2,002 billion in 1980, to $4,372 billion in 1990, to $6,332 billion in 2004.[5]

The economic transformations of the 1980s produced significant social changes and a degree of modernization. These changes incorporated women into the labor force but resulted in a substantial reduction in state revenues. In addition, rather than propping up the institutions of democracy, the new changes helped consolidate a hybrid regime that combined authoritarian and democratic attributes. Dominican leaders have felt comfortable ruling by decree instead of seriously encouraging modernization and consolidation of the state. All of them have been more concerned with macroeconomic stability, at the cost of social polarization and widespread poverty. This has contributed to the development of a society based on social exclusion, where social contestation and political disagreement threaten the social fabric. These are the circumstances in which the Catholic Church reemerged in the 1980s with a nonpartisan strategy to deal with political conflicts. As a mediator, the church became a pillar of the Dominican political architecture, at times preventing endless political crises that could have resulted in bloodbaths.

Institutional Expansion of the Catholic Church

The massive changes experienced by Dominican society had a tremendous impact on the Catholic Church. The church had to make changes of its own to meet the new challenges posed by secularization and the consequent political and social pluralism. Rapid population growth, urbanization, and widespread poverty forced the church to expand and modernize so that it could deliver its religious message and contribute to the solution of problems resulting from socioeconomic transformation and the transition to democracy.

This section focuses on the institutional expansion of the Catholic Church in the Dominican Republic over the last forty years. First, it reviews the development of the Conferencia del Episcopado Dominicano, CED (Dominican Episcopal Conference), the growth and composition of the clergy, and the increase in the number of dioceses. Second, it shows that like the Bolivian and Central American churches, foreign-born religious priests played a vital role in the development of the Dominican church. Finally, it proposes that the enlargement of educational and welfare services expanded the basis of the church as a modern institution. In short, institutional development enabled the church to increase its efficacy, acquire greater visibility in society, and become a major political actor in national affairs.

The Consolidation of the National Church
The establishment of the CED laid the groundwork for national consolidation and modernization of the Dominican church. The first Latin American Episcopal Conference was held in Rio de Janeiro, Brazil, in 1955 and, a year later, the Dominican hierarchy founded the Dominican Episcopal Commission. This commission was the predecessor to the CED, which had its first plenary assembly in July 1963. As noted, Dominican bishops were active against the Trujillo dictatorship and subsequently criticized the Bosch administration. The CED has been noted for the numerous pastoral letters it has issued over the last forty years. It has reflected on numerous political and economic subjects, offered constructive criticism of public authorities, and delegated key bishops to mediate in political conflicts. In church matters, however, it followed in the path of the Bolivian and Central American churches that tried to build themselves up through the importation of foreign religious priests.

The institutional expansion of the last forty years depended on a significant immigration of religious and diocesan priests. These priests arrived in two important waves. The first occurred following the Cuban Revolution in 1959; religious Cuban priests emigrated and many went to the Dominican Republic. This immigration helped the Dominican church by reinforcing its presence at a time when it was small and understaffed. The significance of this immigration can be observed by noting that the *Catholic Directory of 1953* reported forty national priests and 127 religious priests. The church had 187 priests nationwide to serve to the religious needs of over three million people. The directory does not indicate whether native priests were diocesan or religious, but José Luis Sáez, SJ, a distinguished church historian, told me that most local priests were diocesans, and religious priests were generally foreign born (José Luis Sáez, interview with the author, June 26, 1998). The total number of priests had not varied much in the early 1960s, when the first massive immigration of priests arrived from Cuba. This new development was reported in the *Catholic Directory of 1963*, when it reported that 235 religious and 21 diocesans priests had immigrated to the country. It is notable that there were only 5 native religious and 64 native diocesans (See table 4.1).

Table 4.1. Classification of the Clergy into Diocesan/Religious and Nationality, 1936–1976

Priests	Diocesans Dominicans	Foreign Born	Totals	Religious Dominicans	Foreign Born	Totals	Total No. of Priests
1936	28	28	56		15	15	71
1963	64	21	85	5	235	240	325
1971	76	20	96	17	332	349	445
1976	116	385	501	25	366	391	892

Sources: *Boletín Eclesiástico de la Arquidiócesis de Santo Domingo* (1936, 7–12); Tomé (1963, 1965); Secretariado Nacional de Pastoral de Conjunto (1972); Instituto Nacional de Pastoral (1977).

The 1970s saw the second huge immigration, but this time it consisted mostly of diocesan priests. The *Catholic Directory of 1976* reported that 385 of the 501 diocesan priests were foreigners. It also reported that the number of religious priests had increased from 235 in 1963 to 366 in 1976. In 1976, there were 892 priests in the Dominican church, but only 141 were local (see table 4.1). The church's reliance on foreign priests in the Dominican Republic was significantly larger than in Bolivia and Central America. The Dominican church's dependence on an imported pastoral workforce continued through the 1980s, as illustrated by the importation of twenty-five female religious congregations and four male religious congregations (Lluberes 1998, 180). This increase indicates that the Dominican church had not been able to develop a strong local clergy that could provide services to the rapidly changing demographics in the country.

Foreign-born religious priests have been at the center of the institutional development of the Dominican church. Reliance on foreign nationals can be observed in at least two different ways: comparing the proportion of diocesan/religious priests by dioceses and by parishes. When making the comparison by diocese, one finds that religious priests are concentrated in Santo Domingo, the largest population center and the locus of wealth and power. In 2000, the Archdiocese of Santo Domingo had 268 religious and 87 diocesans. In contrast, the Archdiocese of Santiago had 30 religious and 52 diocesans. Similarly, the diocese of La Vega had 37 religious priests and 66 diocesans (see table 4.2).

Staffing parishes is one of the key contributions of foreign-born religious priests to the church. In smaller or recently created dioceses in the Dominican Republic, the proportion of diocesans to religious is more evenly distributed. For example, in 2000, the diocese of Barahona had eleven religious and fourteen diocesans, whereas San Juan de la Maguana had sixteen religious and sixteen diocesans. The other dioceses followed this tendency, except San

Table 4.2. Diocesan and Religious Priests by Diocese, 1993/2000

Name of Diocese	Foundation Date	Religious 1993	Religious 1996	Religious 2000	Diocesan 1993	Diocesan 1996	Diocesan 2000	Total Number of Priests 1993	Total Number of Priests 1996	Total Number of Priests 2000
Archdiocese Sto. Dgo.*	1953	182	278	268	62	111	87	244	389	355
Archdiocese of Stgo.**	1994	46	25	30	54	50	52	100	75	82
La Vega*	1953	42	38	37	29	40	66	71	78	103
La Altagracia	1959	12	15	17	12	16	22	24	31	39
San Juan de la Maguana***	1969	9	10	16	10	12	16	19	22	32
Barahona	1976	14	14	11	8	10	14	22	24	25
Baní	1978	28	14	16	6	13	12	34	27	28
San Francisco de Macoris	1986	11	11	14	23	29	40	34	40	54
Mao-Montecristi	1978	13	13	12	7	12	22	20	25	34
Puerto Plata ****	1997			4			17	0	0	21
San Pedro de Macoris****	1997			6			7	0	0	13
Total		357	418	431	211	293	355	568	711	786

Sources: Instituto Nacional de Pastoral (1993); Rafael Bello Peguero (1996).
*Diocese founded in 1511.
**Diocese elevated to archdiocese in 1953.
***Diocese founded as Prelature "Nullius"in 1953.
****These two dioceses were separated from the Archdioceses of Santiago and Santo Domingo and priests were redistributed. This separation explains the minor reduction in the number of priests in both archdioceses in 2000.

Francisco, which had fourteen religious and forty diocesans. This is largely because the territory of San Francisco used to belong to the Diocese of La Vega, which, over the years, has had the largest concentration of diocesan priests in the country. However, when we examine the number of parishes under the direction of religious priests by diocese in relation to the total number of religious and parishes, the presence of religious priests is indispensable in carrying out the church mission. Religious priests had appointments in 123 of the 285 parishes that existed in 1993 (see web table 4C).

The foreign clergy has helped train national priests in seminaries and thus reduced church dependence on the importation of priests. The result of this instruction is quite noticeable in the regional dioceses. In 2000, the Diocese of La Vega had 103 diocesans, of whom 66 were national diocesans and 37 were foreign (18 Dominicans and 19 foreign-national religious). San Francisco de Macoris had 40 native diocesans and 14 religious (7 nationals and 7 foreigners). Similarly, the Archdiocese of Santiago had 52 diocesans, of whom 49 were national citizens and only 3 were foreigners (see table 4.3). The remaining smaller dioceses have an almost even distribution. However, the Archdiocese of Santo Domingo tips the balance because it has the majority of religious priests, who generally tend to be foreign nationals.

Msgr. Francisco José Arnáiz, former secretary of the CED, told me that in 2000 foreign nationals constituted around 60 percent of the total clergy. However, he was not able to specify the distribution by nationality in the Archdiocese of Santo Domingo (interview with the author, June 26, 1998). In any case, Arnáiz's estimate and the data compiled in table 4.3 reveal a strong pattern of growth in the local clergy. In 2000, there were 786 priests serving in nine dioceses and two archdioceses. Again, this modality of development in the Dominican church is similar to that of Bolivia and Central America, where foreign-born religious priests tended to concentrate in larger cities.

Unlike Bolivia and Central America, where a powerful minority of foreign-born religious priests participated in the popular church, those missionaries who went to the Dominican Republic were less likely to join the popular church. This may be because the Dominican Republic took in many immigrants from Cuba. Many of these priests were quite conservative and came to occupy important positions in the Dominican hierarchy, where their influence was noticeable.

Education and Welfare Programs
Education and welfare programs are two important areas of expansion in the Dominican church. The church has two types of educational institutions: religious and general.

Table 4.3. Distribution of Diocesan/Religious Priests by Diocese and National Origin in 2000

Archdioceses	Dioceses	Dominicans	Diocesans Foreigners	Totals	Dominicans	Religious Foreigners	Totals	Over All Totals
Santo Domingo*		49	3	87	75	15	268	355
Santiago		66	0	52	15	19	30	82
	La Vega	20	2	66	18	6	37	103
	Mao-Montecristi	8	8	22	6	8	12	34
	San Juan de La Maguana	7	7	16	8	8	16	32
	Barahona	19	3	14	3	8	11	25
	La Altagracia	3	4	22	1	16	17	39
	San Pedro de Macorís	12	0	7	4	2	6	13
	Baní	40	0	12	14	2	16	28
	San Fco. de Macorís	17	0	40	7	7	14	54
	Diócesis de Puerto Plata			17	0	4	4	21
TOTAL		241	27	355	76	87	431	786

Source: Author's interviews with Dominican bishops in the summer of 2000.
*The staff at the archives of the Archdiocese of Santo Domingo did not have accurate data on the nationality of priests serving in the archdiocese.

Religious Education
The number of seminaries and seminary students has grown significantly over the last two decades. The number of seminaries increased from five in 1995 to eight in 1996. Seminary students are distributed in different minor seminaries and in Tomás Aquino Seminary in Santo Domingo, the only major seminary in the country. The number of seminary students increased from 252 in 1985 to 400 in 1996, but most of them are at a minor seminary level. Minor seminary students are potential candidates for the major seminary and hope to become Catholic priests (see table 4.4). An increase in the number of ordained priests will surely diminish the church's dependency on the importation of foreign priests, but this is still a goal to be achieved.

The growth of Catholic educational institutions has been formidable. There are now four Catholic universities; one of them, the Pontificia Universidad Católica Madre y Maestra (PUCMM), is recognized as one of the best in the country. The growth of Catholic schools at the primary and secondary levels has been remarkable: the number of Catholic schools increased from 170 in 1977, to 194 in 1993, to 300 in 1996[6] (see table 4.4). These schools are a column upon which the Dominican education system rests.

General Education
Similarly, the church's welfare program in health care has expanded considerably. Church personnel have been involved running national hospitals since 1936 and they have increased over the years. In 1996, the church helped staff some 20 hospitals nationwide and provided services in 220 dispensaries. In both education and health care, the church plays an invaluable role providing basic services that the state is unable to. Unlike their equivalents in Bolivia and Central America, the expansion of church-sponsored educational institutions in the Dominican Republic show sustained growth through the last thirty years. Political instability in Bolivia and Central America explain, in part, the church's inability to produce stable development (see web table 2C).

The Dominican church developed a considerable technical infrastructure to spread its message to the population. This communication is conducted through Catholic radio stations, newspapers and magazines, houses of religious congregations, institutes, and, more recently, a television station (see table 4.5). Radio Santa María of La Vega began transmission in 1956 and became known throughout the nation because of its education programs in the Cibao Valley; today, five other Catholic radio stations broadcast in different regions. The proliferation of houses of religious congregations and religious institutes has also broadened the scope of the church pastoral work. As in all

Table 4.4. Educational and Welfare Assistance Programs

	1936	1953	1963	1965	1971	1977	1985	1993	1996
Seminaries	1	1	1	1	4	5	5	10	8
Seminary students	21	121				127*	252**	221	400***
Parishes	59	63	123	127	183	192	239	285	323
Universities			1	1	1	1	3	4	4
Educational institutions, primary and secondary	7	27	29	150	145	170	179	194	300****
Health centers	4		7	13		45	121	140	240
Hospitals	4	4	7	13	22	22	20	20	20
Dispensaries					13	23	101	120	220****

Sources: Secretariado Nacional de Pastoral de Conjunto (1972), later called Instituto Nacional de Pastoral (1977, 1985, 1993). The version of the 1953 directory used here was included in the 1993 directory. No author appears on the *Boletín Eclesiástico de la Arquidiócesis de S.D.* (1936, 1–12), Mariano Tomé elaborated the *Guía Eclesiástica de la República Dominicana* for 1963 and 1965, and *Rafael Bello Peguero for 1996).
**Situation of 1981, as reported by Msgr. Beras Rojas during his farewell homily. (Conferencia del Episcopado Dominicano, 1990, 422).
***Conferencia del Episcopado Dominicano (1998a, 301).
****Conferencia del Episcopado Dominicano (1998b).

of Latin America, there is a notable difference in the number of males and females who opt for a religious vocation in life. Table 4.5 shows that in 1993 there were 61 non-priest religious brothers and 1,493 religious women. In 1996, the number of men declined to 57, whereas the number of women increased to 1,545. All over Latin America, women are one of the main columns that sustain the church pastoral work, but they are invisible and seemingly powerless within the institution.

The enlargement of the pastoral workforce allowed the creation of new parishes throughout the Dominican Republic. As noted in table 4.4, there has been sustained growth of the number of parishes from the 1950s to the present. The number of parishes increased from 285 in 1993 to 323 in 1996. This pattern continued through the end of the 1990s and the beginning of 2000. In 1998, there were 434 parishes and 408 of them had a priest. web table 2B reveals that the Dominican church compares well with Bolivia and Guatemala in terms of number of parishes and parishes with priests. The churches of Nicaragua and El Salvador have lower numbers, but, in general, all these national churches saw a general increase in the number of parishes with priests.

In conclusion, institutional developments turned the Dominican church into a principal locus of power, with a capacity to respond to social and political crisis in areas in which the state was unable to provide the basic necessities. Religious, educational, and welfare work with the population allowed the church to emerge as a power to be reckoned with when examining Dominican social and political realities. The PUCMM offered a launching pad for the church to emerge as a credible political, social, and cultural actor in society.

The Church, Political Parties in Government, and Financial Resources

The concordat signed with Trujillo framed the relationship between the Catholic Church and the Dominican state. Regardless of what political party comes into the office, the Catholic Church receives public resources. Despite this legal prerogative, the amount of money the church received from the state from 1979 to 2000 declined steadily. During this period, the PRD presidents held office during two terms (1978–1986), the Partido Reformista Social Cristiano, (Reformist Social Christian Party[7]) two terms (1986 to 1994), and the PLD one term (1996–2000).

A caveat is necessary to explain how Dominican governments manipulate the National Budget. I use the data that appear in the national budget as an

Table 4.5. Mass Media and Religious Congregations

	1936	1953	1963	1965	1971	1977	1985	1993	1996
Newspapers and magazines	1	1	2	2		2	8	7	7
Radio stations			1	2	1	4	5	6	5
Non-priest religious brothers	8		98	212	99	102*		61	57
Religious women	75		835	1,153		1,320	1,476**	1,493	1,545
Houses of religious congregations	1		8	20	4	349	166	218	
Male rel. institutes	5	9		21	18	56	27		
Female rel. institutes	4	11		25	35	91	52	69	

Sources: Instituto Nacional de Pastoral (1977, 1985, 1993), Secretariado Nacional de Pastoral de Conjunto (1972), *Boletín Eclesiástico de la Arquidiócesis de S.D.* (1936, 1–12); Tomé (1963, 1965); Bello Peguero (1996).
*Includes the number of non-priest religious brothers and seminary students.
**Conferencia del Episcopado Dominicano (1990, 422).

indicator that there is an association between the Catholic Church, the dominant political parties, and the state.[8] It is hard to explain the strength of this association because of the discretionary manner in which Dominican presidents use the national budget. No one knows exactly how much money allocated for particular items are actually spent for what they were intended to be. Presidents switch items around the budget as they see fit.

It appears that the church received substantially less money during Balaguer's terms (1986–1994), but this is not necessarily true because of the methods used to manipulate the budget (see figure 4.1). In fact, the church received more money during Balaguer's two terms than at any other time in history. In these two terms, the Dominican government helped the church prepare for the five hundredth anniversary of the discovery of the New World and the Fourth Latin American Bishops' Conference of 1992 by launching a huge program of church construction and renovation (see table 4.6). These expenses do not appear in the church's regular budget because Balaguer assigned them through budgets of different ministries and special accounts controlled by the president's office.

In addition, Dominican presidents use their discretionary power to transfer public property to the church. These operations usually involve substantial

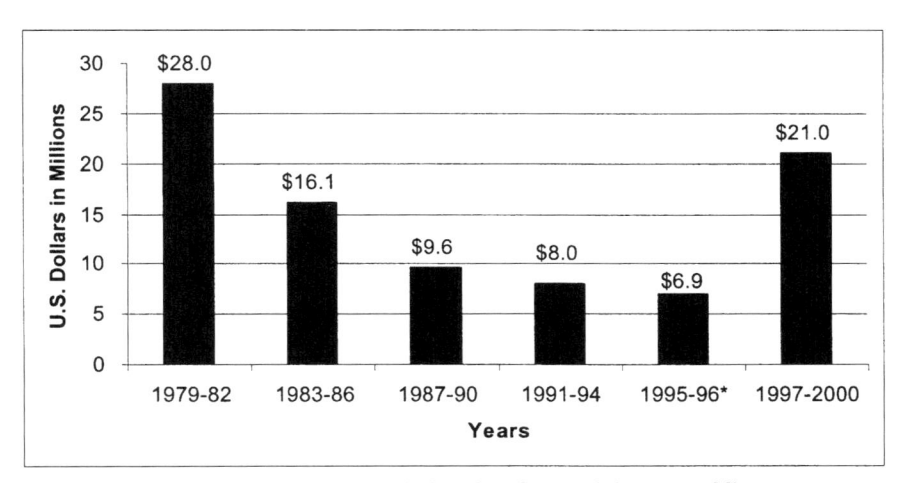

Figure 4.1. State Funding for the Catholic Church, Dominican Republic, 1979–2000
Source: Secretariado Técnico de la Presidencia/Oficina Nacional de Presupuesto, 1979–2000. Volume 1–21. These and subsequent calculations do not take inflation into account, which makes the numbers even more dramatic.
*Represents a two-year period rather than a four-year period.
**The exchange rates from 1979 to 1985 are based on the Mercado Extrabancario a la Venta (Unofficial Exchange Rate). Banco Central de la República Dominicana (1985). The exchange rates from 1985 to 2000 are annual averages and were published as "Tasas de Cambio Promedio para compra y venta de dolares estadounidenses." See Banco Central de la República Dominicana (2005).

Table 4.6. Construction and Renovations of Catholic Institutions by the Dominican State, 1986–1994

Archdioceses of Santo Domingo		Archdiocese of Santiago and other Dioceses	
Institutions	U.S. Dollars	Institutions	U.S. Dollars
House of San Pablo	3,504,818.20	Cathedral Santiago Apostol	3,058,024.37
Cardinal residence	1,977,310.91	Minor Seminary Saint Pious X	238,430.17
Cathedral tunnel	4,611,993.42	San Mauricio Martir Parish	261,032.17
Floors of Cathedral of S.D.	966,863.37	Pilar Constanzo Polytechnic	22,996.87
Mayor Seminary Saint Tomas Aquinas	1,403,040.48	Personal donation to a bishop	129,354.09
Christ the Savior Parish	693,989.98	Personal donation to a priest	126,584.19
Chapel Our Lady of Carmen	513,855.80	Minor Seminary Our Lady of Mercedes	459,969.54
Santa Teresa de Jesús Monastery	336,194.44	Minor Seminary of Santiago Rodríguez	263,909.17
Altar of the Columbus light house	348,970.62	Minor Seminary of Mao	11,627.50
Manresa Loyola residence	58,415.40	Minor Seminary Santo Cura de Ars	101,922.14
Nunciature	127,500.90	Cathedral of the Inmaculada Concepción La Vega	4,499,843.03
		Technological University of the Cibao	1,195,701.43
Subtotal	14,542,953.50	Hotel School of the PUCMM	1,375,339.00
		Cathedral of Santa Ana, SFM	531,601.11
		Basilica of Higuey	243,789.29
		Cathedral of Barahona	312,287.36
		Diocese of San Juan de la Maguana	122,447.36
		Subtotal	12,954,858.78
Total	27,497,812.29		

Source: This table is based on data compiled by Fausto Rosario Adames and published in *Rumbo*, July 27 to August 2, 1994. I converted Dominican pesos into U.S. Dollars based on the average of the exchange rate from 1986 to 1994. It is only an approximation because Adames does not provide data on a yearly basis. He only gives us totals for an eight-year period of what the Dominican state spent on church constructions and renovations. The dollar figure is provided to give the reader a general idea of what was involved in government allocations for the church.

amounts of money and do not appear in the national budget. While I was doing field research for this study, a knowledgeable member of the clergy told me that the church receives far more money outside the framework of the concordat than what is indicated on paper. This makes it difficult, if not impossible, to use government data to explain church-state relationships. Nevertheless, regardless of which political party holds office, the church collects its budgetary allocations and much more as needed.

The decline in regular budgetary allocations to the Catholic Church was principally due to substantial reductions in public spending in the 1980s and early 1990s, and to a lesser degree to ideological considerations (see figure 4.1). The PRD and the PRSC were willing to give funding to the church, but regardless of their political and ideological orientation, they had to cut funding. The Guzmán Fernández administration (1979–1982) gave $28 million to the Catholic Church whereas Jorge Blanco's administration (1982–1986) allotted it $16.1 million. This decline of over $10 million was because of the economic crisis Jorge Blanco faced. He had to sign an agreement with the IMF that required devaluing the peso and making deep cuts in social spending.

Similarly, Balaguer's allotment was significantly reduced to $9.6 million (1987–1990) and $8 million (1991–1994). Like Jorge Blanco, he continued to face economic problems and did not sign an agreement with the IMF until his second term. Balaguer was attentive to the political repercussions of these budgetary cuts and used his last term in office (1995–1996) to increase the church's regular budget to $6.5 million.[9] These increments in church allotments began a new trend, which strengthened during the administration of Leonel Fernández Reina (1997–2000). During his term, Fernández Reina raised the church's budget to $21 million (see figure 4.1 and table 4.7, where I offer a detailed description of government budgetary assignments to the church from 1979 to 2000).

These substantial additions were due to at least two important factors. First, Fernández Reina was aware that his party had not had a good relationship with the Catholic Church going back to the early 1960s when the hierarchy opposed Bosch's government. Bosch's relationship with the church was filled with misunderstanding and distrust. The hierarchy never accepted him because it disagreed with his liberal political thinking. Fernández Reina was aware of this and worked hard to obtain the support of the Catholic hierarchy. It is also important to remember that the PLD was still a small party in the mid-1990s. In fact, it ascended to power thanks to a political alliance with Balaguer. It needed to attract more support from key institutions and groupings in society. (See more regarding Fernández Reina's relationship

Table 4.7. State Allocation for the Dominican Catholic Church, 1979–2000

U.S. Dollars

Institutions of the Catholic Church	1979–82 (PRD)	1983–86 (PRD)	1987–90 (PRSC)	1991–94 (PRSC)	1995–96 (PRSC)	1997–00 (PLD)
1. Archdioceses and dioceses	227,611.35	235,838.25	1,331,914.13	701,927.07	354,808.86	2,204,641.91
2. Institutions of higher education	12,515,448.01	7,187,133.90	2,686,200.27	1,367,912.27	660,540.76	1,247,764.75
3. Polytechnic institutes	4,628,627.25	3,662,200.19	1,644,613.76	1,846,231.91	1,724,681.12	7,615,860.65
4. Schools	145,126.01	17,331.95	62,123.10	190,342.07	123,444.55	301,002.27
5. Seminaries	28,530.67	1,346.50	217,080.28	111,213.78	178,138.24	254,943.01
6. Parishes	19,020.45	33,071.30	121,901.55	282,777.68	174,558.22	1,205,217.50
7. Agencies (Cáritas, Cedail, and CRS)	1,635,561.87	803,292.93	358,769.56	177,331.89	79,544.90	123,097.59
8. Radio Stations	28,530.67	—	53,412.12	186,529.41	97,616.19	450,586.35
9. Associations	145,173.56	525,954.08	277,248.49	786,430.05	1,130,366.61	1,889,947.38
10. Hospitals	4,755.11	1,923.57	3,686.75	2,875.56	1,861.95	16,337.40
11. Medical Clinics	6,657.16	5,597.86	6,075.86	13,852.00	16,215.00	63,425.72
12. Organizations of religious	76,557.30	93,001.93	155,386.30	139,700.58	118,981.28	312,103.35
13. Asylum and assistance centers	155,539.71	126,798.09	219,725.78	461,415.85	550,115.86	1,761,806.30
14. Environmental organizations	8,363,786.08	3,421,609.43	2,533,049.03	1,802,483.18	1,686,026.89	3,563,107.35
Total	27,980,925.19	16,115,099.99	9,671,187.00	8,071,023.28	6,896,900.43	21,009,841.53

Source: Secretariado Técnico de la Presidencia/ Oficina Nacional de Presupuesto, 1979–2000. Volumes 1–21.
The 1995–1996 term represents a two-year period rather than a four-year period.
These and subsequent calculations do not take inflation into account, which makes the numbers even more dramatic. The exchange rates from 1979 to 1985 are based on the Mercado Extrabancario a la Venta (Unofficial Exchange Rates). See Banco Central de la República Dominicana (1985). The exchange rates from 1985 to 2000 are annual averages and were published as "Tasas de cambio Promedio para compra y venta de dolares estadounidenses." See Banco Central de la República Dominicana (2005).

with the evangelicals in chapter 6.) Second, Fernández Reina was able to afford these increments because the economic prosperity of the 1990s allowed him to.

That the church received governmental funds regardless of which political party was in power highlights the fact that it is accepted as one of the pillars that sustains society. The church no longer needs to openly take sides with a particular political party as it did in the early 1960s. It can now present itself as nonpartisan in a conflict-ridden society, where social and political groups need to affiliate themselves with larger political organizations.

The Emergence of the Church as Mediator par Excellence

Transition to democracy in the late 1970s eased political tensions and provided the background for the success of the modernizing orientation of the church. It is worth recalling that this church orientation proposes disengagement from direct, partisan politics in favor of mediating political and social conflicts. Nuncio Clarizio in 1965 and Msgr. Polanco Brito in the early 1970s were the national precursors of this orientation in the Dominican church. Their successful mediations demonstrated that the church could play a moderate role in politics. These accomplishments seem to have persuaded traditional conservative bishops to accept the new modality. The new democratic openings in society diminished the political denunciations of priests associated with the popular church, and many of them came to accept the modernizing orientation as suitable for Dominican reality. The CED pushed mediations in the 1980s and 1990s and it became official ecclesiastical policy.[10]

The church wanted to be recognized as a special actor that could offer a vision of man and society, while not compromising its principles. This framework, however, aligned it with the status quo and reestablished it as a pillar in the political architecture that sustains society. In these circumstances, the church could not claim neutrality vis-à-vis the political system, because it promotes liberal democracy, but it could assert that it was nonpartisan. This has made it possible for the church to fully reintegrate itself into the political system as a special sociopolitical actor whose leadership does not seek office, but the common good.

The Dominican church, like those in Bolivia, El Salvador, and Guatemala, has created a successful modernizing orientation that promotes political mediations. In all cases where the church mediates, one finds weak political institutions under considerable tensions. These tense circumstances are what brings the church to mediate political conflicts and, at the same time, allows it to *appear* to be above political differences. I stress the word appear because of the overlapping interests between the Catholic Church, the state, and the socioeconomic elite in each of the cases selected for study. For example, one can argue that as the church presses the opposition to negotiate, it helps the government regularize a conflictive situation, thus appearing to cooperate with both sides. Considering the influence of the Catholic Church, however, it is nearly impossible for it to be completely nonpartisan. Nevertheless, there is a solid group within the hierarchy that seeks a moderate and neutral role for the church.

The strategy for the full reincorporation of the Dominican church into the political system as a nonpartisan actor emerged on November 30, 1980. The hierarchy published a pastoral letter that outlined the role of the church in relation to government and politics:

> The church neither has nor abrogates a "political formula," but it does have criteria and principles according to which lay Christians should create feasible and correct political formulas. The church would rather offer a framework of a plurality of possible systems, regimes, models and projects, which are opened to lawful and careful human action to face the great challenge of the Continent and our country. The church does not opt for a system or party, but maintains itself free before all of them to opt for man only. It does not do it for opportunistic reasons, but to respect the autonomy of temporal realities, freedom, and the rights of man. At the same time, it urges its faithful laities to responsibly fulfill their unavoidable commitment with the temporal and political world. (CED 1990, 398–99)

This pastoral letter was published in the context of growing social tensions mostly due to social inequality and political exclusion. The business community, government, political parties, and press applauded the church hierarchy's decision to declare itself nonpartisan in a society where nearly everything is politicized. The letter was a signal to all political parties and social movements that the hierarchy was going to play a special role in national politics.

The Church and Mediations in the Dominican Republic

This section centers on the mediating efforts of the church concerning the tripartite dialogue that unfolded in the 1980s and the church's role in the elections of 1986 and 1994. Church participation in these negotiations turned it into the mediator par excellence in Dominican politics and strengthened its reintegration into national life.

The commitment of the church to playing a nonpartisan role moved from theory to practice in 1985, when the Episcopal Conference issued a pastoral letter that reflected on the riots that took place in 1984. These riots had a remarkable impact on a religious hierarchy that saw the social fabric of society under great threat. In the letter, the CED described a true state of anomie, reminding everyone that the poor—the vast majority of Dominicans—were right when they expressed their despair at their economic situations. They proposed dialogue as the key to resolve national issues and recommended a series of norms for the parties in conflict to come to agreements (CED 1985, 507–17). The Pastoral of Dialogue, as it became known, brought praise from the business community, the government, mainstream political parties, and the press.

Church participation in mediation is rather complex and it takes place at various levels of society. I focus on the political mediation sponsored by the Dominican Episcopal Conference through the Universidad Católica Madre y Maestra. This is a mediation that takes place at the national level with social and political organizations that have a nationwide presence. Shortly after the publication of the Pastoral of Dialogue in 1985, the Episcopal Conference recognized Msgrs. Agripino Núñez Collado and Francisco José Arnáiz as coordinators of the church's mediating efforts. The Universidad became a center for international conferences, policy discussions, and a meeting place for parties in conflict. The central idea of these meetings was to bring business, labor, and government together to discuss a series of issues. The participation of these three actors led the organizers of these meetings to call this process the Tripartite Dialogue. From the beginning, they were concerned with the following issues among others: labor, productivity, agrarian reform, social security, taxation, and strategies for dialogue. The first meeting took place in Jarabacoa in 1985, and many others meetings followed in Santo Domingo and at the Universidad in Santiago. In addition to being a forum to discuss public issues, these meetings were also meant to educate participants about the values of the culture of dialogue. International speakers were usually invited to discuss the mediation process elsewhere in Latin America and Spain (Núñez Collado 1993, 43–101).

Tripartite negotiations led to an important agreement in 1988 in which labor, business, and government agreed to extend social security benefits to all family members, revise tax laws, modify the minimum wage, reexamine various important articles in the labor code, include tripartite dialogue in government agencies, increase the pensions of retirees, and create a Permanent Secretariat of Dialogue. In 1990, the government of Joaquín Balaguer (1990–1994) agreed to sign a solidarity pact with both labor and business. He promised to fulfill the agreements of 1988 and to expand on a series of other issues that included balancing the national budget, implementing tributary reform, increasing wages for state workers, indexing the prices of basic goods, and expanding on a program of social assistance. As part of the solidarity pact, business promised to maintain the prices of basic goods for ninety days, increase wages, support the government fiscal reform, deliver dollars generated in international transactions to the government, and cooperate with labor. Labor promised harmonious relations with business, increased productivity, maintenance of public services, and defense of the public order. They promised to organize housewives to support the government, while the government agreed to submit legislation to the National Congress to ban monopolies and promised to create a follow-up commission to assure fulfillment of the pact (Núñez Collado 1993, 141–70).

Despite the enormous effort that went into producing these agreements, cosigners ignored most of them. For example, Balaguer signed the Tripartite Agreement of 1988 to buy time to show that he was not a recalcitrant ruler. Similarly, he signed the Pact of Solidarity in 1990 after he was declared the winner in a controversial election (he won by less than 1 percent of the vote against Juan Bosch, the candidate of the PLD). Bosch did not recognize Balaguer as the winner and called for public demonstrations to press Balaguer to resign, which he never did. Less than a month after his inauguration (August 16, 1990), Balaguer signed yet another agreement in which he made concessions that he could only fulfill partially. Neither business nor labor followed suit with all of their promises either, making the work of the Catholic Church mediators more difficult.

The government's inability to fulfill agreements it signed led many to argue that the tripartite dialogue was a failure. Msgr. Núñez Collado himself acknowledged that Dominican society lacked a culture of dialogue and the bare minimum for political accords. Despite these failures, he believed that the tripartite dialogue brought significant gains in the short run, such as balancing the budget, stopping the emission of money without hard currency in the national reserve, adjusting prices, implementing tributary reform, adjusting wages in the private and the public sectors, exempting wages from taxation, approving a social security law that expands family coverage, ensuring the approval of a new labor code, and promulgating the civil service law (Núñez Collado 1993, 161–69).

Church participation in promoting dialogue and mediation has not been a complete success, but it has secured a special place in the Dominican political system for itself. By the late 1980s, the church's mediators were a fact of life in Dominican politics. While this mediation was taking place at the national level, bishops mediated important conflicts within their dioceses and parish priests did the same at the local level. In the summer of 2001, I interviewed the eleven bishops of the country; they reported that Dominican society was so filled with social and political tensions that they could spend most of their time mediating social and political conflict rather than tending to their religious mission. These kinds of mediation do not receive the same level of coverage in the press as national mediations do, but they are important because they address local issues such as land tenure, agricultural credit, natural disasters, Haitian migration, government support to farmers, and tourism.

The archbishop of Santo Domingo, Nicalás de Jesús Cardinal López Rodríguez, stands out for his frequent comments on nearly every aspect of politics, economics, culture, society, and religion. After his appointment (1981), López Rodríguez became so active in political life that many thought that he was interested in becoming the vice presidential candidate in the 1986 elections. López Rodríguez denied these assertions, saying that he was committed to his vocation as a priest. Nonetheless, under his leadership the CED became one of the main pillars of the Dominican political architecture, while Núñez Collado and Arnáiz are recognized as the public personalities in charge of social and political mediation.

Mediation in Electoral Conflicts
The presidential elections of 1986 and 1994 were the two most important instances of church participation in electoral matters. In 1986, President Salvador Jorge Blanco appointed López Rodríguez to preside over the Commission of Electoral Advisers (CEA) to assist the Junta Central Electoral, JCE (Central Electoral Board). According to Dominican law, the JCE is an electoral tribunal that no other court can override. Local electoral experts and Balaguer himself recommended the appointment of López Rodríguez to the lead the CEA to ensure that the elections were free and fair. The CEA had a difficult job, because its members were appointed just a few days before the elections. Nonetheless, it provided the JCE with a list of technical issues that it had to address. The CEA's recommendations are indicative of the lack of appropriate management and institutional capacity of the JCE. Among other things, it made the following recommendations:

1. Prohibit admission to the main offices of JCE of unauthorized personnel.
2. Prohibit access to data-processing centers of unauthorized personnel.
3. Request two additional copies of the magnetic tape with the data fed to discs, programs, proceedings, and data related to the computation of votes. One of these copies should be kept in a vault outside the JCE.

4. Have the military police provide security to the director and deputy director of the computing center.
5. Ensure the presence of an adequate number of technical experts from the suppliers of computer equipment and air conditioners as well as an electric power generator in case of a blackout. (Document of the CAE/013/86, in Núñez Collado 1996, 168–76)

The institutional weakness of the JCE can be traced back to Balaguer's twelve years in office. Balaguer used the electoral court to reelect himself to office and to ensure that it remained subordinated to him by appointing judges who respected his political orientations. The government of Guzmán Fernández (1978–1982) was able to effect some reforms—for example, allowing all political exiles to return home, restoring democratic freedom, and retiring the most influential military leaders—but it was not able to design economic and social policies that could strengthen the fabric of society or consolidate political institutions such as the JCE. Similarly, the government of Salvador Jorge Blanco (1982–1986) did not make any significant attempts to strengthen the JCE as an institution. Popular mobilizations against implementing IMF recommendations and political divisions within his own party prevented Jorge Blanco from developing the institutions that could enhance the transition to democracy. This is why the CEA had to recommend the implementation of basic institutional procedures to the JCE.

Political divisions within the official party led Jorge Blanco to withdraw his support to Jacobo Majluta, PRD's presidential candidate. As president of the Senate, Majluta made sure that Jorge Blanco did not get approval for IMF international loans. Thus, when Jorge Blanco appointed the CEA at the recommendation of Balaguer, the main opposition candidate, Majluta, and his followers doubted their impartiality and reliability. They perceived that several members of the CEA supported Balaguer. As the electoral campaign came to an end, opinion polls indicated that the election was going to be close. According to one survey, Majluta of the PRD would receive 32 percent, Balaguer of PRSC 31 percent, and Bosch of the PLD 19 percent. The remaining 10 percent was still undecided (letter from Bernardo Vega to Núñez Collado, in Núñez Collado 1996, 186–87). Comparing the results of this survey to the final electoral results, we find that the PRD received 33.5 percent, PRSC 40.5 percent, and the PLD 18.4 percent. The remaining 7.6 percent went to smaller political parties (Espinal 1990, 113). The narrow margin of the election results increased political tensions, thus rendering the work of the CEA more complicated.

The CEA played a crucial role supporting the JCE, so the process of counting the votes was impartial. It received denunciations and complaints from all political parties and responded in timely fashion to the various recommendations that emerged from the political parties. The most difficult issue resulted from examination of the invalidated and monitored votes. The JCE electoral team invalidated 84,695 votes and put 28,707 on the monitored list. Counting these votes occurred in the context of a challenge to two judges who had to be replaced by the deputies. Despite these difficulties, the CEA emerged untarnished by the conflict, and Jacobo Majluta recognized that Balaguer won the elections (Hartlyn 1998, 160–88; Núñez Collado, 1996, 99).

Reform of the Electoral Law and the 1994 Elections
Balaguer did not resolve the credibility problem of the JCE during his new administration (1986–1990). It took another electoral crisis in 1990 for him to start a discussion with the political opposition to address the issue. As a result of negotiations brokered by the Catholic Church, the National Congress passed a new electoral law that increased the number of judges from three to five. The law stipulated that the judges would be appointed by the three principal political parties represented in Congress, and it ordered the creation of a new identity card—the identification and voter registration card—that replaced the old two-identity-card system. It was expected that the new identity card, which included a photograph, would reduce the possibility of electoral fraud, a main complaint in past elections.

Although the major political parties supported the 1992 electoral reform, the credibility issue was not resolved. Opposition parties raised serious questions about the JCE's capacity to freely organize the elections. A national voter registration drive was conducted in February 1993 to replace the old voter registration cards. The number of polling stations (*mesas*) was increased from 6,663 to 9,528. The JCE accepted the technical assistance of the OAS and the International Foundation for Electoral Systems (IFES) to implement the electoral reforms. (IFES is a nongovernmental organization based in Washington, D.C., that provides technical support to electoral processes throughout the world.) Even so, the PRD, the PLD, and the Institutional Revolutionary Party criticized the JCE for being slow, bureaucratic, and inefficient. They still doubted that it was fit to organize free and fair elections.

The opposition's doubts reached a critical point when it appeared that the JCE was not going to implement a public bid for the contract to buy the necessary technology for the data processing center and the photographic equipment needed for the new voter identity card. A pool formed by IBM-Kodak was the principal competitor for the contract. Opposition political parties, however, considered this pool politically connected to high government officials. These fears were confirmed when a vote to open a public bid was three to two. The judges who sympathized with the government voted against the public bid. This rejection raised suspicions about the seriousness of the JCE. The opposition claimed that the fraud was going to take place in the data processing center during voter registration and during the vote count. The government party responded by accusing the opposition of attempting to discredit the JCE before holding the elections. In the midst of this debate, the Catholic Church offered to mediate between the parties in conflict, and it successfully defused a political impasse that could have had serious political consequences.

The OAS and IFES worked with the JCE to produce significant technical improvements in the electoral process of 1993–1994. These advancements, however, were not sufficient to overcome the decision of the parties to politicize the appointment of the judges to the JCE. The judges of the JCE responded to different political parties, and that curtailed their impartiality. This mechanism obviously did not withstand the acid test of Dominican electoral politics, and even before the elections took place the Catholic Church was called in again to mediate as the campaign was unfolding. Violence erupted and several people were killed. Church mediators coordinated with the leading political parties to sign a civility compact that would end the violence. This pact was signed May 10, 1994, six days before the election. Juan Bosch, presidential candidate of the PLD, refused to sign the pact, allegedly because Balaguer never respected the pacts he had signed in the past.

The civility compact was not just about concern with political violence. It required the JCE to provide the final lists of eligible voters to all the political parties so that there would be no doubt as to the transparency of the process. The signers of the pact pledged not to obstruct the activities conducted by rival political organizations or to stage victory celebrations before the JCE officially announced the results. In addition, the parties to the agreement promised to pursue a program of legislative collaboration during the new administration's first year in office. The government promised that it would give every courtesy and facility to enable the members of international delegations of observers to discharge their duties ("Texto del Pacto de la Civilidad" 1994).

Despite technical improvements and international technical support, the JCE was not able to produce free and fair elections. On election day, it became clear that the list of voters the JCE had given to the political parties was not the same as the list it sent to the polling stations. The PRD claimed that over 150,000 people could not vote on election day because their names did not appear on the list at the assigned polling station but instead at polling stations far from the place in which they were assigned to vote. In this context, on May 18, 1994, Balaguer claimed to be the "virtual winner" of the election, with 95 percent of the votes counted, a clear violation of the civility compact. He had apparently received 42.5 percent of the votes and Peña Gómez 41.2 percent. In addition to his claim to victory, Balaguer sent combined units of army and police to make spot inspections of vehicles in search of arms. This was a warning to Peña Gómez and his allies in case they wanted to make public demonstrations. Peña Gómez understood the message and asked his followers to avoid government provocation by abstaining from holding public demonstrations.

International observers and the IFES agreed that there had been irregularities in the election. Representative Stephen Solarz of New York, who led the delegation of the National Democratic Institute, told the *New York Times* that thousands of Dominicans had been "deliberately excluded" from the voting process (French 1994, A5). The PRSC orchestrated a nationalist movement, which claimed that foreign observers and the U.S. Embassy were behind those who accused the JCE of organizing fraudulent elections. Cardinal López Rodríguez joined those who rejected foreign intervention in Dominican affairs, compromising the nonpartisan position of the CED. The political situation became quite polarized because the PRD led a huge national and international campaign to denounce fraud in the election and called for a thorough investigation into what had happened.

International and national political pressures forced the JCE to appoint a verification commission on June 15, 1994, nearly a month after the elections, to investigate the allegations of fraud. The commission presented its report on July 16. Responding to the allegations that there were two voting lists, it said:

> The electoral lists submitted by the Central Electoral Commission to the polling places for the general elections did not match with the lists of electors submitted to the political parties. At least 45 municipalities were reported as affected. The Verification Commission received complaints from over 1,900 polling places. It evaluated no less than 1,468 polling places with an average of 20 substitutes per polling place. It concluded that according to the information reported, around 45,000 voters were deprived of their right to vote and no less than 28,672, according to the information evaluated. (Junta Central Electoral 1994, 31–32)

The commission left no doubt that those irregularities carried out during the election process could have changed the presidential, congressional, and municipal results of the elections. Despite these findings, the JCE declared Balaguer the winner of the 1994 elections. Balaguer and his allies received 42.3 percent, Peña Gómez and his allies received 41.5 percent, Bosch and his allies received 13 percent, and Majluta got 2.3 percent. The JCE had certified an electoral coup d'état, and Balaguer knew that he had to negotiate to get out of this messy political situation.

The Catholic Church joined the OAS to seek a mediated solution to the crisis. Msgr. Núñez Collado and John Graham, general coordinator of the OAS election observers, became key players in the mediation process to get Balaguer and Peña Gómez to agree on a solution to the crisis. After numerous meetings, the two leaders signed what became known as the Pact for Democracy on August 9, 1994, at the Biblioteca Dominicana in Santo Domingo. It includes the following:

1. Prohibition of reelection of the president for two consecutive periods.
2. Reinstatement of Dominican citizenship for those individuals who had assumed the citizenship of another country.
3. Reformation of the judicial system and the passage of two transitory amendments; these limited the presidency and the vice presidency to eighteen months, that is, from August 16, 1994, to February 27, 1996.
4. Elections for president and vice president to be held on November 16, 1995. Those elected would be inaugurated on February 27, 1996.
5. Congressional and municipal authorities elected on May 16, 1994, would remain in office until August 1998.
6. A second round of elections was to be held if no single candidate received at least 40 percent of the votes. ("Texto del Pacto por la Democracia" 1994)

After this pact was signed, the leadership of PRSC in Congress altered it so that President Balaguer would stay in office for two years rather than eighteen months. The second round of elections was raised to 50 percent of the valid votes. Peña Gómez protested these violations of the pact, but in the interest of preventing violence, he canceled a general strike and Balaguer was inaugurated on August 16, 1994. Altering the pact was another fraud, which illustrates the untrustworthiness of Balaguer and his political entourage.

Mediations in the tripartite dialogue and in the elections of 1986 and 1994 confirmed the church's position as a special nonpartisan player. Through the 1990s and the turn of the twentieth century, the government and the political opposition recognized the mediations of Msgr. Núñez Collado as a normal ingredient in the political process. President Fernández Reina appointed him to chair the Commission on National Dialogue promoted by his administration (1996–2000); President Hipólito Mejía Domínguez (2000–2004) named him to chair the Commission to Revise the Constitution. Msgr. Núñez Collado chaired the follow-up commission in charge of mediating numerous conflicts in the Central Electoral Commission before the presidential elections of 2004. He played a key role in resolving what could have been a major political impasse when the Central Electoral Commission appeared to be slow or unwilling to issue bulletins with election results in May 2004. And in the summer of 2005, Núñez Collado coordinated a series of negotiations to discuss the fiscal reforms necessary for the nation to join the Dominican Republic-Central American Free Trade Agreement (DR-CAFTA).

The incorporation of the church as a permanent feature of the Dominican political system is unique as compared to Bolivia and Central America. In those countries, the church mediates political conflicts and issues pastoral letters and messages making observations and suggestions about national political and economic life. In the Dominican Republic, the church goes far beyond calls for national conciliation and occasional mediations, becoming involved in almost every major issue, including fiscal reform, Haitian migration to the Dominican Republic, electoral issues, constitutional reform, and free-trade agreements.

The strong leadership of Msgr. Núñez Collado may help to explain the singularity of the Dominican case. Msgr. Agripino Núñez Collado has developed a career as mediator of political conflicts. He has used his prestige as president of the Pontificia Universidad Católica Madre y Maestra, one of the best universities in the country, and the support of the CED to promote dialogue and mediation as the best ways to resolve national conflicts. The churches of Bolivia and Central America do not have a church official who compares to Núñez Collado on issues of mediation. Dominican political and socioeconomic elites recognize that Msgr. Núñez Collado is a trustworthy mediator who can bring them together in times of crisis. The government, the political parties, and the business communities seem incapable of recognizing the interests of their opponents, and their recurring calls to Núñez Collado through the last three decades have turned him into an indispensable political actor.

In contrast to the Dominican Republic, the political and socioeconomic elites of Bolivia and Central America have not yet found a church official who is willing to dedicate himself almost completely to issues of mediation. Msgr. Arturo Riveras y Damas tried to play a similar role in El Salvador, but he did not have the support of the church hierarchy that Núñez Collado does, and many in the business community saw him as being too close to Christian Democrats. Msgrs. Jorge Manrique in Bolivia and Rodolfo Quezada Toruño in Guatemala played important roles mediating political conflicts in their countries, but their intercessions did not become a permanent feature of the political system. As in El Salvador, the business community believed that these two church figures were too close to the left and considered them biased.

Conclusions

Transition to democracy and the socioeconomic transformation of the 1980s provided the framework for the reemergence of the Catholic Church as the political mediator par excellence in the Dominican Republic. These changes occurred at the same time that the church underwent significant institutional enlargement in the numbers of dioceses, parishes, and educational and welfare programs. Close collaboration with public authorities, regardless of their ideological and political persuasions, continued to facilitate public funding under the concordat of 1954. The cooperation fostered the development and consolidation of the modernizing orientation of the church. This orientation proposed disengagement from direct, partisan politics in favor of a more general stress on highlighting injustice, but suggesting dialogue to resolve political conflicts. The opposing traditional conservative and liberating orientations gradually melted into the mainstream and transformed themselves into a neoconservative orientation that proposes mediation as the best way to achieve consensus.

Most political actors and observers agree that church mediation has been positive and has contributed to social peace and reconciliation. Mediation was a means to reintegrate the church into the architecture of the political system. Because of this reintegration into politics, the church is nonpartisan vis-à-vis the political parties. However, the church defends liberal democracy as the most adequate political system. Through political mediation, the church became a permanent feature in the system. This unique role distinguishes the Dominican church from its counterparts in Bolivia and Central America, where the church mediates political disputes but is not a permanent feature of the political system. I conclude that what makes the Dominican case unique in comparison to our selected cases is the persona of Msgr. Agripino Núñez Collado and the recognition by the Dominican political and socioeconomic elites that he is a trustworthy individual who can resolve their disputes.

Notes

1. This chapter uses information provided to me in interviews with the following: Antonio Camilo González, bishop, Diocese of La Vega; Nicanor Peña, bishop, Diocese of Puerto Planta; Rafael Felipe, bishop, Diocese of Barahona; Ramón Benito de la Rosa Carpio, bishop, Diocese of Altagracia; Francisco Osoria, bishop, Diocese of San Pedro de Macoris; José Grullón, bishop, Diocese of San Juan de la Maguana; Jesús María Moya, bishop, Diocese of San Francisco de Macoris; Tomás Jerónimo Abreu, bishop, Diocese of Mao-Montecristi; Freddy Bretón, bishop, Diocese of Baní; Juan Antonio Flores, archbishop, Diocese of Santiago; Diomedes Espinal de León, auxiliary bishop, Archdiocese of Santiago; and José Francisco Arnáiz, secretary, Dominican Episcopal Conference. It also draws on interviews with the following Catholic priests: José Luis Sáez, José Núñez, José Luis Alemán, Pablo Mella, and Abrahan Apolinario.

2. This figure includes visits by Dominicans who live overseas.

3. This includes the United States, Puerto Rico, Spain, and Venezuela.

4. These figures do not include undocumented migration or the children of Dominicans born in those countries.

5. The most recent increase in the foreign debt is related, in part, to the issuance of two installments of half a billion dollars in "sovereign bonds," paying for the renationalization of two electricity companies (Edesur and Edenorte) and to the financial rescue of three major private banks that collapsed in the summer of 2003 due to corruption and mismanagement. According to the Central Bank, the foreign debt increased by 72 percent during the administration of Hipólito Mejía (2000–2004).

6. The issue of definition comes up in statistics about Catholic educational institutions. Those that refer to primary and secondary schools in table 4.4 also include day care centers, kindergartens, and the general and religious education provided in public schools. This explains why the figures have increased so much. Likewise, statistics dealing with health institutions are defined broadly. Hospitals and dispensaries also include clinics, popular pharmacies, leper clinics, the Oncological Institute, and twenty-two asylums for the elderly. In short, the official Catholic statistics inflate the number of primary and secondary schools by including other educational institutions.

7. Balaguer's Reformist Party became the Reformist Social Christian Party in 1985 because he affiliated it to Christian Democracy.

8. Dominican governments are normally inaugurated on August 16 every four years, but for this examination, each period will begin on January 1 and will conclude on December 31, four years later. That way, one can compare a full year of the annual budget. I consulted various editions of the *Directorio Católico Dominicano* and with historian José Luis Sáez, SJ, to ensure that all institutions included in the national budget did belong legally to the Catholic Church. These institutions were grouped into fourteen different categories, which include archdioceses and dioceses, institutions of higher education, polytechnic institutes, schools, seminaries, parishes, agencies, radio stations, associations, hospitals, medical clinics, organizations of religious, asylum and

assistance centers, and environmental organizations. The list of institutions is too long to include here in detail. I developed a database that includes all the information compiled from the national budget. The only institutions included in these fourteen categories that do not legally belong to the Catholic Church are the Loyola Polytechnic in San Cristobal, the Plan Sierra, and the Plan Cordillera. Nonetheless, I listed them as Catholic institutions because they were established for the Catholic Church to run. The Instituto Superior de Agricultura (Agricultural Institute of Higher Education) was established with seed money provided by U.S. foundations, but administered by the church.

9. As noted below, Balaguer's last term in office was reduced from four to two years after the political impasse created by the electoral fraud of 1994.

10. Portions of this section were published as "The Catholic Church and Political Mediation in the Dominican Republic: A Comparative Perspective" in *Journal of Church and State* 46 (Spring 2004).

CHAPTER FIVE

Building a New Relationship with Society

The implementation of social pastoral programs fueled the development of the Catholic Church as a powerful sociopolitical actor in Dominican society. These programs were oriented toward assistance to the neediest, commitment to transforming society through development, and a liberating education of the impoverished. The church has been rebuilding a new relationship with Dominicans through programs that affect education, health, culture, prisons, human mobility, human rights, peace, ecology, and land. This chapter demonstrates that although all church orientations vocally support social pastoral programs, the clergy who actually work to implement them have been associated with modernizing and liberating orientations.

This chapter assesses the works of Cáritas Dominicana and the Centro Dominicano de Asesorías e Investigaciones Legales, (Dominican Counseling and Legal Research Center), known as Cedail, and analyzes the pastoral work of four dioceses. Cáritas and Cedail are the backbone of the social pastoral work of the Catholic Church in the country. They have a nationwide scope and thus provide an opportunity to examine the challenges faced by the social pastoral programs and how the church rebuilt its connections with society in its transition to democracy and amid the socioeconomic transformations in the 1980s and 1990s.

The social pastoral programs used a mixture of assistentialism and accompaniment (*acompañamiento*) to carry out its programs. Assistentialism is a system in which donors take the lead in the process and beneficiaries meekly receive what the church gives to them. In general, conservative clergymen tend to follow this church orientation. In contrast, accompaniment is of a process whereby the priest or the lay Catholic worker engages beneficiaries in consciousness raising about their potential while providing assistance. It is a process of mutual enrichment because both the worker and the beneficiaries participate in conditions of equality. Liberating and modernizing orientations tend to identify with this pastoral approach. Church social workers design accompaniment to help communities develop their social capital, that is, "connections among individuals—social networks and the norms of reciprocity and trustworthiness that arise from them" (Putnam 2000, 19).

The perception of the accompaniment approach has changed as a result of the democratic transition in Latin America. Under military dictatorships or authoritarian governments in the 1960s and 1970s, accompaniment was a revolutionary method and it was suppressed. In the transition to democracy, accompaniment is no longer revolutionary but a means of strengthening community organizations and civil society. The use of the accompaniment approach is still critical, as it seeks to deepen democracy beyond formalities; it does not threaten the political system because the social and historical contexts have changed drastically.[1]

Unlike the 1960s and 1970s, all political groupings and organizations now accept liberal democracy as a viable regime and do not propose alternatives. It does not seem to be a problem for the neoconservative church orientation to support a social pastoral program of accompaniment as long as the clergy controls it and prevents its politicization. I posit that the development of social pastoral programs following the accompaniment and assistentialism approaches helps the church reinsert itself into society and thus strengthen its ties with the oppressed. A combination of these approaches reinforces the status of the church as the most legitimate and credible institution in Dominican life.

The Development of Social Pastoral Programs

We can observe two important periods in the development of the social pastoral programs of the Catholic Church in the post-Trujillo Dominican Republic. The first period is from the fall of Trujillo to 1982, when the first national pastoral plan (NPP) begins. The second period is divided into two pastoral plans: 1982–1992 and 1992–2002. As noted in chapter 3, during the first period, the church social pastoral work had a twofold nature. First, the Conferencia del Episcopado Dominicano (CED) published pastoral letters in which it sought to raise awareness about the situation of the poor, especially the peasantry, which in the early 1960s, was about 70 percent of the population. In the late 1960s and throughout the 1970s, the church denounced human rights violations, called for agrarian reform, and demanded an end to corruption. Second, it implemented concrete social programs at the diocesan level to help alleviate the lives of the impoverished.

Parishes and *centros de promoción humana*, CPH (Centers for Human Services) implemented social pastoral programs. In many cases, the CPH distributed food, medicine, and clothing donated to the country via the U.S. Agency for International Development through Law PL 480, Catholic Relief Services, and Cáritas Internationalis. At the beginning, the church offered this aid without any conditional ties for recipient communities because it was trying to ease hunger. In the 1980s, the church began to give aid in exchange for work to get beneficiaries involved in solving their own problems. The aid included promoting community producers and developing organizations to provide public services such as building community centers, roads, schools, and irrigation canals (interview with Basilio De la Cruz, head of Cáritas in La Vega, May 26, 2003). In La Vega, Higuey, and Santiago, where bishops were particularly concerned about social issues, small groups of priests supported peasant claims over land tenure and tried to implement pastoral programs that engaged community participation. However, assistentialism rather than accompaniment guided the implementation of these programs.

The development of the social pastoral work received a big push with the implementation of NPPs (1982–1992 and 1992–2002). The first NPP was inspired by the Medellín (1968) and Puebla (1979) meetings of the Latin American Episcopal Conference. In line with the orientation of these conferences, the first NPP (1982–1992) considered five pastoral priorities:

> family, social, community, youth, and mission. Concerning the social pastoral work, it proposed to assume the causes of the poor, to reject poverty and injustice, and to engage the beneficiaries of church social programs. In essence, this meant that the pastoral workforce would increase its presence among the impoverished, live with them, and commit themselves to their causes. The church expects that pastoral workers will promote the culture and education of community leaders and encourage their participation and responsibility. In addition, it seeks the development of community organizations that will help the deprived realize that they can develop their own potential. (Conferencia del Episcopado Dominicano 1985, 24–25)

The first NPP helped begin a process of unification of the social work of the church without threatening the political establishment. It was a national project carried out in all the dioceses simultaneously (interview with Msgr. Diómedes Espinal de León, Archdiocese of Santiago, June 12, 2000).

However, the uneven development of the dioceses, lack of economic resources, and varying levels of clergy commitments to the social pastoral plan yielded mixed results (see below).

In addition, pastoral agents implemented the NPP in a political context that had undergone drastic changes. They put into practice the first NPP during the Dominican transition to democracy, when the church was no longer the "voice of the voiceless." The authoritarian Balaguer was no longer in power, and the PRD-led governments (1978–1982 and 1982–1986) created a democratic opening, which permitted the development of political opposition. In this new context, the "preferential option for the poor" was not a threat to the political establishment, and, on the contrary, it helped alleviate poverty. The NPP contributed significantly to buttressing the church relationship with the people by developing programs that addressed their basic needs. The NPP also helped strengthen the already booming organizations of civil society, which Balaguer had repressed during his years in power (1966–1978). The first NPP was swimming with the current, not against it, and, as such, it enabled the church to accommodate new social and political development at the community and national levels.

The Fourth Latin American Episcopal Conference held in Santo Domingo in 1992 inspired the second NPP (1992–2002). This conference reflected the changes introduced in the church by Pope John Paul II. John Paul II "feared that if base Christian communities and other grassroots organizations are not tied closely to the hierarchy and prohibited from engaging in any non-pastoral or 'political' activities, Catholic doctrinal orthodoxy will be weakened and the church will become analogous to any other national or local interest group" (Stewart-Gambino 1994, 130). This explains, in part, why the conclusions of the Santo Domingo conference do not contain the social and political critiques that the Medellín and Puebla conferences did.

The second NPP states that it assumes the commitment of the Fourth Latin American Episcopal Conference. It addresses four needs: integral education for the new evangelization, human promotion that assumes preferential option for the poor, inculturation of the Gospel that takes into account local culture, and the need to organize the pastoral at all levels and areas of the ecclesiastical life.[2] The NPP mandates the organization of pastoral councils in dioceses and parishes. It recommends the development of a national structure that articulates the social pastoral at national and diocesan levels (Conferencia del Episcopado Dominicano 1994, 27–34).

In 2000, the CED published the *Primer Concilio Prelenario Dominincano: Documento Final* (*First Dominican Plenary Council: Final Document*) and it affirmed the key postulate of the second NPP. It makes it explicit that "dignity and human promotion are the backbone of the social pastoral." However, rather than talking about the "preferential option for the poor," it repeats the Gospel command: "defend the poor with a preferential love" (Conferencia del Episcopado Dominicano 2000, 276–77). This change in language reveals that the Dominican hierarchy of the church, with Vatican approval, wanted to distance itself from the critical and progressive voices of the past. Similarly, the Plenary Council does not use the term "ecclesiastical base communities," but "communities at the basic level," which means that they are integrated as part of the hierarchical structure of the church (Conferencia del Episcopado Dominicano 2000, 164–66). The church wants to form communities, but it wants to make sure that they are under control of the clergy, not operating as grassroots organizations with "political" goals. The hierarchy allows a pastoral of accompaniment because the clergy can exert control over its process of development and implementation. These new guidelines obviously limit the work of clergymen associated with the liberating orientation.

In general, the second NPP helped consolidate the developments initiated during the first pastoral plan. It continued to promote human development and community organization, strengthened the relationship of the church with the impoverished, and enhanced its credibility and legitimacy in the country. During this time, the National Pastoral Commission emerged to coordinate pastoral work at the national level, lending considerable support to dioceses through Cáritas and Cedail, key institutions in the development of the social pastoral.

Cáritas Dominicana and the Social Pastoral Work

This section examines a selected group of dioceses to study the ways in which Cáritas and the social pastoral programs helped the church build bonds with local communities. It also evaluates the challenges confronted by social pastoral programs. I examine the dioceses of Mao-Montecristy, La Vega, Barahona, and San Juan de la Maguana. I selected these dioceses because their bishops supported teams of social pastoral workers to implement innovative methods to conduct their activities. The work of these teams illustrates how a social pastoral program of accompaniment contributes to strengthening the role of the church in society.

Cáritas opened its first office in Santo Domingo in 1961, following the assassination of Rafael L. Trujillo. Trujillo had not allowed Cáritas to operate in the country because, according to him, "there were no poor people in the country." Cáritas expanded from the Archdiocese of Santo Domingo to other dioceses and now operates an office in each of the nine dioceses and two archdioceses. At the diocesan level, the director of Cáritas works directly with the person in charge of the social pastoral programs. In some cases, the director of Cáritas is also in charge of the social pastoral work in the diocese. Social pastoral workers face challenges that vary from diocese to diocese, but there are similar patterns nationwide. These include poverty, social injustice, housing shortages, inadequate financial and human resources, migration and immigration difficulties, problems in education, environmental degradation, and insufficient involvement of priests in the social pastoral work (interviews with Rafael A. Reyes, head of Cáritas and the social pastoral programs in the Diocese of Mao-Montecristi, June 5, 2003, and Fr. Lucas Cruz, head of the social pastoral programs in the Archdiocese of Santiago, June 30, 2003).

Cáritas has a nationwide project to support the social pastoral work in every diocese. The national office serves as a channel to provide financial resources to diocesan offices. Cáritas investments have increased significantly over the last few years to support pastoral work in all the dioceses. These increments were initially the result of the disasters caused by Hurricane George, which hit the island in 1998. Because of its increased money, Cáritas was able to influence international and local donors. The success of the Cáritas fund-raising campaign allowed it to initiate housing projects in all the dioceses, not just those affected by the storm.

The Diocese of Mao-Montecristi
The Vatican established the Diocese of Mao-Montecristi in 1978 in a region that belonged to the Diocese of Santiago. The new diocese is in the northwest of the Dominican Republic and it stretches from Santiago Province to the northwest borders with Haiti. It includes the provinces of Valverde, Montecristi, Dajabón, and Santiago Rodríguez. Poverty and inequality surround these provinces despite richness in agriculture, salt mining, and industry. In an attempt to address these issues, Cáritas and the social pastoral programs built on the efforts of Jesuit priests who had been working at the Haitian border since the 1930s. The social work of Fr. Regino Martínez, SJ, in the 1980s and 1990s illustrates a social pastoral program of accompaniment.

Fr. Martinez helped organize an agricultural confederation called Unión Campesina Autónoma (Autonomous Peasant Union) to recover an agrarian settlement numbered AC-372, located near the border with Haiti, from large landowners. In 1989, the Dominican government declared that this settlement was available for public use. Despite this, the peasants were not able to recover the lands immediately because local landowners wanted the settlement for themselves. Fr. Martínez lived with peasants for eleven months until they were able to recover it. He drew an important lesson from this experience:

> We believe the power of organization is the only way for the poor to participate in a democracy in order to obtain what they need. Politicians, the World Bank and other international agencies do not consider these communities as social subjects. This is why poverty increases every day despite the large development programs to combat poverty that are conceived in air-conditioned offices. Salaries, administration, and per diem consume the money generated by these programs. Poor people do not participate in the elaboration and execution of these programs. This is why poverty keeps increasing by the day. (interview with Fr. Martínez, head of Solidaridad Fronteriza, May 30, 2003)

With support from Msgr. J. Tomás Abreu Herrera, bishop of the Diocese of Mao-Montecristi, Fr. Martínez founded and directed Solidaridad Fronteriza (Border Solidarity), an institution dedicated to the development of popular organizations and the defense of human rights. Solidaridad Fronteriza helped organize centers for mothers in Loma de Cabrera, Dajabón, Partido, and Restauración. It also promoted the foundation of the Asociación de Mujeres la Nueva Esperanza (The Good Hope Women's Association), a group of more than 700 women who buy secondhand clothes at the border with Haiti and resell it in the open markets of Santiago, Puerto Plata, and Dajabón. It also contributed to the organization of the Comité de Defensa de los Derechos del Pueblo (Committee for the Defense of People's Rights), a group that operates in four neighborhoods in Dajabón whose objective is to build popular housing with Cáritas support. In addition, Solidaridad Fronteriza put together La Red de Organizaciones (Network of Organizations), which includes mothers, peasants, youth, and cultural associations in four municipalities. It also operates on the Haitian side of the border as Solidarité Frontalier, where it promotes the defense of human rights and the development of community organizations similar to those found on the Dominican side of the border. Cáritas works through the various peasant associations that exist in the diocese. It expects communities to channel their petitions for help through these associations and parochial councils. Members of these communities participate in public discussions concerning Cáritas projects in the Diocese of Mao-Montecristi (see table 5.1).

Pastoral workers select beneficiaries based on their level of poverty and their willingness to contribute unskilled labor to build homes. The houses built in the diocese have forty-eight square meters, including a small gallery, living and dinning room, a small kitchen, two bedrooms, and a bathroom. In April 2003, these houses cost from $1,702 to $2,042. The beneficiary had to

Table 5.1. Cáritas Dominicana Projects in the Diocese of Mao-Montecristi

Period	Project	Location	Quantity	Amount Invested in U.S. Dollars*
1999–2000*	Housing construction	Dajabón	10	27,487.63
	Houses repaired	Various communities	33	90,709.18
		Various communities	76	19,790.16
Subtotal				137,986.97
2001–2003 Phase I	Housing construction	Dajabón, La Meseta, El Dajao, Mao	30	78,083.94
	Community education and preventive medicine	16 communities		14,689.37
Subtotal				92,773.31
2001–2003 Phase II	Housing construction	Various	15	47,631.21
	Community education and preventive medicine	16 communities		34,126.59
Subtotal of projects				81,757.80
Total Investment				312,518.07

Source: Cáritas Dominicana (2003).
*For this and subsequent tables I used the average of the exchange rate to convert Dominican pesos to U.S. dollars.

contribute $681 and provide unskilled labor and food for neighbors who helped. Rafael A. Reyes concludes that he is beginning to see changes in people's attitudes regarding community organizations and self-reliance, but he admits that there is a long way to go to accomplish the goals of the accompaniment approach because most people in the diocese are not yet organized.

> It is difficult to implement the accompaniment approach because the institutions of state and society implement paternalistic approaches, which normally turn people into parasites and thus create a relationship of dependency. In addition, we live in an individualistic society and, as the social and economic crisis hit, individualism and egocentrism tend to strengthen. (interview with Rafael A. Reyes, head of Cáritas and pastoral social in the Diocese of Mao-Montecristi, June 5, 2003)

Despite these challenges, the works of Cáritas, the social pastoral programs, and Solidaridad Fronteriza reinforce the ties of the Catholic Church with remote communities generally disregarded by the state. The social work of these organizations strengthens the church's standing, providing it with legitimacy and credibility.

The Diocese of La Vega
The Vatican created the Diocese of La Vega in 1953, in the heart of the Cibao Valley, the richest agricultural region of the country. In 1978, it was subdivided to create the Diocese of San Francisco de Macoris as part of a larger program to reinforce the missionary and social pastoral work of the church. Presently, the Diocese of La Vega includes the provinces of Salcedo, La Vega, Jarabacoa, Constanza, Monseñor Noel, and Sánchez Rámirez. Despite its agricultural development and industry, the provinces that comprise the Diocese of La Vega confront widespread poverty and lack social services.

La Vega's is one of the most experienced dioceses in terms of the implementation of social pastoral programs. When the Vatican named Msgr. Juan Flores Santana to the post of bishop of La Vega in 1966, he built on already existing programs such as Radio Santa María, the first Catholic radio station in the country. Radio Santa María has been broadcasting since 1956, and most people know it throughout the Cibao Valley because of its effective educational programs, especially its literacy programs that have helped lower illiteracy rates in the region. In addition, for many years Radio Santa María served valley communities by airing programs that not only addressed the needs of the population but also provided communication when the region's road network was not yet well established.

The first centro de promoción humana was established in La Vega in 1973. The CPH focused its work on the peasantry in line with the tenets of the CED, which then emphasized a rural pastoral program. These centers began conducting social pastoral work with peasants evicted from their lands and towns by mining companies such as Falconbridge and La Rosario Mining Company. Falconbridge operated in Bonao, extracting iron and nickel, and La Rosario mined gold in Cotui. The operations of these companies created enormous social conflicts in the region. Through its social pastoral programs, the church helped the peasants who faced environmental degradation, landlessness, and abandonment (interview with Msgr. Flores Santana, June 14, 2000).

Cáritas opened its offices in the diocese in 1968 and began to serve as a channel to fund the diocesan pastoral programs. Although social pastoral programs were based on assistentialism and paternalism, they made significant contributions to help the peasants cope with their conflicts with the mining companies. Cáritas, for example, was accustomed to receiving donations and distributing them in communities. However, the implementation of the NPP stimulated Cáritas and the social pastoral not only to expand their programs but to promote human development. With Cáritas's support, the social pastoral work expanded its concerns to nutritional education, agro-forestry, ecology, horticulture, wood, agriculture, disaster prevention, infrastructural projects such as water and sanitation, production of furniture, and housing construction (interview with Basilio de la Cruz, head of Cáritas in La Vega, May 26, 2003; see table 5.2).

Like the Diocese of Mao-Montecristi, La Vega faces overwhelming social challenges. The most pressing problems include lack of economic resources, an insufficient amount of reliable and committed volunteers, and the constant pressure of internal and international migration. There is also a lack of coordination of social work with government agencies and nongovernmental organizations (NGOs) and of recognition by priests and nuns that the social pastoral work must be one of their priorities (interview with Basilio De la Cruz, head of Cáritas in the Diocese of La Vega, May 26, 2003).

The diocese has the same social problems found elsewhere in the country such as lack of adequate health services, insufficient schools, and widespread poverty. Cáritas has a staff of seven persons working in the diocese who coordinate their work with various volunteer groups at the parish level. These volunteers constitute the backbone of Cáritas's work with the communities. However, lack of employment for community leaders creates great difficulties, which Cáritas is unable to resolve. Many of the trained volunteers need to migrate to resolve their own personal problems, forcing Cáritas and the

Table 5.2. Cáritas Dominicana Projects in the Diocese of La Vega

Period	Project	Location	Quantity	Amount Invested in U.S. Dollars
1999–2000	Housing construction	Cevicos	19	51,076.02
	Houses repaired	Las Matas, Cotui	82	17,730.83
Subtotal				68,806.85
2001–2003 Phase I	Housing construction	El Yagal	30	69,661.84
	Prevention and mitigation of disasters			
	Integral environm. education	Entire diocese		2,677.59
	Production and trade of furniture	Jarabacoa		31,864.88
		Zambrana		28,607.79
Subtotal				132,812.09
2002–2003 Phase II	Housing construction	El Higo	34	118,458.10
		Zambrana	24	73,522.48
	Aqueduct construction and environ. sanitation	La Vega and Cotuí	11 hydraulic construction projects	47,129.80
Subtotal projects				239,110.38
Total investment				440,729.32

Source: Cáritas Domicana (2003).

social pastoral to constantly find new people to train. The complexity increases when local parish priests do not make the social pastoral work one of their priorities. This may be why, despite good intentions, the social pastoral program remains based on an assistentialist approach rather than on human promotion and accompaniment. Fr. Francisco Contreras, head of the social pastoral program in the Diocese of La Vega, stated:

> We have started a process of human promotion, but in what regards the commitment of lay Catholics, we have not yet moved from a pastoral based on assistentialism to human promotion. When we evaluate our social work it becomes clear that we have not yet moved from assistentialism. For example, we can see it when there is an urgent need such as a natural disaster or the death of a person in a community. People immediately show their solidarity by being willing to help the neediest, but when we invite them to participate in activities of social promotion that require a degree of commitment and accompaniment, their willingness diminishes. (interview with Fr. Francisco Contreras, June 26, 2003)

These critical reflections suggest that Cáritas and the social pastoral work are not meeting all their objectives in the Diocese of La Vega regarding the commitment of lay Catholics, priests, and nuns in the development of human promotion and accompaniment. The perceived lack of progress speaks to the inability of the Cáritas social pastoral program to effectively reach its objectives. However, it does not mean that landless peasants and poor urban dwellers, the prime beneficiaries of the program, do not value their work. My observations and conversations with beneficiaries in at least four dioceses reveal that they may not have increased their attendance at mass on Sunday or committed themselves to community organizing, but they appreciate it when church personnel work with them to resolve particular issues. This appreciation is what increases the credibility of the church in local communities and society in general.

The Diocese of Barahona
The Vatican founded the Diocese of Barahona in 1976 as part of a larger effort to strengthen the presence of the church in relatively untended remote regions. Located in the Dominican southwest, the new diocese includes the provinces of Baoruco, Independencia, Pedernales, and Barahona, which had been part of the Diocese of San Juan de la Maguana. Like other regions bordering Haiti, Barahona was never a desirable place for government officials and the clergy. In 1976, road conditions were deplorable and communications between towns within the province were difficult, if not nearly impos-

sible. The road network set up by the government has improved considerably, and transportation between Barahona and Santo Domingo or between Barahona and its various adjacent provinces and towns is no longer difficult. The national government also built an international airport near the city of Barahona to attract foreign and national investors to develop tourism facilities on the beaches and nearby Lake Enriquillo, the largest saltwater lake on the island. However, investors have not flocked to Barahona and the airport is hardly ever used. Despite the improved public infrastructures, Barahona is still one of the poorest provinces in the country and it does not yet meet the basic needs of the population.

The social pastoral work of the Catholic Church has sought to address the needs of the poorest population through various programs on education, sanitation, ecology, immigration, agriculture, and rural issues. The section below focuses on some of the pastoral programs implemented by Lemba at the Centro de Formación Diocesana de Cabral, CFDC (Cabral Center for Diocesan Education). Lemba is one of the oldest and largest social pastoral programs in the Diocese of Barahona.

The Cabral Center for Diocesan Education and Lemba
When the Vatican established the Diocese of Barahona, the CFDC was already working under the direction of religious from the Order of the Immaculate Heart of Mary, also known as the Belgian priests. The center had been involved in the promotion of catechism and human development. The bishop of Barahona renamed it the Centro de Formación Diocesana de Cabral and refocused its work. In the early days of its social pastoral work, the CFDC was concerned with rural pastoral programs, following the conceptual orientation then promoted by the CED. Msgr. Fabio Mamerto Rivas, the first bishop of Barahona, authorized Lemba to conduct the social pastoral work at the CFDC.

Lemba was a group of lay Catholics who wanted to incorporate the accompaniment approach into the rural pastoral work. That this group chose to name itself Lemba is evocative of their social pastoral approach. Juan Sebastian Lemba was an African slave who rebelled against Spanish slavery in 1522 (Tujibikile 1993, 55–74). Traditional historians have not included Lemba among the heroes of the nation, such as the Indian rebel Enriquillo, but this group of lay Catholics thought Lemba should be their hero because he had taken the first steps to defend the rights of black slaves. "Lemba did in his days what we have to do today: to struggle against a modern form of slavery" (interview with Carlos Naveo and Felicia Fermín, founders of Lemba, June 28, 2004).

The social pastoral work of Lemba consisted of promoting human development in Cabral, Cabeza de Toro, Tamayo, the city of Barahona, and various other neighboring towns. With approval from Msgr. Rivas in 1982, a small team of lay Catholic workers from Lemba set out to organize woodcutters in the community of Cabeza de Toro. Lemba social pastoral workers claimed to be following the guidance of the NPP, which called for a "preferential option for the poor." They moved to the community to learn about social conditions, especially cutting and trading charcoal, railroad ties, poles, and buttresses. They learned that peasants did not manage the dry wood forest rationally and that landowners, intermediaries, and business people profited handsomely from the wood business. Because of the inadequate methods used to cultivate the dry wood forest, the region was quickly losing its woods. Without the woods, there would be no rain, and without rain, farm crops could not be cultivated.

The woodcutting business operated through intermediaries who advanced money to cutters who used the money to cover their basic family expenses. For example, intermediaries would pay twelve pesos for a sack of charcoal and resell it for twenty-five to intermediaries who worked for Pedro A. Rivera, a wealthy industrialist from La Vega. Pedro A. Rivera had an intermediary working for him who controlled thirty trucks, which, on a weekly basis, loaded an average of 2,500 sacks of charcoal. Rivera's intermediaries in the region had power in the communities surrounding Cabeza de Toro. The intermediaries who bought poles, buttresses, and railroad ties for sugar mills and other enterprises operated in a similar manner.

The goal of Lemba's organizers was to teach peasants how to manage the dry wood forest rationally while making a profit, but without intermediaries. Rational management of the dry wood forest consists of using the dry wood without touching the green. In addition, the organizers raised awareness among the peasantry about the need to classify the wood into pieces that were good for poles, railroad ties, buttresses, or simply for charcoal. Furthermore, they introduced issues of land tenure and used it in conversations with the peasants. It turned out that many of these lands were public and that landowners did not have titles to lands they claimed (interview with Carlos Naveo and Felicia Fermín, founders of Lemba, June 28, 2004).

The social pastoral approach used by Lemba ran into problems when it affected the interests of the intermediaries and their powerful backers. Lemba's teams effectively organized the community of Cabeza de Toro and its surrounding areas, and the community was soon ready to talk to the local forestry authorities. In 1986, Pedro de Jesús Candelier, the national director of forestry, visited Cabeza de Toro to meet with the community. Backed by the presence of Msgr. Rivas, community leaders made four important demands to Candelier:

- that the national director of forestry not send its agents to supervise the burning of charcoal because the community will exercise this role on a voluntary basis;
- that the government ban Pedro A. Rivera's fleet of trucks from the area. They would only tolerate trucks from the community. Each truck would make no more than a trip a week and not carry more than 200 sacks of charcoal;
- that the national director of forestry not order trucks to come in without community approval;
- that each truck owner pay one peso for each sack of charcoal. This peso would go to a community fund, which would be used to promote community affairs. (interview with Manuel Antonio Pérez, founder and president of Lemba, June 26, 2003)

Candelier told the community that he would raise these issues with President Balaguer, but he could not make any promises. Candelier could not make any promises because Pedro A. Rivera was a close political ally of the president and there were powerful interest groups associated with the buying and selling of charcoal, railroad ties, poles, and buttresses. Aware that Msgr. Rivas was behind community demands, Balaguer approved the peasants' demands despite the complex web of interests groups that were involved in these issues. His approval reveals that he did not want to get into problems with the Catholic Church shortly after his inauguration (1986–1990), nor did he want to appear recalcitrant to international donors who supported sustainable development.

The next step in dealing with intermediaries and government officials was to train community leaders to develop social capital outside their communities. Social capital resides in relationships and, by definition, it empowers both individuals and communities. Building these relationships within the bureaucracy of the Consejo Estatal del Azúcar, CEA (State Sugar Council) and the privately owned sugar mills was a milestone for communities around Cabeza de Toro. These were the main customers for railroad ties, poles, and buttresses. Lemba launched a program to train key community leaders on how to navigate the system, that is, how to develop social capital that would enable them to deal with both the CEA and the privately owned sugar concerns. This social capital worked well prior to the privatization of many CEA sugar mills, but when the government privatized them in the late 1990s,

Lemba and the communities had to use their previous experience to develop new social capital.

Lemba's social pastoral work also included other programs that followed the same philosophy of accompaniment. These include a micro-credit office that lends money to woodcutters and to women who operate small businesses, a program dealing with gender issues and domestic violence, and a beekeeping program, which is not only meant to generate revenue for the community but also to put a claim on lands in dispute. With Cáritas's support, Lemba and the social pastoral program implemented a variety of projects (see table 5.3).

Notwithstanding Lemba's success, it is important to keep in mind that it is composed of a relatively small number of lay Catholics who work with volunteers distributed in different communities. They face overwhelming challenges, such as insufficient community organizations, lack of awareness about community problems, and a sense of dependency in most communities.

Another point worth remembering is that Lemba works in a region where most social assistance programs, Catholic or government sponsored, are based on assistentialism and not on the accompaniment approach. As in the dioceses of Mao-Montecristi and La Vega, the number of priests, lay Catholics, and nuns who use the accompaniment approach is rather small. Further, in these dioceses, particularly in the Archdiocese of Santiago, most priests and *presidentes de asambleas* (delegates of the word) do not make the social pastoral work a priority in their parishes (interview with Fr. Tobias De la Cruz, head of the social pastoral in the Archdiocese of Santiago, June 6, 2003). Thus, a social pastoral program based on an accompaniment approach is still a goal.

The Diocese of San Juan de La Maguana

In 1953, Pope Pious XII established a Prelature "Nullius" in San Juan de la Maguana, but it did not become a diocese until 1969. As noted above, in 1976, the Vatican subdivided dioceses to establish the Diocese of Barahona. The Diocese of San Juan de la Maguana includes the provinces of Azua, San Juan de la Maguana, and Elías Piña, which borders Haiti. Except for San Juan de la Maguana, located in a rich and fertile valley, Elías Piña and Azua mirror the poverty and isolation that is common in the southwest of the Dominican Republic.

The Diocese of San Juan de la Maguana developed a comprehensive census of the existing social conditions in its three provinces. The Vatican named Msgr. José Dolores Grullón bishop of the diocese in 1991, and he currently presides over the National Commission of the Social Pastoral. When Msgr. Grullón began his numerous pastoral visits to all the communities in

Table 5.3. Cáritas Dominicana Projects in the Diocese of Barahona

Period	Project	Location	Quantity	Amount Invested in U.S. Dollars
1999–2001	Housing construction	Arroyo Seco	39	56,430.17
	Latrines		39	6,526.75
	Reparation of a clinic	Paraiso	1	13,577.20
Subtotal				76,534.12
2001–2003 Phase I	Housing construction	Batey Cuchilla	15	44,819.82
		Villa Nizao	30	80,000.47
		Polo	20	59,767.60
		Granado y Guanarate	53	168,936.75
	Start-up production of 225 tareas	Arroyo Seco		11,865.07
Subtotal				365,389.72
2001–2003 Phase II	Housing construction	Batey 3	20	71,711.71
		Villa Nizao		14,117.73
	Houses	Cabeza de Toro	60	303,110.57
	Start-up production of 225 tareas	Arroyo Seco		2,638,330.00
	Houses repaired	Barahona		11,394.66
	Environ. sanitation	Villa Jaragua		26,510.51
	Reforest fruit trees	Arroyo Seco		30,415.68
Subtotal projects				459,899.19
Total investment				901,823.03

Source: Cáritas Dominicana (2003).

his diocese, he conducted a census to determine the scope of social problems. His data revealed that the three provinces that composed the diocese had overwhelming problems involving nutrition, sanitation, schooling, health, eating habits, deforestation, and so on. He found that over 17 percent of the inhabitants did not possess identity documents; 40 percent of school-aged children (seven to thirteen years) were not attending school; 37 percent of the houses did not have toilets or latrines; and 28 percent did not eat fruits and vegetables. Armed with these statistics, Msgr. Grullón began to develop a comprehensive social pastoral program to address the situation (interview with Msgr. José Dolores Grullón, June 23, 2003).

In 1992, the Diocese of San Juan de la Maguana established the Fundación de Desarrollo de Azua, San Juan y Elías Piña, known as Fundasep (Foundation for the Development of Azua, San Juan, and Elías Piña) to support the social pastoral work within its territory. The bishop mandated Fundasep to support and strengthen other associations that sought to protect natural, socioeconomic, and human resources in the region. In addition to requesting funds from traditional Catholic services agencies, such as Cáritas, Catholic Relief Services, and Miserior, Fundasep was expected to raise funds from international and national sources for the diocese to carry out its social projects. Through a well-orchestrated campaign, Fundasep has enlisted the support of an array of international agencies that include the Fundación Interamericana, the European Union, Manos Unidas de España, the Kellogg Foundation, USAID, and Fondo Menorquín de Cooperación. National sources include the Dominican government and the León Jiménes Group. Unlike other dioceses, where Cáritas is the backbone of the social pastoral program, in San Juan de la Maguana Fundasep became very independent because of its many sources of revenues.

The support Fundasep receives from external and internal sources enabled the diocese to launch an array of social pastoral programs throughout the 1990s, which continues up to the present. As can be seen in table 5.4, the diocese has been able to invest a significant amount of money to help resolve community problems that the state has scarcely addressed. The diocese says it is aware that the government is also working to resolve many of the same problems that it seeks to resolve, but, unlike the government, it uses a method based on accompaniment. According to Msgr. Grullón, the government builds aqueducts to deliver potable water to communities, constructs houses for the victims of hurricanes, and promotes health plans through the Ministry of Health. Once the projects are completed, the government hands them over to a state agency to collect regular service fees. What is different about the church programs? Msgr. Grullón explains:

We work on communities' projects based on the accompaniment approach. We do not build an aqueduct; the community builds it. These are small aqueducts, small community projects that enhance the institutions of the community. The community learns how to build its aqueduct. It asks for it and participates in the project design and its execution. At the end of the project, we have two products: the aqueduct and a more developed community. If the pipe breaks, they will know how to build it and how to repair it rather than waiting for the government's help. This philosophy inspires each of the projects we promote within our diocese. We want to break away from the attitude of dependency that exists in our communities. We want people to become self-reliant rather than dependent. (second interview with Msgr. Grullón, bishop of the Diocese of the Diocese of San Juan de la Maguana, June 23, 2003)

The social pastoral program plays an important role whenever natural disasters occur. When Hurricane George hit the island, Fundasep collaborated with government authorities and civilian organizations to provide relief help for the victims. The social pastoral program worked on two fronts: building houses for the victims of the storm and supporting a prefabricated housing project in collaboration with the Banco Nacional de la Vivienda, BNV (National Housing Bank). With support from Cáritas Dominicana, the diocese helped hurricane victims build their own houses (see table 5.5). A selected beneficiary would borrow $2,043 from the BNV and bring it to the diocese. The social pastoral program would build a small house with two bedrooms, kitchen, bathroom, dining, and washing place in fifteen days. In 2003 prices, a person would pay $10.21 monthly to the BNV, which is significantly lower than the $17.02 or more they would pay for rent.

Table 5.4. Investments in the Diocese of San Juan de la Maguana, 1992–2001

Project	Amount Invested in U.S. Dollars
Environmental sanitation	653,913.29
Potable water	829,704.08
Health	255,339.76
Rural housing	3,484,644.67
Prefabricated houses	2,446,632.62
Agro-forestry and natural resources	757,738.85
Adult literacy programs	571,741.08
Chapels	318,120.50
Const.: school, dispensary, comm. ctr.	71,207.47
Community roads	360,416.22
Total	9,749,458.54

Source: Fundasep (2002).

Table 5.5. Cáritas Dominicana Projects in the Diocese of San Juan de la Maguana

Period	Project	Location	Quantity	Amount Invested in U.S. Dollars
1999–2000	Housing constr.	San Juan	50	161,258.93
Subtotal				161,258.93
2001–2002 Phase I	Housing constr.	San Juan	50	188,639.83
	Potable water + irrigation systems	Padres Las Casas		38,249.91
Subtotal				226,889.74
2001–2002 Phase II	Housing constr.	San Juan	100	452,689.30
	Potable water + irrigation systems	Padres Las Casas		36,558.39
Subtotal of projects				489,247.70
Total investment				877,396.37

Source: Cáritas Dominicana (2003).

The social pastoral programs implemented in the three provinces that make up the Diocese of San Juan de la Maguana have had a significant impact on the living conditions of the population. For example, from 1997 to 2002, the effectiveness of the social pastoral program decreased the number of undocumented persons by 7 percent and the number of houses without bathroom/latrines decreased from 37 to 27.46 percent. Church programs helped diminish the number of children out of school, age seven to thirteen, from 40 percent to 18.20 percent, and the number of persons age fourteen and over who cannot read and write went from 27 percent to 18.82 percent (see web table 5A). Despite the success of these social pastoral programs, Msgr. José Grullón believes that a social pastoral work based on accompaniment remains a goal. After consulting and speaking with all the communities of his diocese, he remains convinced that

> dependence is the greatest national challenge. People are dependent on politicians and the church; they expect others to resolve their problems. For example, when Hurricane George hit our region, we obtained some monetary donations from the USAID and other institutions to build houses. Most people did not want to contribute to build their own houses. We had to tell them that if they did not contribute they would not be beneficiaries of the diocese's project. They finally accepted our conditions, but it took a lot of dialogue to make them understand that they needed to become part of the solution to their own problem. (second interview with Msgr. Grullón, Bishop of San Juan de la Maguana, June 23, 2003)

Social pastoral workers in the other dioceses I studied share Bishop Grullón's concern with dependency. Like Msgr. Grullón, they all believe that accompaniment is the preferred method to implement the social pastoral programs because it seeks to transform beneficiaries into autonomous social actors. However, the reality is that social pastoral workers have not yet organized most communities. The Diocese of San Juan has made significant inroads to promote a social pastoral based on accompaniment to reduce paternalism and assistentialism, but the formation of self-reliant communities remains an objective.

Cedail, Social Pastoral Work, and Human Rights

This section examines Cedail's contribution to the social pastoral work in the nine dioceses and two archdioceses of the country. The first portion focuses on Cedail's program to document children twelve years old and under and on its community education programs. The second analyzes Cedail's human rights work concerning the Haitian immigrants and Dominicans of Haitian descent. Like Cáritas, Cedail implements programs geared to strengthening existing community institutions, developing new ones, and enhancing the role of the church in society.

The CED established Cedail in 1979 following the Third Latin American Bishops' Conference held in Puebla, Mexico. This conference stimulated the national bishops' conference to promote programs that respond to the needs of the poor. It is in this context that Miserior, a German Catholic foundation, allocated seed money for a two-year program to provide legal defense for Haitian migrant workers in the Dominican Republic. Msgr. Priamo Tejeda, auxiliary bishop of the Archdiocese of Santo Domingo and in charge of social pastoral programs, asked Dr. Luisa Campo to lead the agency.

Dr. Campo was a nun/attorney who worked with Jesuit priests in the northern districts of Santo Domingo. She was familiar with the legal needs of the barrios because she was already involved providing legal aid to youths arrested by the police. Miserior had earmarked the funding for the legal defense of Haitian immigrants, but she insisted the program cover poor Dominicans because they had multiple legal needs as well. Dr. Campo was not allowed to use the money to cover Dominicans, but she became instrumental in persuading the CED to establish Cedail as a nonprofit institution providing legal assistance to both Haitians and Dominicans (interview with Luisa Campo, founder of Cedail, June 30, 2004 and Plinio Ubiera, May 27, 2003).

In the following two decades, Cedail developed into a nationwide service agency that coordinates the church's work in human rights. In 2002, Cedail had a four-story building in Santo Domingo, a national office with one executive director, an administrator, three attorneys, and support staff. It also had an attorney in each of the dioceses in charge of the local legal assistance program. The staff of twenty-five persons coordinates its nationwide operations with a budget slightly over $284,203.

Cedail, Undocumented Children, and Building Social Capital

The problem of people without proper identify papers has compounded Cedail's efforts to provide legal counsel to communities in rural and urban settings. Without identity documents, citizens cannot conduct normal legal activities such as declaring a child at the official registry, attending school, voting, or buying a piece of property. Like most issues tackled by the Catholic Church, providing identity documents should be done by the Dominican state, an entity that appears unwilling or unable to launch national registration campaigns. As a small social service agency, Cedail cannot resolve this problem completely, but it can alleviate conditions and raise awareness about it.

Government officials and political observers have attributed children's lack of identity papers to illiteracy, lack of resources, and careless parents who do not register their children at birth. Despite the fact that every municipality in the country has an office to register children at birth, the Encuesta Demográfica y de Salud (Demography and Health Survey), or Endesa 2002, estimates that 40 percent of children fourteen and under do not have identity papers (Molina Achécar 2003).

According to Dominican Law 659 of 1944 (modified as Law 13/93), if parents do not register their children within sixty days (urban) or ninety days (rural) after their birth, they have to apply for late birth registration. This process is usually complex and costly because people must travel to visit all the civil registries within their province to obtain certificates indicating that they are not registered in those offices. In addition, the law mandates that to obtain a late birth registration, a person needs to provide eleven pieces of documentation and obtaining it is usually burdensome.[3] To speed up this process, the president of Cedail, Msgr. José Dolores Grullón, negotiated an agreement with the JCE (Central Electoral Board), the government institution in charge of the civic registry, to coordinate its programs in both urban and rural communities. These programs consist of helping undocumented persons obtain their identity papers in each diocese. In short, the JCE and Cedail agreed to

- coordinate programs of birth registration through Cedail's diocesan centers;
- coordinate with judicial authorities to speed up the ratification of birth certificates registered by the birth registration programs;
- coordinate the exemption of payment to the civil registry in each birth registration program;
- conduct censuses and establish receiving centers for the reception of documents;
- coordinate birth registration programs with parishes, institutions, and organizations in places identified for such purpose. (Cedail 2001, 15)

The JCE authorized Cedail to organize birth registration programs in designated parishes and communities. With financial support from CRS and UNICEF, Cedail developed birth registration programs that have three components: preliminary registration, registration, and postregistration. Preliminary registration is the initial organization of the process, in which

Table 5.6. Cedail Educational and Legal Programs, 2001–2002

Project	Place	Amount Invested in U.S. Dollars
Legal ed. of Haitian immigrants and Dominicans of Haitian descent (CRS)	Esperanza, Mao	39,689.94
Democracy, rule of law and participation (PID)	La Vega	24,641.70
Pastoral of human rights (CRS)	In all dioceses	2,281.10
Birth registration programs (UNICEF)	Sto. Dgo. , Mao, S. Frco., San Pedro, Stgo, Pto. Plata, La Altagracia, and Baní	7,210.36
Institutional evaluation (CRS)	In all dioceses	67,961.73
Internship for students from the Catholic university-PUCMM (CRS)	Esperanza, Mao	813.79
Office equipment (own funds)	Santo Domingo, La Vega, Mao	2,094.39
Outsourced staff	Santo Domingo	9,217.13
Total		96,472.38

Source: Cedail (2002).

Cedail educates the community and local authorities through workshops on the importance of identity papers for citizens. It also provides the community with information regarding the documents people need to register their children twelve years old and under. The registration phase involves submitting the necessary documentation to Cedail's lawyers. Postregistration consists of moving the documents through the bureaucratic process until they reach the civil registry and it issues the certificates (interview with Noemí Méndez, a Cedail lawyer in charge of the eastern region, June 4, 2003; see table 5.6).

The success of the birth registration program depends on the training and reliability of paralegal personnel in beneficiary communities. The education of paralegal personnel entails educating community leaders to provide basic assistance on human rights issues. Cedail organized a two-year program in Esperanza, Mao, to train fifty paralegal community workers who can now provide legal assistance and prepare their communities for the birth registration programs. As a result of this training, these paralegal workers helped register 540 Dominican children of Haitian descent who live in a Haitian neighborhood (*batey*) near the city of Esperanza, Mao (interview with Desiré Del Rosario, Cedail lawyer in charge of the northern region, July 7, 2003).

Table 5.7. The Activities of Cedail in Social Pastoral Programs, 2001–2002

Issue	Number of Cases Resolved
Criminal	2,500
Civil	1,795
Sexual violation	465
Land tenure	876
Family violence	1,579
Abuse of minors	543
Birth registration	15,621
Labor	150
Migration	275
Municipal	39
Assistance to prisoners	1,325
Total	25,168

Source: Cedail (2002).

Cedail's training of community leaders goes beyond legal issues. With financial support from the Programa para Iniciativas Democráticas, PID (Program for Democratic Initiatives), Cedail developed a series of workshops in La Vega to educate people on the rule of law and democratic participation. In addition to a series of lectures given by Cedail lawyers, beneficiary communities received a series of brochures dealing with human rights, the prison system, social security, democratic participation and government, agrarian reform and property rights, and the like.

They also provided assistances to communities nationwide on sexual violence, family violence, abuse of minors, prisons, migration, and penal and civil issues (see table 5.7). These programs all provide assistance and build social capital through a social pastoral program of accompaniment where both individuals and communities learn to resolve their own problems. Those served by Cedail and the social pastoral in general develop an admiration for the church, even if they do not go to Sunday mass.

Cedail, Haitian Immigration, and Human Rights

We must put Cedail's pastoral work with Haitian immigrants in context to understand why Dominican authorities have implemented laws and regulations that exclude them from economic, social, and political life. Haitian-Dominican relations have been conflict ridden for nearly two centuries. It is important to remember that the Dominican Republic is the only country in the Americas that obtained its independence from another Latin American country. Haiti had invaded the emerging Dominican Republic in 1821 and occupied it for twenty-two years. When Dominicans declared their independence in 1844, Haiti did not recognize it. During the next ten years, Haiti waged war against the new nation state, which led to further animosities between the two countries. In the twentieth century, as already noted in chapter 2, Trujillo ordered the army to conduct mass killings of Haitian immigrants in 1937, which complicated the relationships between the two countries.

Haitian immigration and subsequent human rights violations are not new issues in the Dominican Republic. The twentieth-century story of these violations began when sugar plantations developed in the eastern and southern regions of the country. Initially, sugar companies, with government aid, evicted Dominican peasants from their lands to open fields for cane sugar cultivation at the turn of the twentieth century. These evictions constituted the first important rounds of gross human rights violations in the twentieth century.

At the same time, sugar companies imported cane cutters from Haiti to work in sugar plantations because Dominican peasants did not want to cut cane at the price paid by sugar companies. They could do much better working on their own plots. Sugar companies brought Haitian workers to live in isolated ethnic neighborhoods called *bateyes*, whose living conditions were subhuman. Terrible working and living conditions was the second round of human rights violations.

During the Trujillo dictatorship (1930–1961), Dominican workers organized labor unions, but the regime suppressed them when workers asked for better working conditions and higher wages. Following the overthrow of Trujillo in 1961, labor unions organized again and partially succeeded in gaining basic labor rights. Peasants were unable to organize during the Trujillo dictatorship, but during the Balaguer regime (1966–1978) they formed organizations with support from local priests. They exerted political pressure on the regime to implement agrarian reform. In the 1980s, Cedail emerged as a provider of legal advice to labor unions in the sugar sector. In fact, it joined international human rights organizations that requested visits by the International Labor Organization to investigate conditions in the bateyes and in the state-owned sugar mills (interview with Freddy Báez, a Cedail lawyer in charge of the southern region, June 4, 2003).

Sugar production declined in the 1980s, and today it is no longer an important dynamic sector in the economy. The Dominican government privatized the state-owned sugar industry, forcing thousands of workers into unemployment. Privatization legislation has forced both Dominican and Haitian workers to migrate to the urban centers in search of jobs in the construction industry, agriculture, and petty commerce. Many Haitian cane cutters have become unskilled construction workers in the cities of Santo Domingo and Santiago. However, older Haitian workers, who spent their lives in the sugar field, no longer have the strength to work in agriculture or construction. The government and sugar companies left them behind in the bateyes with no pension or health coverage. Worse, they do not have identity papers, which the Vicini and the Central Romana Corporation require to honor their pensions. Cedail established birth registration programs to enable both Dominican and Haitian workers to obtain identity papers and has set up programs to provide legal assistance to laid-off workers, both Dominican and Haitian, who claim pensions.

The agrarian reform promoted by Balaguer in the 1970s did not resolve most land tenure claims, and many Dominican peasants remain landless or live on lands without proper titles. As the sugar industry a century ago, today the tourism industry is the fastest-growing sector in the eastern region. It needs all the land it can get, either near the beaches or in the flat plains to develop golf courses. Investors in the tourism industry found peasants living on the lands they wanted to develop. The peasants had lived on those lands for generations but lacked legal titles to them. Cedail counsels peasant communities who fight eviction from their lands, this time by the tourism industry (interview with Noemí Méndez, a lawyer in charge of the eastern region for Cedail, June 4, 2003).

The conditions of Haitians and Dominicans of Haitian descent are much worse than those of Dominican citizens. The vast majority of Haitian workers work long hours at low wages and have no job security. Their living conditions are precarious and they have no legal protection to make any claims in their jobs. This means that the Dominican state and society routinely discriminate against them and exclude them from many aspects of life. Historically, Haitian bateyes have lacked basic social services such as electricity, potable water, and sanitation. In 2000, this situation had not improved. Law 141-97, the Privatization of Public Enterprise Law, does not require private investors to take care of the basic needs of the bateyes. Most bateye dwellers live in barracks, and less than a quarter live in duplex houses. Over half the bateyes are located on lands that belong to the CEA (State Sugar Council), and two-thirds do not have potable water or sanitation. Education and health services are meager: 16 percent of the bateyes do not receive health services; 4 percent do not have a medical dispensary; and 3 percent of rural clinics and small-scale pharmacies are available only in 2 percent of the communities. Thirty percent of the bateyes do not have a formal school, which explains why there is 33 percent illiteracy among the population who live in these communities (PNUD 2005, 141).

In addition to these depressing conditions, Haitian immigrants and Dominicans of Haitian descent confront mass deportation because of their illegal status in the Dominican Republic. Following the downfall of the Duvalier dynasty in 1986, Haitian migration to the Dominican Republic increased because of political and economic instability in Haiti. Despite the importance of Haitian immigration, no one knows exactly how many Haitians live in the country. This is a controversial issue. On the one hand, right-wing nationalist groups believe that Haitians are invading the country; on the other hand, Dominican farmers and construction firms want to maintain the status quo because they want cheap labor.

Nationalists probably exaggerate when they claim that over a million Haitians live in the country. The Dominican Census of 1991 estimated the number of Haitian immigrants to be 245,737. This figure does not include the number of Dominicans of Haitian origins who are not immigrants. Unfortunately, ten years later, the Dominican census did not ask about national origins, so we do not know what the population is now. We know, however, that through the 1990s and early in the twenty-first century, the worsening political and economic crises in Haiti forced people to migrate. Field observations, newspapers articles published in the Dominican press, and conversations with experts indicate that Haitian immigration has increased significantly over the last ten to fifteen years. The estimates of the United Nations Development Program in the Dominican Republic indicate that this increase was substantial (see web table 5B). This immigration is no longer restricted to the sugar industry, which has nearly disappeared, but is spread all over the country in the most important sectors of the economy, including agriculture, poultry, cattle, construction, and small businesses.

The Dominican government has tried to stop Haitian immigration through forced deportations. It stepped up deportations in 1991 when, at the United Nations, Haitian president Jean Bertrand Aristide denounced the treatment that his compatriots received in the Dominican Republic. Dominican president Joaquín Balaguer (1990–1994) who, at the time, faced an economic crisis at home, took advantage of this opportunity to retaliate by increasing deportations. Although declining now, deportations remained strong through the 1990s and continued in the next decade (see figure 5.1).

Dominican security forces deport Haitian workers on the grounds that they lack legal status in the country and that they are acting within the framework of international law, which recognizes the sovereign rights of states to regulate their borders. However, the Dominican government does not comply with the American Convention on Human Rights, which establishes minimal due process protections to ensure fair deportation adjudica-

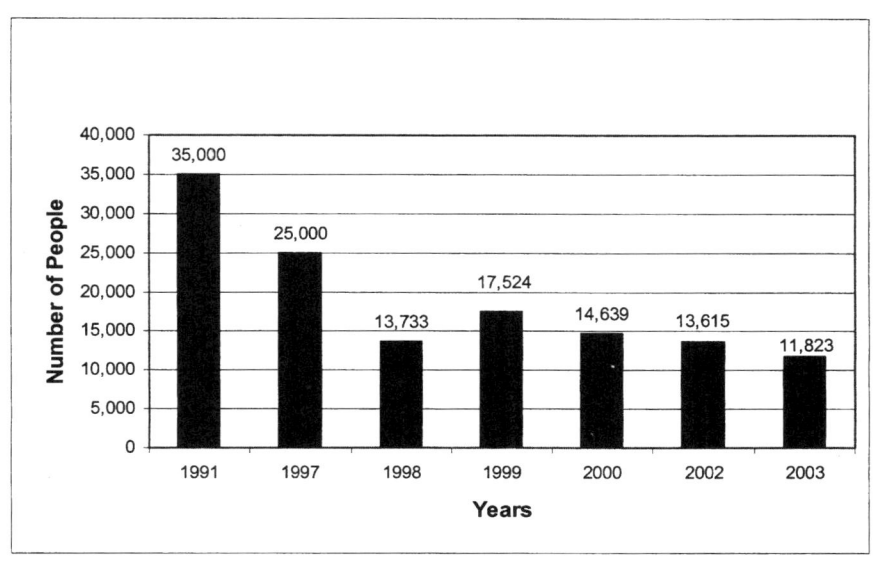

[Figure: Bar chart showing Number of People by Year — 1991: 35,000; 1997: 25,000; 1998: 13,733; 1999: 17,524; 2000: 14,639; 2002: 13,615; 2003: 11,823]

Figure 5.1. Haitians Deported from the Dominican Republic, 1991–2003
Source: PNUD (2005, 128).

tion. Nor does it abide by the Protocol of Understanding, which it signed with the Haitian government in 1999. This agreement establishes procedures regulating the time, place, and manner of deportation. For example, the Protocol of Understanding declares that Dominican authorities must not separate families and that deportees can have their possessions at all times. Dominican authorities must notify their Haitian counterparts at the border about deportations. Deportees must receive any nonfraudulent documentation (República Dominicana y República de Haití, 1999).

Human rights workers at the northern and southern border told me that Dominican authorities do not meet any of these conditions. The Dominican police detain expellees in irregular manners, whether they are at work or walking on the streets. They separate families, and children are often left abandoned. When Haitians are detained, Dominican guards take all their possessions and never return them. Deportees receive little food and water and are subject to arbitrary treatment. They are transported in harsh conditions and have to remain inside a bus for hours or days at a time (interview with Xavier Lejeune and Alejandro Robles, human rights workers for Solidaridad Fronteriza in Dajabón, May 30, 2003; interview with Fr. Pedro Ruquoy, parish priest at Batey Cinco, Barahona; Fletcher and Miller, 2004).

Deportation of Haitian immigrants and Haitians of Dominican descent led to protests from international human rights organizations, Cedail, and other local NGOs. In the 1970s and 1980s, international and national human rights organizations focused their attention on the recruiting system and the living conditions of Haitian in the bateyes. In the 1990s, organizations such as Americas Watch, National Coalition for Haitian Refugees, Caribbean Rights, and the AFL-CIO pressed the U.S. government to make the Dominican Republic ineligible for the generalized system of preference because of its violations of the rights of Haitian cane cutters and free-trade-zone workers. Despite these denunciations, the Dominican government continued to deport Haitians through the 1990s, but, at the same time, it charged the Dirección General de Migración, DGM (General Migration Office), to begin issuing identity cards to migrant workers. From 1998 to 2000, the DGM issued around 12,787 identity cards, mostly to Haitian workers in the agricultural sector. Similarly, the government introduced a system to issue entry visas to Haitians, which has led to a notable increase in the movement of people across the border (interview with Franc Báez Evertsz, July 10, 2004). These political pressures were effective, but as deportations declined, organizations such as Cedail and local NGOs that work with Haitian immigrants have been left to provide basic assistance to immigrant workers.

The problem of documenting the children of Haitian immigrants remains a formidable challenge to Cedail and to Dominican society if the Dominican government does not change the birth registration law. In a study of an urban Haitian community in a northern district of Santo Domingo, Franc Báez Evertsz found that 89 percent of heads of households born in the country reported having some kind of identification, but only 66 percent of those born in Haiti reported having one.

The longer people from Haiti live in the country, the higher the probability that they have identity documents, but the difference is insignificant. Women are less likely than men to have some kind of personal document of identification. Fifty-nine percent of men have some kind of documentation and only 54 percent of women reported identify documents. The situation with youth and children is the most problematic: 59 percent of the children do not have identification documents. This figure increases to 69 percent when one looks at children under the age of five years old (Báez Evertsz 2001, 66–71). My observations and conversations with Cedail lawyers indicate that the situation is much worse in the countryside, where both Haitians and Dominicans have fewer opportunities to register their children.

The problems confronted by Haitian immigrants and their children are overwhelming. Because most of these workers are undocumented, they pass this status on to their children who are born in the Dominican Republic. The Dominican state does not grant citizenship to Haitian children, because they are "foreigners in transit." Consequently, Dominican authorities deny Haitians the rights and privileges enjoyed by all Dominicans, such as obtaining identity documents and attending public schools. Denial of access to public schools to Haitian children is an old issue in the country. It was even made official in 1999, when it appeared in the Reglamento de Instituciones Educativas Públicas (Rules and Regulation of Institutions of Public Education), which was approved by Consejo Nacional de Educación (National Council of Education). This prohibition contradicts the International Convention of the Rights of Children and the Code for the System of Protection of Children and Adolescents, which was agreed on by the Dominican State (PNUD 2005, 142).

This action allows human rights organizations to accuse the Dominican government of failing to comply with its international obligations. As noted earlier, Cedail has established programs to help the children of Haitian immigrants, but it cannot resolve this problem until the Dominican Congress changes birth registration laws. As of now, Dominican laws do not recognize birthrights of Dominicans of Haitian descent. If nothing more, Cedail's social pastoral programs of accompaniment with Haitian immigrants shows that the church is acting in areas neglected by the state.

Conclusion

Cáritas and Cedail have been instrumental in supporting the church's social pastoral programs and carrying both legal and social assistance in poor communities neglected by the Dominican state. These agencies aim at developing social capital, empowering communities, and resolving pressing community issues such as housing, land ownership, identity documents, migration, and human rights violations. However, Cedail's and Cáritas's accomplishments in fostering a pastoral program of accompaniment in communities located in all the dioceses and archdioceses are modest. Their work retains an assistentialist character and still needs to enlist the support of most parish priests, whose involvement in the promotion of a pastoral program of accompaniment is rather limited.

This research reveals that while it is true that the social pastoral work contributes to the strengthening of ties between church and communities, its achievements are poor. My examination of four dioceses where bishops have pushed for the implementation of a social pastoral program based on accompaniment exposes these limitations: the social pastoral work is still based on assistentialism and accompaniment is still a goal to be achieved. These shortcomings are obviously associated with the limited resources available for church personnel to carry out its mission, but the task is overwhelming due to issues of underdevelopment, widespread poverty, and the subsequent dependent mentality created by years of church- and state-sponsored asistentialism. Notwithstanding this inadequacy, social pastoral work tends to contradict the hegemonic neoconservative orientation that seems to be so close to the power structure of society. The social pastoral programs show that the church is a multifaceted institution that seeks to appeal to the entire society, not just to one sector of it. Church social welfare programs contribute immensely to enhance the perception that it is engaged in solving local and national issues rather than just mediating to resolve the disputes of the elite.

Notes

1. This chapter draws extensively on interviews with the following bishops: Msgr. Antonio Camilo González, Diocese of La Vega; Jose Grullón, Diocese of San Juan de la Maguana; Tomás Jerónimo Abreu, Diocese of Mao-Montecristi; and Rafael Felipe, Diocese of Barahona. It also draws on interviews with the following Catholic priests: José Luis Sáez, Antonio Lluberes, José Núñez, Antonio Fernández, Regino Martínez, and Pedro Ruquoy. I also acknowledge information provided to me by the following nuns: Luisa Campos, Margarita Ruiz, Amelia Encarnacion, Sonia Adames, Altagracia Contreras, and Elvira Minaya.

2. Inculturation means "the process of discerning where God is at work in a culture and articulating a theology sensitive to the local context" (Cleary 2005, 4).

3. (a) A letter from the mayor (if born in rural areas) or a certificate from a clinic or hospital.
  (b) A certificate from the church indicating whether the person was baptized.
  (c) A certificate from the school if the person is studying.
  (d) A certificates from all the civil registries that correspond to the person's place of birth.
  (e) Copies of the parents' identity and electoral cards.
  (f) If the parents are deceased, copies of the death certificates.
  (g) If the parents are married, a copy of their marriage certificate.
  (h) A sworn and signed statement by a witness over fifty years old. A copy of the identity and electoral cards must be included.
  (i) A letter addressed to the president of the Central Electoral Board requesting the birth certificate.
  (j) A letter addressed to the president of the Central Electoral Board requesting a certificate if the person has an identity and electoral card.
  (k) Two 2 x 2 photos.

CHAPTER SIX

Evangelicals and Politics: Challenges and Opportunities

Today it is impossible to discuss organized religion and politics in Latin America without taking into account the emergence of the evangelical movement. As elsewhere in Latin America, evangelicals are the fastest-growing religious group in the Dominican Republic. This chapter looks at their integration into the mainstream of Dominican life. It examines this phenomenon in the context of changes in the religious field in Latin America. These changes have affected the Dominican state, which needs to confront new ecclesiastical institutions seeking societal recognition. This analysis centers on the political implications of evangelicalism, not on their religious significance. To accomplish this, I first examine changes in the Latin American religious arena and then look at the Dominican case as an illustration of the evangelicals' incorporation into politics. I argue that the rapid growth of the evangelical movement in the Dominican Republic is the result of mutations in the religious field that occurred in the context of profound socioeconomic and cultural transformations. These changes were largely but exclusively imposed from abroad. Evangelicals broke the Catholic religious monopoly and have begun to carve out a space in Dominican society and politics and as such challenge both the Catholic Church and the state.[1]

Changes in the Latin American Religious Field

The Latin American religious field saw dramatic changes in the latter part of the twentieth century. The Catholic Church monopolized this arena for nearly five hundred years and became one of the main pillars of legitimization of political power. Following independence from Spain and Portugal (1810–1824), Protestant missionaries arrived in many parts of Latin America, but they did not have a significant impact beyond small groups of people who were mostly merchants and immigrants from Protestant countries.

Protestants were generally well educated and situated within modern social sectors (i.e., they were workers, small property owners, schoolteachers, employees, etc.). Many Latin Americans who converted to Protestantism in the nineteenth century tended to support a type of radical liberalism that opposed the political influence of the Catholic Church. Therefore, Protestants participated in the important democratic struggles of the second half of the nineteenth and the first half of the twentieth centuries. Members of Protestant congregations supported the antislavery campaigns in Brazil (1870–1889), Cuban wars of independence (1868–1898), the Mexican Revolution (1910–1940), the *tenentes*' (lieutenants'') movement in Brazil (1920 and 1930), the citizens' movement (*movimiento civilista*) in Peru (1920–1940), agrarian revolution in Guatemala (1944–1954), and the Cuban Revolution (1959) in its early stage (Bastian 1986b). A tiny minority of citizens who were concerned with promoting liberal democracy came from a Latin American Protestantism that emerged from the political culture of radical liberalism, Masonic lodges, and educational institutions.

After the 1950s, the religious landscape changed radically in Latin America. People who converted to Protestantism were no longer just from small social enclaves. Unlike historical Protestants, the new Protestants, known as evangelicals, or Pentecostals in Latin America, have become a mass religious movement whose social and cultural consequences are already changing the region's political landscape. From the 1950s to the 1990s, over 50 million Latin Americans converted to evangelical Protestantism, that is, approximately 11 percent of the total population. Political scientist Fr. Edward Cleary acknowledges that "religious conversion is the single greatest social process changing Latin America and the Caribbean in the twentieth and twenty-first centuries. Conversions from and within religious groups have rocked the region and changed the face of religion. The process has taken place through a series of quiet explosions that are only now becoming clear" (Cleary 2004, 50). Undoubtedly, the massive presence of evangelicals in Latin American societies has implications that go beyond religion and affect other areas.

The Incorporation of Evangelicals into Latin American Politics
Changes in the religious field have introduced a new dynamic to the political participation of Protestants. Unlike historical Protestants in the nine-

teenth and early twentieth centuries, evangelicals constitute a popular religious movement whose political orientation is not homogeneous. There are at least two important political constituencies evolving within the Latin American evangelical community.

The first constituency is composed of traditional evangelical leaders who do not want to take sides with particular political parties; they prefer to develop a strategy to gain the recognition of public authorities. These leaders want, above all, to be legitimate bearers of salvation goods. They want to be in a position that would allow them to influence the changing Latin American religious scene and need, therefore, to develop a relationship with established public authorities rather than political parties.

The second constituency is made up mostly of the so-called neoevangelical leaders, also called neo-Pentecostal, who claim to be more flexible than traditional evangelicals regarding religious norms. Neoevangelical leaders apparently want to take advantage of conflicts between the Catholic Church and the state to advance their political and religious interests. This was the case of Chile under Augusto Pinochet in the 1970s and 1980s, Guatemala under Efraín Ríos Montt and other military rulers in the 1980s, and Nicaragua under the Sandinistas in the 1980s. As noted in chapter 2, the Catholic Church in Chile and Guatemala opposed repressive political measures that caused the disappearance of thousands of political opponents. In Nicaragua, the Catholic Church opposed the Sandinista Revolution for different reasons. Archbishop Obando y Bravo claimed that the Sandinistas were an atheist regime that undermined the Catholic religion. He perceived Sandinista support for the popular church as leading to a division within the church, and he was not going to allow it. This explains why he tacitly supported the counterrevolution as a way of getting rid of a regime that appeared to question his authority. In all three cases, prominent evangelical pastors tried to take advantage of these conflicts to gain legitimacy in the eyes of public authorities (Bastian 1986a, 48–54).

During the democratic transition that unfolded in the 1980s, many neoevangelical leaders promoted the formation of evangelical political parties. They believed that the evangelical community was large enough to play a greater role in politics. Political organizations with close ties to evangelical churches sought elected office at the local, provincial, and national levels. From 1980 to 1994, evangelicals organized twenty-four political parties in eleven countries: Argentina, Bolivia, Brazil, Chile, Colombia, El Salvador, Guatemala, Mexico, Peru, Venezuela, and the Dominican Republic. These parties are small, however, and their influence is still limited.

Unlike historical Protestants, the evangelicals constitute a popular movement whose political orientation is not different from that of the general population. Public opinion surveys show that church affiliation has little to do with party affiliation in Latin America. Steigenga's findings suggest that this is also true in Central America. Roderic Camp found similar results in Mexico when he compared Catholic and non-Catholic voting preferences (Camp 1997, 120–21; Smith, 1998, 43–44; Steigenga, 2001, 51–62). Nevertheless, evangelical political parties and ecclesiastical institutions have introduced a new ingredient into the Latin American political stew. The Dominican Republic illustrates how evangelicals have begun their transition into the mainstream of politics and society as a whole.

Evangelicals and Politics in the Dominican Republic

The remaining portions of this chapter examine the emergence of evangelicals and their integration into the mainstream in the Dominican Republic. It reviews the presence of historical Protestant, or mainline, churches in the country; the growth of evangelicalism since the 1960s; their challenges to the Catholic Church and the Dominican state; and their integration into mainstream politics. Most Dominican evangelical leaders seek state recognition as carriers of salvation goods who want to exert their influence in religious and political arenas. As noted below, only a tiny minority entertains the possibility of creating a confessionary political party. Here I examine how mainstream evangelicals use politics to obtain prerogatives that would allow them to succeed in the religious arena.

The Historical Background of Dominican Protestantism

The presence of historical Protestantism in the Dominican Republic is rather weak. The first important appearance of Protestants occurred in 1824, when Haitian president Jean-Pierre Boyer (1818–1843) authorized missionaries to bring six thousand free American blacks to take up residence on the island of Hispaniola. Historian George Lockward reports that most of them went to Haiti, but the Haitian government distributed some 2,400 in different areas of the eastern portion of the island. The Haitian government allocated them in three different trips: 1,200 were supposed to disembark in Santo Domingo, 200 would be sent to Samaná, and 1,000 were to go offshore in Puerto Plata (Hoetink 1994, 29–31; Lockward 1982, 43).

Soon after, Protestant pastors established the first Methodist Wesleyan Society in Puerto Plata, where missionaries built a chapel with a capacity for two hundred people. Methodist missionaries founded the second society in

Samaná and established a congregation with sixty members. In both cases, the preaching was done in English, but it promoted education in Spanish as a means to have an influence in society. The activities of the missionaries did not receive major opposition from the Catholic Church until 1861, when Spain reannexed the Dominican Republic. As noted in chapter 1, the Vatican appointed Don Bienvenido Monzón y Puente archbishop of Santo Domingo and introduced a series of strict religious regulations, including abolishing Protestant societies and churches.

Fearing religious persecution, Protestant missionaries wrote President Abraham Lincoln asking for protection from Spanish authorities. It was this fear that led many Protestants—the so-called Americans from Puerto Plata and Samaná—to join forces with Dominican nationalists when they fought to force Spain to leave the country in the War of Restoration of Independence (Lockward 1982, 234–40). In a way, this war gave Dominican Protestants a "birth certificate" and, like their Cuban, Brazilian, and Mexican counterparts, allied them with progressive liberal nationalist forces. Despite this identification with national politics, Protestants continued to form their own societies and preached in English to their followers.

The Free Methodist Church was the first to start breaking out of isolation by preaching in Spanish and promoting education. Pastor Samuel E. Mills of the Free Methodist Church of Ashtabula, Ohio, took up residence in the Dominican Republic and, in 1889, began to preach in Spanish in the northern city of Monte Cristi. Mills later moved to Santiago and then to San Francisco de Macoris. In both places, the Free Methodist Church left a legacy of education. In Santiago, it founded the Instituto Evangélico (Evangelical Institute) in 1917, and in San Francisco de Macoris, the Colegio Lincoln (Lincoln school) in 1916. In spite of its progress in promoting education, Rev. Israel Brito, seemingly the official historian of the Free Methodist Church, recognizes its slow growth during its first seventy years. The Free Methodist Church grew from less than 1,000 members in 1935 to 7,170 in 1975. Brito attributes this sluggish growth to the "lack of concern for the organization of statistics to reveal the increase or decrease of membership" (Brito 1978, 42, 77), but the Dominican religious field remained under Catholic monopoly, which made it difficult, if not impossible, for Protestant churches to grow. In short, for many Dominicans the Free Methodist Church still was a foreign church that ministered mostly to urban middle-class people.

The Episcopal, Evangelical, and Moravian churches directed their evangelizing efforts only to English-speaking workers in the southeastern regions of the Dominican Republic. These regions saw the development of the sugar industry in the latter third of the nineteenth century. American, Cuban, and

Italian capitalists invested in the sugar industry, expanded towns into cities, enlarged ports, and built railroads to connect sugar mills with seaports. The wages paid by the sugar companies were low, and Dominican peasants, unfamiliar with intensive capitalist exploitation, preferred to retreat to their plots of land rather than cut sugar cane for foreign corporations. A significant number of peasants formed guerrilla forces to fight the sugar companies to keep their land and way of life (Calder 1984, 115–32). Foreign firms first imported workers from the English-speaking Lesser Antilles and then brought thousands of workers from Haiti. The companies preferred the more skilled English-speaking workers to operate machines in the industrial phase of sugar production.

The relationship of Protestants with U.S. sugar companies and the U.S. military government installed in the country from 1916 to 1924 varies significantly from church to church. The Dominican Episcopal Church illustrates a case of close collaboration with both the U.S. occupation of 1916–1924 and sugar capitalists. The Church of England in the Lesser Antilles sent Reverend William Wyllie to work in San Pedro de Macoris, the heartland of sugar production, to conduct missionary work. By the time Wyllie arrived, Rev. Benjamin I. Wilson had already been working with both the English- and Spanish-speaking populations in San Pedro for twenty-two years. Rev. Wyllie arrived two years after the U.S. military occupation of the Dominican Republic (1916–1924), discontinued ministering to the Spanish-speaking population, and asked the military government for assistance to establish his work among foreigners. He also established a small day school for American children, which lasted the entire time of the military occupation. The successors to Rev. Wyllie did not establish services in Spanish until 1952, and the first native Dominican, Telesforo Isaac, was not ordained until 1958 (Wipfler 1966, 131–47).

The growth of the Episcopal Church was very modest in the first half of the twentieth century. In the early 1960s, the church had eighteen congregations located in five different centers. Its growth took place mostly after 1955, when the Episcopal Church began to minister in Spanish. In the early 1960s, it continued its educational work by operating eight parochial day schools, an evening high school, a domestic science program, and two day nurseries with 1,700 children. Despite this progress, the Episcopal Church was still very small with a membership of just over 3,000 with communicants reaching 1,300 (Wipfler 1966, 16).

Unlike the Episcopal Church, the Dominican Evangelical Church was more cautious in its relations with the U.S. military government. The decisive event in establishing the church in the Dominican Republic occurred in

1919, when Dr. Samuel G. Inman, the executive secretary of the Committee on Cooperation in Latin America, visited. Dr. Inman made his recommendations to five different missionary boards, which agreed to begin missionary work there. A budget of $80,000 was earmarked for the Dominican mission, and the board named Rev. Philo W. Drury as the first superintendent of the Dominican Evangelical Church. Dr. Nathan Huffman of the evangelical United Brethren in Puerto Rico accompanied Rev. Drury. They bought property in Santo Domingo and found a Puerto Rican pastor to take charge of it. With help from Puerto Rican volunteers, they established two missions: San Pedro de Macoris and La Romana.

The leaders of the Dominican Evangelical Church wanted to lay solid foundations in Dominican soil. They recognized positive and negative elements in the U.S. military occupation of the country. On the positive side, the military government facilitated travel, stimulated interest in health and education, and welcomed Protestant leaders. On the negative side, influential Catholics linked Protestant missionaries to the military occupation. Because of this, the leadership of the church avoided excessive fraternization with the U.S. military government (Wipfler 1966, 158–60).

Local authorities have recognized the work of the Dominican Evangelical Church in health and education. It began its medical missions in 1921, and by 1932 established the International Hospital in Santo Domingo, which offered its services for twenty-five years. The Dominican Evangelical Church also organized the first nursing school in the country and prepared nearly 150 young women in that profession. Julio Postigo, one of the first converts to evangelicalism, founded the Librería Dominicana, which opened to sell Bibles but went on to sell books and became known as a cultural center that promoted literacy, live theater, literature, and talks by well-known Dominican intellectuals. The success of these activities led Postigo to add a second story to the library and a printing shop, which published the church's periodicals. To stimulate Dominican writers, Postigo established contests to give awards to young authors and published anthologies of famous Dominican authors. Postigo led the Librería Dominicana for twenty-nine years (1937–1966) and made an important contribution both to Dominican culture and the promotion of the Protestant religion (Martínez 1994, 101–37).

Despite its success with the medical mission and the librería, the Dominican Evangelical Church remained very small. In 1960, the church reported eighty congregations and 3,000 full members and about the same amount of related individuals. The church transformed the medical missions into baby clinics and closed the International Hospital in 1957. The church operated a network of schools in six cities. In 1963, these schools had 2,300 children enrolled. Although Protestants considered it the most indigenous of the historical Protestant churches, it was financially dependent on the Board of Christian Work in New York City (Wipfler 1966, 15).

The Moravian Church was another historically Protestant church that ministered to the West Indian sugar workers. A Moravian pastor established it in 1911, with 147 English-speaking members in San Pedro de Macoris. The pastor's sympathy for the sugar workers' plight helped church membership increase rapidly. Only three years later, it had grown to 1,144 members. Rev. D. E. Phillips, a native of St. Thomas and head of the church of San Pedro, identified himself with labor unions and rejected any race-based discrimination. His activities eventually led to his resignation from the church and departure from the country. Later, the Dominican government deported many of his followers to their country of origin.

Lack of resources prevented the Moravian Church from expanding its mission beyond English-speaking workers. In 1914, it had 1,444 members, and by 1936 when the Dominican government began to favor national workers over imported ones it had reached 2,100. Many members of the Moravian Church returned to their home countries and the church completely stopped working with the non-English speaking population. In 1960, Moravian church authorities transferred the properties of the local church to the Dominican Evangelical Church (Lockward, 1982 302–13).

Historically Protestant churches did not make any significant penetration into the Dominican religious field because most of them conducted their missionary work in English and they apparently did not have the will or the funding to expand their operations. Similarly, their impact on local and national politics was insignificant because missionaries and their followers were mostly foreigners.

Changes in the Dominican Religious Field

The post-Trujillo Dominican society slowly began to see a transformation in the religious field. Changes occurred in the context of the vast cultural, political, ideological, social, and economic adjustments discussed in chapters 3 and 4. The political and economic systems that developed prepared the conditions for what Dominican sociologist Marcos Villamán called the "binomial of modernity-modernization" (Villamán, 1993, 111–14). The popular sectors, particularly those in urban settings, were included in the models of consumption of a modern lifestyle through communication and urbanization. This type of inclusion was not possible at the material level because this type of capitalist modernization did not leave any room for the popular sectors in the formal labor market. In fact, it relegated them to the informal market and widespread poverty. The social conditions created by Dominican capitalist modernization left the popular sectors living in a situation of relative overpopulation and social misery. They were thus vulnerable to symbolic responses to real social problems. According to Villamán:

> The social conditions of people living in settings of relative overpopulation and the perception that they have of this situation constitute suitable circumstances for the reception of the Pentecostal paradigm. The practical and organizational support of the Pentecostal model seeks to respond to religious needs that result from a situation of wretchedness that have not been adequately cared for by the dominant and established religious systems. (Villamán 1993, 113–16)[2]

The emergence of the evangelical religious movement is a noteworthy change in the Dominican religious landscape. Unlike Catholics and mainline Protestants, evangelicalism emphasizes divine healing, belief in speaking in tongues, the filling of the Spirit, deep emotional fervor, adherence to a kind of "holiness doctrine," the importance of prayer and receiving answers to prayer, and a type of literal biblicism that takes the Bible seriously but naively. This religious view calls attention to the inevitability of the present. It preaches that humans cannot do anything to change it. Only God can intervene to provide a solution that would resolve the overwhelming problems of humanity. Thus, conversion is the only opportunity to overcome the current condition of misery and desperation.

Unlike historically Protestant churches that worked with foreigners, evangelical churches carry out their entire mission in Spanish; evangelicals tend to live and work with the poorest sectors of the population and inculturate their version of Protestantism to the practices and values of local people. Evangelicalism becomes Dominican by adapting local musical rhythms, emotional singing styles, and folk Catholicism.

> They reinterpret local belief and superstition in light of the Christian message rather than ridicule it. For the uneducated man, the "evil-eye," spirits, charms, healing, etc., has a significance that no one can destroy by derision. Evangelical sects have attempted to grapple with these beliefs and relate them to the new dispensation of Christ. They continue to be part of the environment, but once a man has accepted Christ they are no longer either a necessity or a threat for him. (Wipfler 1966, 25)

The style of emotional celebration conducted by evangelicals seems to fit quite well with popular culture in Latin America and, in particular, in the Dominican Republic, where people like to dance to all kinds of musical rhythms. Contrary to mainline Protestant churches, evangelicals included local folklore into their services and adapted to local circumstances.

Adaptation to local culture is not limited to the religious field. In the Dominican Republic and in all of Latin America, the tendency for evangelicals is to surrender responsibility for authority to the hands of one man: the pastor. Evangelicals adapt the authoritarian style that is so common in Latin America. In a way, pastors become caciques, local bosses, in their congregations and, when they rise up through the upper ranks of the church hierarchy, they tend to become caudillos, strong regional and national leaders, in a way that resembles authoritarian political developments in the region. In fact, authoritarianism contributes significantly to the fragmentation of evangelicals; pastors use their authority to carve out their space within competitive religious denominations.

The Rise of Evangelicalism

Evangelical Protestantism grew slowly in the first half of the twentieth century. Individual preachers went to San Pedro de Macoris to jump-start their mission in the most cosmopolitan city of the country at that time. One such preacher was Salomón Feliciano, a native of Puerto Rico, who arrived in San Pedro de Macoris in 1918. He built up a modest congregation, but because of lack of funds, he had to leave the country the following year. His followers continued the congregation, but they eventually joined the Dominican Evangelical Church, although its doctrine was substantially different.

Evangelicalism really established its contemporary roots during the Trujillo dictatorship (1930–1961), when the four largest evangelical denominations began their missionary work. These denominations include the Assemblies of God, the Church of God, the Church of God of the Prophesy, and the Church of God Pentecostal. Francisco Hernández González arrived from Puerto Rico in 1930 to begin the work of the Assembly of God. Although he was not a pastor or a professional preacher, he claimed the Holy Spirit had called on him to dedicate his life to God. Hernández established his base of operation in San Pedro de Macoris at the residence of one of his followers. He later expanded his operation to San Pedro de Macoris, Ramón Santana, la Romana, Santo Domingo, and Santiago.

The Pentecostal Church of God sent various other Puerto Rican preachers to the country, but most had to stop their missions because of lack of resources and inability to find supplementary employment to finance their activities. This changed in 1941, when missionaries arrived directly from Missouri to organize the church and to hold a series of conventions to promote it. Pastors preached exclusively in Spanish, and the central church in the United States allowed for a degree of autonomy in the local church. This was a radical departure from the tradition of historically Protestant churches, which directly controlled missionary work. In fact, since 1940, the superintendent of the church, the executive with the highest rank within the Assemblies of God has been a Dominican. Thus, early on, evangelicals sought to adapt to the local society and culture in their preaching style and acceptance of Dominican folkways.

The Church of God began its missionary work in 1939, when Silvestre Jorge arrived from the Bahamas. He began his work in Santo Domingo but soon moved to Santiago, where a group had broken away from the Pentecostal Evangelical Church. Subsequently, Jorge and his associates moved to Puerto Plata and Sánchez, where there was a legacy of Protestantism. Afterward, he wrote in detail to the Church of God in the United States asking for help to establish a mission in the country. The Church of God of the Prophesy emerged in a similar way when Trajano Adrián, a Haitian preacher who had lived in Cuba, started to develop a group of faithful evangelicals in Santo Domingo, particularly in the eastern section of the country. He, too, requested help from the Church of God of the Prophesy in the United States, which sent a fact-finding mission that subsequently recommended absorbing Adrián's mission.

The Church of God Pentecostal and the Assemblies of God have a common origin in the Dominican Republic. Salomón Feliciano, the first evangelical preacher in the Dominican Republic, had worked with Juan L. Lugo in Puerto Rico. Lugo was the pioneer of Puerto Rican evangelicalism and promoted Feliciano's efforts in the Dominican Republic. These arrangements continued until 1956, when the executives of the Assemblies of God and the Puerto Rican evangelical leadership decided to work separately. Nonetheless, preachers of the Puerto Rican Church of God Pentecostal continued to visit the country. On February 23, 1963, Rev. Alberto Martínez registered the Church of God Pentecostal with public authorities (Alvarez Vega 1996, 101–23; Lockward 1982, 132–36).

Measuring the Growth of Evangelicals
Measuring evangelical growth is elusive because of the fragmentation of the movement and the lack of updated lists of church membership. My evaluation of the evangelical growth is based on data gathered by Cornelio Hegeman and Eufemio Ricardo Luis for the "Directorio de Iglesias Evangélicas Dominicanas" (Directory of Dominican Evangelical Churches) (1988) and the Demos and Endesa surveys. Hegeman and Ricardo Luis compiled their data on evangelical churches based on membership lists provided to them by

pastors. They also used statistics compiled by Dario Platt (1981) and data supplied by the *World Christian Encyclopedia*. The validity of these data is questionable, but given subsequent developments in terms of evangelical growth, they do suggest that a pattern had begun to emerge.

Hegeman and Ricardo Luis classified Protestant churches into seven different categories. These categories include traditional (TP) and independent Pentecostal (IP), traditional fundamentalist evangelical (TFE), independent fundamentalist evangelical (IFE), Haitian and Dominican evangelical (HDE), historically Protestant (HP), and Adventist Church (AC).

The difference between TP and IP is the model of church government and its administration. TP is a network of churches organized under one denomination, whereas the IP churches are autonomous. The roots of TFE and IFE churches can be traced back to the Anabaptists or churches of the radical reform. Protestant churches rose against the Catholic Church, but the radical reform churches were not satisfied with the Protestant churches and opposed their liberal form of Protestantism. The difference between these denominations refers to administration and autonomy. The HDE churches are not a denomination but a grouping of small independent churches that include independent Pentecostal and Baptist. The HP refers to the mainline denominations and the AC, which is not evangelical but is a non-Catholic denomination, and grouped as a form of Protestantism.

Despite efforts by evangelical preachers during the Trujillo dictatorship, they were unable to challenge Catholicism's religious domination. In the early 1960s, they were a tiny minority of no more than 45,000 persons out of a population of 3 million (Wipfler 1966, 13). In the 1970s and the 1980s, their numbers began to grow. The TP and IP churches experienced the greatest rate of growth (see table 6.1). The TP include the Assemblies of God, the Church of God, and the Church of God of the Prophesies, which are the largest evangelical denominations in the country. These churches tripled their membership in less than fifteen years, whereas the IP churches doubled their membership. TFE and IFE and HDE churches grew significantly as well. AC and HP grew rapidly, too, but on a slightly smaller scale. In sum, all the non-Catholic religious denominations grew in membership.

Full membership in Protestant churches grew moderately from 1.05 percent of the total population in 1960 to 2.07 percent in 1987. However, the number of affiliates and church attendance grew significantly with respect to the general population (4.15 percent and 6.18 percent respectively for 1987) (see table 6.2).

These data show that the evangelicals had emerged as a new religious group and that Catholicism no longer monopolized the religious landscape.

Table 6.1. Growth of Evangelicals in the Dominican Republic: 1974 and 1988

	Years	Members	Affiliates*	Number of Groups**
TP	1974	16,280	?	290
	1988	49,184	est. 166,298	779
IP	1974	10,000	est. 20,000	Est. 125
	1988	20,000	est. 40,000	Est. 250
TFE	1974	13,122		202
	1988	20,513		440
IFE	1974	360		9
	1988	2,865		40
HDE	1974	620		5
	1988	10,596		426
HP	1974	8,856		51
	1988	10,625	23,866	172
AC	1974	8,319	16,316	?
	1988	25,000	est. 35,000	256
Totals	1974	75,353		765
	1988	138,783		3564

Source: Hegeman and Ricardo Luis (1988).
*Refers to attendees who are not yet members.
**Figures include parishes and preaching centers.
(TP) = Traditional Pentecostal
(IP) = Independent Pentecostal
(TFE) = Traditional Fundamentalist Evangelical
(IFE) = Independent Fundamentalist Evangelical
(HDE) = Haitian-Dominican Evangelical
(HP) = Historically Protestant
(AC) = Adventist Church

Evangelical pastors gave Hegeman and Ricardo Luis the data to build the Directorio. Because many of these pastors might have wanted to show that church membership was higher than what it actually was, I looked at the data collected by research groups accepted by the Dominican academic community, government institutions, and the United Nations. These research groups are the Encuesta Nacional de Cultura Política y Democrática, or Demos (National Survey of Political and Democratic Culture), affiliated with the Pontificia Universidad Católica Madre y Maestra, and the Encuesta Demográfica y de Salud, or Endesa (Demography and Health Survey), associated with the Centro de Estudios Sociales y Demográficos (Center for Social and Demographic Studies). These two surveys show that the number of people who identify themselves as evangelicals has been growing steadily

Table 6.2. Evangelicals and the Dominican Population: 1974 and 1987

Characteristic	Year	Population	Total Membership	Full % of Pop.	# of Affiliates	% of Pop.
Full membership	1974	4,200,000*	75,353	1.79	150,000?	3.57?
	1987	6,707,710	138,783	2.07	276,000?	4.15?
Affiliate membership	1974	4,200,000	150,000 est.	3.57 est.		
	1987	6,707,710	276,000 est.	4.15 est.		
Church attendance	1974	4,200,000	225,353	5.37		
	1987	6,707,000	414,783	6.18		

Source: Hegeman and Ricardo Luis (1988, 89).
*Hegeman and Ricardo Luis point out that these figures are tentative and that the margin of error is bigger in IP churches.

Table 6.3. Growth of Evangelicals according to Three Surveys

Survey	Year	Catholics	All Protestants	Evangelicals	No Religion
Demos	1994	70.4	9.2		21.2
Demos	2001	67.5	12.1		20.9
Endesa	2002	64.3	12.1	9.1	22.8

Sources: Duarte et al. (1996); Duarte et al. (2002); Molina Achécar (2003).
The Demos survey (Duarte et al.), mixes evangelicals with historical Protestants; Endesa (Molina Achécar) reports them separately and shows that evangelicals are the largest Protestant group.

through the 1990s. The number of Catholics has been decreasing slightly from 70.4 percent in 1994 to 64.3 percent in 2002. In contrast, evangelicals (historical Protestants included) have increased from 9.2 percent in 1994 to 12.1 percent in 2001. Looking at evangelicals alone, they comprise 9.1 percent of the population (see table 6.3). The increase in the number of people who do not profess a religion is the most astonishing fact. People who declared no religion increased from 21.2 percent in 1994 to 22.8 percent in 2001 (see table 6.3). This is quite revealing because it indicates that evangelical growth is not necessarily associated with a decrease in the number of people who profess Catholicism as their religion. The bottom line is that the number of evangelicals has increased to 748,996 out of a total population of 8,230,722 (the preliminary figure of the 2002 census).

The Endesa survey (see web table 6A) offers a wide assortment of data showing evangelical growth according to a variety of variables that allows us to understand their location in society. The Endesa team interviewed 27,135 households selected randomly from a population of 8,230,722. According to Endesa, 7.7 percent of males and 10.5 percent of females identified themselves as evangelicals; whereas 61.4 percent of males and 67.3 percent of females self-identified as Catholics. The responses given to the Endesa surveyors deal only with religious identification and do not tell us much about whether people attended religious services regularly or live by the moral standards set by their church. Alvarez Vega (1996 137–40), citing interviews with leaders of the evangelical churches, reported that membership and attendance consisted mostly of women (Assemblies of God, 80 percent; Church of God Pentecostal, 60 percent; Church of God of the Prophesy, 65–70 percent). These data indicate that evangelicalism is like Catholicism in that women's attendance at church is much greater than men's. More in-depth research and field observations are necessary to learn what religious identification really means for both males and females.

The Endesa survey shows that evangelicalism has tended to grow more in the northern and eastern provinces. It is worth recalling that Protestants took residence in those provinces in the nineteenth and early twentieth centuries. Endesa reported the following results for three northern provinces: Puerto Plata, 12.7 percent; Ma. T. Sánchez, 13.1 percent; and Samaná, 21.2 percent. In the eastern provinces, La Romana had 24.5 percent of its population as Protestants; San Pedro had 13.1 percent; La Altagracia had 15.5 percent; El Seibo had 13.7 percent; and Hato Mayor had 11 percent (see web table 6A).

These are the provinces where historically Protestant churches carried out their religious missions. Does that mean that evangelicals are mere continuations of the historically Protestant churches? There is a connection, but it is not as direct as it may seem. As discussed above, Protestant church services were not conducted in Spanish in the northern provinces until 1898, and it was not until the first half of the twentieth century that missionary activities were carried out among English-speaking workers in the eastern provinces. The descendants of these workers, bearers of the Protestant religion, did not succeed in promoting it. In fact, the *chorchas*, as historically Protestant churches are known in the eastern provinces, always had slow growth (Rev. Adalberto Martínez, former vice minister of education, interview with the author, July 10, 2001, and Alfredo Ossers Veras, director of postgraduate education at the Universidad Evangélica in Santo Domingo, interview with the author, June 25, 2004).

In 2002, the chorchas represented 1.2 percent of the historically Protestant population distributed throughout the country. Despite their small size, the chorchas laid some of the groundwork for evangelicals because they were the first to begin preaching Protestantism and exerted a degree of influence in the local society. The growth of evangelicals in provinces where there was no Protestant legacy shows that the religious explosions are complex issues. For example, according to Endesa there was significant growth in the following southern provinces: Santo Domingo, 11 percent; San Cristobal, 11.5 percent; Barahona, 15.7 percent; and Pedernales, 14.4 percent. Evangelicals have also grown from 5 to 8 percent in thirteen other provinces (see web table 6A). This means that this is a nationwide phenomenon, not just a continuation of the historically Protestant churches.

The growth of evangelicals is the product of mutations in the religious field. These transformations were the result of a number of factors, including cultural changes, socioeconomic transformations, and a type of modernization that leaves the vast majority of the population in widespread poverty. These developments are not a mere imposition from outside, but rather the result of the interplay of complex internal and external sociocultural changes. Unlike the chorchas that isolated themselves from the mainstream of society, evangelicals have embraced Dominican culture, especially folk Catholicism. They go where the Catholic Church has limited or no presence at all, which is one reason for their success.

Incorporation of Evangelicals into Dominican Politics

This section examines the incorporation of evangelicals into the political process from the downfall of the Trujillo dictatorship in 1961 to 2004. I divide the period into two parts: the first looks at the process from 1961 to 1994 and the second from the 1994 to 2004. During the first period, individuals acting independently from their churches participated in politics. In the second period, the leadership of ecclesiastical institutions participated in the process of political integration.

There were two types of political tendencies among those individuals who sought to participate in politics from 1961 to 1994. One group wanted to be part of mainstream politics and a second one was critical of the political establishment and proposed to create organizations that encouraged social change. Among the first group, Julio Postigo, Rev. Luis King, and Andrés Reyes stand out as the most prominent evangelical leaders who participated in mainstream politics during the period under study. The second attempted to establish short-lived organizations as noted below.

Incorporating Individual Evangelicals into Politics

Julio Postigo was perhaps the most prominent evangelical leader during the Trujillo dictatorship. As noted above, Trujillo recognized the director of the Librería Dominicana and his activities. In 1955, the Ministry of Education appointed Postigo to the National Commission on Children's Literature and the government sent him to Europe to promote the Feria de la Paz y de la Confraternidad del Mundo Libre (Fair for Peace and Confraternity of the Free World), a major cultural activity the government used to celebrate Trujillo's twenty-fifth anniversary in power. Notwithstanding this recognition, in 1956 security forces arrested Postigo for allegedly participating in communist activities. Francisco Prats Ramírez, a well-connected individual with the local elite, was influential in getting Postigo freed three days later. Prats Ramírez argued that keeping Postigo in jail could lead the Free Methodist Church to denounce the government. Subsequently, the central government appointed Postigo council member of Santo Domingo and vice president of the city council (Martínez 1994, 87–96).

Following the fall of Trujillo, Postigo joined the Dominican Revolutionary Party (PRD) and was elected city council member, a post from which he had to resign because the government chose him as a substitute member in the Junta Central Electoral, JCE (Central Electoral Board). In 1965, when the revolution broke out, Postigo did not side with Bosch's PRD, but joined the government of national reconstruction ostensibly to "soften frictions and collaborate against the chaos" that resulted from the revolution (Postigo 1994). Acceptance of the post caused Postigo significant problems with the Free Methodist Church because the church perceived that his involvement in government in the midst of a revolution brought the Librería Dominicana under suspicion. Postigo resigned from the government in August 1965, but his problems over his post at the Librería did not end and, as a result, he had to retire in 1966 (Martínez 1994, 162–68).

Evangelicals used social connections to resolve political problems and to obtain prerogatives from the state. The story of Reverend Luis M. King of the northern province of Nagua illustrates the case of an evangelical leader whose social activism brought him into conflict with civil authorities. Like Postigo, Rev. King was a member of the Free Methodist Church who was involved in community affairs. Rev. King supported community strikes in the early 1970s and came under government suspicion as a result. Government forces went to Nagua, arrested Rev. King, and took him to the headquarters of the National Police in Santo Domingo. The government had accused him of organizing the strikes in Nagua in 1971 and 1972. Rev. Angel Severino Cáceres, a former general superintendent of the Free Methodist Church, asked General Juan René Beauchamps Javier, minister of the armed forces, and Fernando Alvarez Bogart, director general of the state sugar council, to mediate with President Balaguer to obtain the reverend's release.

These two important government officials were good friends of Rev. Cáceres and Rev. King. They mediated with President Balaguer and convinced him that Rev. King was not a political instigator but rather a strong moral force in the community and that he could be useful to the government. Balaguer met with Rev. King and asked him to accept the post of governor of the province of Nagua. Apparently aware of the conflicts the Free Methodist Church had over Postigo's conflict with the church over the acceptance of a government post in 1965, Rev. King told Balaguer that his church agreed, but under the following conditions:

- Rev. King will not attend government dedications of public works in the province on Sundays because the pastor must be at his church on those days.
- He will not be involved in partisan politics in his community.

- He will use his post of governor to promote social activities in the community. (Rev. Angel Severino Cáceres, former superintendent of the Free Methodist Church, interview with the author, June 16, 2004)

Balaguer accepted the conditions and said that he did not want a politician in Nagua, but rather a person who would take care of social needs of the province; he would not have to attend government dedications of public works.

Social and political connections enabled the Free Methodist Church to obtain prime real estate to consolidate its educational activities in Santiago. The Evangelical Institute of Santiago was on land that belonged to the city. A problem arose when private builders asked municipal authorities to relocate the institute to land near the main campus of the Catholic University in Santiago. These builders wanted to construct a large office building across from the city government, where the evangelical institute was located. Local evangelical leaders opposed the transfer, but rather than fighting it out in the streets, used their connections with the city mayor as well as Fernando Alvarez Bogart and Juan René Beauchamps Javier, both of whom had important posts in a new Balaguer administration (1990–1994). They argued that a transfer of the institute to the outskirt of the city would cause an uproar among evangelicals, which would inconvenience President Balaguer. Again, through their intermediaries, evangelicals convinced Balaguer to donate 6 million square meters to the Free Methodist Church, the owner of the evangelical institute (Rev. Angel Severino Cáceres, former superintendent of the Free Methodist Church, interview with the author, June 16, 2004).

Participation in political parties was another method used by some evangelical leaders to press their demands. Andrés Reyes represents one of the most outstanding cases of an evangelical leader who joined a political party. Despite opposition from the Free Methodist Church, in 1974, he ran for congressional representative for the Santiago Accord, a large political alliance that included parties from the extreme left to the extreme right that opposed Balaguer. Reyes's party, the PRD, was the largest political force in the coalition. As noted in chapter 3, the Santiago Accord withdrew from the electoral race, but it did give Reyes an opportunity to participate in a significant political event. In 1979, Guzmán Fernández named him minister of education (1978–1982). This was the second time an evangelical leader occupied a ministerial post. (The first was Alfonso Lockward, who briefly served as minister of planning during Balaguer's twelve-year regime [1966–1978].)

Subsequently, in 1991, at Reyes's urging, the PRD established a commission of religious affairs that he cochaired with Fabio Solis, an ex-Catholic priest. The aim of this commission was to attract evangelicals to the party and to develop relationships with their churches. When the PRD returned to power in 2000, President Hipolito Mejía Domínguez named Reyes president of the Consejo Nacional de Educación (Nacional Council of Education) (Andrés Reyes, interview with the author, June 22, 2001).

The accounts of these three prominent evangelicals show that they all come from the Free Methodist Church, a historically Protestant church that was heavily involved in promoting education. At the same time that it was promoting education, the Free Methodist Church was able to establish excellent relationships with the upper middle class of Santiago and Santo Domingo, and those relationships were important when the church ran into problems with prominent builders from Santiago or when security forces arrested Rev. King in Nagua. The Free Methodist Church did not allow their participants to join political parties or accept prominent jobs in government, but it made some exceptions, as the cases of Postigo and Rev. King illustrate. In the late 1970s, the church appeared to be more tolerant and apparently did not make a serious objection when Andrés Reyes took up the position of minister of education.

The second tendency in the early political involvement of evangelicals was of leaders to be critical of the status quo. This was a secular student movement with no official links to the churches. Those affiliated with this movement thought that Protestants ought to have a commitment to justice and social change. In San Pedro de Macoris, the most prominent members of this movement included José Dunker Lambe, Rev. Telésforo Issaac, and Rev. Nestor Lira (José Dunker Lambe, psychiatrist and former leader of the Federation of High School Students in San Pedro de Macoris, interview with the author, June 17, 2004).

In the early 1960s, Temístocles Montás organized the Movimiento Estudiantil Cristiano (Christian Student Movement) in Santo Domingo and took a stance against the status quo. A decade later, Próspero Juan, a prominent Protestant, became leader of the progressive Sindicato Unido de la Romana (La Romana Unified Labor Union), known for its combativeness in defending workers' interests. These movements were small and never had sufficient force or followers. We cannot compare them to the Catholic popular church movement. However, although the Episcopal Church and the Dominican Evangelical Church did not allow its members to get involved in politics, all the individuals named here belonged to these political movements (Bienvenido Alvarez Vega, director of *Hoy*, interview with the author, June 11, 2001).

Toward the Institutional Incorporation of Evangelicals into National Politics

The integration of evangelicals into the mainstream of Dominican society took place from 1994 to 2005. This brought a competitor to the Catholic Church, not only in the area of religion but also in politics. For practical reasons, the state and mainstream political parties began to recognize the legal and economic prerogatives demanded by evangelicals. The year 1994 was a turning point in the political incorporation of the evangelical leadership because in that year public authorities and opposition political parties invited the evangelical leaders to witness the signing of the Pact for Democracy. Since then, evangelical leaders have participated with the Catholic Church in national political mediations.

Evangelical Institutional Ecclesiastical Institutions and the Political Process
The development of national ecclesiastical institutions provided the platform for government recognition of evangelicals. The initial steps to create national ecclesiastical institutions started in the 1970s, when a number of evangelical pastors began to acquire national publicity; some denominations began to administer their own affairs rather than depending on external supervision. Evangelical denominations did not yet coordinate their activities because they still lacked national ecclesiastical institutions.

The Confraternidad Evangélica Latinoamericana, CONELA (Latin American Evangelical Confraternity) noted this disadvantage when a delegation visited the country in 1983. It suggested the creation of a national ecclesiastical institution. It was due to CONELA's recommendation that the Confraternidad Evangélica Dominicana, CONEDO (Dominican Evangelical Confraternity) was established in 1983. CONEDO grouped most of the evangelical churches together for about nine years until a new ecclesiastical organization emerged. This new institution was called the Confraternidad de Unidad Evangélica, CODUE (Confraternity of Evangelical Unity). CODUE was established in 1992 as a result of a division within CONEDO. About 80 percent of evangelical churches transferred their membership to CODUE. CONEDO was left with roughly 20 percent of the evangelical membership (Rev. Manuel Bello, superintendent of the Assemblies of God and former president of CODUE, interview with the author, July 12, 2001).

In interviews with several past presidents of CONEDO[3] and CODUE,[4] most did not want to elaborate much on why these two institutions had separated. Only Rev. Andrés Rincón was willing to address the issue:

> The division was the result of conflict of interests among superintendents. I was not a superintendent and presided over CONEDO. Subsequently, Rev. Braulio

Portes presided over CONEDO when he was not a superintendent. Then, people became upset. How can you lead without being superintendent within your council? The statutes of CONEDO allowed you to preside without being a superintendent. This brought jealousy. Above anything else, it was jealousy that divided CONEDO. (Rev. Andrés Rincón, national administrative bishop of the Church of God, interview with the author, June 30, 2004)[5]

The fact that the vast majority of councils[6] or denominations transferred their membership to CODUE suggests that the division was not just over personality or hierarchical issues. Although their leaders tend to minimize their differences in public over the years, there are important differences between CONEDO and CODUE. The councils that left CONEDO to form CODUE seemed more traditional and concerned with pastoral, spiritual, and ministerial issues, whereas those that remained tended to show a greater interest for social and political issues. For example, when evangelicals call for a convention dealing with religious issues or church business, CODUE usually takes the lead. On the other hand, when the call deals with political or social participation, CONEDO tends to call for it. At times, it seems that CONEDO is the social branch of the evangelicals and CODUE the more religious, pastoral type of institution (José Dunker Lambe, interview with the author, June 17, 2004).

CONEDO and CODUE do not account for all the evangelicals in the country. At the time of their split, some smaller groups were left out and subsequently others emerged that did not feel represented within the two national ecclesiastical institutions. These groups include the Red Pastoral (the Pastoral Network), led by Georgie Reynoso; the Asociación de Ministros Evangélicos, ASIMILE (Association of Evangelical Ministers), led by Pablo Villanueva; and the Consejo Nacional de Iglesias Evangélicas, CONIN (National Council of Evangelical Churches). The Red Pastoral brings together elite groups of neoevangelical churches that operate mostly in Santo Domingo, whereas ASIMILE is the most traditional and fanatic. These groups believe that CODUE and CONEDO are not the true representatives of Christianity. CONIN represents a diversity of evangelicals who are interested in political issues. Except for the Free Methodist Church, affiliated with CODUE, historically Protestant churches such as the Adventist Church, Episcopal Church, and Dominican Evangelical Church are not members of CONEDO or CODUE. Dominican mainline Protestant churches follow in the tracks of mainline Protestantism elsewhere in Latin America, in that it does not seem to get along with evangelicals due to different governmental structure, theological concepts, and worshiping methods.

Political Parties and the Evangelicals

In the late 1980s, Dominican politicians became aware of the emergence of CONEDO as a national ecclesiastical institution. José Francisco Peña Gómez and Juan Bosch noticed this new social development and its political consequences. Peña Gómez attended services at a Free Methodist Church during his youthful years and became known among evangelicals for his poetry recitals. This participation in religious activities brought him a particular awareness about the evangelical movement. In the 1980s and 1990s, Peña Gómez met many times with associations of pastors in the different regions of the country, presented his government programs to them, and asked for their suggestions. These meetings allowed Peña Gómez and his party, the PRD, to begin developing a political constituency within the evangelical religious movement. This is why his party, in 1991, established a religious affairs commission to cultivate a political relationship with the evangelical community (Rev. Pedro de la Rosa, pastor at the Primera Asamblea de Dios in Santiago, interview with the author, July 9, 2004). Peña Gómez's early start attracted the largest following of evangelicals among the main political parties.

Unlike Peña Gómez, Juan Bosch did not have any association with religious institutions. On the contrary, many within the Catholic Church and the evangelical movement believed he was an atheist. Bosch was keenly aware that evangelicals represented a new important group and his party, the Partido de Liberación Dominican, PLD (Dominican Liberation Party) needed to court their votes. In the electoral campaign of 1990, Bosch tried to attract evangelicals to his party. When asked about the evangelical churches during the 1990 electoral campaign, Bosch said that they would get the same treatment as the Catholic Church. The Catholic hierarchy did not welcome this declaration, but the evangelical leadership took note of it because it meant that another mainstream politician took them into account. Soon after, the PLD set up a religious affairs commission to improve its relation with evangelicals, many of whom believed that Bosch was a Marxist, if not communist (Querina Alcequiez, member of the PLD's Religious Affairs Commission, interview with the author, June 28, 2001). Joaquín Balaguer of the PRSC (Reformist Social Christian Party) established a religious affairs commission to deal with evangelical issues. Contrary to other politicians, Balaguer had used his power in office to dispense favors to evangelicals, hoping to exert his political influence among their movement. The three most important political parties developed commissions of religious affairs to attract the evangelical vote.

My interviews with over twenty-five evangelical leaders and long-term observations of Dominican elections reveal that, as elsewhere in Latin American, there is no such a thing as an evangelical or Catholic vote in the Dominican Republic. Although the possibilities for developing a church-affiliated party are as slim as elsewhere in Latin America, a group of evangelicals have pushed for the creation of a Christian political alternative. The groups that have emerged include the Movimiento Cristiano por la Paz y la Democracia (Christian Movement for Peace and Democracy) led by Rev. Nelson Arias, Movimiento de Integración Evangélica Nacional (Movement for Evangelical Integration) led by Ana Inez Polanco, and Partido Quisqueyano Democrata Cristiano (Quisqueyan Christian Democratic Party) led by the Rev. Elías Wessín Chávez.

Despite major efforts by its leaders, the first two evangelical movements were not able to gather enough signatures to register with the JCE and have tended to disappear from the political scene. However, the third was able to obtain it. The success of Rev. Wessín Chávez was due, in part, to the fact that his father, General Elías Wessín y Wessín, had founded the Quisqueyan Democratic Party in the late 1960s to compete against Joaquín Balaguer. His party was made up mostly of conservative veterans who were dissatisfied with Balaguer's regime (1966–1978). Rev. Wessín Chávez inherited the party from his father and renamed it the Quisqueyan Christian Democratic Party (Rev. Nelson Arias, interview with the author, June 26, 2001). He was able to win a seat in Congress because of a political alliance developed with larger parties. This is how he became director of the National Passport Office. In this sense, Rev. Wessín Chávez is not different from many other Dominican politicians who tried to carve out a small space in the political arena.

Evangelicals and Political Mediation
Political parties and the state facilitated the integration of evangelical leaders and their ecclesiastical institutions into the political mainstream in the 1990s. The recognition that evangelicals are a new religious group whose members can vote and possibly affect the results of elections introduces a new ingredient to the political scene.

The crisis that resulted from the 1994 elections marked a watershed in the relationship of evangelical ecclesiastical institutions with politics. As discussed in chapter 4, in 1994 the Catholic Church and the Organization of American States mediated the Pact for Democracy. This pact is significant because the government and the political parties agreed to invite the leaders of the national evangelical institutions, CONEDO and CODUE, to witness its signing. They sat next to Msgr. Agripino Núñez Collado, the mediator par excellence, and shared the spotlight as nationally recognized ecclesiastical institutions. Although they did not make any claims about competing with the Catholic Church, the fact that they were at the meeting was the beginning of a sort of competition. Evangelicals were here to stay, and the public authorities were aware of their importance.

In the administrations of Leonel Fernández (1996–2000) and Hipólito Mejía Domínguez (2000–2004), evangelical leaders were invited to participate in political mediations along with Msgr. Agripino Núñez Collado. Thus, President Fernández invited the leaders of CONEDO and CODUE to take part in the national dialogue meetings that were held during his administration, and they participated in the discussions that led up to the reform of the Constitution. During the Mejía Domínguez administration, the National Dialogue Commission invited Rev. Reynaldo Franco Aquino of CODUE to join Msgr. Núñez Collado in the follow-up commission that was established to advise the JCE authorities in the process of organizing the elections of 2004. In the fall of 2003 and the spring of 2004, Franco Aquino and Núñez Collado advised the JCE in handling the crisis that eventually led to the political division of the PRD. No one denies that Msgr. Núñez Collado is the mediator par excellence and that he occupies the center stage as far as mediation of political conflict is concerned. However, we cannot ignore the fact that evangelical leaders such as the Reverends Franco Aquino, Ezequiel Molina, Braulio Portes, Manuel Estrella, Silverio Manuel Bello, and others are nationally recognized religious leaders whose influence is acknowledged by political parties and the state.

The participation of evangelical leaders in political mediation has not caused any frictions with the Catholic hierarchy. In the late 1980s and early 1990s, the Catholic Church had some frictions with evangelicals whom it accused of trying to win Catholic devotees (Alvarez Vega, 2003, 11). These disappeared in the 1990s, and the church accommodated evangelical leaders in the mediation process and in the discussion of national problems. At times of crisis caused by hurricanes and other natural catastrophes, evangelical pastors and Catholic priests have come together to help the population. Despite this collaboration, both Catholic and evangelicals conduct their pastoral programs separately. Similarly, neither church has signaled any interest toward ecumenical issues.

Evangelicals and the Search for Influence in Society

Notwithstanding their participation in political mediation, the main concern of Dominican evangelicals is to expand their influence in society and to obtain privileges from the state that would allow them to have an impact on the religious field.

Let us first examine how they seek to influence society and then explore what kinds of prerogatives they want to extract from the state. We should bear in mind that participation in political mediation and calling for moderation is a significant part of the process to influence society. Likewise, making concrete proposals to advance the general interest of the population is another way of obtaining credibility and legitimacy in society. For example, at a seminal meeting held in La Vega on December 4, 1993, prominent evangelical leaders that included Rev. Braulio Portes, J. Adalberto Martínez, Alfredo Ossers Veras, and others drafted a document called "Lineamientos Generales para la Elaboración de una Agenda de Consenso para el Pueblo Dominicano" (General Guidelines to Elaborate a Consensus Agenda for the Dominican People). This document included an array of issues ranging from education, human rights, national resources, transportation, and foreign relations. The framers of this groundbreaking document established a few key points that are evocative of their religious agenda.

- Update current laws, decrees, and resolutions on religious matters.
- Facilitate the development of churches, ministries, and the religious movement in general through the promulgation of a religious affairs law that guarantees the establishment and operation of religious institutions through the following mechanisms:
  a) Establish and formalize specific accords that would permit different religious groups to help the Dominican state deliver services that benefit the diverse sectors of the population.
  b) Respect public order and custom and balance the diversity of religious practices nationwide.
  c) Implement a national registry of religions where each religious organization can deposit its definitive data according to creed, organization, and representatives. This national registry would give them the necessary protection and representation in an environment that would allow them to carry out their activities with equal rights. (CONEDO 1994)

CONEDO promoted this document among all evangelicals and played an important role in establishing connections with government authorities. For Rev. Braulio Portes, a former president of CONEDO, evangelical churches must participate in civil society and contribute to the consolidation of national institutions and strengthen the rule of law, governance, social justice, and equity in the distribution of national wealth. This is why CONEDO joins with nongovernmental organizations in promoting social and religious objectives. Rev. Portes believes that evangelical leaders are still timid concerning their participation in civil society (Rev. Braulio Portes, former president of CONEDO, interview with the author, June 16, 2001).

Rev. Portes is not alone in promoting these issues. Rev. Manuel Estrella, former president of CONEDO, Rev. Ezequiel Molina of the Ministry Battle for the Faith, and, more recently, Reynaldo Franco Aquino of CODUE have participated in important political mediations. With these new developments, participation of the evangelical leadership in political mediation has become part of the political landscape.

Similarly, issuing communiqués or giving press conferences to call attention to major social and political issues has become a normal occurrence. For example, in September 1998, at a time of an intense power struggle between Congress and the executive over the economic and political orientation of state policies, CONEDO and CODUE issued a joint communiqué noting that in the past political parties had used Congress and the executive for sectarian purposes. They believe that political parties must abandon this type of political practice and replace it with a gesture of humility. For them, this is the only way to end unnecessary uncertainties and anxieties in the population (CODUE 1998a, 2). This type of message contributes to the general recognition that evangelical ecclesiastical institutions support the common good and appear to be nonpartisan in a conflict-ridden and tense society. In this sense, evangelical ecclesiastical institutions follow in the path of the Catholic Church, which has developed a strong relationship with the state.

The traditionally less critical and political CODUE has become increasingly aware of its social responsibilities and frequently issues messages where it critiques public authorities for failing to meet their obligations. In May 2003, it issued a communication in which it proclaimed that "tricks, corruption, concealment, insensitivity, rebelliousness and contempt are the dominant factors in Dominican culture and political practice." "It is urgent," the message added, "[to make] a radical change in the direction of the country to escape mediocrities and to elevate the political discourse" (Martínez 2003, 11). Rev. Ezequiel Molina of the Battle for the Faith Ministry went even further stating, "the country is ruled by a tiny group of three or four lions regardless of the person that occupies the presidency" (Cárdenas 2003, 1). These messages reflect critical positions issued by leaders who seek a long-term relationship with the Dominican state, not just a temporary association with a particular occupant of the presidential palace.

Evangelicals and the Search for Prerogatives

Evangelicals also pressed state authorities to recognize their prerogatives in education and legal matters. Contrary to their expectations, they made significant gains during the administration of Leonel Fernández Reina (1996–2000). Their expectations had been low because Juan Bosch had left a legacy in his party that stressed the secular nature of state and society, leaving little room for religion. Fernández Reina moved swiftly to invite evangelicals to government functions and to listen to their recommendations. Because of his meetings with evangelicals, he agreed to a modification of the Law 66-99 on general education. The modifications introduced included two important items that evangelicals had been demanding for a long time. First, the modified law reassured the representation of delegates from evangelical ecclesiastical institutions in the Consejo Nacional de Educación, CONE (National Council of Education), the state agency that oversees all matters concerning national education. Second, the modified version says that the Ministry of Education would provide biblical instruction at the primary, intermediate, and secondary levels. It establishes that programs and teaching methods will be proposed by the Conferencia Episcopal Dominicana, CED (Dominican Episcopal Conference) and CODUE. These two institutions will send the programs of biblical instructions to CONE for its approval. They will also send representatives to CONE and nominate the appropriate candidates to teach biblical instructions when the Ministry of Education creates teaching posts for such topics. The CED and CODUE will train the personnel that currently teach human and religious education in public schools (Wessin Chávez 2000, 4–5; Rev. Adalberto Martínez, former vice minister of education, interview with the author, July 10, 2001).

The Fernández administration also ordered the Ministry of Finances to recognize CONEDO and CODUE as the prime channels to request tax exemption status. They were empowered to coordinate and approve all tax-exempt importation of vehicles for church use as well as tax-exempt travel by church personnel (CODUE 1998b).

These measures strengthened a pattern that political parties recognized. Figure 6.1 and table 6.4 offer detailed data on public financial resources allocated to evangelical ecclesiastical institutions.[7] These data show that evangelical organizations have been receiving money from the National Budget for quite some time. A review of the budgetary allocations to the religious organizations from 1979 to 2000 reveals that the PRD, the PRSC, and the PLD have increased appropriations. These figures obviously are not comparable to the resources assigned to the Catholic Church, but they are an indication of the incorporation of evangelicals into the mainstream.

Table 6.4. State Allocation for the Dominican Evangelical Institutions, 1979–2000

U.S. Dollars

Evangelican Institutions	1979–82 (PRD)	1983–86 (PRD)	1987–90 (PRSC)	1991–94 (PRSC)	1995–96 (PRSC)	1997–00 (PLD)
Evangelical federations, confederations, and confraternities	—	—	—	—	—	393,278.06
Evangelical assemblies and associations	1,011,017.54	571,843.80	322,675.71	601,369.01	553,330.83	1,202,214.76
Protestant educational institutions	—	2,558.85	167,137.64	335,563.55	93,240.09	389,098.43
Evangelical schools	2,377.56	1,820.02	1,370.93	1,870.55	2,514.70	115,488.18
Evangelical churches	—	—	9,178.89	2,073.18	4,607.68	380,162.85
Adventist churches	—	—	—	—	—	9,887.83
TOTAL	1,013,395.09	576,222.68	500,363.17	940,876.30	653,693.30	2,490,130.11

Source: Secretariado Técnico de la Presidencia/Oficina Nacional de Presupuesto, 1979–2000. Volume 1-21.
The 1995–1996 term represents a two-year period rather than a four-year period.
These and subsequent calculations do not take inflation into account, which makes the numbers even more dramatic. The exchange rates from 1979 to 1985 are based on the Mercado Extrabancario a la Venta (Unofficial Exchange Rates). See Banco Central de la República Dominicana (1985). The exchange rates from 1985 to 2000 are annual averages and were published as "Tasas de cambio Promedio para compra y venta de dolares estadounidenses." See Banco Central de la República Dominicana (2005).

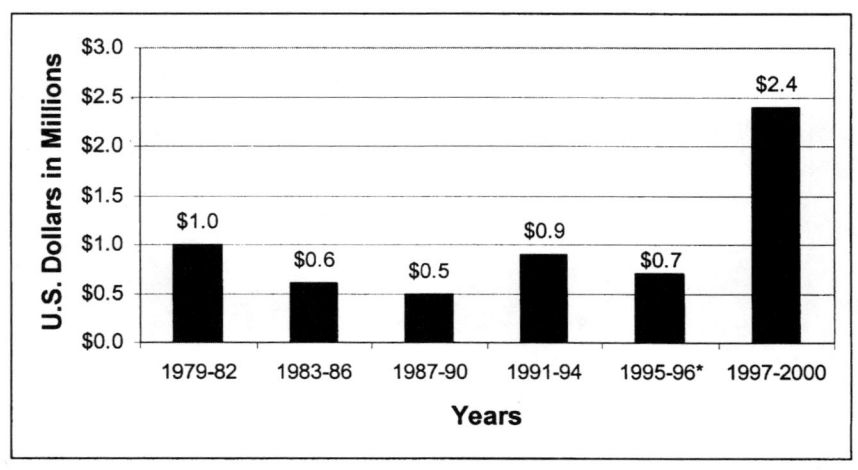

Figure 6.1. State Funding for the Evangelical Churches, Dominican Republic, 1979–2000
Source: Secretariado Técnico de la Presidencia/Oficina Nacional de Presupuesto, 1979–2000. Volume 1–21.
Notes: *Represents a two-year time period rather than a four-year time period. The exchange rates from 1979 to 1985 are based on annual averages calculated by the Departamento de Cuentas Nacionales y Estadísticas Económicas/División de Precios. These exchange rates are annual averages based on the Mercado Extrabancario a la Venta (Unofficial Exchange Rates). See Banco Central de la República Dominicana (1985). The data on the exchange rate from 1985 to 2000 were published as "Tasas de CambioPromedio para compra y venta de dolares estadounidenses." See Banco Central de la República Dominicana (2005).

Figure 6.1 shows that Fernandez Reina gave more financial resources to the evangelical than any other previous president. This was part of his strategy to attract new groups to his party, which was still a small organization in the mid-1990s. It is worth recalling that he used the same policy with the Catholic Church to attract its support. Fernández Reina was not alone in trying to attract evangelicals to his party. In the context of the presidential electoral campaign of 2004, President/candidate Hipólito Mejía Domínguez signed a "social pact" with evangelical leaders that broadened Fernández Reina's previous concessions.

This pact included broad participation in education, recognition of evangelical institutions in the administration of public health programs, integration into state-sponsored patronage in health and education program, provision for the assimilation of evangelical chaplaincy in the armed forces and national police, acceptance of civil marriage performed by evangelical pastors, creation of the legal framework for evangelical media, and allowance of tax exemption status to religious items and vehicles deemed necessary for church use (El Estado Dominicano y las Iglesias Evangélicas y Protestantes 2004, 10). This pact was subsequently approved by both houses of Congress, but as of February 2007, the new Fernández administration (2004–2008) has not signed it into law.

Most analysts and even a number of evangelical leaders understood that President Mejía Domínguez's willingness to sign this pact was a means to attract evangelical voters to the official party. He was seeking reelection during a profound social, economic, and political crisis. Most polls showed him losing the race. Evangelical leaders acted opportunistically to obtain prerogatives they had been asking for; the president's special political circumstances opened a opportunity and they seized it. This is another indication of how evangelicals take advantage of whatever turns up to integrate themselves into the political system. Thus, they followed in the footsteps of other Latin American evangelicals who took advantage of the Catholic Church's conflicts with military regimes such as those in Chile and Guatemala or the Sandinista Revolution in Nicaragua.

Conclusions

Evangelicals have successfully adapted to Dominican culture and politics and have begun to carve out their space in society. They have profitably challenged the Catholic religious monopoly and set themselves as legitimate religious groups. The roots of evangelicals in the Dominican Republic can be traced back to the nineteenth and early twentieth centuries when Protestantism was alienated from the mainstream of society. While it is true that there is a link with historically protestant churches in northern and eastern provinces of the country, the evangelical growth is the result of mutations in the religious field. I conclude that these mutations occurred in the context of a number of factors, including cultural changes, socioeconomic transformations, and a type of capitalist modernization that left the vast majority of the population in widespread poverty. Unlike the early Protestants that immigrated to the country, evangelicals have embraced Dominican culture, especially Dominican folk Catholicism. In a way, evangelicals have followed in the footsteps of the Catholic Church, which adapted itself to the cultural environment of the New World. Thus, the growth of evangelicals is not simply the result of foreign influences, but rather the consequence of interplay between external and internal sociocultural factors.

It is still too early to tell whether evangelicals will strengthen or weaken the democratic process in Latin America. What is certain is that they are quickly learning how to accommodate the political system by developing strategies to demand legal and social prerogatives that will enable them to exert influence in the religious arena. Groups of evangelicals have already formed church affiliated political parties across the region, but the vast majority of evangelical leaders only seek recognition from public authorities so they can carry on their religious mission. It is also certain that evangelical are helping reshape the Latin American political landscape, but it does not necessarily mean that they will be the standard bearers of capitalist development and liberal democracy, as Max Weber saw Protestantism in the beginning of capitalism in Europe.

Dominican evangelicals are successfully accommodating to society and politics. In the past four decades, they moved from political insignificance to full recognition by both mainstream political parties and the state. Since the 1990s, they have been participating in political mediations along with the Catholic Church, they have increased their influence in society, and they have begun to successfully pressure the state to obtain legal and social prerogatives. In sum, evangelicals have emerged as another source of legitimacy, which neither the state nor the Catholic Church can ignore.

Notes

1. This chapter draws on interviews with the following evangelical leaders: Pedro de la Rosa, Jose Dunker Lambe, Alfredo Ossers Veras, Lorenzo Mota King, Oscar Arocha, Ezequiel Molina, Lucy Cosme, Reynaldo Franco Aquino, Angel Severino Cáceres, Norberto Batista, Andrés Rincón, Manuel Estrella, Pedro Piñeiro, Adalberto Martínez, Silverio Manuel Bello, Bienvenido Alvarez Vega, Nelson Arias, Andrés Reyes, Braulio Portes, and Querina Alcequiez.

2. I have kept the term Pentecostal here because this is a translation from Spanish, but as noted earlier, in Latin America the terms evangelical and Pentecostal are generally used as synonyms.

3. Rev. Braulio Portes and Rev. Manuel Estrella.

4. Rev. Silverio Manuel Bello and Rev. Reynaldo Franco Aquino.

5. The superintendent has two functions: administrative and pastoral. He administers the resources of the church as an executive and operates as the pastor of all the pastors. He is the spokesperson for the denomination or council.

6. Councils or denominations are institutions that bring together a group of churches that work with the same religious philosophy and bear the same name.

7. I grouped evangelical institutions into six categories that include evangelical federations, confederations and confraternities, evangelical assemblies and associations, Protestant educational institutions, evangelical schools, evangelical churches, and Adventist churches.

General Conclusions

This research shows that the Dominican church was a factor of cohesion that facilitated social and political domination in the nineteenth and twentieth centuries. The church developed a cozy relationship with both the social and political elites that stretches back to the colonial period and continues until the present. It used its religious and social status to legitimate the power of the elite in the midst of widespread poverty, human rights violations, and political exclusion. Church leaders perceived that both the state and the socioeconomic elite had the resources it needed to carry out its evangelical mission and that it had no choice but to develop a close relationship with the powers that be. In this sense, the Dominican church was not different from its equivalents in Central and South America because they all shared a neo-Christendom orientation that sought state protection to fight liberalism, Protestantism, and secularization in the nineteenth century. In the twentieth century the church found another reason to support conservative and dictatorial regimes because it needed to fight socialism and communism.

The study examined the reincorporation of the Catholic Church to Dominican politics in the post-Trujillo society and draws comparisons with the churches of Bolivia and Central America. The collapse of the Trujillo dictatorship and the subsequent Revolution of 1965 rocked Dominican society to its foundation and forced the church to reassess its relationship with the state and society. Despite the gravity of the situation, it took the local hierarchy more than five years to realize that it needed to distance itself from the conservative social and political elite. Only cautious guidance from the Vatican could steer the local hierarchy away from the Trujillo dictatorship. Similarly, it was the nuncio, not the local hierarchy, who mediated between the Constitutionalists and the U.S. during the military occupation of the country.

Despite Vatican introduction of important changes in the composition of the church leadership following the Revolution of 1965, the Dominican church hierarchy remained conservative and closely tied to the Balaguer regime. The church was able to stay put with its conservative position because of the U.S. military strategic defeat of the left-leaning revolutionary forces and Balaguer's restoration of the authoritarian regime. Balaguer respected the concordat Trujillo signed with the Vatican and continued to support the church financially. This relationship allowed the hierarchy to operate as if nothing had changed and inhibited any church movement—such as the popular church—that could challenge Balaguer. The church became a factor of social and political cohesion, which enabled Balaguer and subsequent leaders to strengthen their rule over a conflict-ridden society.

Hugo Eduardo Polanco Brito and Agripino Núñez Collado were the two great church mediators in the aftermath of the 1965 Revolution. These clergymen represent two important moments in the process of church reintegration into politics through mediation. The mediations of Polanco Brito during Balaguer's twelve-year period (1966–1978) raised the profile of the church in Dominican life. Balaguer tolerated church involvement in political mediation because it allowed him to eradicate what he considered to be "undesirable" individuals. The church, in turn, gained political visibility and legitimacy in the eye of the population because it aided political prisoners or revolutionaries involved in political kidnapping to leave the country. Though Balaguer and the church had different goals, they agreed on the need to create a stable political climate.

Polanco Brito opened up the conservative hierarchy to the realization that the church needed to update and modernize its approach to politics. In the early 1980s, the church hierarchy embraced mediation wholeheartedly when it noted that successive strikes and riots threatened the very fabric of society. Traditional conservative bishops had no choice, but to join the modernizing orientation that Polanco Brito had proposed in the 1970s. Clearly, pressing political circumstances drove the church leadership to get involved in mediation. This conservative attitude parallels those of Bolivia and Central America, where the church hierarchies participated in political mediation as a result of massive political repression to strikers and other political opponents in Bolivia or civil wars in Central America.

The transition to democracy and the socioeconomic transformations that occurred in the Dominican Republic in the 1980s provided the framework for church participation in political mediation. These two transitions occurred simultaneously, making it difficult for the government and the opposition to reach agreements without a legitimate broker. The complexity of the phenomenon resulted from at least two factors: Dominican democracy is delegative and fragile, and the economic transformations of the 1980s tended to deepen a process of social exclusion that threatened the social fabric society. These circumstances opened the opportunity for the church to consolidate its reincorporation into the mainstream of society as the mediator par excellence.

The mediations of Agripino Núñez Collado, from the early 1980s to the turn of the century, deepened the participation of the church in the political process. These interventions were priceless for the Dominican government, the political opposition, and the church. They helped government and political parties to resolve crucial impasses that otherwise could have ended in bloodshed. In exchange for its public service, again, the church gained greater credibility and legitimacy with the higher echelons of society. The activities and mediations of Núñez Collado have made him a permanent factor in the political system. Friends and foes recognize him as a key ingredient in the political system. However, these mediations do not make the church hierarchy less conservative or neutral regarding the Dominican political system. In fact, the church continues to be a factor of cohesion for the political system and mediation is a mechanism employed to sustain the political architecture.

Like its counterparts in Bolivia and Central America, the Dominican church claims to be nonpartisan, but its promotion of liberal democracy as the only political alternative and its overlapping interests with the government and the socioeconomic elite turn it into a defender of the status quo rather than a true nonpartisan actor. This research demonstrates that regardless of which political party is in office, the Dominican church receives its ordinary financial allotments through the national budget, extraordinary government allowance for special construction projects, and, on occasions, transfer of public assets to set up training schools and other social services. This complex set of circumstances makes it difficult, if not impossible, for the clergy to be truly nonpartisan when it comes to the defense of the Dominican political establishment.

Despite weakness and inertia at various points, the church played a significant role in the transition to democracy in the countries under study. It fostered the ecclesiastical base communities, peasant and labor movements, and human rights organizations. These entities helped to lay a foundation upon which a solid civil society could emerge. The church hierarchy critiques of governments and political opponents, its continuous calls for dialogue, and national reconciliation turned into an institution that political actors can count on in times of crisis. These circumstances, in turn, transformed the church into a special political actor that does not seek secular power, but exerts considerable influence on those who do.

The reinsertion of the church into the Dominican political scene contrasts sharply with that of its counterparts in Bolivia, Guatemala, and El Salvador. Unlike the Dominican revolution of 1965, the revolutions that rocked these nations were not strategically defeated by direct U.S. military interventions. These revolutions helped to democratize these societies and as such opened up social and political spaces that prepared the social conditions for the growth of the popular church and other social movements. These developments also allowed for the progress of a modernizing orientation within these countries' churches. The failure of the Dominican revolution delayed the process of democratization, and the clergy did not receive strong pressures from rank and file priests. As a result, bishops associated with the modernizing orientation were more conservative and unwilling to support the popular church. These developments parallel the Nicaraguan case.

In Nicaragua, the revolution successfully took power, retained it for ten years, and democratized society. However, it came into conflict with the hierarchy, which saw its relationship with the popular church as a threat to the official church. The Nicaraguan hierarchy opposed the Sandinista Revolution and the growth of the popular church and inhibited the development of the modernizing orientation within its ranks.

None of the cases examined here parallels the Dominican experience regarding political mediation. In the Dominican case, Msgr. Agripino Núñez Collado became a seemingly permanent mediator. Three important factors partly explain the permanence of Núñez Collado as the chief church official in political mediations: (1) He has the public support of the hierarchy to mediate since the early 1980s; (2) the government, the political opposition, and the business community recognize him as a mediator par excellence; and (3) the weakness of the Dominican political institutions make his presence practically indispensable. Bolivia and Central America did not have such a key mediator. Msgr. Arturo Rivera y Damas (deceased in 1994) of El Salvador would be the closest comparison to Núñez Collado. However, unlike Núñez Collado, he did not have the support of the Salvadoran hierarchy, the socioeconomic elite, and most of the political establishment.

Political stability is another important element that distinguishes the Dominican experience from that of its equivalents in Bolivia and Central America. Unlike Central America, the Dominican Republic did not have a long civil war or the unstable political situation of Bolivia. This situation made it possible for the Dominican church to implement two ten-year pastoral programs that consolidated its institutions and brought it closer to the impoverished sectors of the population. Notwithstanding this advantage, the social pastoral programs of the Dominican church have been mostly assistentialist and only moderately based on the accompaniment approach.

Cáritas and Cedail pushed for a pastoral program of accompaniment in accordance with the precepts of the Medillín and Puebla bishopric conferences, but their work kept an assistentialist character despite attempts to promote a pastoral program of accompaniment. My examination of four dioceses (Mao-Valverde, La Vega, Barahona, and San Juan de la Maguana) shows similar developments: the social pastoral work is still based on assistentialism, and accompaniment is still a goal to be achieved. Despite these shortcomings, the social pastoral program shows that the church is a multifaceted institution that seeks to appeal to the entire society, not just one sector of it. Church welfare programs do contribute to enhance the perception that it is engaged in solving local and national issues rather than just mediating in the political disputes of the elite.

Concerning the emergence of the evangelical movement, the Dominican Republic mirrors the larger reality of Latin America where it has broken the Catholic religious monopoly and begun to insert themselves into the political field. I traced the roots of Dominican evangelicals back to the nineteenth and early twentieth centuries when Protestant churches established themselves in the eastern and northern provinces. Although there is a link between these churches and the current upsurge of the evangelical movement, it is mainly a result of mutations in the religious field. These mutations occurred in the context of profound capitalist socioeconomic and cultural transformations that were largely but not exclusively imposed from the outside. Mutations in the Dominican religious field are not the equivalent of a religious reformation per se, but a sort of religious syncretism where folk Catholicism and elements of Protestantism combine to form a creolized Dominican version of Protestantism. Thus, the growth of evangelicals is not merely the outcome of overseas influence, but the upshot of a complex process of internal and external sociocultural changes.

Evangelicals are also rapidly learning and adapting to Dominican political culture. They have accommodated the political system by designing strategies that enable them to achieve legal and social recognition. Like their counterparts in Latin America, groups of Dominican evangelical leaders have attempted to organize church-affiliated parties to participate in politics, but these endeavors have not yet been quite fruitful because few have been elected to office. However, the leaders of the national ecclesiastical institutions have sought and obtained some legal and financial prerogatives from the state, though not on as regular a basis as the Catholic Church, which has a concordat that frames its relationship with the state.

The participation of the evangelical leadership in political mediations along with the Catholic Church since the early 1990s has brought it a wider recognition in society. Mainstream political parties established special commissions to address their needs as it became obvious that pastors could have an influence on the voting behavior of their followers. Even the Catholic hierarchy recognizes the evangelical leadership and invites them to discuss national issues. Notwithstanding these facts, evangelicals still do not have enough connections in high places that would allow them to have agreements to frame and regulate their relationships with the state.

It may be premature to judge whether evangelicals will reinforce or deteriorate democratic values in the Dominican Republic. What seems to be certain is that they are helping to reshape the political landscape and they are beginning to develop a new political identity. However, this does not mean that evangelical churches will be the standard bearers of capitalist development or that because Dominican society has an authoritarian culture some form of democracy cannot fruitfully develop. Despite this inadequacy, political pluralism is taking root in the Dominican society, and it has already opened a space for evangelicals to grow into a new religious and political identity.

What seems certain for the near future is that both Catholics and evangelical institutions will play important roles in society and politics. The presence of the clergy is necessary to mediate political conflicts because of the weakness of Dominican democracy and the incapacity of political parties to reach significant agreements regarding lasting political and economic reforms. However, in the end, the clergy's mediation clergy may run into problems and lose credibility because it is an intercession without arbitration—that is, Núñez Collado and his evangelical colleagues mediate conflicts, but they do not have any mechanism to ensure implementation of what is agreed on by political actors. Dominican society does not seem prepared for arbitration because it does not have a political culture of negotiation. This is why political mediation has become a permanent feature in a political system based on a zero-sum game—a system where the winner takes all the power.

Bibliography

Interviews Conducted by the Author

Abreu, Tomás Jerónimo. 2000. Bishop, Diocese of Mao-Montecristi. Interviewed June 24. Mao.

Adames, Fausto Rosario. 1998. Author and journalist. Interviewed June 12. Santo Domingo.

Adames, Sonia. 2001. Teacher and school administrator. Interviewed June 4. Santo Domingo.

Alcequiez, Querina. 2001. Member of the PLD's Religious Affairs Commission. Interviewed June 28. Santo Domingo.

Alemán, José Luis, SJ. 1998. Professor of Economics at the Pontificia Universidad Católica Madre y Maestra. Interviewed June 9. Santo Domingo.

Alvarez-Vega, Bienvenido. 2001. Director of the newspaper *Hoy*. Interviewed June 11. Santo Domingo.

Arias, Nelson, Rev. 2001. Pastor of the Iglesia Metodista Libre y Activista Político. Interviewed June 26. Santo Domingo.

Arnáiz, Francisco José, Fr. 1998. Secretary of the Dominican Episcopal Conference. Interviewed June 26. Santo Domingo.

Arocha, Oscar, Rev. 2004. Pastor Iglesia Bautista de la Gracia. Interviewed July 8. Santiago.

Apolinario, Abrahan. 2001. Parish priest in Villa Mella. Interviewed June 12. Santo Domigo.

Báez Evertsz, Franc. 2004. Sociologist and specialist in international migration. Interviewed July 10. Santo Domingo.

Báez, Freddy. 2003. Cedail lawyer in charge of the southern region. Interviewed June 4. Santo Domingo.

Batista, Norberto, Rev. 2004. Pastor de la Primera Iglesia de la Cristianización de Santiago. Interviewed July 7. Santiago.
Bello, Silverio Manuel, Rev. 2001. Superintendent of the Assemblies of God and former president of CODUE. Interviewed July 12. Santo Domingo.
Bretón, Freddy. 2001. Bishop, Diocese of Baní. Interviewed June 10. Baní.
Cáceres, Angel Severino, Rev. 2004. Former superintendent of the Free Methodist Church. Interviewed June 16. Santo Domingo.
Camilo González, Antonio. 2000. Bishop of the Diocese of La Vega. Interviewed June 12. La Vega.
Campo, Luisa. 2004. Founder of Cedail. Interviewed June 30. Santo Domingo.
Cela, Jorge. 1998. Director of the Journal Estudios Sociales. Interviewed, July 11. Santo Domingo.
Contreras, Altagracia. 2001. Community organizer at El Milloncito, Sabana Perdida. Interviewed June 4. Santo Domingo.
Contreras, Francisco, Fr. 2003. Head of the Social Pastoral in the Diocese of La Vega. Interviewed June 26. La Vega.
Cosme, Lucy, Rev. 2004. Pastor Iglesia Puerta de Bendición y Libertad para todas las Naciones. Interviewed June 24. Santo Domingo.
De la Cruz, Basilio. 2003. Head of Cáritas in the Diocese La Vega. Interviewed May 26. La Vega.
De la Cruz, Tobias, Fr. 2003. Head of the Social Pastoral Archdiocese of Santiago. Interviewed June 6. Moca.
De la Rosa, Pedro, Rev. 2004. Pastor of the Primera Asamblea de Dios. Interviewed July 9. Santo Domingo.
De la Rosa Carpio, Ramón Benito. 2000. Bishop, Diocese of La Altagracia. Interviewed June 21. Higuey.
Del Rosario, Desiré. 2003. Cedail lawyer in charge of the northern region. Interview July 7. Santo Domingo.
Díaz Santana, Juan Bolivar. 1998. Author and journalist. Interviewed June 11. Santo Domingo.
Dunker Lambe, José. 2004. Psychiatrist and former leader of the Federation of High School Students in San Pedro de Macoris. Interviewed June 17. Santo Domingo.
Encarnación, Amelia. 2001. Teacher and school administrator. Interviewed June 11. Santo Domingo.
Espinal de León, Diómedes. 2000. Auxiliary bishop in the Archdiocese of Santiago. Interviewed June 12. Santiago.
Estrella, Manuel, Rev. 2004. Former president of CONEDO and president of the Servicio Social de Iglesias Dominicana. Interviewed June 17. Santo Domingo.
Felipe, Rafael. 2000. Bishop, Diocese of Barahona. Interviewed June 22. Barahona.
Fernández, Antonio. 2003. Parish priest at Nuestra Señora de la Altagracia in Paraíso, Diocese of Barahona. Interviewed June 27. Barahona.
Ferrand, Fernando. 2001. Former priest and journalist. Interviewed June 12. Santo Domingo.

Flores Santana, Juan, Msgr. 2000. Archbishop, Diocese of Santiago. Interviewed June 14. Santiago.

Franco Aquino, Reynaldo, Rev. 2001. Former president of CODUE. Interviewed June 16. Santo Domingo.

Guigni, José Luis. 2004. Head of Catholic Relief Services in Santo Domingo. Interviewed June 22. Santo Domingo.

Grullón, José Dolores, Msgr. 2000. Bishop of San Juan de la Maguana. Interviewed June 22. San Juan de la Maguana.

———. 2003. Bishop of San Juan de la Maguana. Second interview, June 23. San Juan de la Maguana.

Lafleur, Lucas, Fr. 2000. Parish priest of La Altagracia in Santiago. Interviewed June 13. Santiago.

Lejeune, Xavier and Robles, Alejandro. 2003. Human rights workers at Solidaridad Fronteriza in Dajabón. Interviewed May 30. Dajabón.

Lluberes, Antonio, SJ. 2001. Rector of the Politécnico Loyola in San Cristobal. Interviewed, June 15. San Cristobal.

Lucas Cruz, Fr. 2003. Head of the Social Pastoral in the Archdiocese of Santiago. Interviewed June 30. Santiago.

Marrero, Tomás, Fr., SJ. 2001. Founder and promoter of CEB movement in Santiago Domingo. Interviewed July 10. Baní.

Martínez, J. Adalberto, Rev. 2001. Former vice minister of education. Interviewed July 10. Santo Domingo.

Martínez, Regino, Fr., SJ. 2003. Head of Solidaridad Fronteriza. Interviewed May 30. Dajabón.

Mella, Pablo. 2001. Professor and researcher at the Centro Bonó. Interviewed June 4. Santo Domingo.

Méndez, Noemí. 2003. Cedail lawyer in charge of the eastern region. Interviewed June 4. Santo Domingo.

Minaya, Elvira. 2001. Teacher and community organizer. Interviewed June 20. Santo Domingo.

Molina, Ezequiel, Rev. 2004. President Batalla por la Fe. Interviewed June 24. Santo Domingo.

Molina, Uriel, Fr. 1997. Former advisor to the Sandinista government. Interviewed July 17. Managua, Nicaragua.

Mota King, Lorenzo, Rev. 2004. President of the Servicio Social de Iglesias. Interviewed June 17. Santo Domingo.

Moya, Jesús María. 2000. Bishop, Diocese of San Francisco de Macoris. Interviewed June 9. San Francisco de Macoris.

Naveo, Carlos, and Felicia Fermín. 2004. Founders of Lemba. Interviewed, June 28. Santo Domingo.

Nuñez, José, SJ. 2001. Director of the Jesuit Refugee Center. Interviewed June 27. Santo Domingo.

———. 2003. Director of the Jesuit Refugee Center. Second interview June 17. Santo Domingo.

Osoria, Francisco. 2000. Bishop, Diocese of San Pedro de Macoris. Interviewed June 21. San Pedro de Macoris.
Ossers Veras, Alfredo, Rev. 2004. Director of postgraduate education at the Universidad Evangélica. Interviewed June 25. Santo Domingo.
Peña, Nicanor. 2000. Bishop, Diocese of Puerto Plata. Interviewed June 15. Puerto Plata.
Pérez, Manual Antonio. 2003. Founder and president of Lemba. Interviewed June 26. Barahona.
Pimentel, Franklyn. 2001. Parish priest in the Diocese of Baní. Interviewed June 16. Santo Domingo.
Piñeiro, Pedro, Rev. 2004. Pastor of the Iglesia Buenas Nuevas. Interviewed June 22. Santo Domingo.
Portes, Braulio, Rev. 2001. President of Confraternidad Evangelica Dominicana. Interviewed June 16. Santo Domingo.
Reyes, Andrés, Rev. 2001. President of the Religious Affairs Commission of the Dominican Revolutionary Party. Interviewed June 22. Santo Domingo.
Reyes, Rafael Anibal. 2003. Head of Cáritas and the social pastoral program in the Diocese of Mao-Montecristi. Interviewed June 5. Mao-Valverde.
Rincón, Andrés, Rev. 2004. National Administrative Bishop of the Iglesia de Dios. Interviewed June 30. Santo Domingo.
Ruiz Bergés, Margarita. 2001. Author and theologian. Interviewed June 26. Santo Domingo.
Ruquoy, Pedro, Fr. 2004. Parish priest at Batey Cinco and defender of immigrant rights in Barahona. Interviewed June 11. Barahona.
Sáez, José Luis, SJ. 1998. Church historian and professor at the Universidad Autónoma de Santo Domingo. Interviewed June 26. Santo Domingo.
———. 2000. Author's correspondence with José Luis Sáez, SJ, March 10–August 4. Santo Domingo.
Ubiera, Plinio. 2003. Executive director of Cedail. Interviewed May 27. Santo Domingo.

Published and Unpublished Materials

Note: All newspapers cited are published in Santo Domingo unless otherwise indicated.
Adames, Fausto Rosario. 1994. "La Iglesia en la Danza de las Construcciones." *Rumbo* 27 (July–August): 8–15.
Alemán, José Luis, SJ. 1982. *27 Ensayos sobre Economía y Sociedad Dominicana*. Santiago: Universidad Católica Madre y Maestra.
Alfau Durán, Vetillo. 1975. *El Derecho de Patronato en la República Dominicana*. Santo Domingo: Editora Educativa Dominicana.
Althusser, Louis. 1971. *Lenin and Philosophy and Other Essays*. New York: Monthly Review Press.
Alvarez Vega, Bienvenido. 1996. "Movimiento Pentecostal Dominicano." In *El Campo Religioso Dominicano en la Década de los 90: Diversidad y Expansión*, ed. Mar-

cos Villamán. Santo Domingo: Departamento de Estudios de Sociedad y Religión, Inc., Decir.
Alvarez Vega. 2003. "Comunidad Evangélica y Opinión Pública." Unpublished paper delivered at the Segunda Expo Feria del Libro Cristiano. Santo Domingo, October, p. 11.
Báez Evertsz, Franc. 2001. *Vecinos y Extraños. Migrantes y Relaciones Interétnicas en un Barrio Popular de Santo Domingo*. Santo Domingo: Servicio Jesuita a Refugiados.
Banco Central de la República Dominicana. 1985. "Precio del dólar efectivo en el mercado extraordinario. Promedios mensuales (ventas 1969–1985)."
Banco Central de la República Dominicana. 2005. "Tasas de cambio promedio para compra y venta de dolares estadounidensesl." htpp: www.bancentral.gov.do/ (accessed May 13, 2005).
Barnadas, Joseph. 2000. *El Cardenal Maurer de Bolivia, 1900–1990: Breve Biografía en el Centenario de su Nacimiento*. Sucre, Bolivia: Editorial Judicial.
Bastian, Jean-Pierre. 1986a. *Historia del Protestantismo en América Latina*. Mexico City: Centro de Comunicación Cultural CUPSA.
———. 1986b. "Religión Popular Protestante y Comportamiento Político en América Central: Clientela Religiosa y Estado Patrón Guatemala y Nicaragua." *Nueva Antropología, Revista de Ciencias Sociales* 24 (88): 48–57, 151–78.
———. 1992. "Les Protestantismos Latino-Américain: Un Objet à Interroger et à Construire." *Social Compact* 39 (3): 329.
Bello Peguero, Rafael (ed.). 1996. *Provincias Eclesiásticas de Santo Domingo y Santiago de los Caballeros: Cifras Estadísticas*. Santo Domingo: Amigo del Hogar.
———. 1997. *Sínodos Diocesanos, 1851, 1878, y 1938*. Santo Domingo: Amigo del Hogar.
Belza, Juan Esteban. 1976. *El Pastor de los Pobres y su Mitra de Plomo*. Santo Domingo: Talleres Gráficos de ITESA.
Bendaña, R. 1985. "Guatemala." In *Historia General de la Iglesia América Latina*, Vol. 6, *América Central*, ed. E. Dussel, R. Cardenal, J. E. Arellano, M. Carias, M. Picado, and W. Nelson. Salamanca, Spain: CEHILA/Ediciones Sígueme.
Berryman, Philip. 1984. *The Religious Roots of Rebellion: Christians in Central American Revolutions*. Maryknoll, NY: Orbis Books.
———. 1994. *Stubborn Hope: Religion, Politics, and Revolution in Central America*. Maryknoll, NY: Orbis Books.
Betances, Emelio. 1995. *State and Society in the Dominican Republic*. Boulder, CO: Westview.
Betto, Frei. N.d. *What Are Ecclesial Base Communities?* Managua, Nicaragua: Centro Valdivieso.
Blancarte, Roberto. 1992. *Historia de la Iglesia Católica en México*. Mexico City: El Colegio Mexiquense/Fondo de Cultura Económico.
Boletín Eclesiástico de la Arquidiócesis de Santo Domingo. 1936. 1 (5) January.
Booth, John and Mitchell Seligson. 1989. *Elections and Democracy in Central America*. Chapel Hill: University of North Carolina Press.

Bourdieu, Pierre. 1971. "Genèse et Structure du Champ Religieux." *Revue Française de Sociologie* (December): 328–29.
Bosch, Juan. 1964. *Crisis de la Democracia de América en la República Dominicana.* Mexico City: Centro de Estudios y Documentación.
———. 1998. *Discursos Políticos*, Vol. 1. Santo Domingo: Impreso en los Talleres de la Editora Corripio.
Brett, Edward T. (2002). "Archbishop Arturo Rivera y Damas and the Struggle for Social Justice in El Salvador." Unpublished paper presented at the Henry Institute Symposium on Religion and Politics, May 3–4, pp. 1–25.
———. 2003. *The U.S. Catholic Press on Central America: From Cold War Anticommunism to Social Justice.* Notre Dame, IN: University of Notre Dame Press.
Brito, Israel 1978. *Historia de la Iglesia Metodista Libre Dominicana.* Santo Domingo: Editora Educativa Dominicana.
Brockman, James R. 1999. *Romero: A Life.* Maryknoll, NY: Orbis Books.
Bruneau, Thomas C. 1974. *The Political Transformation of the Brazilian Catholic Church.* Cambridge, UK: Cambridge University Press.
———. 1982. *The Church in Brazil: The Politics of Religion.* Austin: University of Texas Press.
Calder, Bruce J. 1970. *Crecimiento y Cambio de la Iglesia Católica Guatemalteca, 1944–1966.* Ciudad Guatemala: Editorial José de Pineda Ibarra.
———. 1984. *The Impact of Intervention: The Dominican Republic during the U.S. Occupation of 1916–1924.* Austin: University of Texas Press.
———. 2001. "The Role of the Catholic Church and Other Religious Institutions in the Guatemalan Peace Process, 1980–1996." *Journal of Church and State* 43 (Autumn): 779, 793.
Camp, Roderic A. I. 1997. *Crossing Swords: Politics and Religion in Mexico.* Oxford, UK: Oxford University Press.
Cañas, Antonio. 1989. "La Guerra en los Primeros Cien Días de ARENA." *Estudios Centroamericanos (ECA)* (July–December): 669–81.
Cardenal, Rodolfo. 1996. "La segunda Visita de Juan Pablo II: El Desafío de la Justicia y la Reconciliación." *Estudios Centroamericanos* 567–72 (January–June): 29–45.
Cárdenas, Luis M. 2003. "Evangélicos Señalan Vías Lograr Tranquilidad." *Hoy*, February 1.
Cardoso, Fernando Henrique. 1979. "Overview of the Bureaucratic-Authoritarian Model." In *The New Authoritarianism in Latin America*, ed. David Collier. Princeton, NJ: Princeton University Press.
Cáritas Dominicana. 2003. *Informe de Cáritas Dominicana, 1999–2003.* Santo Domingo. May 20.
Cassá, Roberto. 1995. "Recent Popular Movements in the Dominican Republic." *Latin American Perspectives* 22 (3): 80–93.
Castillo de Aza, Zenón. 1961. *Trujillo y Otros Benefactores de la Iglesia.* Ciudad Trujillo, Dominican Republic: Editora Handicap, C x A.

Castor, Suzy. 1983. *Migración y Relaciones Internacionales: El Caso Haitiano- Dominicano*. Mexico City: Siglo XXI.
Cedail. 2001. *Los Operativos de Declaración de Nacimientos*. Santo Domingo: Publicaciones Cedail.
———. 2002. *Informe Económico Elaborado para la Conferencia del Episcopado Dominicano: Proyectos Educativos y Jurídicos*. June 1, 2001 to May 31, 2002.
Centro de Promoción del Laicado. 1985. *Bolivia: La Iglesia y la Política Económica del Gobierno de Paz Estenssoro*. La Paz: CEPROLAI.
Chea, José Luis. 1988. *Guatemala: La Cruz Fragmentada*. San José, Costa Rica: Editorial Departamento Ecuménico de Investigaciones (DEI).
Chester, Eric Thomas. 2001. *Rag-Tags, Scum, Riff-Raff, and Commies: The U.S. Intervention in the Dominican Republic, 1965–1966*. New York: Monthly Review Press.
Clark, James. 1967. *The Church and the Crisis in the Dominican Republic*. Westminster, MD: Newman Press.
Cleary, Edward. 1985. *Crisis and Change. The Church in Latin America Today*. Maryknoll, NY: Orbis Books.
———. 2004. "Shopping Around: Questions about Latin American Conversions." *International Bulletin* 28 (2): 50.
———. 2005. "Missionaries and the Indigenous Resurgence in Latin America." Submitted to the *Bulletin of Missions*, p. 4.
CODUE. 1998a. "Sólo CODUE y CONEDO Podrán Tramitar Exoneraciones Ante el Poder Ejecutivo." *Voz de CODUE*, September–October.
———. 1998b. "Llamado Urgente al País de CODUE y CONEDO" in *Voz de CODUE*, September–October.
CONEDO. 1994. *Lineamientos Generales para la Elaboración de una Agenda de Consenso para el Pueblo Dominicano*. Santo Domingo: CONEDO.
Conferencia del Episcopado Dominicano (CED). 1985. *Plan Nacional de Pastoral*. Santo Domingo: Editora Amigo del Hogar.
———. 1990. "Homilía de su Eminencia Card: Beras en su Despedida." In *Documentos de la Conferencia del Episcopado Dominicano 1955–1990*. Santo Domingo: Editora Amigo del Hogar.
———. 1994. *Segundo Plan Nacional de Pastoral*. Santo Domingo: Amigo del Hogar.
———. 1998a. *Documentos de la Conferencia del Episcopado Dominicano 1991–1997*. Santo Domingo: Editora Amigo del Hogar.
———. 1998b. *Mensaje de la Conferencia del Episcopado Dominicano*. July.
———. 2000. *Primer Concilio Plenario Dominicano: Documento Final*. Santo Domingo: Susaeta Ediciones Dominicanas.
Conferencia Episcopal de Bolivia (CEB). 1992. *Mensajes y Exhortaciones de la Conferencia Episcopal de Bolivia, 1979–1992*. La Paz, Bolivia: CEB.
Conferencia Episcopal de Nicaragua (CEN). 1979. *Carta Pastoral Compromiso Cristiano para una Nueva Nicaragua*. November.
Crassweller, Robert. 1968. *Trujillo: La Trágica Aventura del Poder Personal*. Barcelona: Editorial Bruguera, S.A.

Cuello, José Israel. 1985. *Documentos del Conflicto Dominico-Haitiano de 1937*. Santo Domingo: Editora Taller, C x A.

de Agar, Martín 2000. *Raccoolta di Cocordi, 1950–1999*. Vatican City, Rome: Librería Editrice Vaticana.

De Broucker, José. 1966. "La Verdad Desnuda Tras la Polémica Actuación del Nuncio Clarizio." *Ahora!* 132, May 16.

De la Cruz, Víctor Manuel. 1998. *Juan Bosch, Lautico García y la Iglesia Católica*. Santo Domingo: Editora Búho.

Departamento de Cuentas Nacionales y Estadísticas Económicas. División de Precios, 1969–1985. Santo Domingo, República Dominicana.

Diamond, Larry, Juan Linz, and Seymour Martin Lipset (eds.). 1989. *Democracy in Developing Countries: Latin America*, Vol. 4. Boulder, CO: Lynne Rienner.

Draper, Theodore.1968. *The Dominican Revolution: A Case in American Policy*. New York: Commentary.

Duarte, Isis and Ramonina Brea. 2002. *Hacia Dónde va la Democracia Dominicana? (Demos 1994–2001)*. Santo Domingo: Pontifica Universidad Católica Madre y Maestra/Asociación Dominicana Pro-Bienestar de la Familia.

Duarte, Isis, Ramonina Brea, Ramón Tejada, and Clara Báez. 1996. *Cultura Política y Democracia en República Dominicana (Demos, 94)*. Santo Domingo: Impresora G & G.

Dussel, Enrique (ed.). 1992. *The Church in Latin America. 1492–1992*. Maryknoll, NY: Orbis Books.

Dussel, Enrique, R. Cardenal, R. Bendaña, J. E. Arellano, M. Carias, M. Picado, and W. Nelson (eds.). 1985. *Historia General de la Iglesia en América Latina*, Vol. 6, *América Central*. Salamanca, Spain: CEHILA/Ediciones Sígueme.

Eagleson, John, and Philip Scharper (eds.). 1979. *Puebla and Beyond*. Maryknoll, NY: Orbis Books.

El Estado Dominicano y las Iglesias Evangélicas y Protestantes. 2004. "Pacto Social Firmado por el Presidente Hipólito Mejía y las Iglesias Evangélicas." *Rescate*, Santo Domingo: No 17, Fourth year.

Ellacuría, Ignacio. 1989. "El Diálogo en los Primeros Cien Días de Cristiani." *Estudios Centroamericanos (ECA)* 489–94 (July–December): 683–93.

Espinal, Rosario. 1990. "The Defeat of the Dominican Revolutionary Party in the 1986 Elections: Causes and Implications." *Bulletin of Latin American Research* 9 (1): 103–15.

Espinal, Rosario, and Jonathan Hartlyn. 1999. "The Dominican Republic: The Long and Difficult Struggle for Democracy." In *Democracy in Developing Countries: Latin America*, ed. Larry Diamond, Jonathan Hartlyn, Juan Linz, and Seymour Martin Lipset. Boulder, CO: Lynne Rienner.

Estudios Centroamericanos. 1988. "Editorial: El Significado del Debate Nacional." *Estudios Centroamericanos* 477–82 (July–December): 713–29.

Fazio, Carlos. 2004. "El Ex Embajador de E.U. en El Salvador Señaló a D'Abuisson como el Autor Intelectual Clave: El Testimonio de Robert White en el Caso del Asesinato de Monseñor Romero." *La Jornada*, Mexico City, September 24.

Figueredo, Sergio. 1971. "El Nuncio y la Iglesia Dominicana." *Ahora!* 383, March 15.
Fleet, Michael, and Brian H. Smith. 1997. *The Catholic Church and Democracy in Chile and Perú*. Notre Dame, IN: University of Notre Dame Press.
Fletcher, Laurel, and Timothy Miller. 2004. "New Perspectives on Old Patterns: Forced Migration of Haitians in the Dominican Republic." *Journal of Ethnic and Migration Studies* 30 (4): 659–79.
French, Howard. 1994. "With Balaguer Holding Tiny Lead, Dominican Fraud is Charged." *New York Times*, May 19, A5.
Frente Sandinista de Liberación Nacional (FSLN). 1983. "Comunicado Oficial de la Dirección Nacional del FSLN sobre la Religión." *La Iglesia en Nicaragua*. Madrid: IEPALA.
Fundación de Desarrollo de Azua, San Juan y Elías Piña (FUNDASEP). 2002. No. 5, November. Fifth year.
Gaceta Oficial del Gobierno Dominiano. 1954. Gaceta No. 7720, *Resolución No. 3874, del Congreso Nacional, que Aprueba el Concordato y el Protocolo Final Suscrito entre la República Dominicana y la Santa Sede*. Ciudad Trujillo, Dominican Republic: Imprenta J. R. Vda. García. Sucesores.
García Lluberes, Leonidas. 1934. "Influencia de la Iglesia Católica en la Formación de la Nacionalidad y en la Creación de la República Dominicana." *Boletín Eclesiástico de Santo Domingo* 44 (128–129): 184.
Gleijeses, Piero. 1978. *The Dominican Crisis: The 1965 Constitutionalist Revolution and American Intervention*. Baltimore and London: Johns Hopkins University Press.
González, Antonio Camilo. 2001. *Fray Rocco Coccchia*. Santo Domingo: Amigo del Hogar.
Gramsci, Antonio. 1971. *Selections from the Prison Notebooks*. New York: International Publisher.
Greene, Anne. 1993. *The Catholic Church in Haiti: Political and Social Change*. East Lansing: Michigan State University Press.
Guerrero Cano, María Magdalena. 1991. *El Arzobispo Monzón*. Serie Hombres de Iglesia, 7. Santo Domingo: Amigo del Hogar.
Guerrero, Miguel. 1993. *El Golpe de Estado: Historia del Derrocamiento de Juan Bosch*. Santo Domingo: Editora Corripio.
Gunther, Richard, P. Nikiforos Diamandouros, and Hans-Jurgen Puhle (eds.). 1995. *The Politics of Democratic Consolidation: Southern Europe in Comparative Perspectiva*. Baltimore: Johns Hopkins University Press.
Gutiérrez, Gustavo. 1971. *Teología de la Liberación*. Lima: Perspectivas, CEP.
———. 1973. *A Liberation Theology: History, Politics, and Salvation*. Maryknoll, NY: Orbis Books.
———. 1990. "Church of the Poor." In *Born of the Poor: The Latin American Church since Medellín*, ed. Eduard Cleary. Notre Dame, IN: University of Notre Dame Press.
Hartlyn, Jonathan. 1998. *The Struggle for Democratic Politics in the Dominican Republic*. Chapel Hill and London: University of North Carolina Press.

Harto de Vera, Fernando. 1993. "La Resolución del Proceso de Negociaciones de Paz." *Estudios Centroamericanos (ECA)* 531–36 (January–June): 29–38.

Hegeman, Cornelio, and Eufemio Ricaro Luis. 1988. "Directorio de Iglesias Evangélicas Dominicanas: 1988." In *La Historia de las Iglesias Evangélicas desde Lutero hasta la República Dominicana*, ed. Ricardo Oostendorp. Santo Domingo: Universidad Nacional Evangélica/Escuela de Teología.

Hennelly, Alfred T. (ed.). 1993. *Santo Domingo and Beyond: Documents and Commentaries from the Historic Meeting of the Latin American Bishops' Conference.* Maryknoll, NY: Orbis Books.

Henríquez Ureña, Max. 1991. *El Arzobispo Valera.* Serie Hombres de Iglesia, 6. Santo Domingo: Amigo del Hogar.

Hoetink, Harry. 1994. *Santo Domingo y el Caribe: Ensayos sobre Cultura y Sociedad.* Santo Domingo: Fundación Cultural Dominicana.

Instituto Nacional de Pastoral. 1977. *Directorio de la Iglesia en la Republica Dominicana, 1977.* Santo Domingo: Amigo del Hogar.

———. 1985. *Directorio de la Iglesia en la Republica Dominicana.* Santo Domingo: Amigo del Hogar.

———. 1993. *Directorio de la Iglesia en la Republica Dominicana.* Santo Domingo: Gráficos de Editora Tele-3.

Jiménez, Ramón Emilio. 1987. *El Arzobispo Novel.* Serie Hombres de Iglesia, 3. Santo Domingo: Amigo del Hogar.

Jonas, Susanne. 2000. *Of Centaurs and Doves: Guatemala's Peace Process.* Boulder, CO: Westview.

Junta Central Electoral. 1994. "Proceso Electoral 1994." *Informe de la Comisión de Verificación.* Santo Domingo, July 12.

Keogh, Dermot (ed.). 1990. *Church and Politics in Latin America.* New York: St. Martin's Press.

Kirk, John M. 1992. *Politics and the Catholic Church in Nicaragua.* Gainesville: University of Florida Press.

Klaiber, Jeffrey. 1998. *The Church, Dictatorships, and Democracy in Latin America.* Maryknoll, NY: Orbis Books.

Klein, Herbert S. 1992. *Bolivia: The Evolution of a Multi-Ethnic Society.* New York: Oxford University Press.

Lalive d'Epinay, Christian. 1969. *Haven of the Masses: A Study of the Pentecostal Movement in Chile.* London: Lutterworth Press.

Latin American Episcopal Council (CELAM). 1970. *Second General Conference*, Vol. 1, *Position Papers*, Volume 2, *Conclusions.* Bogotá: CELAM.

Leveque, Kart. 1972. "La Iglesia en Tres Crisis Dominicana." *Ahora!* 473, December 4.

Levine, Daniel H. 1981. *Religion and Politics in Latin America. The Catholic Church in Venezuela and Colombia.* Princeton, NJ: Princeton University Press.

———. 1996. "From Church and State to Religion and Politics and Back Again." In *Democracy in Latin America: Patterns and Cycles*, ed. Roderic Ai Camp. Wilmington, DE: SR Books.

Linz, Juan J. 1990. "Transitions to Democracy." *Washington Quarterly* 13: 156.
Lluberes, Antonio, SJ. 1998. *Breve Historia de la Iglesia Dominicana, 1493–1997*. Santo Domingo: Editora Amigo del Hogar.
Lockhart, James, and Stuart Schwartz. 1996. *Early Latin America: A History of Colonial Spanish America and Brazil*. Melbourne: Cambridge University Press.
Lockward, Alfonso. 1993. *Intolerancia y Libertad de Cultos en Santo Domingo*. Santo Domingo: Editora Taller.
Lockward, George. 1982. *El Protestantismo en Dominicana*. Santo Domingo: Editora Educativa Dominicana.
Lowenthal, Abraham. 1972. *The Dominican Intervention*. Cambridge, MA: Harvard University Press.
McPherson, Alan. 2003. "Misled by Himself: What the Johnson Tapes Reveal about the Dominican Intervention of 1965." *Latin American Research Review* 38 (2): 127–46.
Maduro, Otto. 1980. *Religión y Conflicto Social*. Mexico City: Centro de Estudios Ecúmenico.
Mainwaring, Scott. 1986. *The Catholic Church and Politics in Brazil, 1916–1985*. Stanford, CA: Stanford University Press.
Mainwaring, Scott, Guillermo O'Donnell, and J. Samuel Valenzuela (eds.). 1992. *Issues in Democratic Consolidation: The New South American Democracies in Comparative Perspectives*. Notre Dame, IN: University of Notre Dame Press.
Maldonado Villagrán, David. 1991. *Resumen Histórico: 500 Años de Evangelización en Bolivia*. La Paz, Bolivia: Empresa Editora "Urquizo" S.A.
Malloy, James M. and Eduardo Gamarra. 1988. *Revolution and Reaction: Bolivia, 1964–1985*. New Brunswick, NJ: Transaction Books.
Martin, David. 1990. *Tongues of Fire: The Explosion of Protestantism in Latin America*. Oxford, UK, and Cambridge, MA: Blackwell.
Martínez, J. Adalberto. 1994. *Julio Postigo: La Librería Dominicana. Semblanza e Historia*. Santo Domingo: Fundación Editorial Evangélica Dr. Julio D. Postigo.
Martínez, Luis. 1995. "The Sword and Crucifix: Church-State Relations and Nationality in the Nineteenth Century Dominican Republic." *Latin American Research Review* 30 (1): 75.
Martínez, Víctor. 2003. "Evangélicos Critican Mañas de Políticos." *El Nacional*, January 5.
Metzler, Josef (ed.). 1991. *America Pontificia Primi Saeculi Evangelizationis, 1493–1592*, Vol. 1. Vatican City, Rome: Librería Editrice Vaticana.
Meyer, Jean. 1999. *Historia de los Cristianos en América Latina: Siglos XIX y XX*. Mexico City: Editorial JUS.
———. 2000. *Samuel Ruiz en San Cristóbal*. Mexico City: Tusquets Editores.
Molina Achécar, Martiza. 2003. *Encuesta Demográfica y de Salud, Endesa 2002*. Santo Domingo: Editorial Gente.
Montgomery, Tommie Sue. 1983. "The Church in the Salvadoran Revolution." *Latin American Perspectives* 10 (1): 69–75.

Moreno, José A. 1970. *Barrios in Arms: Revolution in Santo Domingo.* Pittsburgh, PA: University of Pittsburgh Press.

Moya Pons, Frank. 1973. "Notas para una Historia de la Iglesia en Santo Domingo." *Eme-Eme, Estudios Dominicanos* 1 (6): 3–17.

Nouel, Carlos. 1913. *Historia Eclesiástica de la Arquidiócesis de Santo Domingo: Primada de América,* Vol. I. Rome: Oficina Poligráfica Italiana.

———. 1914. *Historia Eclesiástica de la Arquidiócesis de Santo Domingo: Primada de América,* Vol. 2. Santo Domingo: Imprenta "La Cuna de América" Vda. de Roques y Ca.

Núñez Collado, Agripino. 1993. *Concertación: La Cultura del Diálogo.* Santiago: Departamento Editorial PUCMM.

———. 1996. *Testigo de una Crisis. . . Diez Años Después.* Santo Domingo: Editora Taller.

O'Donnell, Guillermo. 1994. "Delegative Democracy." *Journal of Democracy* 5 (January): 59–60.

———. 1996. "Illusions about Consolidation." *Journal of Democracy* 7 (2): 34–51.

Oxhorn, Philip, and Graciela Ducatenzeiler (eds.). 1998. *What Kind of Democracy? What Kind of Market? Latin America in the Age of Neoliberalism.* University Park: Pennsylvania State University Press.

Pepén, Juan Félix. 1954. *La Cruz Señaló el Camino: Influencia de la Iglesia en la Formación y Conservación de la Nacionalidad Dominicana.* Ciudad Trujillo, Dominican Republic: Editorial Duarte.

———. 2003. *Un Garabato de Dios. Vivencias de un Testigo.* Santo Domingo: Ediciones Peregrino.

Peralta Brito, Rafael, and José Chez Checo. 1979. *Religión, Filosofía y Política en Fernando A. de Meriño 1857–1906.* Santo Domingo: Amigo del Hogar.

Pérez, César. 1996. *Urbanización y Municipio en Santo Domingo.* Santo Domingo: Instituto Tecnológico de Santo Domingo.

Pérez, César, and Artiles Leopoldo. 1992. *Movimientos Sociales Dominicanos: Identidad y Dilemas.* Santo Domingo: Instituto Tecnológico de Santo Domingo.

Pérez Memén, Fernando. 1984. *La Iglesia y el Estado en Santo Domingo (1700–1853).* Santo Domingo: Editora de la UASD.

———. 1985. *El Arzobispo Fernando Carvajal y Rivera: Un Crítico de la Política Colonial Española (y Otros Ensayos Históricos).* Santo Domingo: Universidad Nacional Pedro Henríquez Ureña.

Pittini, Ricardo. 1949. *Memorias Salesianas de un Arzobispo Ciego.* Buenos Aires: Editorial Poblet.

Platt, Dario. 1981. *Nueva Esperanza para Santo Domingo.* Santo Domingo: Publicaciones de la Universidad INTEC.

PNUD. 2005. *Informe Nacional de Desarrollo Humano: República Dominicana.* Santo Domingo: Editora Corripio.

Polanco Brito, Hugo Eduardo. 1948. *Seminario Conciliar Santo Tomás de Aquino.* Ciudad Trujillo, Dominican Republic: Imprenta "San Francisco" de la Papelera Industrial Santo Domingo.

———. 1969. *Recortes de Periódicos de Polanco Brito, 1966–1970–1972–1973*. "Carta Circular del Arzobispado," *Listín Diario*, June 6; and "Obreros Explican," *El Nacional*, July 28. (All the *Recortes de Periódicos de Polanco Brito* are located at Biblioteca Central of the Pontificia Universidad Católica Madre y Maestra, Santiago, Dominican Republic.)

———. 1970a. "Diario de Polanco Brito." *Documentos sobre el Secuestro del Coronel Donald J. Crowley*. (Located in the Sala Hugo Eduardo Polanco Brito at the Biblioteca Central of the Pontificia Universidad Católica Madre y Maestra. Santiago, Dominican Republic.)

———. 1970b. *Documentos sobre el Secuestro del Coronel Donald J. Crowley*. "Polanco Va Aeropuerto para Recibir Cadáver," *El Nacional de Ahora!* May 28.

———. 1970c. *La Iglesia Católica y la Primera Constitución Dominicana* (Discurso en el Día de la Constitución. San Cristóbal, 6 de noviembre). Santo Domingo: Editora del Caribe, C x A.

———. 1971. *Recortes de Periódicos de Polanco Brito, 1971–1975*. "Prelado Requiere Pongan Coto a la Banda," *El Caribe*, 24 May.

———. 1972a. *Recortes de Periódicos de Polanco Brito, 1969–1970–1972–1973*. "Solicitan Ampliar Plazo en Pro de Buscados," *Listín Diario*, January 24; "Harry se Asila," *El Nacional*, January 24; "Rechaza Asilo: Monseñor Polanco Pide que Plinio Reflexione" and "Matos Moquete Afirma se Quedará en el País," *El Nacional*, January 25.

———. 1972b. *Recortes de Periódicos de Polanco Brito, 1969–1970–1972–1973*. "Sacan a Macorís: Burlan Justicia," *El Nacional*, March 18.

———. 1972–1973. *Recortes de Periódicos de Polanco Brito, 1969–1970–1972–1973*. "Episcopado Pide se de Permiso Salida a Presos," *Listín Diario*, December 26; and "Obispos Revelan JB Prometió Amnistía," *El Nacional*, January 5.

———. 1973a. *Recortes de Periódicos de Polanco Brito, 1966–1970–1972–1973*. "Carta de Polanco Brito a Rafael Herrera, Editor of *Listín Diario*," *Listín Diario*, February 22.

———. 1973b. *Recortes de Periódicos de Polanco Brito, 1966–1970–1972–1973*. "Toman Rehén Hijo Embajador México: Presidente Dispone Salvo Conducto a Asilado," *Listín Diario*, September 27.

———. 1974a. *Recortes de Periódicos de Polanco Brito, January–May, 1974*. "Obispo Santiago Apoya Ocupación Iglesias," *La Noticia*, May 4; and "Obispo Persuade Evacuen Templo," *Listín Diario*, May 4.

———. 1974b. *Recortes de Periódicos de Polanco Brito, January–May, 1974*. "Celebran Hoy Elecciones. Acuerdo Mantiene Abstención," *El Sol*, May 16; and "Texto de la Declaración Emitida Anoche por la Misión Mediadora entre los Partidos Políticos Signatarios del Acuerdo de Santiago y el Gobierno en Relación con la Abstención Electoral del Bloque Oposicionista," *Listín Diario*, June 16.

———. 1974c. *Recortes de Periódicos de Polanco Brito, January–May, 1974*. "Declaración de Saturnino Gil Morales, Líder del PRD," *El Nacional de Ahora*, May 17.

———. 1974d. *Recortes de Periódicos de Polanco Brito, 1971–1975*. "El Arzobispo Exhorta Esfuerzo Común," *Listín Diario*, May 20.

———. 1974e. *Recortes de Periódicos de Polanco Brito, June–December, 1974.* "Monseñor Confía logro Arreglo," *Listín Diario,* June 3; and "Monseñor me Desconcierta," *Listín Diario,* June 4.

———. 1974f. *Recortes de Periódicos de Polanco Brito, 1971–1975.* "Texto Integro de la Homilía de Polanco Brito en Honor a Nuestra Señora de las Mercedes," *El Sol,* September 25.

———. 1974g. *Diario de Polanco Brito in Secuestro en el Consulado de Venezuela, September–October,* Vol. 2, "Diplomáticos Hablan a Terroristas: Reanudan Suministro Alimentos," *El Caribe,* October 3; "Decisión Varia Ambiente," *Listín Diario,* October 5; and "Terroristas Aceptan Dejar el País: Comando Viajaría a Panamá," *El Caribe,* October 9.

———. 1975. *Recortes de Periódicos de Polanco Brito, 1975.* "Monseñor Pepén Renuncia Obispado de la Altagracia," *El Caribe,* May 12; "Pepén Renuncia de Higuey por Razones de Salud: Envían a Monseñor Polanco Brito., *El Sol,* May 12; "Obispo Afirma Corrientes no Rompen Unidad Iglesia," *El Sol,* July 26; "Gulf and Western Trasladó a Pepén," *Cometa,* November 23; "Polanco Brito Critica Latifundismo de Gulf y Terratenientes en el Este," *Última Hora,* November 29; "Monseñor Polanco Brito Pide Liberación de Presos Políticos," *El Nacional,* November 29.

———. 1976. *Recortes de Periódicos de Polanco Brito, 1976.* "Arzobispo Exhorta Adquirir Terrenos," *Listín Diario,* April 8; "Balaguer Acusa Inescrupulosos Facilitar Tierras a Extranjeros," *El Sol,* April 9; and "Arzobispo Anticipa Primer Voto Nacionalizar Gulf and Western," *Última Hora,* October 4.

———. 1980. "Aporte de la Iglesia en el Cibao a la Causa Nacional, 1844–1880." *Eme Eme, Estudios Dominicanos* 8, (48): 22–24.

———. 1981. *Síntesis de la Historia de la Iglesia en Santo Domingo.* Higuey, Dominican Republic (publisher is not indicated).

Postigo, Julio. 1994. Carta a Don Antonio Imbert, Presidente del Gobierno de Reconstrucción Nacional. In *Julio Postigo: La Librería Dominicana. Semblanza e Historia,* ed. Adalberto Martínez. Santo Domingo: Amigo del Hogar.

Presidencia de la República del Salvador, FDR, and FMLN. 1987. "Comunicado Conjunto de la Tercera Reunión de Diálogo." *Estudios Centroamericanos (ECA)* (July–December): 746–47.

Przeworski, Adam. 1991. *Democracy and the Market: Political and Economic Reforms in Eastern Europe and Latin America.* Cambridge, UK: Cambridge University Press.

Putnam, Robert. 2000. *Bowling Alone.* New York: Simon and Schuster.

Ramírez López, Berenice P. 1987. "El Trasfondo Histórico de la Revolución Salvadoreña." In *Centroamérica: Una Historia sin Retoque,* ed. María Teresa Gutiérrez-Haces. Mexico City: Instituto de Investigaciones Económicas, UNAM and El Día.

República Dominicana y República de Haití. 1999. *Protocolo de Entendimiento sobre Mecanismos de Repatriación entre la República Dominicana y la República de Haití.* Suscrito el 2 de diciembre de 1999. Santo Domingo, Dominican Republic.

Rivera y Damas, Arturo. 1987. "Esquipulas es una Esperanza." *Estudios Centroamericanos (ECA)* 465–70 (July–December): 859–63.

Rochet Coronado, Rosa María. 1987. "Las Raíces del Diálogo entre la Iglesia Católica y el Gobierno Nicaragüense." *Avance* 65, Universidad de Costa Rica/FLACSO, 7.

Rodríguez de León, Francisco. 1996. *Balaguer y Trujillo: Entre la Espada y la Palabra*. Santo Domingo: Artes y Ediciones Caribe.

Rodríguez Demorizi, Emilio. 1969. *Santana y los Poetas de su Tiempo*. Santo Domingo: Editora del Caribe, C x A.

———. 1973. *Samaná, Pasado y Porvenir*. Santo Domingo: Editora del Caribe.

Rodríguez Núñez, José Carlos. 1991. *La Diócesis de Santiago de los Caballeros: Apuntes para su Historia*. Santo Domingo: Editora Corripio.

Ruiz Bergés, Margarita. 1987. "La Función Ideológico-Política de la Iglesia Católica en la República Dominicana. 1960–1980." Unpublished Masters dissertation, Universidad Iberoamericana. Mexico City.

———. 2001. "Memoria Histórica de la Vida Religiosa Femenina en República Dominicana, 1959–1999." Unpublished manuscript. Santo Domingo, Dominican Republic.

Sáez, José Luis, SJ. 1979. *Testigos de la Esperanza: Historia de la Vida Religiosa en Santo Domingo*. Santo Domingo: Amigo del Hogar.

———. 1988. *Los Jesuitas en la República Dominicana*, Vol. 1, *Los Primeros Veinticinco Años (1936–1961)*. Santo Domingo: Museo Nacional de Historia y Geografía y Archivo Histórico de las Antillas.

———. 1990. *Los Jesuitas en la República Dominicana*, Vol. 2, *Hacia el Medio Siglo (1962–1986)*. Santo Domingo: Archivo Histórico de las Antillas.

———. 1993. *Cinco Siglos de la Iglesia Dominicana*. Santo Domingo: Ediciones MSC-Amigo del Hogar.

———. 1994. *La Iglesia y el Negro Esclavo en Santo Domingo: Una Historia de Tres Siglos*. Santo Domingo: Colección Quinto Centenario, Serie Documentos 3.

———. 1996a. *El Arzobispo Portes*. Serie Hombres de Iglesia, 12. Santo Domingo: Amigo del Hogar.

———. 1996b. *Génesis y Evolución de la Provincia Eclesiástica de Santo Domingo*. Santo Domingo: Editora Amigo del Hogar.

———. 1999. *Lino Zanini: Diplomático y Agente de Cambio, 1909–1997*. Santo Domingo: Editora Amigo del Hogar.

———. 2001. *El Arzobispo Mena*. Santo Domingo: Editora Amigo del Hogar.

———. 2002. *Monseñor Pittini*. Santo Domingo: Editora Amigo del Hogar.

———. 2005. "Nuncios Apostólicos en la República Dominicana, 1930–1998." Unpublished manuscript. Santo Domingo, Dominican Republic.

Safa, Helen. 1999. "Women Coping with Crisis: Social Consequences of Export-Led Industrialization in the Dominican Republic." *The North South Agenda*, Paper 36, (April): 2.

———. 1995. *The Myth of the Male Breadwinner: Women and Industrialization in the Caribbean*. Boulder, CO: Westview.

Samandu, Luis, Siebers, Hans, and Sierra, Oscar. 1990. *Guatemala: Retos de la Iglesia Católica en una Sociedad en Crisis*. San José, Costa Rica: Editorial Departamento Ecuménico de Investigaciones (DEI).

Schmitter, Philippe. 1994. "Dangers and Dilemmas of Democracy." *Journal of Democracy* 5 (April): 57–74.
Secretariado Nacional de Pastoral de Conjunto. 1972. *Directorio de la Iglesia Católica en Republica Dominicana*. Santo Domingo: Amigo del Hogar.
Secretaría Status Rationarium Generale Ecclesiae. 1973. *Annuarium Statisticum Ecclesiae*, 1970 Vol. Vatican City, Rome: Typis Polyglottis Vaticanis.
———. 1982. *Annuarium Statisticum Ecclesiae*, 1980 Vol. Vatican City, Rome: Typis Polyglottis Vaticanis.
———. 1992. *Annuarium Statisticum Ecclesiae*, 1990 Vol. Vatican City, Rome: Typis Polyglottis Vaticanis.
———. 2000. *Annuarium Statisticum Ecclesiae*, 1998 Vol. Vatican City, Rome: Librería Editrice Vaticana.
Secretariado Técnico de la Presidencia/Oficina Nacional de Presupuesto. 1979–2000. "Informe de Ejecución Presupuestaria." Vols. 1–21. Santo Domingo: Gobierno Dominicano.
Selser, Irene. 1989. *Cardenal Obando*. Mexico City: Centro de Estudios Ecuménicos.
Slater, Jerome. 1970. *Intervention and Negotiation: The United States and the Dominican Republic*. New York: Harper and Row.
Smith, Brian H. 1982. *The Church and Politics in Chile: Challenges to Modern Catholicism*. Princeton, NJ: Princeton University Press.
———. 1998. *Religious Politics in Latin America: Pentecostal vs. Catholic*. Notre Dame, IN: University of Notre Dame Press.
Sobrino, Jon. 1986. "La Iglesia y la Solución del Conflicto Salvadoreño." *Estudios Centroamericanos (ECA)* 447–52 (January–June): 84–85.
———. 1993. "The Winds of Santo Domingo and the Evangelization of Culture." In *Santo Domingo and Beyond: Documents and Commentaries from the Historic Meeting of the Latin American Bishops' Conference*, ed. Alfred T. Hennelly. Maryknoll, NY: Orbis Books.
Spalding, Hobart. 1977. *Organized Labor in Latin America: Historical Case Studies of Urban Workers in Dependent Societies*. New York: Harper Torchbooks; Stanford, CA: Stanford University Press.
Steigenga, Timothy J. 2001. *The Politics of the Spirit: The Political Implications of Pentecostalized Religion in Costa Rica and Guatemala*. Lanham, MD: Lexington.
Stein, Andrew J. 1997. "The Church." In *Nicaragua without Illusions: Regime Transition and Structural Adjustment in the 1990s*, ed. Thomas W. Walker. Wilmington, DE: SR Books.
———. 1998. "The Consequences of the Nicaraguan Revolution for Political Tolerance: Explaining Differences among the Mass Public, Catholic Priests, and Secular Elites." *Comparative Politics* 30 (3): 342.
Stewart-Gambino, Hannah. 1992. *The Church and Politics in the Chilean Countryside*. Boulder, CO: Westview.
———. 1994. "Church and State in Latin America." *Current History* 93 (581): 130–31.

Stoll, David. 1990. *Is Latin America Turning Protestant? The Politics of Evangelical Growth*. Berkeley: University of California Press.
Testimonios de Cristianos. 1976. *Bolivia: 1971–76—Pueblo Estado Iglesia, Testimonios de Cristianos*. Lima: Centro de Estudios y Publicaciones.
"Texto del Pacto de la Civilidad." 1994. *Listín Diario*, May 11.
"Texto del Pacto por la Democracia." 1994. *Listín Diario*, August 11.
Tischler Visquera, Sergio. 1998. *Guatemala 1944: Crisis y Revolución—Ocaso y Quiebre de una Forma Estatal*. Puebla, Mexico: Universidad Autónoma de Puebla and Universidad de San Carlos de Guatemala.
Tomé, Mariano, SJ. 1963. *Guía Eclesiástica de la República Dominicana*. Santo Domingo: Amigo del Hogar.
———. 1965. *Guía Eclesiástica de la República Dominicana*. Santo Domingo: Amigo del Hogar.
Tujibikile, Pedro Muamba, CICM. 1993. *Sebastian Lemba. Mártir de la Iglesia Naciente y Héroe de los Excluídos*. Santo Domingo: Ediciones CEDEE.
Valda Palma, Roberto. 1995. *Historia de la Iglesia de Bolivia en la República*. La Paz, Bolivia: Imprenta Publicidad Papiro.
Vallier, Ivan. 1970. *Catholicism, Social Control, and Modernization in Latin America*. Englewood Cliffs, NJ: Prentice Hall.
Veeser, Cyrus. 2002. *A World Safe for Capitalism: Dollar Diplomacy and America's Rise to Global Power*. New York: Columbia University Press.
Vega, Bernardo. 1984. *Los Estados Unidos y Trujillo*, Vol. 1. Santo Domingo: Fundación Cultural Dominicana.
———. 1985. *Nazismo, Fascismo y Falangismo en la República Dominicana*. Santo Domingo: Fundación Cultural Dominicana.
———. 1988. *Trujillo y Haití*, Vol. 1, *1930–1937*. Santo Domingo: Fundación Cultural Dominicana.
———. 1995. *Trujillo y Haití*, Vol. 2, *1937–1938*. Santo Domingo: Fundación Cultural Dominicana.
———. 1999. *Los Estados Unidos y Trujillo: Los Días Finales, 1960–1961*. Colección de Documentos del Departamento de Estado, la CIA y los Archivos del Palacio Nacional Dominicano. Santo Domingo: Fundación Cultural Dominicana.
———. 2004. *Cómo los Americanos Ayudaron a Colocar a Balaguer en el Poder en 1966*. Santo Domingo: Fundación Cultural Dominicana.
Vilas, Carlos M. (ed.). 1993. *Democracia Emergente en Centroamérica*. Mexico City: Universidad Nacional Autónoma de México.
———. 1995. *Between Earthquakes and Volcanoes: Market, State, and the Revolutions in Central America*. New York: Monthly Review Press.
Villamán, Marcos. 1993. *El Auge Pentecostal: Certeza, Identidad, Salvación*. Mexico City: Centro Antonio de Montesino (CAM).
Wallerstein, Immanuel. 1974. *The Modern World-System*, Vol. 1. New York: Academic Press.

———. 1979. *The Capitalist World-Economy: Essays*. Cambridge, UK: Cambridge University Press.

———. 2003. "The Three Instances of Hegemony in the History of the Capitalist World-Economy." In *Social Theory: Roots and Branches*, ed. Peter Kivisto. Los Angeles: Roxbury Publishing Company.

Wessin Chávez, Elías. 2000. "La Ley de Lectura Bíblica en las Escuelas." *La Voz de CODUE* 7, July–August.

Wiarda, Howard. 1965. "The Changing Political Orientation of the Catholic Church in the Dominican Republic." *A Journal of Church and State* 8 (2): 239–54.

Willems, Emilio. 1967. *Followers of the Faith: Culture Change and Protestantism in Brazil and Chile*. Nashville, TN: Vanderbilt University Press.

William, Philip J. 1989. *The Catholic Church and Politics in Nicaragua and Costa Rica*. Pittsburgh, PA: University of Pittsburgh Press.

Wipfler, William. 1966. *The Churches of the Dominican Republic in the Light of History: A Study of the Root Causes of Current Problems*. Cuernavaca, Mexico: Centro Intercultural de Documentación, Sondeos No. 11.

———. 1980. *Poder, Influencia e Impotencia: La Iglesia como Factor Socio-político en República Dominicana*. Santo Domingo: Ediciones CEPAE.

Zavaleta Mercado, René. 1970. El Poder Dual en América Latina: Estudios de los Casos de Bolivia y Chile. Mexico City: Siglo XXI.

Index

aggiornamento, 50
agrarian reform, 117
authoritarian regime, 2

Báez, Buenaventura, 26
Balaguer, Joaquín, 3, 43–44, 113–16, 117–19, 126, 231
Bolivia: agrarian reform, 57; Atezama, Abel, 60; Banzer, Hugo, 58; Barrientos Ortuño, René (general), 58; Bolivian Workers Confederation (COB), 58; Church and Society in Latin America (ISAL), 64; crisis, 65–67; "Dignity and Liberty," 66; diocesan and religious priests, 59, 97n2; Dominicans, 59; "Evangelio y Violencia" ("Gospel and Violence"), 62; García Meza, Luis (general), 66; growth and consolidation of the church, 59–60, 65; hierarchy, 60; human rights, 64; hunger strike, 65; Justice and Peace Commission, 63; Lechín, Juan, 58; Manrique, Jorge, 60; Maurer, Vincent (cardinal), 60; mediation, 60–66; National Revolutionary Movement (MNR), 57; nonpartisan actor, 68; Oblate of Mary Immaculate, 59; Paz Estenssoro, Víctor, 58; Permanent Assembly of Human Rights, 64; political activity, 57–58; political landscape, 58; political prisoners, 63; popular church, 61; presidential decree 21060, 67; radical priests, 64–65; repression, 61–63; role of progressive priests, 63; Siles Suazo, Hernán, 58; Society of Maryknoll, 59; Spanish Missionary Society for Cooperation with Latin America (OCSHA), 64; Terrazas, Julio, 67
Bosch, Juan, 101–2, 113, 123, 170, 231

Caamaño, Francisco, 103
caciques, 10, 11, 16n5
capitalist modernization, 2, 216
Catholic Church, 15n1
Catholic community leaders and revolutionary commandos, 107
Catholic cultural traditions, 1

Catholic hierarchy and conservative regimes, 19; military governments, 52; U.S. government, 57
caudillismo, 12, 16n8
caudillo, 10, 11, 16n4
Christian commitment, 52
church institutional crisis, 26–27; church-state relations after Spanish departure, 27; Cocchia, Rocco, 27; European apostolic vicar, 27; reestablishment of Spanish colonial rule, 27
church's influence, 4
church-state relations: church financial resources, 157–61; integration of church and state, 20–21, 39; privileges, 19, 24–26; ruptures, 19–20; subordination of church to the state, 21–22; types, 19–22
church-Trujillo crisis: benefactor of the church, 24; Dominican Episcopal Conference, 40; Holy See, 43; negative press coverage, 41; Panal, Francisco, 41; Trujillo, Ramfis, 43; U. S. Embassy in Santo Domingo, 41–42
clergy: dependent church model, 44; development of the clergy, 32; Eudists, 32; importation of foreign clergy, 28; nationalist project, 44
colonial church: Casas, Bartolomé de las, 22; indigenous, 22; *Inter Caetera*, 22; Montesino, Antón de, 22; *Real Patronato* (Royal Patronage), 22; Royal and Supreme Council of Indies, 46n1; *Universalis Ecclesiae Regimini* (papal bull), 22
Communist Party and agrarian reform, 118
comparative historical perspective, 17
Conciliar Seminary, 25, 32
concordat, 20, 29, 37–39, 46n3
conferences: Bolivian Episcopal Conference (CEB), 60; Conference of Diocesan Priests in Guatemala (COSEGUA), 72; Conference of Latin American Religious (CLAR), 56; Conferences of Medellín (1968) and Puebla (1979), 50, 54; First Latin American Bishop Conference (1955), 39; Fourth Latin American Bishops' Conference, 56, 180; Latin American Episcopal Conference (CELAM), 49; Medellín Conference and Ecclesiastical Base Communities, 52–53; Nicaraguan Episcopal Conference (CEN), 84
conservatives, 19–20
conservative shift, 54–55
constituent assembly, 23
Cortes de Cadiz, 24, 46n2
council of state, 44
credibility and legitimacy, 2–3
Cuban Revolution, 8

declaration on the rural situation, 118
Dios, Patria y Libertad (God, Fatherland, and Freedom), 24
Dominican National Guard, 34
Dominican Republic
—anti-communist hysteria, 102
—Balaguer regime, 113–15
—Banda Colorada, La (The Red Band), 122
—building a new relationship with society: *centros de promoción humana* (Centers for Human Services, CPH), 179, 186; defending the poor with a preferential love, 181; demands of community leaders, 191; Dominican Sugar Council (CEA), 191; perception of the accompaniment approach, 178; social pastoral approach of Lemba, 190

—Casado Villar, Manfredo, 124
—Cedail: *bateyes* (isolated ethnic neighborhoods), 202; birth registration programs, 199; Campo, Luisa, 198; documenting children of Haitian immigrants, 206; education of paralegal personnel, 200; effects of privatization, 202; foreigners in transit, 207; foundation of Cedail, 198; Grullón, José Dolores, 199; human rights workers in the border, 205; late birth registration, 199; legal advice to labor, 202; organized labor, 202; people without identity papers, 198, 206; training of community leaders, 201
—church financial resources, 157–61
—church role in society, 163; actions of Polanco Brito, 120; church's approach to the peasants, 117; diminished political denunciations, 163; Polanco Brito's leadership, 116
—Constitutionalists, 103
—Constitutionalist zone, 110
—Diocese of Barahona: Cabeza de Toro, 191; Cabral Center for Diocesan Education, 189; Candelier, Pedro de Jesús, 190; Consejo Estatal del Azúcar (State Sugar Council, CEA), 191; interests of intermediaries, 190; Lemba, 189; Lemba Social Pastoral Workers, 190; microcredit office, 192; rational management of the dry forest, 190; Rivas, Fabio Mamerto, 189; Rivera, Pedro A., 191; social issues, 188; woodcutting business, 190

—Diocese of La Vega: impact of social pastoral programs, 188; migration, 186; pressing problems, 186; Santana, Juan Flores, 185
—Diocese of Mao-Montecristi: Abreu Herrera, J. Tomás, 183; Autonomous Peasant Union (UCA), 182; beneficiary of Cáritas housing projects, 183; Border Solidarity, 183; Good Hope Women's Association (ASOMONEDA), 183; Martínez, Regino, 182–83
—Diocese of San Juan de la Maguana: Banco Nacional de la Vivienda (National Housing Bank, BNV), 195; building houses for victims, 195; dependence, 197; effectiveness of pastoral programs, 197; Foundation for the Development of Azua, San Juan, and Elías Piña (Fundasep), 194; Grullón, José Dolores, 192; Hurricane George, 195; scope of social problems, 194
—Dominican governments' manipulation of the national budget, 157
—economic activity, 145–48; Caribbean Basin Initiative, 146; Central Bank of the Dominican Republic, 146; diminished capacity of the state, 148; Dominican fund held in U.S. banks, 44; foreign debt, 149; free trade zones, 146–47; growth of Dominican exports, 114; Gulf and Western Corporation, 118; Jorge Blanco, Salvador, 148, 168; land ownership, 118; new economic policy, 148; reduction

of state revenues, 148; remittances from abroad, 147; social and economic transformation, 145, 149; sugar production in the 1980s, 202; tourism industry, 146, 203; women in the labor force, 147–48
— electoral politics: Central Electoral Board, 167–68; Central Electoral Commission, 173; Civility Compact, 170; Commission of Electoral Advisers (CEA), 167; delegative democracy, 144; electoral law, 169; electoral reform, 169; institutional weakness of the Central Electoral Board (JCE), 168; International Foundation for Electoral Systems, 169; Organization of American States (OAS), 104; political exclusion, 164; process of inclusion/exclusion, 147; reelection of the president, 144; triumvirate government, 106
— Fiallo, Viriato A., 101
— growth and consolidation of the church, 149; diocesan and religious priests, 151; educational institutions, 155; foreign-born religious priests, 151; foreign clergy and the training of priests, 153; institution of expansion of the church, 149; massive immigration of priests, 150; parishes, 157; pastoral workforce, 151–53, 157; Pontificia Universidad Católica Madre y Maestra, 155; proportion of religious to diocesan priests, 151; Radio Santa María, 155–56, 185; religious women, 157; Universidad Católica Madre y Maestra, 14, 141n6, 155, 165, 173, 221
— Haitian people: American Convention of Human Rights, 204; Aristide, Jean Bertrand, 204; Dominican nationalists and Haitian immigration, 204; General Migration Office (DGM), 206; Haitian immigration, 202, 204, 206; human rights workers, 205; mass deportations, 204, 206; peasants without legal titles, 203; Protocol of Understanding, 205; public schools and Haitian children, 207; social conditions of Haitians residing in the Dominican Republic, 203
— hierarchy: Adames, Roque, 118–19; Arnáiz, Francisco José, 153, 165; Beras Rojas, Octavio, 107; Castellano, Rafael, 35; Catholic religious dominance, 220; Christian reaffirmation, 102; church congresses, 105; construction of the basilica, 106; departure of Beras Rojas from war zone, 107; ecclesiastical governments, 17; Ecclesiastical Province of Santo Domingo, 36; García, Lautico, 101; hierarchy involvement in politics, 19; individual declarations of bishops, 118; influence of popular church on hierarchy, 135; Jesuit presence, 100–101; López Rodríguez, Nicolas (cardinal), 167; nunciature, 108; papal nuncios, 55; Pérez Sánchez, Eliseo, 35; Pittini, Ricardo, 35–37; Pittini's close collaboration with Trujillo, 37; Pittini's ecclesiastical government, achievements of, 36;

Reilly, Thomas, 41; *Si Magna et Excelsa* (papal bull), 36; social background of Catholic hierarchy, 102
—inequality, 164
—legacy of revolutionaries, 139
—Loyalists, 103
—mainstream political parties: Dominican Communist Party (PCD), 178; Dominican Liberation Party (PLD), 125, 162, 166, 168, 170, 231; Dominican Revolutionary Party (PRD), 100, 104, 113, 140n3, 168, 180, 227; foundation of the Dominican Revolutionary Party, 100; leftist parties, 100; National Civil Union (UCU), 101; Reformist Party (PR), 113, 139, 175n7; Social Christian Revolutionary Party (PRSC), 100–102, 107, 168, 171
—military presence of the United States, 103
—nationalist protests against the American occupation, 32
—Nouel and development of the clergy, 32
—Pepen's resignation, 130
—political mediations of Clarizio, 108–9, 141n5
—political mediations of Núñez Collado, 166, 173, 223; church as permanent feature of the political system, 173; Commission on National Dialogue, 173; Commission to Revise the Constitution, 173; Graham, John, 172; leadership of Núñez Collado, 173; nationally recognized mediators, 122; neutrality, 163; nonpartisan, 163; overlapping interests of the church and the state, 164; Pact for Democracy, 172; pastoral letter of November 1980, 164; Pastoral of Dialogue, 165; Permanent Secretariat of Dialogue, 165; reincorporation of the church in the political system, 164–65; Solidarity Pact, 165–66; special sociopolitical actor, 163; Tripartite Agreement, 165; Tripartite Dialogue, 165; tripartite negotiations, 165; Universidad Católica Madre y Maestra, 165; Verification Commission, 171
—political mediations of Polanco Brito, 120; Anti-reelection Unified Command, 120; Brito, Polanco, 141n6, 120–30; Crowley, Donald J., 120–21; freedom of political prisoners, 122, 124; Gómez, Maximiliano, 121–22; guerrilla movement, 123; mediating commission, 126; Méndez Vargas, Radhamés, 129–30; Mexican Embassy, 121, 124; Moquete, Matos, 122; national police, 121; relatives of political prisoners, 122–24; revolutionary commando, 128; Santiago Accord, 125–27; Venezuelan Consulate, 128–30; voice of the voiceless, 2, 52, 128, 136
—popular church: Adrian Dominican Sisters, 112, 134; *animadores*, 138; background of priest who started CEBs, 136–37; Catholic youth, 106; Cela, Jorge, 138; contribution of CEBs, 136; Daughters of Charity, 134; dissenting priests, 133; Dubert, Ramón, 131; Ecclesiastical Base Communities (CEBs), 53, 136;

equipos comunitarios (community groups), 138; experiment of the CEBs, 136; Figueredo, Sergio, 131, 135; González Buelta, Benjamín, 137; Guachupita, 138; Guerrero, Tomás, 138; Hermanas del Colegio de Santo Domingo, 112; Jesuit priests as target of harassment, 131; Lafleur, Lucas, 131; living as part of a CEB, 138; Lumen Vitae Institute, 137; Movement of Committed Christians, 133; occupation of Catholic temples, 124; occupation of churches, 133; parish of Dajabón, 132; parish of San Miguel, 110; popular church as social movement, 130; progressives within the church, 119; repression of foreign priests, 131; Sisters of Cardinal Sanchas, 134; Sisters of Mercy, 112; three priests of San Miguel, 109; worker-priests of Paris, 110
—reliance on foreign priests, 28
—social pastoral programs: accompaniment, 177, 178, 192, 194; assistentialism, 177, 186, 188, 192; Cárita Internationalis, 179; Cáritas, 186; Cáritas Dominicana, 177, 181–82; Catholic Relief Services, 179; Dominican Counseling and Legal Research Center (CEDAIL), 177; First Dominican Plenary Council, 180; grassroots organizations, 181; human promotion, 180; inculturation of the Gospel, 180; National Pastoral Commission, 181; national pastoral plans (NPP), 178–80; perception of the accompaniment approach, 178;

preferential option for the poor, 180; social capital, 178, 191
—Tapley Bennett, William, 103
—Wessín y Wessín, Elías (general), 103, 125–26, 140n3, 232

El Salvador: bishops and political elites, 96; Central America Common Market, 88; Chávez González, Luis, 90–91; conservative Salvadoran bishops, 92; Cristiani, Alfredo, 95; Delegates of the Word, 91; Duarte, José Napoleón, 93–94; expansion of the armed forces, 89; Farabundo Martí Front for National Liberation (FMLN), 89; fourteen families, 88; growth and consolidation of the church, 90; hierarchy, 90–91, 95; Human Rights Commission, 89, 94; human rights violations, 89; institutional development, 90; mediation of the church, 92–94; national debate for peace, 94; National Renovating Alliance (ARENA), 94; papal visit to El Salvador, 95; paramilitary groups, 89; pastoral workforce, 90; popular church, 91–92; rebel-controlled territory, 93; Revolutionary Democratic Front (FDR), 89; Rivera y Damas, Arturo, 92–93; Romero, Oscar, 91–92; Romero's assassination, 98n5; Sáenz Lacalle, Fernando, 95; Salvadoran military, 88; Salvadoran social movements, 88; U.S. economic and military support, 89
Escuela Normal, 29
evangelicalism, 217
evangelical leaders: Dunker Lambe, José, 228; Instituto Evangélico de Santiago, 227; Juan, Próspero, 228;

King, Luis (reverend), 225, 226; Mejía Domínguez, Hipólito, 228, 233; Montás, Temístocles, 228; political involvement of evangelicals, 228; Reyes, Andrés, 227–28

evangelical political mediation: Aquino, Reynaldo, 232; evangelical incorporation into politics, 232; Pact for Democracy, 232

evangelicals, 15n2; Assemblies of God, 219; Catholic religious monopoly, 209; Christian Student Movement (MEC), 228; Church of God, the, 219; Church of God of the Prophesy, the, 219; evangelical adaptation to local culture, 218; evangelicalism as a popular movement, 212; evangelicalism during the Trujillo period, 218; evangelical movement, 2, 5; evangelical participation in political parties, 227; evangelical political parties, 211; evangelical Protestantism, 218; evangelicals seeking to exert influence, 234; Feliciano, Salomón, 218; growth of evangelicals and mutation of the religious field, 224; Hernández, Francisco, 218; holiness doctrine, 217; integration of evangelicals into society, 229; Latin American religious field, 209; mutation in the Dominican religious field, 245; neoevangelical leaders, 211; neoevangelicals, 211; new Protestants, 210; Pentecostal Church of God, 218; Pentecostal Evangelical Church, 219; Protestants and democratic struggles, 210; religious conversion, 210; salvation goods, 211, 212; survey research on evangelicals, 221; traditional leaders, 211

evangelicals and political institutions: Confraternity of Evangelical Unity (CODUE), 229; Dominican Evangelical Confraternity (CONEDO), 229; ecclesiastical institutions, 229; Latin American Evangelical Fraternity (CONELA), 229; Pact for Democracy, 229; Pastoral Network (Red Pastoral), 230; Rincón, Andrés (reverend), 229; superintendent, 240n5

evangelicals and political parties: church-affiliated parties, 232; evangelicals accommodate political system, 245; evangelical vote, 232

evangelicals' growth, 219–25; Adventist Church, 220; Alvarez Vega, Bienvenido, 223, 228; *chorchas*, 224; English-speaking workers, 224; evangelical preachers, 220; Haitian and Dominican Evangelical Church, 220; Independent Fundamentalist Church, 220; Independent Pentecostal Church, 220; mutations in the religious field, 224; religious identification, 223; Traditional Fundamentalist Evangelical Church, 220; Traditional Pentecostal Church, 220

evangelicals' search for influence: Estrella, Manuel, 235; evangelical as nonpartisan, 235; evangelical critiques, 235; evangelical demands recognized, 236; evangelicals in national budget, 236; Martínez, Adalberto, 234; political impact of evangelicals, 236; Portes, Braulio, 234; prerogatives, 234; proposals, 234; Social Pact, 238

Fernández Reina, Leonel, 161–63, 173, 233, 236, 238

folk Catholicism, 10, 217, 225
foreign religious priests, 32

Gaudium et Spes ("The Pastoral Constitution of the Church in the Modern World"), 50
general amnesty, 105
Gómez, Maximiliano, assassination of, 120–21, 141n7
Guatemala: Arévalo, Juan José, 69; army's campaigns against the indigenous, 76; Assembly of Civil Society (ASC), 77; Casariego Acevedo, Mario, 70–71; Catholic Social Action, 73; Cerezo, Vinicio, 75; Confederation of Guatemalan Religious (CRG), 74; Esquipulas II, 76; foreign-born religious priests, 73; Gerardi, Juan, 74, 78; growth and consolidation of the church, 69–71; Guatemalan economic growth, 73; guerrilla warfare, 76; Human Rights Office, 78; institutional basis of the church, 71; liberal oligarchs, 68; mediation, 75–78; mediation of Rodolfo Quezada Toruño, 76; missionaries in Guatemala, 73; National Dialogue Commission, 77; National Guatemalan Revolutionary Union (URNG), 76; pastoral workforce, 68, 71, 72–78; peasant leagues, 74; Penados del Barrio, Próspero, 75; political activity, 70–75; political division of the hierarchy, 75; reforms, 69; Rossel Arellano, Mariano, 69; Rufino Barrios, Justo, 68; Ubico, Jorge, 69; United Fruit Company, 69; Ydígoras Fuentes, Miguel, 70
guerrilla movements, 51
Gutiérrez, Gustavo, 50
Guzmán Fernández, Antonio, 168

hacienda, 10, 16n6
Haitian liberalism, 23
Haitian massacre, 47n9
Haitian occupation, 23; church-inspired plot, 23; Dominican Constitution, 24; Dominican independence, 23; Hispanophile, 23, 25; Portes, Tomás (vicar general), 23–26; Portes's nationalist project, 28; Valera Jiménez, Pedro (bishop), 23
Hasbum, Amin Abel, 121
Hermanos de la Salle, 135
Heureaux, Ulises, 29
historical Protestants, 209, 212, 216, 220, 224; adaptation to local culture, 218; Americans of Samaná and Puerto Plata, 213; Brito, Israel, 213; Colegio Lincoln, 213; Dominican Episcopal Church, 212, 214; Dominican Evangelical Church, 214, 215; Dominican religious field, 216; Drury, Philo W. (reverend), 215; emotional celebration, 217; Free Methodist Church, 213, 226–28; growth of the Episcopal Church, 214; inculturate, 217; Inman, Samuel G., 215; Instituto Evangélico, 213; International Hospital in Santo Domingo, 215; La Romana, 215; Librería Dominicana, 215; medical mission, 215; Methodist Wesleyan Society, 212; Mills, Samuel E. (pastor), 213; Moravian Church, 213, 216; Pentecostal paradigm, 217; Postigo, Julio, 215, 225; Protestant collaboration with U.S. occupation, 214; religious persecution, 213; San Pedro de Macoris, 214; Wyllie, William (reverend), 214
historic circumstances of the New World, 22

Hostos, Eugenio María de, 29. *See also* Escuela Normal
human rights, 51, 135

inalienable rights, 2
inculturation, 10
institutional development of Colombian church, 21
institutional incorporation of evangelicals: models of the church, 16n3; modern historiography, 2; mutation of the religious field, 10
Inter-American Peace Force, 104
interpretations of religion and politics: Bastian's notion of religious mutation, 6, 10; Bourdieu's theory of the religious field, 11; institutional analysis, 6; schools of thought on evangelicals, 9–10; world system theory, 13

John Paul II (pope), 54–57, 86, 180
Juárez, Benito, 19
juridical personality, 34–35

Latin American religious landscape, 210
legacy of colonialism, 18
liberal democracy, 57
liberalism, 18
liberals, 19–20
liberating education, 51
liberation theology, 52
López Trujillo, Alfonso, 53

Majluta, Jacobo, 168
Medellín Conclusions, 51
Meriño, Fernando, 28–29
military rulers of Central America, 115
minor seminary of Santo Cerro, 35
Monzón, Bienvenido, 27
mutations of popular religious culture, 10

national congress, 31
nationalist protest, 31
new evangelization, 56
Nicaragua: Barrios de Chamorro, Violeta, 87; Calderón y Padilla, Octavio José, 80; Carballo, Bismarck, 85; Cardenal, Ernesto, 82; church hierarchy, 82; Contras, 84–85; corruption under Anastasio Somoza Debayle, 80; ecclesiastic jurisdiction, 81; educational institutions, 81; General Ortega, Humberto, 87; Giglio, Paolo, 86; growth and consolidation of the church, 80–81; Lezcano y Ortega, José Antonio, 80; mediation, 86–87; Molina, Uriel, 82; National Commission of Reconciliation, 86; National Literacy Crusade, 84; Nicaragua earthquake, 79; Nicaraguan educational policies, 84; Obando y Bravo, Miguel, 85–86; pastoral letters of the CEN, 84–85; pastoral workforce, 83; political behavior of priests, 83; popular church, 81–82; populist approach, 97n3; priests and support for Sandinista Revolution, 82; radical priests, 82; religious community of Solentiname, 82; Revolutionary Christian Movement, 82; Sandinista Front for National Liberation (FSLN), 84; Sandino, Augusto César, 80; Sapoá agreement, 86–87; Somoza Debayle, Luis and Anastacio, 79; Somoza García, Anastasio, 78
nineteenth-century liberalism, 18
nonpartisan political mediation, 2
Nouel (archbishop), 30–32

orientations within the church: Christendom, 7; liberating, 8;

modernizing, 8; neo-Christendom ecclesiology, 7, 18, 39; neoconservative, 8, 68; re-Christianizing society, 18; traditional, 7

Pacem in Terris ("Peace on Earth"), 50
"pact of domination," 13
Paradis, Collin de, 29
Patronato (patronage), 22, 29
Peña Gómez, José Francisco, 123, 171, 231
political mediation, 2
political regime, 13
power of the clergy, 1
process of inclusion/exclusion, 147
Puebla Conference, 54

Reagan, Ronald, 89
relationship of dependence, 11
religious field, 12
religious marketplace, 12
Rockefeller, Nelson, 56
role of papal nuncios, 55
Rufino Barrios, Justo, 19

Saéz, José Luis, 4–5
socialist revolution, 20
social justice, 1
socioeconomic change, 2

Spanish annexation, 26–27
spiritual cohesion of the nation, 4
state, definition of, 13

tenets of Vatican Council II, 49–50
Third Latin American Bishop Conference, 54
traditional historical studies, 3
transition to democracy, 2, 68
Trujillo, Rafael, 32–35, 37–40, 42–45

University of Santo Domingo, 34–35
U.S. aid to Central America, 86
U.S. military occupation, 31, 46n6, 99, 104
U.S. State Department, 41

Vásquez, Horacio, 34
Vatican and changes in local church, 116
Vatican Council II, 1–2
Vatican-initiated changes in Dominican church, 119
Venezuelan Consulate, abduction at, 129
Vicariate of Solidarity, 52

weak political institutions, 2
Wessín Chavez, Elías (reverend), 232
World Life Program, 56

About the Author

Emelio Betances earned his PhD in sociology in 1989 from Rutgers University and has taught at the Benemérita Universidad Autónoma de Puebla in Mexico (1982–1988), the City University of New York (1989–1990), and Gettysburg College (1991–2006). In 1991 he founded Gettysburg College's Latin American Studies Program and served as its director (1991–2001). He is the author of *State and Society in the Dominican Republic* (1995) and the editor, with Hobart Spalding, of *The Dominican Republic Today* (1996). Betances's areas of interest include political and historical sociology, economic development, religion, and social movements.